# a guide to

# A LEVEL
# ECONOMICS

## A N D R E W   T I B B I T T

Thomas Nelson and Sons Ltd
Nelson House   Mayfield Road
Walton-on-Thames   Surrey
KT12 5PL   UK

51 York Place
Edinburgh
EH1 3JD   UK

Thomas Nelson (Hong Kong) Ltd
Toppan Building 10/F
22A Westlands Road
Quarry Bay   Hong Kong

Thomas Nelson Australia
102 Dodds Street
South Melbourne
Victoria 3205

Nelson Canada
1120 Birchmount Road
Scarborough   Ontario
M1K 5G4   Canada

First published by Thomas Nelson and Sons Ltd 1986

ISBN 0-17-448119-5
NPN 9 8 7 6 5

Printed in Hong Kong.

# Contents

# INTRODUCTION

1 This guide is a realistic attempt to help students studying courses in A Level Economics. It is designed to be used, it is not something that should just occupy space in a locker or on a bookshelf.

2 It has been designed to fulfil three main functions.
   (a) As a *Study Guide*, to provide an overview of the main topics when they are first encountered.
   (b) As a *Course Companion*, through the provision of essential information, straightforward explanations of key concepts, and exercise material which monitors the development of understanding and hopefully encourages further research and inquiry.
   (c) As a *Revision Guide*, by presenting material in clear annotated form and with revision exercises.

3 This guide is *not* a traditional Economics textbook, nor is it intended to be a substitute for one. It is likely that most A level students will have access to both a teacher (or tutor or lecturer) and a standard textbook. Teachers can normally help clarify matters as long as students have some appreciation of the topic and appropriate language, but teachers are not always available for consultation. Textbooks are always available for reference, but many contain daunting passages of prose and cannot answer the questions of puzzled readers. *A Guide to A Level Economics* is designed to complement these traditional sources.

4 Each Unit in the *Guide* includes the following sections:
   (a) *Preview material* to outline the key issues covered in the Unit.
   (b) *Essential information*, presented in annotated form and complemented, where appropriate, by diagrams to highlight key concepts.
   (c) *Exercises*, which for the most part check the reader's understanding of the information presented in the immediately preceding sections, although some require further research or cross-reference work.
   (d) *Review material*, to show the key questions answered by the Unit, the terminology introduced, and some test material.
   (e) *Answer section*, for the exercises and review questions—with some explanation and guidance as to how the answers have been obtained.

5 The Units in the *Guide* cover the main syllabus areas prescribed by the Examination Boards. The material included in Economics courses is subject to constant change. This *Guide* aims to keep pace with the new developments, e.g. in comparative economics, in the 'Keynesian' and 'Monetarist' debate, in international developments and in discussing the causes and effects of deindustrialisation and privatisation.

6 Where appropriate each Unit contains both theoretical and applied information: the theory being qualified by observations from the real world and illustrated by case study material (both hypothetical and real); the applied information organised through a framework of theory.

7 The exercise material is designed to mirror the ways used by the examination boards using:
   (a) multiple choice questions,
   (b) data response questions—based on either statistical data or written commentaries,
   (c) case studies,
   (d) essay questions.
   Additionally some exercises contain short answer questions and some others require simple graphical or diagrammatic representation of data. The majority of the exercises have been tested 'in the field'.

8 The answers, provided at the end of each Unit include some explanation of the method used in generating the answer. The essay plans are not designed to be model answers but brief outlines of a possible approach. Many of the answers provided for the data response and case studies will be open to discussion. You are most welcome to disagree as long as you can defend your point of view!

Andrew Tibbitt
May 1986

# Economic systems

## 1.1 Preview

1  Economic activity involves combining resources to produce goods and services.
2  Countries organise their economic activity in different ways.
3  The economic system chosen has to answer basic issues as to what is produced, how it is to be produced, who is to be able to consume what is produced, and how total production can be increased.
4  These issues are aspects of the basic economic problem that is common to all societies, namely how to satisfy unlimited wants with only limited resources (the total sum of wants vastly exceeds the available supply of goods and services).

## Exercise 1

1  **An appointment in Prague**
   Following the first leg of a European soccer Cup match in Watford, where nearly 20,000 fans saw Watford defeated 2–3 by Sparta Prague, the team, officials and press corps arrived in Czechoslovakia for the second leg.
   'We were directed to a press conference in the airport lounge. Elton John (Watford FC Chairman) is very big news in Prague. His Russian tour was such a success that he has Big Brother's rubber-stamp of approval throughout the Soviet bloc. He is rated the number one pop star. He was big enough on the black market before that tour but he is rated a superstar now.
   Tickets for the match have all been sold. Party members, government officials, sports club members and "best factory workers of the month" have first choice. It is almost impossible for the ordinary Czech fan to obtain a ticket unless he falls into one of those categories.'
   (a) Who, or what, decided that Elton John's music should be made available in Czechoslovakia? Who, or what, would make that decision in Britain?
   (b) What is a black market? Do you find black markets in Britain?
   (c) Contrast the ways that tickets may have been allocated for the matches in Britain and Czechoslovakia.
   (d) Why are 'best factory workers of the month' selected in Czechoslovakia? How are factory workers motivated in Britain?

2  **Speech to Communist Party Central Committee**
   In a speech, given by the late Yuri Andropov, to the Communist Party Central Committee in December 1983, he called for 'tighter discipline by the labour force to fulfil the current five year plan'.

'People have been working with greater desire. In general a change for the better in the national economy has begun to show ... the most important thing now is not to lose the tempo .... In the conditions of the present international situation which has been sharply aggravated through the fault of the aggressive imperialistic circles, the strict implementation of the state plan becomes not just an obligation but also a patriotic duty of every Soviet person. There has to be proper order in meeting the planned targets. Bottlenecks have to be eliminated.'

In demanding better consumer goods the speech revealed that 'Soviet trade organisations had rejected as substandard: 50,000 TV sets, 115,000 radios, almost 250,000 cameras, 1,500,000 clocks and watches and 160,000 refrigerators offered by factories for retail in 1984'.

The State's retail buyers refused to purchase because of 'the disparity between the quality and assortment of these goods and the demands made by the consumers'.

(a) What would be contained in 'the current five year plan'? Does Britain have a five year plan?

(b) How would bottlenecks be removed in the Soviet Union? How would they be eliminated in Britain?

(c) What do you think is the function of the State's retail buyer in the Soviet Union? Has the consumer any choice as to the goods and services he buys in the Soviet Union?

(d) What might happen to factories producing sub-standard goods in the Soviet Union? What would happen to firms producing sub-standard goods in Britain?

(e) Are there similarities between the Soviet and British economies?

## 1.2 Types of economic system

1   Two extreme forms of economic system can be identified:
   (a) centrally planned (also known as command economies, and
   (b) free market (also known as free enterprise or *laissez-faire* or capitalist economies).

   *Centrally planned* economies have the following features:
   (a) resources are allocated by a central planning authority (CPA),
   (b) resources are owned by the state,
   (c) factories are owned and run by the state,
   (d) prices are fixed by the CPA.

   *Free market* economies by contrast have the following features:
   (a) resources are allocated by the workings of the price mechanism in a free market,
   (b) resources are privately owned,
   (c) factories are privately owned,
   (d) producers are motivated by the chance to earn private profits.

2   In practice few countries' economic systems conform to either of these extreme positions. Most involve a mix of characteristics from both types. For example:

(a) Britain is fundamentally a free market economy but some industries are state owned (nationalised industries, e.g. British Rail and the Steel industry) and some markets are controlled (e.g. agriculture).

(b) Yugoslavia is described as a market socialist economy where market forces fix prices, but factories are owned by the workers.

(c) The Soviet Union has basically a centrally planned economy but some products can be produced and sold privately.

(d) The United States is predominantly a free market economy, but some activities are operated by the government (e.g. NASA space exploration).

# 1.3 Basic components of an economic system

1 There are six basic components, or building blocks, of an economic system.

(a) *Ownership of resources*—are resources owned by private individuals, or the state?

(b) *The role of private profit*—are profits the property of private individuals or are the surpluses the property of the state?

(c) *Allocation of resources*—are resources allocated by the price mechanism in free markets, or are they allocated by directions from the central planning authority?

(d) *Ownership of production units*—are factories owned by private individuals, workers or the state?

(e) *Degree of freedom of choice*—can producers make what they want or are they directed as to what to produce? Can consumers choose between alternative suppliers of goods or are they restricted to those approved by the state?

(f) *The role of the government*—does the government keep out of most economic matters or is it directly involved in all aspects of economic activity?

2 Table 1.1 gives a summary of the building blocks of three types of economic system.

| Building block | Free market | Centrally planned | Market socialist |
|---|---|---|---|
| Ownership of resources | Private | State | State |
| Private profit | Yes | No | Yes |
| Allocation of resources | Price mechanism | CPA | Price mechanism |
| Ownership of production | Private | State | Workers |
| Freedom of choice | Yes | No | Yes |
| Role of government | None | High | Some |

Table 1.1 Three types of economic system.

# 1.4 Economic systems—terms defined

**1 The price mechanism**

In free markets prices have two functions:

(a) to signal to consumers the cost of purchasing a good or service, and

(b) to signal to producers the revenue they will receive from selling the good or service.

Normally the higher the price of a good or service:

(a) the less consumers will want to buy the good or service,

(b) the more producers will be willing to provide the good or service.

So, if there is a shortage of a good or service and the price rises, less will be purchased and more will be supplied, so that the shortage disappears.

### 2 Consumer sovereignty

Consumer sovereignty exists if consumers have the power to determine what is produced for, and sold in, the market. In a free market economy consumers exercise sovereignty through their purchases of goods and services.

### 3 Planners sovereignty

In centrally planned economic systems the CPA has the power to determine what is produced. If consumers want a good or service that is not part of the plan, their want will remain unsatisfied.

### 4 Public goods/service

Public goods are goods which provide benefit for everybody, but for which consumers cannot express a meaningful demand through their purchases in the market. Public goods, e.g. national defence, are therefore provided by the state.

### 5 Merit goods/service

Some goods that are provided by the government provide particular benefit to individuals as well as general benefit to society. These are called merit goods. The government may provide such goods as it is felt that consumers, if left to make their own spending plans, would under-consume or be unable or unwilling to afford these goods. Common examples of merit goods are provision of a national health service, state education and the fire service.

### 6 De-merit goods

Some goods purchased by individuals do harm to their consumers and thereby impose costs on society in general. These are called de-merit goods.

### 7 Free goods

Goods which are not scarce, i.e. where supply exceeds demand, have no price and are said to be free goods.

### 8 Private good/service

Goods and services which provide benefit to individuals and which are provided by firms are said to be private goods or services.

### 9 Externalities

A decision taken in one area of the economy can cause a change in economic conditions elsewhere. Such consequences are known as externalities or social costs and benefits. For example, building a new motorway has direct costs such as construction costs and loss of use of the land, but will also change traffic conditions in by-passed towns and reduce transport costs.

# 1.5 The role of the economic system

1 An economic system is necessary to provide an answer to the fundamental economic problem of reconciling unlimited wants with limited sources.

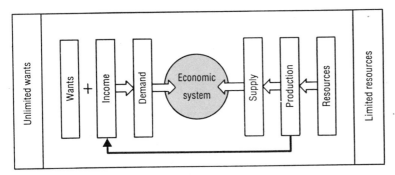

**Figure 1.1** The two sides of the economic system

2 The economic system must therefore find answers to the following problems.
   (a) *What is to be produced?*—e.g. consumer goods or machinery, defence weapons or hospitals?
   (b) *How, and where, are the goods to be produced?*—e.g. with new technically advanced machinery or through more labour intensive methods?
   (c) *For whom is the production to be made available?*—e.g. for people with the most money or those with special needs and qualifications?
   (d) *How can more be produced?*—e.g. what forms of incentives make workers produce goods more efficiently?

# 1.6 An evaluation of alternative economic systems

1 The variety of economic systems in the world indicates that no one system provides a universally acceptable solution to the basic economic problems.
2 The extent to which a country is satisfied with its economic system will depend on what it hopes the system will achieve. The objectives or aims of societies are produced by political power and political systems.
3 Here are some criteria for assessing the different economic systems.
   (a) *How evenly are incomes and wealth distributed?*—Is it acceptable to have wide differences between income and wealth levels within a society?
   (b) *Who decides how resources are to be allocated?* Should the consumer be sovereign? Does the CPA know what is best for its citizens?
   (c) *Is there likely to be employment for all those who want it?* Is it acceptable to have, say, only 90% of the working population at work?

5

(d) *How is economic power distributed?* Which individuals or groups should have the power to decide what form the economic activity should take?

(e) *Should citizens enjoy complete economic freedom?* Should they be able to choose whether or not to work, and if so, where to work?

4  There are other criteria that need to be considered, and remember that the importance attached to each point is a subjective judgement, i.e. one based on individual opinion.

---

## Exercise 2

1  Most economic systems involve a mix of characteristics from free market and centrally planned systems. From what you know, or can find out, place the economic systems of the following countries on a spectrum of economic systems, ranging from complete free market systems on the right, to complete central planning systems on the left. The UK has been marked in as a guide.

Cuba, Australia, USA, Yugoslavia, West Germany, Soviet Union, Italy

Complete central planning  ⟸  ⟹  Completely free market

2  Place in order the features of an economic system that you would consider to be important.

List the components such an economic system would require.

---

## 1.7 Problems associated with free market economic systems

1  Free market economic systems fail in number of ways.

(a) *Under-production of public goods.* Individuals cannot express a meaningful demand for public goods so they have to be provided by the state, e.g. in 1984 the British government spent about £300 per head on national defence, some £17bn in total.

(b) *Under-provision of merit goods.* Consumers may be unable or unwilling to buy merit goods in quantities that are thought to be socially desirable, e.g. individuals may go without health treatment if they feel they cannot afford to pay the bills.

(c) *Over-consumption of de-merit goods.* Individuals may buy and consume goods that do themselves and society in general harm, and government may aim to discourage purchases of such goods, e.g. cigarettes and addictive drugs.

(d) *Monopoly elements.* Powerful producers or groups within the economy can distort prices, and this in turn distorts the allocation of resources. For example, powerful unions in the printing industry ensure certain wage and staffing levels in their industry at the expense of newspaper owners and the consumer.

(e) *Externalities.* Free market decisions are taken on the basis of private costs and benefits and ignore any social costs and benefits. For example, loss-making telephone boxes may not be provided by a private telephone company even though the boxes provide social benefits to the community as a whole.

(f) *Instability of markets.* Some markets are inherently unstable and free market forces cause output and prices to fluctuate, e.g. foreign exchange markets and agriculture.

(g) *Insecurity.* Economic resources in a free market system may not be in demand and hence will be forced to lie idle, e.g. over one in four school leavers could not find work in 1984 in Britain.

(h) *Inequalities of wealth and income.* Ownership of resources in free market economies is one source of wide differences in wealth and incomes. For example, in Britain the least wealthy 50% of the population share only 5% of the total wealth of the country.

(i) *National strategic considerations.* Free markets may not ensure production in markets which are considered of national strategic importance, e.g. the shortage of British merchant shipping as highlighted by the Falklands crisis.

# 1.8 Problems associated with centrally planned economic systems

Centrally planned economic systems are also thought to fail in a number of ways.

(a) *Bureaucratic.* Planners and government agencies are necessary to formulate and enforce planning decisions. There is no 'invisible hand' at work (i.e. the price mechanism) allocating resources as in the free market system.

(b) *Inflexibility.* Adjusting plans to unforeseen circumstances is difficult and laborious, e.g. shortages of food cause long queues at food shops rather than a quick increase in supply.

(c) *Lack of choice.* Consumers have to accept the decisions of the planners, e.g. Soviets cannot buy *Levi* jeans unless the planners allocate the foreign currency for their importation.

(d) *Lack of positive incentives.* Workers and managers cannot achieve direct increases in their standards of living through hard work, and may therefore be less willing to work hard and efficiently, e.g. they produced the sub-standard goods mentioned by Yuri Andropov (see Exercise 1 in this unit).

## Exercise 3

1 To what extent does the British government allow the following goods or services to be provided by the free market? Explain why the situation is as it is.
(a) Lighthouses
(b) Lifeboats

(c) Agricultural products
(d) Agricultural machinery
(e) Letter delivery
(f) Telephone installation
(g) Central banking (Bank of England)
(h) High Street banking (e.g. Barclays Bank)
(i) Police security
(j) Private security (e.g. Securicor)

2 Four Salford University students left Keswick for Seathwaite on the Lakeland Mountain Goat bus service. They planned to climb Scafell Pike, the highest mountain in England.

From Seathwaite they climbed up the newly repaired footpath beyond Stockley's Bridge where thousands of previous walkers, enjoying the free access to the National Park, had caused serious erosion.

By Piers Gill they took time off to try some rock scrambling. One fell and broke his leg. Two of the party descended to Wasdale Head to call out the Mountain Rescue Service. The injured student was eventually airlifted to hospital by an RAF helicopter. The others, safely back in the George Hotel in Keswick that evening, contributed willingly to the Mountain Rescue collection box.

(a) Why do you not have to pay to climb Scafell Pike? Is it a free good?
(b) Would you classify the students' education at Salford University as a public, merit or private service?
(c) Is the bus service a public good? Why is it provided at a subsidy by the Cumbrian County Council?
(d) Should the injured student have been asked to pay for the RAF helicopter service?
(e) Who provides the Mountain Rescue Service? Is this a free good?
(f) The hospital the student was taken to was a National Health Service hospital. Was his treatment an example of a merit service?

3 **Essay**
What are the key characteristics of free market and centrally planned economic systems? Why does the UK operate a mix of both systems?

## 1.9 Wants and demands

1 One side of the basic economic problem is that wants (for all practical purposes) are unlimited. Although demand for some goods and services can be satisfied there are always other goods and services that people would buy if they had the money to do so.

2 Wants are determined by:
(a) *customs and culture*—e.g. few French people want cricket bats,
(b) *Climate*—e.g. few British homes have air-conditioning,

(c) *a hierarchy of wants*—purchases of necessities will be satisfied before purchases of luxuries, e.g. households want food and clothing before colour TV sets.

3 Economists are concerned with *demand* more than wants. *Demand* is defined as a want supported by the ability to pay for it.

4 Demand can be classified in a number of ways.
   (a) *Goods and services*—e.g. a car is a good, but car repairs are a service.
   (b) *Final and intermediate products.* Final goods are demanded as an end product, e.g. electricity to heat a room; but intermediate goods are demanded to help produce something else, e.g. electricity to run machinery.
   (c) *Consumer, consumer durable and producer goods.* Consumer goods provide immediate benefit and are then used up, e.g. food. Consumer durables provide benefit to a household over a period of time, e.g. a food processor. Producer goods (capital goods) provide producers with additional resources used in the production of other goods, e.g. the machinery needed to make the food processors.

# 1.10 Resources (factors of production)

1 The other side of the economic problem is that economic resources are limited in supply.

2 Resources can be classified as follows:
   (a) *Land* (or natural resources)—i.e. anything which occurs naturally and is available for economic use e.g. coal, North Sea oil.
   (b) *Labour* (or human resources)—e.g. coal miners, teachers, office workers.
   (c) *Capital* (or artificial resources)—e.g. machinery, buildings, vehicles.
   (d) *Enterprise*—i.e. the organisers of the other factors of production, the risk takers in the economy who seek a profit, e.g. Marks & Spencer, Shell and BP.

3 Efficiency of an economy refers to the output of goods and services from a certain input of resources or factors.
   (a) Efficiency can normally be increased if human factors specialise in doing what they are relatively good at, and then exchange the goods and services produced for other goods and services.
   (b) Larger scale operation will normally produce increased efficiency up to a certain point (known as economies of scale), but thereafter efficiency will fall again (known as diseconomies of scale) (see *Unit 4.9*).
   (c) *The Law of Variable Proportions* (or diminishing marginal returns) suggests that efficiency will vary as extra units of a variable factor are introduced alongside certain fixed factors, e.g. the addition of more workers to a factory working with a set amount of machinery. The marginal production of each additional variable factor (e.g. worker) is likely to rise at first but then start to fall, and may even become negative.

9

**4 Production possibility (or transformation) curves** show the quantities of two goods or services that a country can produce with its limited resources.

*Observations from Figure 1.2*
☐ Resources can either be used to make good A or good B.
☐ With existing resources it is possible to combine quantity a1 of good A with quantity b1 of good B, or a2 of A with b2 of B.
☐ Production possibility curves normally slope like this because:
(a) of the incidence of economies and diseconomies of scale,
(b) of the Law of Variable Proportions,
(c) some resources are not suitable for the production of both goods.
☐ Production possibility curves are drawn subject to the following assumptions:
(a) the level of resources is fixed,
(b) the state of technical knowledge is fixed,
(c) goods can be made in a variety of ways requiring various combinations of factors,
(d) each unit of the resources is identical (or homogenous).
☐ It is impossible for a country to produce combinations of goods beyond its production possibility curve.
☐ A combination of goods within the curve indicates that some resources are not fully employed.
☐ An increase in resources, or increased technology, will cause the curve to shift its position outwards, allowing more of both goods to be produced.

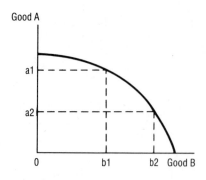

**Figure 1.2** Production possibility curve

# 1.11 Opportunity cost

**1** As wants exceed production (i.e. are relatively scarce) much economic activity is concerned with exercising choices, e.g. what to buy and what to go without, what to make and what not to make.

**2** The basis for making such choices is the concept of *opportunity cost*. The cost of undertaking one form of action is seen as the benefit foregone by not doing the next best alternative. For example the opportunity cost to a company of spending £10m on new machinery is the benefit the company foregoes by not spending the £10m in other ways.

**3** If goods and services are not scarce, i.e. if supply exceeds demand, and no one has been able to secure or exercise ownership rights to the relevant resources, then the goods or services will have no price. They are said to be free goods or services and have no opportunity cost.

## Exercise 4

**1** Classify the following in two ways—as either consumer, consumer durable or producer goods or services, and as either public, merit or private goods or services:
(a) the service of a newsagent
(b) a printing press

(c) a *Mars* bar
(d) a National Health Service hospital
(e) the service provided by traffic wardens
(f) a television
(g) the service of television repair man
(h) a motorway
(i) a fire engine
(j) a council house

2  Classify the following resources as either land, labour, capital or enterprise:
(a) a juggernaught lorry
(b) its driver
(c) its owner
(d) coal
(e) the President of the National Union of Mineworkers
(f) a reservoir
(g) bauxite (the basis of aluminium)
(h) a self-employed window cleaner
(i) the window cleaner's van
(j) the window cleaner's ladder

3  Which of the four kinds of resources (or factors of production) would be involved in the production of the following?
(a) wine
(b) motor cars
(c) the advice from a firm of accountants
(d) a feature film

4  Two Australian scientists become stranded on an island in the Great Barrier Reef. They estimate that if they each spend half a day fishing and half a day hunting they will catch the following:

|  | Fish | Wallabies |
|---|---|---|
| Greg | 3 | 1 |
| Bruce | 2 | 2 |

(a) If they both fish and hunt what will be the total combined catch?
(b) If they decide to specialise in what they are relatively good at, what will the total catch be?
(c) Bruce feels that he could repair their radio if the devoted two full days to this task.
  (i) What is the opportunity cost of repairing the radio?
  (ii) What is the opportunity cost of not repairing the radio?

5  Three classmates are faced with the following situations.
   Pupil X works in a supermarket on Saturdays and earns £25 a day. She is picked to play for the school hockey team who have fixtures on Saturday mornings. She wants to play properly so she buys a new stick costing £15.
   Pupil Y wants to go on the school ski trip. The total cost will be about £300. Her parents say she can go and that they will pay.
   Pupil Z loses her Economics textbook which had cost the school £8. She was asked to pay £4 towards replacing the lost book.

| Good X | Good Y |
|--------|--------|
| 0 | 24 |
| 14 | 21 |
| 26 | 18 |
| 36 | 15 |
| 44 | 12 |
| 50 | 9 |
| 54 | 6 |
| 56 | 3 |
| 57 | 0 |

| Number of assistants | Total value of sales/hour |
|--------|--------|
| 1 | 25 |
| 2 | 70 |
| 3 | 100 |
| 4 | 120 |
| 5 | 130 |
| 6 | 120 |

(a) What was the opportunity cost of Pupil X playing hockey?

(b) What was the opportunity cost to Pupil Y of going on the skiing holiday?

(c) What was the opportunity cost of the skiing holiday to her parents?

(d) What was the opportunity cost to Pupil Z of losing her textbook?

(e) What was the opportunity cost to ratepayers?

6 A country can produce the combinations shown on the left of Goods X and Y from its available resources.

(a) Construct the country's production possibility curve.

(b) What is the opportunity cost of producing 12Y instead of 9Y?

(c) What is the opportunity cost of producing the 57th X?

(d) What can be said about the economy of the country if only 30X are being produced with 12Y?

(e) Is it possible for the country to produce 45X with 18Y?

7 A motorway service station notices that the value of sales from its snack bar varies with the number of assistants employed (see left).

(a) At what point do the returns from employing an extra assistant start to fall?

(b) At what point does the marginal return become negative?

(c) Does this situation conform to the Law of Variable Proportions? Is it at all realistic?

## Review

### Unit 1 will have helped provide answers to the following questions

1 What are the main components of an economic system?

2 What are the main types of economic system chosen by countries?

3 What are the main functions of an economic system?

4 What are the main drawbacks of a free market economic system?

5 What are the main drawbacks of a centrally planned economic system?

6 What are the main ways that economists classify wants and resources?

7 What information is shown in a production possibility curve?

8 What are the advantages and disadvantages of specialisation?

9 What is the concept of opportunity cost?

### Unit 1 has introduced the following terminology

Capital
Centrally planned economic systems
Command economy
Consumer durable goods
Consumer goods
Consumer sovereignty
De-merit goods
Economic efficiency
Economic problem
Economic system
Enterprise
Externalities
Factors of Production
Final goods
Free goods
Free market economic systems
Hierarchy of wants
Intermediate goods
Labour
Land
Law of Variable Proportions
Merit goods
Mixed economic system
Opportunity cost
Planners sovereignty

Price mechanism
Producer goods
Production possibility curves
Public goods
Resources

## Multiple choice questions

1 The Law of Variable Proportions states that as
   additional units of a variable factor are introduced
   to a fixed factor arrangement:
   (a) the marginal and average product will rise at
       first but then fall
   (b) the marginal product will fall continuously,
       while the average product rises continuously
   (c) the average product will rise at first then fall,
       while the marginal product will fall at first then
       rise
   (d) the marginal product will rise until it equals
       the average product
   (e) marginal and average product are constant

2 The demand for a good is:
   (a) the ambition to own it
   (b) the response of quantity bought to a change in
       price
   (c) the amount of a good that will be bought at a
       given price
   (d) the amount of a good that increases a
       consumer's total satisfaction
   (e) the amount of a good that firms are willing to
       produce at a given price

3 A mixed economy is one where:
   (a) there is a well-balanced industrial structure
   (b) people of all races work in industry
   (c) there are some examples of primary, secondary
       and tertiary economic activity
   (d) part of the economy is state owned and
       controlled
   (e) all economic activity is controlled by the
       government

4 Which of the following could not happen in a free
   market economic system?
   (a) private ownership of property
   (b) government control of prices in some markets
   (c) consumers can influence the type and quality
       of production
   (d) free working of the price mechanism
   (e) producers seeking to earn profits

5 Consumer sovereignty means that consumers can:
   (a) satisfy all their needs
   (b) influence the volume of output of different
       goods
   (c) change their purchases if prices change
   (d) form economic pressure groups
   (e) outnumber producers in most markets

6 A key characteristic of centrally planned economies
   is that:
   (a) great emphasis is placed on consumer
       sovereignty

   (b) profits of private manufacturing industry are
       subject to government control
   (c) managers are the ultimate decision takers
   (d) directives rather than prices are used for the
       allocation of resources
   (e) governments may offer incentives to firms to
       locate in depressed regions

7 If goods are described as being relatively scarce it
   means that:
   (a) there are very few of those goods available
   (b) there are insufficient of those goods to meet
       total demand
   (c) the goods are limited in supply
   (d) there are not enough of the goods to satisfy all
       the wants of the consumers
   (e) the goods are high in the hierarchy of wants

8 The economic problem common to all societies is:
   (a) how to allocate scarce resources
   (b) how to test economic theories
   (c) how to achieve full employment
   (d) how to stop people wanting more and more
   (e) how to stabilise prices

9 Markets are necessary because:
   (a) people need to be able to shop around
   (b) people do not know the opportunity costs
   (c) producers and consumers are often not the
       same people
   (d) consumers benefit if they specialise
   (e) barter is inefficient

10 The cost to the country of developing transplant
   surgery techniques is:
   (a) the taxpayers' money used for its development
   (b) the value of the other goods that could have
       been provided with the money
   (c) over £10 m
   (d) benefits to other medical programmes
       discovered in the transplant operations
   (e) the cost of development of other hospitals

11 Specialisation occurs for all but one of the
   following:
   (a) people have different abilities
   (b) places have different characteristics
   (c) people work better when they concentrate on
       one activity
   (d) specialisation makes the job more interesting
   (e) specialisation makes better use of scarce
       resources

12 Which of the following must be found together for
   the basic economic problem to arise?
       (i) wants are unlimited
       (i) wants are subject to a hierarchy of wants
       (iii) resources are limited
       (iv) resources can be combined in a number of
       ways

   (a) (i) and (ii) only
   (b) (i) and (iii) only
   (c) all four

(d) (iii) and (iv) only

(e) (i), (ii) and (iii) only

# Answers

## Exercise 1

1 (a) Officials of the Central Planning Authority under direction from the Soviet Communist Party. Market forces determine sales in Britain.

(b) A black market exists alongside a controlled market. Where demand exceeds supply at the controlled price, market forces push up the black market price. Black markets do exist in Britain.

(c) In Britain tickets were available to those that choose to spend some of their income (£2.30) on buying a ticket (as supply exceeded demand at this price). In Czechoslovakia tickets were allocated as a reward for approved political and economic behaviour.

(d) In Britain workers are motivated by, amongst other things, chances to increase their personal incomes. In Czechoslovakia the pursuit of private individual gain is subordinated to the pursuit of national targets.

2 (a) Five year plans would allocate resources and set production targets. In Britain the government controls the economy through indirect measures e.g. taxation and government spending, and it does have a medium term plan to cover this activity.

(b) In the Soviet Union more resources would be allocated to this area by the central planners. In Britain prices would rise providing an incentive for firms to make a profit by providing the good or service in question.

(c) The retail buyer appears to control the quality of output from producers and to distribute goods to shops. Choice of goods is limited (unless the consumer obtains some foreign currency).

(d) Workers and managers may suffer penalties. In Britain consumers would stop buying goods from the firm and the firm would go out of business.

(e) Both economies have to find an answer to the basic economic problem of unlimited wants and limited resources.

## Exercise 2

2 Refer to the features in *Unit 1.6* and the components in *Unit 1.3*.

## Exercise 3

1 (a) Lighthouses—taxpayer

(b) Lifeboats—charity RNLI

(c) Agricultural products—controlled market

(d) Agricultural machinery—free market

(e) Letter delivery—monopoly of Post Office

(f) Telephone installation—monopoly of British Telecom

(g) Central banking—nationalised Bank of England

(h) High Street banking—private firms operate these banks, entry of foreign banks controlled by government.

(i) Police security—state provision, but public may have to pay (e.g. at big public events)

(j) Private security—private firms provide the service for private clients

The question is designed to show the somewhat arbitrary division between goods and services the state produces in Britain and those that the private sector is allowed to provide.

2 (a) The Lake District is a free gift of nature. There was no supply price. There are social costs involved, e.g. footpath repair.

(b) Salford University is part state financed and part financed by private enterprise. To the students their education is probably a merit service.

(c) Transport is normally considered a merit service. It is subsidised because there are externalities involved, e.g. encouragement of tourism.

(d) There was cost to the taxpayer involved, and the benefit was specifically for the student. But it would be unacceptable to leave him there if he could not afford the rescue price.

(e) Volunteers. No, the resources involved could have been used for other things.

(f) Generally health care is a merit service, although there are aspects of public service about it.

3 Suggested essay plan.

Introduction: Definition of terms (i) Economic system (ii) Free market (iii) Centrally planned (iv) Mixed economy

## Exercise 2

1

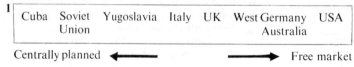

| Cuba | Soviet Union | Yugoslavia | Italy | UK | West Germany | USA |
| | | | | | Australia | |

Centrally planned ← → Free market

Main paragraphs:   (i) Basic components (see *Unit 1.3*) (ii) Problems with free market economies (see *Unit 1.7*) (iii) Problems with centrally planned economies (see *Unit 1.8*)

Conclusion:   Mixed economies seek the best of both systems.

## Exercise 4

**1**

|  | Consumer, consumer durable, producer goods/service | Public merit or private goods/service |
|---|---|---|
| Newsagent | consumer service | private |
| Printing press | capital good | private |
| *Mars* bar | consumer good | private |
| NHS hospital | capital good | public/merit |
| Traffic wardens | consumer service | public |
| Television | consumer durable | private |
| TV repairman | consumer service | private |
| Motorway | capital good | public |
| Fire engine | capital good | public/merit |
| Council house | capital good | merit |

**2** (a) capital     (f) capital
   (b) labour     (g) land
   (c) enterprise     (h) enterprise
   (d) land     (i) capital
   (e) labour     (j) capital

**3** All four types of factors would be needed. Very little can be produced without combining all types of factors.

**4** (a) 5 fish (3 + 2) and 3 wallabies (1 + 2).
   (b) 6 fish (3 × 2 from Greg) and 4 wallabies (2 × 2 from Bruce).
   (c) (i) The loss of his hunting, i.e. 8 wallabies (if they specialise) or 4 fish and 4 wallabies (if they do not specialise).
   (ii) Benefit foregone through not being rescued.

**5** (a) The benefit she forgoes by not having £40 to spend in the first week and £25 afterwards.
   (b) Nothing—she goes without nothing as her parents pay.
   (c) The goods and services her parents could have bought for £300.
   (d) The goods and services she could have bought with £4.
   (e) The goods and services the ratepayers went without from wasting £4.

**6** (a) Plot quantity of Good X on vertical axis against quantity of Good Y on the horizontal axis.
   (b) 6X will be lost (50 down to 44).
   (c) 3X will be lost (3 down to 0).
   (d) Unemployment of some resources, or some resources not operating at full capacity.
   (e) Not at present. The country needs more resources e.g. from economic growth.

**7** (a) After 3 assistants (Marginal sales of 3rd = 30, of 4th = 20)
   (b) After 5th assistant (Marginal sales of 6th = − 10)
   (c) Yes. Yes!

## Multiple choice answers

**1** (a) See *Unit 1.10 (3)*.
**2** (c) See *Unit 1.9*.
**3** (d) See *Unit 1.2*.
**4** (b) There is no government intervention in free markets.
**5** (b) See *Unit 1.4 (2)*.
**6** (d) See *Unit 1.3*.
**7** (d) i.e. there is no opportunity cost involved if things are not relatively scarce.
**8** (a) See *Unit 1.5*.
**9** (c) Markets bring producers and consumers together.
**10** (b) i.e. opportunity cost.
**11** (d) Over-specialisation may make the job boring.
**12** (b) Limited resources to satisfy unlimited wants.

# UNIT 2　Demand

## 2.1 Preview

1　Demand refers to purchases of goods and services.
2　The level of purchases of a product will be affected by a number of variables, including its price, the price of other connected products and the income levels of consumers.
3　The relationship between quantity demanded and the price of the good is shown in the demand curve for the product. Normally demand curves slope downwards to the right, i.e. as price rises quantity demanded falls, and vice versa.
4　Demand curves can be generated through two theoretical approaches: (a) utility analysis and (b) indifference curve analysis.

## 2.2 Some definitions

1　**Effective demand**
   Economists are concerned with realistic wants, i.e.wants that are supported by the ability to pay for them.

2　**The quantity demanded**
   The amount of a good or service that is purchased over a given period of time at a given price.

3　**A demand curve**
   A line connecting a series of points which show the quantity of a good demanded at various price levels.

4　**Individual consumer's demand**
   The quantity of goods and services purchased by an individual.

5　**Market demand**
   The total quantity demanded of a particular good or service. Market demand is the sum of all individuals' demand for a good or service.

6　**Consumer equilibrium**
   Consumers are said to be in equilibrium when they are spending their incomes so as to get maximum satisfaction, i.e. they cannot change their pattern of expenditure and increase their total satisfaction.

## 2.3 Assumptions about consumer behaviour

1　The two theoretical approaches to generating demand curves outlined below are based on specific assumptions as to how consumers behave, the nature of the products available to be purchased, and conditions of the market place where the goods and services are purchased.

2  These assumptions are:
   (a) *Rationality*—consumers will spend their incomes in order to get maximum satisfaction.
   (b) *Perfect knowledge*—consumers know all the relevant information about the prices, quality and availability of goods.
   (c) *Homogeneity*—each unit of a good or service is identical; the output of one firm is the same as the output of another firm.
   (d) *Divisibility*—goods can be purchased in the exact quantity desired.
   (e) *Many buyers*—no single consumer can influence the market price by adjusting his level of purchases.
   (f) *Fixed wants*—consumers are consistent in their preferences for products.

## 2.4 The relationship between price and quantity demanded

1  In most situations, as price rises the quantity demanded of a product falls, and as price falls quantity demanded rises.
   *Observations from Figure 2.1*
   ☐ At price P1, quantity demanded of Good X is Q1.
   ☐ At lower price P2, quantity demanded is higher at Q2.
   ☐ The demand curve is drawn on the assumption that all other factors that affect quantity demanded (e.g. incomes and prices of other goods) are constant. For convenience, economists refer to this assumption through the Latin phrase *ceteris paribus* (other things being equal).

2  This commonsense relationship between price and quantity demanded can be derived from two theoretical approaches:
   (a) Utility analysis (see *Unit 2.5*) and
   (b) Indifference curve analysis (see *Unit 2.6*).

3  There are some exceptional demand curves where the quantity demanded of a product rises as price rises (see *Unit 2.10*).

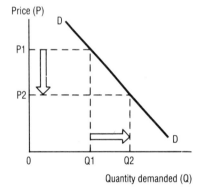

**Figure 2.1**  Demand curve for Good X

## 2.5 Utility analysis

1  **Utility** is the name economists use for the satisfaction, benefit or usefulness of a good or service for the consumer.

2  **Total utility** is the combined utility obtained from the consumption of a number of units of a good or service, i.e. the total benefit gained from drinking ten cans of *Coca Cola* in an afternoon.

3  **Marginal utility** is the extra utility obtained from the consumption of the last unit of a good or service, i.e. the additional benefit gained from drinking the tenth can of *Coca Cola*.

4  Utility is a difficult concept because:
   (a) *it is subjective*—i.e. it depends on the preferences of individuals,
   (b) *it has no units of measurement*—although different levels of utility can be detected and ranked.

5 Utility analysis is based on two principles.

(a) *Diminishing marginal utility*. For most goods, the extra utility gained from the consumption of additional units of a product falls after a certain level of consumption.

*Observations from Figure 2.2*

☐ Consumption of Q1 goods generates marginal utility MU1.

☐ Consumption of Q2 goods generates lower marginal utility at MU2.

(b) *Equi-marginal returns*. A consumer will get maximum satisfaction from spending his income if he allocates his expenditure so that for all goods the ratio of marginal utility to price of the good is the same.

$$\frac{MUa}{Pa} = \frac{MUb}{Pb} = \frac{MUc}{Pc} = \text{etc.}$$

where MUa = the marginal utility received from consumption of the last unit of good A

Pa = the price per unit of good A

If the consumer allocates his expenditure according to the principle of equi-marginal returns he will be in equilibrium and acting rationally.

6 There are four steps to deriving the demand curve relationship.

(a) Assume price of good A rises. MUa:Pa no longer equals MUb:Pb.

(b) To re-establish the principle of equi-marginal returns the consumer will have to raise the level of marginal utility received from good A.

(c) According to the concept of diminishing marginal utility this can be done by reducing the quantity of good A consumed.

(d) So, a rational consumer, when faced with the rise in price of good A reacts by cutting down his purchases of good A.

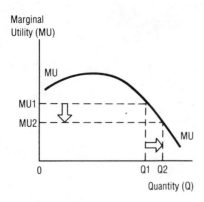

**Figure 2.2** Marginal utility curve

# Exercise 1

1 A consumer attempts to measure the total satisfaction he receives from the consumption of different quantities of three goods, A, B and C.

| Quantity | Total utility | | |
|---|---|---|---|
| | from A | from B | from C |
| 1 | 9 | 16 | 27 |
| 2 | 17 | 33 | 51 |
| 3 | 24 | 49 | 75 |
| 4 | 30 | 61 | 99 |
| 5 | 34 | 69 | 109 |
| 6 | 36 | 73 | 113 |
| 7 | 36 | 72 | 110 |

There is £40 per month available to be spent on these goods. The unit price of good A is £2, of good B £4, and of good C £8.

(a) What would be the consumer's total utility from consumption of these goods if he bought:
　　(i) 4 units of A + 2 units of B + 3 units of C
　　(ii) 2 units of A + 7 units of B + 1 unit of C
　　(iii) 2 units of A + 3 units of B + 3 units of C

(b) For each combination of purchases in part (a) above calculate the ratio of marginal utility and price for each good.

(c) Why do the results from (b) above show that none of these combinations is the best combination possible?

(d) Which combination of purchases would give the consumer maximum satisfaction?

(e) If the price of good C fell to £6 per unit what would happen to his combination of purchases?

(f) As a result of the fall in price of good C what has happened to the level of demand for good C?

## 2.6 Indifference curve analysis

1　**An indifference curve** is a line which shows combinations of two goods that give a consumer equal levels of satisfaction, i.e. the consumer is indifferent about which combination is purchased because both yield the same level of utility.
*Observations from Figure 2.3*
☐ The consumer can spend his income on either clothes or entertainment.
☐ Combinations C1 + E1, C2 + E2 and C3 + E3 all yield the same level of total satisfaction.
☐ As the consumer reduces the level of consumption of one good the remaining units of that good become more important, i.e. marginal utility rises, so there must be a substitution of larger numbers of units of the other good (where marginal utility is now low) to compensate.
☐ The gradient at each particular point on the indifference curve is known as the *marginal rate of substitution* of the one good for the other.

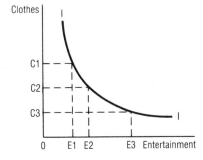

**Figure 2.3**　An indifference curve

2　**An indifference map** is a collection of indifference curves, each curve representing a different level of total satisfaction for the consumer.
*Observations from Figure 2.4*
☐ In theory there are an infinite number of indifference curves on the indifference map.
☐ The indifference curves cannot cross. They each represent a different 'contour' of satisfaction.
☐ The further away from the origin the indifference curve is drawn, the higher level of total satisfaction it represents.

3　**A budget line** shows two key pieces of information:
(a) *the consumer's budget constraint*—i.e. the number of the two goods the consumer could buy with his income.
(b) *the relative price levels of the two goods*—a change in unit price of either good will change the number of units it is possible to buy with a given level of income, and hence alter the gradient of the budget line.

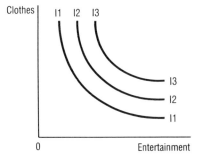

**Figure 2.4**　An indifference map

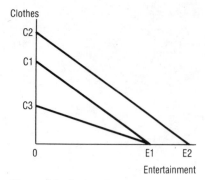

**Figure 2.5**  Budget lines

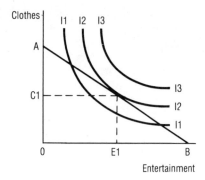

**Figure 2.6**  Consumer equilibrium

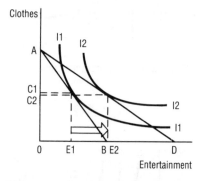

**Figure 2.7**  The effect of a fall in price of entertainment

*Observations from Figure 2.5*
□ If all the consumer's budget is spent on clothes quantity C1 can be bought. If all the income is spent on entertainment quantity E1 can be bought.
□ If the consumer's budget increases and the prices of clothes and entertainment stay the same purchases of the two goods can be increased to C2 and E2 respectively.
□ If the price of clothes rises, and the consumer's income stays the same, then fewer clothes can be bought from the fixed budget, i.e. quantity C3.
□ In summary, the position of the budget line shows the level of income of the consumer, the slope of the line shows the relative price levels of the two goods.

**4   The relationship between price and quantity demanded**
(a) Indifference curves show what consumers might do.
(b) Budget lines show what consumers can do.
(c) Combining the two shows what consumers will do.
(d) The consumer will be in equilibrium when he is getting the maximum satisfaction possible from spending his income, i.e. when he is consuming at a point on the highest possible indifference curve given his budget level. This is represented by the point where the budget line forms a tangent to the indifference curve.
*Observations from Figure 2.6*
□ I1, I2 and I3 represent indifference curves for a consumer.
□ AB represents the consumer's budget constraint (budget line).
□ The consumer will be in equilibrium when he consumes C1 clothing and E1 entertainment. At this combination the consumer is on the highest possible indifference curve.

**5   The effect of a change in price of entertainment**
*Observations from Figure 2.7*
□ AB represents the consumer's original budget constraint, and C1 and E1 the consumer's original combinations of purchases.
□ AD represents the new budget constraint when the price of entertainment falls, because more entertainment can now be bought.
□ The new equilibrium position for the consumer is C2 and E2 because here the consumer is consuming at a point on the highest possible indifference curve.
□ The result of the fall in price of entertainment was for the quantity of entertainment consumed to rise, and the quantity of clothes bought to fall slightly.

## 2.7  Income and substitution effects

1   The overall effect of changing price incorporates two separate elements.
   (a) *A substitution effect*—because one good is now relatively cheaper than the other good.
   (b) *An income effect*—because the purchasing power or real value of the consumer's income has changed.

2   These separate effects can be shown with the use of indifference curve analysis.

*Observations from Figure 2.8*

☐ AB is the original budget line. C1 and E1 are the original combination of purchases.

☐ Line XX isolates the substitution effect by changing the gradient of AB to reflect the new price relationship following the fall in the price of entertainment, but leaving real income unchanged, and is tangential to the original indifference curve I1.

☐ The substitution effect alone would move the point of consumption to C2/E2.

☐ The income effect is isolated by allowing XX to move parallel to AD, indicating a rise in real income, but no further change in relative prices.

☐ Purchases now move to combination C3/E3, which indicates the new equilibrium position and the overall price effect.

☐ In summary, the overall price effect is the sum of separate substitution and income effects.

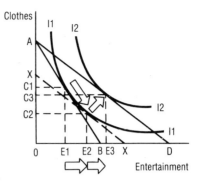

**Figure 2.8** The substitution and income effects

## 2.8 Links between the two theoretical approaches

1 Two obvious links between utility analysis and indifference curve analysis are:

(a) the shape of the indifference curve is governed by the principle of diminishing marginal utility,

(b) at the equilibrium point of consumption the gradient of the indifference curve equals the gradient of the budget line. So at the point of tangency:

$$\frac{MU \text{ (clothes)}}{MU \text{ (entertainment)}} = \frac{P \text{ (clothes)}}{P \text{ (entertainment)}}$$

which can be re-written to coincide with the relationship observed in the principle of equi-marginal returns (see *Unit 2.5 [5]*).

## Exercise 2

1 A consumer can spend his income on books or leave it in money form. He calculates the combinations of books and money remaining for three different levels of satisfaction.

| Level 1 | | Level 2 | | Level 3 | |
|---|---|---|---|---|---|
| £ | Books | £ | Books | £ | Books |
| 100 | 6 | 100 | 25 | 80 | 63 |
| 80 | 10 | 80 | 30 | 60 | 65 |
| 60 | 16 | 60 | 35 | 50 | 67 |
| 50 | 23 | 50 | 40 | 40 | 75 |
| 40 | 30 | 40 | 50 | 35 | 85 |
| 25 | 50 | 25 | 75 | 30 | 105 |
| 15 | 60 | 20 | 95 | 20 | 125 |

(a) Draw the indifference map which results from these calculations.

(b) If the level of income is £100 per month construct budget lines when the price of books is: i) £0.80p each, ii) £1.25 each, iii) £2.50 each

(c) What will be the quantity of books purchased at each price level?

(d) Use this information to construct the consumer's demand curve for books.

2   For an overweight boy the following purchases of chocolate bars and thick shakes each week yield the same level of satisfaction.

| Thick shakes | Chocolate bars |
|---|---|
| 2 | 9 |
| 3 | 7 |
| 4 | 5.5 |
| 5 | 4.5 |
| 7 | 3 |
| 10 | 2 |

(a) How many chocolate bars is he prepared to go without if he buys 3 thick shakes instead of 2?

(b) What is his marginal rate of substitution at the point of 3 thick shakes and 7 chocolates bars on the indifference curve?

(c) What can be inferred about the relative prices of the two products if he does buy 7 thick shakes and 3 chocolate bars?

(d) If his preferred combination changed to 10 thick shakes and 2 chocolate bars what would have happend to the relative prices of the two products?

3   If a consumer's budget line was not straight but concave to the origin which of the assumptions listed in *Unit 2.3* could not be operative?

4   **Essay**
How do rational consumers react to changes in prices of the goods they buy?

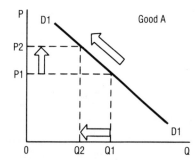

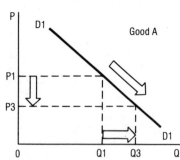

**Figure 2.9**  Movement along demand curves

## 2.9 Movements along and shifts in demand curves

1   **A change in quantity demanded** refers to the change in the level of demand for a product following a change in price of that product. It is shown by a *movement along* the original demand curve. *Observations from Figure 2.9*

☐ A rise in price of Good A from P1 to P2 causes a fall in quantity demanded, from Q1 to Q2, and is shown by a movement along the original demand curve D1.

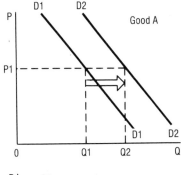

□ A fall in the price of Good A from P1 to P3 causes a rise in quantity demanded from Q1 to Q3, and is shown by a movement along the original demand curve D1.

2  **A change in demand** refers to the change in the level of demand for a product following a change in any other factor, other than the price of the product itself. It is shown by a *shift* in the position of the whole demand curve.
*Observations from Figure 2.10*
□ A rise in demand for Good A is shown by a movement of the demand curve from D1 to D2. At the original price P1 more of the good is now demanded, Q1 to Q2.
□ A fall in demand for Good A is shown by a leftwards movement of the demand curve from D1 to D3. At the original price P1 less of the good is now demanded, Q1 to Q3.

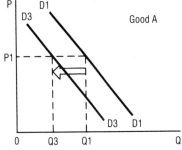

**Figure 2.10**  Shifts in demand curves

3  **Factors leading to a change in demand**
There are several factors which cause a change in demand for a product.
(a) *Change in the size and composition of the population*—e.g. a rise in the number of elderly people causes increased demand for health and social services.
(b) *Change in the size and distribution of incomes*—e.g. a fall in personal incomes leads to a fall in the demand for durable goods.
(c) *Change in the price and availability of complementary goods*— e.g. a fall in the price of salad foods leads to an increase in the demand for salad cream.
(d) *Change in the price and availability of substitute goods*—e.g. cheaper coach travel will lead to a fall in demand for rail travel.
(e) *Changes in fashion and taste*—e.g. the rise and fall in demand for skateboards in the 1970s.
(f) *Changes in marketing strategy and advertising*—e.g. the development of good promotional videos for pop music records.
(g) *Changes in the expectations of future price levels*—e.g. the rise in the demand for petrol in the days before a budget.
(h) *Changes in the law*—e.g. if wearing rear seatbelts became law then there would be an increased demand for them.
(i) *Changes in quality and reputation*—e.g. the fall and rise of sales of Jaguar cars in the United States in the late 1970s and early 1980s.
(j) *The introduction of a new product*—e.g. the rise of sales of personal (walkman) radios.
Students should be able to think of many more factors which will affect the demand levels of particular products.

┌─ Exercise 3 ─────────────────────────────

1  For each of the following situations state whether a change in demand would be illustrated by:
    i) a shift to the left of the demand curve
   ii) a shift to the right of the demand curve
  iii) a movement along the original demand curve

| Question | Product | Circumstance |
|---|---|---|
| (a) | Pan-Am flights to USA | New, successful advertising by British Airways |
| (b) | Beer sales in public houses | Stricter enforcement of breath tests for motorists |
| (c) | Jogging suits | Increased passion for fitness |
| (d) | Apples | Fall in the price of apples |
| (e) | Apples | Fall in the price of oranges |
| (f) | Baby foods | Fall in the birth rate |
| (g) | New model of a car | Strike at the factory where the car was produced |
| (h) | Telephone calls | Rise in postal rates |
| (i) | Bus travel | Increase in subsidies from local councils |
| (j) | Dishwashers | Big redundancy pay paid to local workers |
| (k) | Steel | General fall in the level of economic activity |
| (l) | Whisky | Budget next week |
| (m) | Computer programs | Growth of use of computers in business |
| (n) | Pop record | Appearance on *Top of the Pops* |
| (o) | Shares in London Brick PLC | News of a take-over bid for the company |

2   In May 1983 Sony launched its 2″-screen Watchman TV in Britain. The set was the visual companion to the highly successful Walkman portable stereo radio/cassette player. Initially the Watchman was priced at £250.

Sony leapt into the lead with its flat display tube because the rival British product designed by Sir Clive Sinclair was held up by a five week sit-in at the Timex plant in Dundee where it was being produced.

The launch of the Sony product, however, guaranteed advance publicity for the Sinclair set which appeared to be of superior design, e.g. its rechargeable batteries last eleven hours instead of Sony's two-and-a-half, and would retail for only £60.

Bus queues, parks and sports grounds were thought likely places to 'sprout' the Watchman, for it had already proved a huge success in the United States and Japan.

(a)   Describe the various factors influencing the level of demand for Watchman TVs in the summer of 1983.

3   **Essay**

Distinguish between a change in quantity demanded and a change in demand. With reference to a specific good or service of your choice, state why the quantity of the product demanded at a given price will vary from time to time.

## 2.10 Exceptional demand curves

1 **Perverse demand curves** are those which refer to goods where demand rises as price rises.
*Observations from Figure 2.11*
☐ At price P1 quantity demanded is Q1.
☐ At higher price P2, quantity demanded has risen to Q2.

2 Possible explanations for this behaviour include:
(a) *Speculative purchases*—consumers may think the price rise is an indication of even further price rises.
(b) *'Snob' purchases*—consumers may regard the goods as a status symbol whose high price makes them a rarity.
(c) *'Giffin goods'*—are those which are inferior (i.e. have a negative income elasticity of demand (see *Unit 3.5*) and form a large proportion of a consumer's expenditure.

3 In many cases the demand curve may not be perverse, but only appear to be so, as the change in price causes a change in some other important factor and thus causes both a movement along and shift in the demand curve at the same time.
*Observations from Figure 2.12*
☐ A fall in the price of shares from P1 to P2 causes an increase in demand for them, from Q1 to Q2.
☐ The fall in price is taken as an indication of further falls in price so the demand curve for the shares shifts to the left, D1 to D2, and a fall in quantity demanded to Q3.
☐ The combination gives the effect of a perverse demand curve, D3.

## 2.11 Other terms defined

1 **Joint demand**
Goods that are demanded for joint use, e.g. electricity and electrical goods are said to be in joint demand. This is similar to the concept of complementary goods developed in *Unit 3*.

2 **Composite demand**
When a good can be used for several purposes, e.g. trains can be used for business travel or leisure travel, the demand for that good is said to be a composite demand.

3 **Competitive demand**
Goods that are very close substitutes for each other, e.g. daily newspapers, are said to be in competitive demand.

4 **Derived demand**
Goods that are not bought for their own sake, but as components or inputs for the manufacture of some other good, e.g. employees in a factory, are said to have a derived demand (see *Unit 8*).

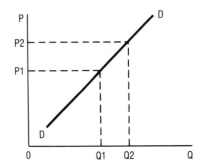

**Figure 2.11** Perverse demand curve

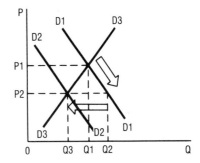

**Figure 2.12** Price and quantity demanded of shares

# Review

## Unit 2 will have helped provide answers to the following questions

1 What are the basic assumptions about consumer behaviour which are the basis for utility and indifference curve analysis?
2 How is the relationship of price and quantity demanded derived from utility analysis?
3 How is the above relationship derived from indifference curve analysis?
4 How can it be shown that the overall price effect is made up of separate substitution and income effects?
5 What is the difference between a change in quantity demanded and a change in demand?
6 What may cause a demand curve to shift its position?
7 What may cause a movement along a demand curve?
8 Why do some demand curves appear to slope upwards to the right?

## Unit 2 has introduced the following terminology

Budget lines
*Ceteris Paribus*
Change in demand
Change in quantity demanded
Competitive demand
Composite demand
Derived demand
Diminishing marginal utility
Effective demand
Equilibrium (of the consumer)
Equi-marginal returns
Giffen goods
Income effect
Indifference curves
Individual consumer demand
Joint demand
Marginal rate of substitution
Marginal utility
Market demand
Movement along (a demand curve)
Perverse demand
Rational behaviour
Shift (of a demand curve)
Substitution effect
Utility

## Multiple choice questions

1 A rational consumer is one who:
   (a) behaves in a sensible way at all times
   (b) is not influenced by advertising
   (c) knows the prices of all goods and buys the cheapest
   (d) purchases goods so as to get maximum satisfaction from spending his income
   (e) has perfect knowledge of the market

2 The total utility derived by a consumer from eight records less the total utility derived from seven records is the:
   (a) consumer surplus of the eighth record
   (b) marginal utility of eight records
   (c) derived demand for records
   (d) equilibrium level of demand for records
   (e) marginal utility of the eighth record

3 A consumer will be in equilibrium when income is spent according to the:
   (a) law of diminishing marginal utility
   (b) principle of increasing returns
   (c) law of supply and demand
   (d) principle of equi-marginal returns
   (e) marginal consumption principle

4 A consumer will stop buying *Mars* bars when:
   (a) marginal utility from the last bar falls to zero
   (b) total utility from all bars falls to zero
   (c) total utility from all bars is negative
   (d) the marginal utility to price ratio for bars equals the ratio for other goods
   (e) the 'fridge is full'

5 The Law of Diminishing Marginal Utility states that:
   (a) the more of a good you buy the less extra benefit you receive from additional purchases of the good,
   (b) the more of a good you buy the more total utility will fall,
   (c) as more units of a good are bought so the price of the good will fall,
   (d) as more of a good is bought the marginal rate of substitution will fall,
   (e) the more of a good that is bought the more benefit consumers receive from extra purchases.

6 Which of the following will *not* affect the marginal utility of a commodity or service?
   (a) the price of the good
   (b) the quantity of the good purchased
   (c) a change in tastes
   (d) a change in consumers' needs
   (e) changes in fashion

7 The movement of a budget line to a parallel position to the right of the original line indicates that:
   (a) there has been a change in relative prices
   (b) there has been a change in absolute prices
   (c) consumers' tastes for each good has risen
   (d) consumers' real income has risen
   (e) the marginal rate of substitution for both goods has risen

8 If a consumer is allocating income between two goods so that at the chosen combination of goods the budget line forms a tangent to an indifference curve, the consumer:
   (a) is buying too much of both goods
   (b) is buying the same quantity of both goods

(c) is paying the same price for both goods
(d) cannot increase satisfaction without an increase in income
(e) cannot be acting rationally

**9**

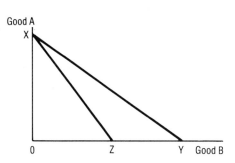

**Figure 2.13** Budget lines

In Figure 2.13 which could have caused a shift of the budget line from XY to XZ?
(a) a rise in real income
(b) a rise in the absolute price of A
(c) a fall in the absolute price of B
(d) a rise in money income
(e) a rise in the absolute price of B

**10** Which of the following best defines derived demand?
(a) wants backed up by the ability to pay for them
(b) the amount of a good demanded over a period of time at different price levels
(c) demand arising out of the joint use of two goods
(d) demand for factors of production arising from the nature of demand for the final good
(e) demand for goods that are very close substitutes

## Answers

### Exercise 1

**1** (a) i) 138 (30 from A, 33 from B, 75 from C)
ii) 116 (17 from A, 72 from B, 27 from C)
iii) 141 (17 from A, 49 from B, 75 from C)
(b) i) 3:1 (MU from 4th A = 6, Price of A = 2)
17:4 (MU from 2nd B = 17, Price of B = 4)
3:1 (MU from 3rd C = 24, Price of C = 8)
ii) 4:1 for A, −1:4 for B, 27:8 for C
iii) 4:1 for A, 4:1 for B, 3:1 for C
(c) MU:P ratio is not the same for all goods. The principle of equi-marginal returns is not upheld,
(d) 4A, 4B and 2C (Total utility = 142, MU:P for all goods is 3:1)
(e) 2A, 3B and 4C (Total utility = 165, MU:P for all goods is 4:1)
(f) Quantity of C bought has risen from 2 to 4, the result expected from a fall in price

### Exercise 2

**1** (a)

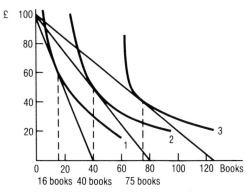

**Figure 2.14** A consumer's demand for books

(b) i) At price £0.80p each can buy 125 books and have £0 left
ii) At price £1.25 each can buy 80 books and have £0 left
iii) At price £2.50 each can buy 40 books and have £0 left
(c) i) 75 books
ii) 40 books
iii) 16 books—found where budget line is a tangent to highest indifference curve
(d) Demand curves show the quantity demanded at various prices, here a line joining points: i) price £0.80/quantity 75 books ii) price £1.25/quantity 40 books iii) price £2.50/quantity 16 books.
N.B. the demand curve slopes downwards to the right.

**2** (a) 2
(b) Between 1.5 and 2 chocolate bars for 1 thick shake. Marginal rate of substitution is the gradient of the indifference curve.
(c) At this point budget line must have some gradient as indifference curve, and the gradient of the budget line indicates relative prices. Thick shakes are about half the price of chocolate bars if he consumes at this point.
(d) Thick shakes would have become cheaper relative to chocolate bars.

**3** The consumer would be able to influence the price of the products he was buying, i.e. he would not be one of many consumers.

**4** Suggested essay plan.
Introduction:  Definition of terms i) Rational consumer behaviour
Main paragraphs:  i) Utility analysis (see *Unit 2.5* *[1 to 6]*)
ii) Indifference curve analysis (see *Unit 2.6* *[1 to 5]*)
iii) Normal shaped demand curves.
Conclusion.

**Exercise 3**

**1**

| a | shift left | Pan-Am and British Airways compete. More people fly BA |
|---|---|---|
| b | shift left | Legal changes cause fall in demand for beer in public houses |
| c | shift right | Fashion leads to increase in demand |
| d | movement along | Price fall leads to increase in quantity demanded |
| e | shift left | More oranges are bought, less competing apples are demanded |
| f | shift left | Change in age structure of population |
| g | shift left | Lack of availability may cause purchases to shift elsewhere |
| h | shift right | Fewer communications by letter, more by telephone |
| i | movement along | Subsidy cuts the cost of fares, more bus journeys demanded |
| j | shift right | Rise in incomes (at least in the short run) |
| k | shift left | Demand for steel derived from demand for final goods |
| l | shift right | Prices are expected to rise as excise duty is raised |
| m | shift right | Software and hardware are complementary |
| n | shift right | An example of successful marketing |
| o | shift right | More demanded as chance of a capital gain emerges |

**2** Watchman TVs—factors tending to lower demand: i) better product being developed, ii) prices expected to fall, iii) support for the British producer (?) —factors tending to increase demand: i) people become more familiar with the product ii) proven product already selling overseas iii) doubts about production and availability of Sinclair product.

**3** Suggested essay plan.
Introduction:   Definition of terms i) Change in quantity demanded refers to change in price, shown by movement along demand curve ii) Change in demand refers to change in any other factor, shown by shift of demand curve.
Main paragraphs:   Chosen product and influence of factors in *Unit 2.9 (3)* and others. Diagrams to show shift in demand curve.
Conclusion.

## Multiple choice answers

**1** (d)  By definition.
**2** (e)  i.e. the extra utility from the eighth record.
**3** (d)  Following equi-marginal returns maximises satisfaction.
**4** (d)  i.e. the consumer conforms to the principle of equi-marginal returns.
**5** (a)  Marginal utility decreases as the quantity consumed increases.
**6** (a)  Marginal utility is a subjective value with which price is compared.
**7** (d)  No change in gradient indicates no change in prices.
**8** (d)  i.e. the consumer is on the highest indifference curve possible.
**9** (e)  Consumers can buy less B with their income if the price of B rises.
**10** (d)  By definition.

# Elasticity of demand UNIT 3

## 3.2 Demand and revenue curves

1 **Total revenue** (or outlay) is the quantity sold (or bought) multiplied by the price of the good.
2 **Average revenue** is total revenue divided by the price of the good, i.e. average revenue equals the price of the good.
3 **Marginal revenue** is the additional revenue received by a firm from selling the last unit of a good.
4 **Revenue and demand curves**
   *Observations from Figure 3.1*
   ☐ If the firm charges P1 for its good it can sell Q1.
   ☐ At price P1 total revenue received will be indicated by the rectangle described by 0P1/0Q1.
   ☐ At lower price P2 the firm can sell quantity Q2, and will receive revenue 0P2/0Q2.
   *Observations from Figure 3.2*
   ☐ If average revenue slopes as shown in AR1, total revenue (TR) will rise at a decreasing rate and then begin to fall, and marginal revenue (MR) will be half-way between AR1 and the vertical axis and have twice the gradient of AR1.

## 3.3 Price elasticity of demand

1 **Price elasticity of demand (PED)** is a measure of the responsiveness of quantity demanded to a change in the price of the good.
2 It is calculated as:

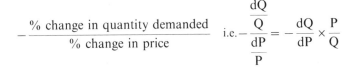

$$-\frac{\% \text{ change in quantity demanded}}{\% \text{ change in price}} \quad \text{i.e.} - \frac{\dfrac{dQ}{Q}}{\dfrac{dP}{P}} = -\frac{dQ}{dP} \times \frac{P}{Q}$$

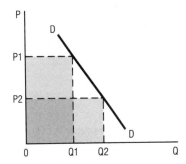

**Figure 3.1** Demand curve

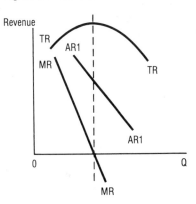

**Figure 3.2** Revenue curve

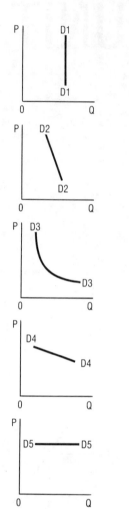

**Figure 3.3** Price elasticity of demand

where dQ = the change in quantity demanded
Q = the original quantity demanded
dP = the change in price of the good
P = the original price of the good

The minus sign is added for convenience so that all PEDs are positive.

3 **Specific demand curves**
*Observations from Figure 3.3*
☐ Demand curve D1 shows perfectly inelastic price elasticity of demand, i.e. there is no change in quantity demanded when price changes. PED = 0.
☐ Demand curve D2 shows relatively inelastic price elasticity of demand, i.e. there is only a small change in quantity demanded when price changes. PED is between 0 and 1.
☐ Demand curve D3 shows unitary price elasticity of demand, i.e. the proportionate change in quantity demanded is exactly the same as the proportionate change in price. PED = 1.
☐ Demand curve D4 shows relatively elastic price elasticity of demand, i.e. there is a large change in quantity demanded when price changes. PED lies between 1 and infinity.
☐ Demand curve D5 shows perfectly elastic price elasticity of demand, i.e. there is an infinitely large response in quantity demanded to a change in price. PED = infinity.

4 The PED of a downward sloping (to the right) straight line demand curve is *not* constant, but falls as price falls and quantity demanded increases.
☐ The equation for calculation of PED shown in *Unit 3.3(2)* shows that PED does not simply equal the gradient of the demand curve.
*Observations from Figure 3.4*
☐ If a fall in price leads to an increase in total revenue marginal revenue must be positive, and PED relatively elastic.
☐ If a fall in price leads to no change in total revenue then marginal revenue must be zero, and PED will be unitary.
☐ If a fall in price leads to a fall in total revenue then marginal revenue must be negative, and PED is relatively inelastic.
☐ In the case shown here PED falls from above 1, through 1 to a value below 1.

# 3.4 Factors affecting price elasticity of demand

1 The response of quantity demanded of a good to a change in price will depend on a number of factors.
(a) *The availability of substitutes*—e.g. a rise in the price of the *Guardian* may cause a significant drop in sales as people switch to other daily newspapers.
(b) *Habit*—e.g. people who habitually buy the *Guardian* will think twice before switching newspapers.
(c) *Proportion of income spent on the good*—e.g. buying newspapers normally takes only a small proportion of a household's income so people will not react too much to a change in price of newspapers.
(d) *Absolute price level*—e.g. newspapers are relatively low in price compared to, say, Teletext TV sets. A 10% rise in price

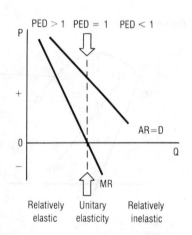

**Figure 3.4** Examples of PED

of newspapers will have less effect on newspaper sales than a 10% rise in the price of Teletext TVs would have on TV set sales.

(e) *Usefulness of the good*—e.g. people who consider reading the *Guardian* as a luxury will react more to a change in price than, say, an A level economics student who likes to keep up to date with economic developments by reading the *Guardian*.

(f) *Time*—e.g. some people may over-react to the price change of a newspaper but others may take time to adjust their purchases in the light of the new price level.

## Exercise 1

**1** A firm finds it can sell the following quantities of shrubs each day if it changes the prices as shown (see right).
  (a) Draw the demand curve facing the firm for its shrubs.
  (b) Calculate for each price level the firm's total revenue.
  (c) Calculate the marginal revenue received per shrub from increasing sales from (i) 4 to 8 (ii) 20 to 24 (iii) 32 to 36.
  (d) Calculate the PED for the firm's shrubs at the point on the demand curve indicating:
   (i) a fall in price from £10 to £9 each
   (ii) a fall in price from £6 to £5 each
   (iii) a fall in price from £3 to £2 each

| Price (£) | Quantity sold/day |
|---|---|
| 1 | 40 |
| 2 | 36 |
| 3 | 32 |
| 4 | 28 |
| 5 | 24 |
| 6 | 20 |
| 7 | 16 |
| 8 | 12 |
| 9 | 8 |
| 10 | 4 |

**2** A family live in a house that has gas central heating, and they cook on a gas cooker. Their gas bill is £180 each winter quarter and £100 each summer quarter. Their income is below the national average at £8000 p.a. The price of gas rises by 6%.
  (a) Suggest how the family might react to the rise in the price of gas.
  (b) In general, with reference to the points outlined in *Unit 3.4*, state why you think the demand for gas is probably relatively inelastic.

**3 Essay**
What factors affect the price elasticity of demand for a product. Illustrate its relevance to decisions taken by government.

## 3.5 Income elasticity of demand

**1 Income elasticity of demand (YED)** is the responsiveness of quantity demanded of a good to a change in the level of incomes.

**2** It is calculated as:

$$\frac{\% \text{ change in quantity demanded}}{\% \text{ change in income}}$$

**3** If YED is +ve the good is said to be *normal*.
 If YED is −ve the good is said to be *inferior*.

**4 An income consumption curve** can be drawn to show the effect of a rise in income on the consumption of two goods.

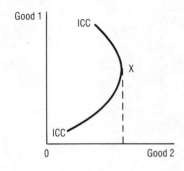

**Figure 3.5** Income consumption curve

*Observations from Figure 3.5*

☐ The income consumption curve (ICC) joins the points of tangency of successive budget lines and indifference curves (see *Unit 2.6*).

☐ After point X the quantity of Good 2 demanded starts to fall back. Good 2 has become inferior.

## 3.6 Cross-price elasticity of demand

1  **Cross-price elasticity of demand (XED)** is the responsiveness of quantity demanded of a good to a change in the price of another good.

2  It is calculated as:

$$\frac{\% \text{ change in quantity demanded of one good}}{\% \text{ change in price of another good}}$$

3  If XED is +ve the goods are said to be *substitutes*.
   If XED is −ve the goods are said to be *complements*.
   If XED is 0 the goods are said to be *independent*.

---

## Exercise 2

1  In 1984 holiday tour companies planned to sell over 8m holidays. The big five tour operators (Thomsons, Intasun, Horizon, Global and Cosmos) became involved in a price cutting war chopping up to £150 off some holiday prices.

   The market for package holidays has a number of features. Often a holiday is a large item of expenditure from a family's budget, and a foreign package holiday is a luxury item of expenditure. There are many firms competing for business and consumers can obtain clear and accurate information about all the holidays from travel agents. The holiday is largely a consumption good, lasting on average 10–14 days.

   (a) What would you anticipate the price elasticity of demand to be for overseas package holidays? Explain your answer.

   (b) In 1984 there were over 3m unemployed, and the personal incomes of those with a job were rising only slowly. What effect would these factors be expected to have on the demand for overseas package holidays?

   (c) What would you expect to be the value of cross-price elasticity of demand for overseas package holidays with respect to changes in the price of (i) new cars, (ii) new furniture and (iii) food?

2  The data in the table is compiled from the *Annual Abstract of Statistics*. (HMSO)

   (a) Analyse how expenditure on the goods or services shown has changed with changes in disposable income.

   (b) From the data can it be concluded that food is an inferior good or a normal good?

   (c) What other factors may have caused the expenditure changes outlined in the data?

| Year | Index of Income[1] | Expenditure as % of total expenditure on | | | |
|------|------|------|------|------|------|
| | | Food | DHG[2] | Transport | Housing |
| 1972 | 91.0 | 24.9 | 7.4 | 14.2 | 12.6 |
| 1973 | 95.7 | 24.4 | 7.9 | 13.6 | 13.5 |
| 1974 | 90.8 | 24.5 | 7.8 | 13.4 | 13.8 |
| 1975 | 90.5 | 24.8 | 7.4 | 13.8 | 13.1 |
| 1976 | 92.5 | 24.9 | 6.6 | 13.2 | 14.9 |
| 1977 | 94.0 | 24.7 | 6.9 | 13.5 | 14.4 |
| 1978 | 98.7 | 24.1 | 7.0 | 13.6 | 14.8 |
| 1979 | 101.8 | 23.2 | 7.5 | 13.9 | 14.6 |
| 1980 | 100.0 | 22.7 | 7.0 | 14.6 | 15.0 |
| 1981 | 99.5 | 21.7 | 7.5 | 14.9 | 15.8 |

[1] = index of gross disposable income at constant market prices
[2] = durable household goods

**3  Essay**
What are the common elasticities of demand? Why would it be essential for a businessman to have some knowledge of these elasticities for his products?

## Review

### Unit 3 will have helped provide answers to the following questions

1  How do you measure price, income and cross-price elasticity of demand?
2  What is the relationship of price elasticity of demand and a normal demand curve which slopes downwards to the right?
3  What are the important factors which determine the level of price elasticity of demand?
4  Why is elasticity such an important concept for business and government?

### Unit 3 has introduced the following terminology

Average revenue
Complementary goods
Cross-price elasticity of demand
Income consumption curves
Income elasticity of demand
Independent goods
Inferior goods
Marginal revenue
Normal goods
Perfect elasticity
Perfect inelasticity
Price elasticity of demand
Substitute goods
Total revenue
Unitary elasticity

### Multiple choice questions

1  If, after a reduction in price, total expenditure on a good falls even though quantity demanded has risen the PED of the good is:

(a) perfectly elastic
(b) relatively elastic
(c) unitary
(d) relatively inelastic
(e) perfectly inelastic

2  If the price of *Pot Noodles* rises by 10% and the expenditure on *Pot Noodles* rises by 10%, price elasticity of demand for *Pot Noodles* is:
(a) 0
(b) between 0 and 1
(c) 1
(d) between 1 and infinity
(e) infinity

3

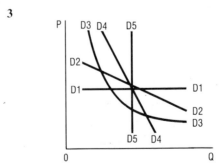

**Figure 3.6 (a)**  Demand curves

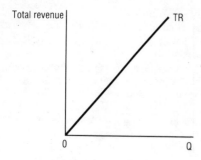

**Figure 3.6 (b)**  Total revenue curve

Which of the demand curves shown in Figure 3.6(a) would produce a total revenue curve as shown in Figure 3.6(b)?
(a) D1   (b) D2   (c) D3   (d) D4   (e) D5

**4** If a firm raises the price of its product from 10p to 15p per unit and, as a result, sales per week fall from 5000 to 4000 units the price elasticity of demand for the good (ignoring the minus sign) is:
(a) 3   (b) 2.5   (c) 1.5   (d) 0.4   (e) 0.33

**5** In a situation where the demand curve for a product slopes downwards to the right, price elasticity of demand:
(a) is zero at all points
(b) is falling as the quantity demanded increases
(c) is unitary at all quantities of demand
(d) is the same at all quantities of demand
(e) is rising as the quantity demanded increases

**6** If imports rise in price by 10% following a depreciation of the sterling exchange rate and the price elasticity of demand for imports is known to be 0.5 what would happen to the value of goods imported?
(a) rise
(b) fall by a factor of 2
(c) stay the same
(d) impossible to say
(e) fall by a factor of 0.5

**7**

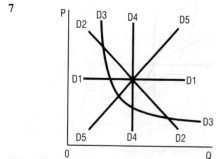

**Figure 3.7**  Demand curves

Which of the demand curves in Figure 3.7 has unitary price elasticity of demand?
(a) D1   (b) D2   (c) D3   (d) D4   (e) D5

**8** Which of the following would tend to make the price elasticity of demand for a product low?
(a) few substitutes are available
(b) the good is considered an essential purchase
(c) the absolute price level of the good is low
(d) the good takes only a small share of the consumer's incomes
(e) all of the above

**9** British Rail charges higher prices to rush-hour travellers than to off-peak travellers. They do this because the demand for rush-hour travel is:
(a) more price elastic
(b) less price elastic
(c) negative at off-peak times
(d) more income elastic
(e) less income elastic

**10**

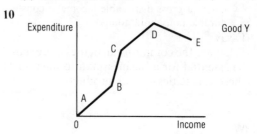

**Figure 3.8**  Response of expenditure to changes in income

Figure 3.8 shows the level of expenditure on Good Y at different levels of income.
Good Y is a normal good between points:
(a) A & B only
(b) A & D
(c) C & D only
(d) D & E only
(e) A & E

**11** If as a result of a rise in income of 10% consumers increase their holiday expenditure by 20% their income elasticity of demand for holiday expenditure is:
(a) 0.5   (b) 0.75   (c) 1   (d) 2   (e) 5

Questions 12, 13 and 14 refer to the following definitions:
  i) Goods for which income elasticity of demand is negative.
  ii) Goods for which cross-price elasticity of demand is zero.
  iii) Goods for which cross-price elasticity of demand is negative.
  iv) Goods for which price elasticity of demand is infinite.
  v) Goods for which income elasticity of demand is positive.

**12** Which definition is a description of complementary goods?
(a) i   (b) ii   (c) iii   (d) iv   (e) v

**13** Which definition is a description of independent goods?

(a) i  (b) ii  (c) iii  (d) iv  (e) v

**14** Which definition is a description of inferior goods?
(a) i  (b) ii  (c) iii  (d) iv  (e) v

**15** The quantity of computer software bought from a shop rose by 20% when the price of home computers fell by 50%. The value of cross-price elasticity for computer software with respect to the price of home computers is:
(a) 0
(b) 0.4
(c) 1
(d) 2.5
(e) impossible to calculate from this information

# Answers
## Exercise 1
**1** (a) Price plotted on vertical axis, quantity demanded on horizontal axis.
(b) Total revenue = price × quantity i.e. 40, 72, 96, 112, 120, 120, 112, 96, 72 and 40 respectively.
(c) Marginal revenue is extra revenue received from selling one more unit of a good i.e. from 40 to 72 when selling 8 rather than 4 or 8 per shrub, revenue stays at 120 when sales rise from 20 to 24 (MR = 0), total revenue falls from 96 to 72 when sales rise from 32 to 36, hence MR = −4 per shrub.
(d) Using formula shown in *Unit 3.3 (2)*:
  i) in range from 10 to 4.5
  ii) in range from 1.2 to 0.83
  iii) in range from 0.375 to 0.22

**2** (a) Some points:
  i) they cannot shift to other fuels straight away
  ii) may embark on immediate economy drive
  iii) gas bills form significant proportion of expenditure
  iv) fuel is an essential purchase.
(b) See *Unit 3.4*.

**3** Suggested essay plan.
Introduction:  Definition of terms i) Price elasticity of demand
Main paragraphs:  i) List factors in *Unit 3.4*,
  ii) Elasticity, demand curves and revenue links,
  iii) Examples of importance to government, e.g. raising taxes to generate more tax revenue, increasing the prices charged by nationalised industries, influencing changes in the exchange rate to improve the balance of payments position.
Conclusion.

## Exercise 2
**1** (a) Relatively price elastic because:
  i) high proportion of income spent on holidays
  ii) a luxury purchase

iii) many substitutes
iv) good knowledge of market from agents
v) consumption good, but all these may be offset by habit
(b) Overseas package holidays are probably normal goods, i.e. they have +ve income elasticity of demand. Fall in incomes would lead to fall in demand.
(c) Cars and furniture may be substitutes for holidays, i.e. +ve cross-price elasticity of demand. Food and holidays independent, XED = 0.

**2** (b) Comparing income changes and changing share of expenditure does not necessarily show normal or inferior status of a good, e.g. rising income, rising expenditure could be consistent with falling share of expenditure.
(c) Changes in prices, e.g. of mortgage rates for housing, of petrol for transport. Changes in credit availability, e.g. HP terms durable household goods.

**3** Suggested essay plan.
Introduction:  Definition of terms i) Elasticity
Main paragraphs:  i) Three common types are price, income and cross-price elasticity, ii) Contrast price elastic, price inelastic, normal, inferior, substitute, complementary and independent goods, iii) Businessmen need to know because, e.g. (a) predict demand changes, (b) predict effects of changing price, (c) predict effects of tax or subsidy changes.
Conclusion.

## Multiple choice answers
**1** (d) Change in price causes low response in quantity demanded.
**2** (a) There has been no change in quantity demanded.
**3** (a) Extra goods sold at a constant price causes total revenue to rise at a constant rate.
**4** (d) % change in quantity demanded is 20% change in price is 50.
**5** (b) See *Unit 3.3(4)*.
**6** (a) Import prices rise by 10%, quantity of imports falls by 5%, value of imports rises.
**7** (c) See *Unit 3.3(3)*.
**8** (e) See *Unit 3.4*.
**9** (b) People have to go to work. Often they do not have to pay all their fares.
**10** (b) Normal goods are those where expenditure on the good rises with income.
**11** (d) % change in quantity is 20, % change in income is 10.
**12** (c) See *Unit 3.6*.
**13** (b) See *Unit 3.6*.
**14** (a) See *Unit 3.5*.
**15** (b) % change in quantity is 20, % change in price of other good is 50.

# UNIT 4 Costs and supply

## 4.1 Preview

1 Goods and services are produced by firms.
2 The quantity of goods or services that a firm is willing to provide for a market over a given period of time is called the supply.
3 Firms will normally produce for a market if they can earn a profit by doing so.
4 A firm's profit is the difference between their costs and their revenue.
5 The behaviour of firms is governed by a consensus of aims of various groups operating within the firm.
6 A firm's ability to control the price charged for products and the quantities they can sell will depend on the amount of competition they face from rival producers.

## 4.2 Definitions

1 **Supply**
The quantity of a good or service that producers are willing to place on the market over a given period of time at a given price level.

2 **Firms**
Productive units supplying markets. They are organisations that make economic goods and services.

3 **Market supply**
The total supply from all firms making a particular product.

4 **The supply of an individual firm**
The quantity of a product produced by a firm in a certain period of time.

## 4.3 Conventional supply curves

1 For most products the supply curve will slope upwards to the right.
*Observations from Figure 4.1*
☐ The higher the market price the more producers will be willing to supply to the market, e.g. at price P1 they will supply quantity Q1, but at higher price P2 they will increase supply to Q2.
☐ Producers react this way as higher market prices allow them to earn higher profits (assuming costs stay constant).

## 4.4 Elasticity of supply

1 **Elasticity of supply** is the response of quantity supplied to a change in the price of the good, and it is measured as:

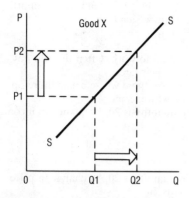

***Figure 4.1*** Supply curve for Good X

$$\frac{\% \text{ change in quantity supplied}}{\% \text{ change in price}} = \frac{\dfrac{dQ}{Q}}{\dfrac{dP}{P}} \quad \text{or} \quad \frac{dQ}{dP} \times \frac{P}{Q}$$

where dQ = change in quantity supplied
dP = change in price
Q  = original quantity supplied
P  = original price charged

## 2  Specific supply curves

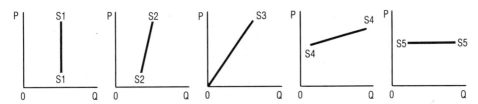

**Figure 4.2**  Specific supply curves

*Observations from Figure 4.2*

☐ Supply curve S1 shows perfect inelasticity of supply, i.e. there is no change in quantity supplied when price changes.

☐ Supply curve S2 shows relative inelasticity of supply, i.e. there is only a small change in quantity supplied when price changes.

☐ Supply curve S3 shows unitary elasticity of supply. Indeed any straight line supply curve that passes through the origin will have unitary elasticity. This means that the proportionate change in price is exactly matched by the proportionate change in quantity supplied.

☐ Supply curve S4 shows relative elasticity of supply, i.e. there is a large change in quantity supplied following a change in price.

☐ Supply curve S5 shows perfect elasticity of supply, i.e. the firm will supply any quantity required at the given market price.

# 4.5 Movements along and shifts in supply curves

1  A supply curve shows the relationship between quantity supplied and market price. It is drawn on the assumption that everything else that influences supply decisions is unchanged (*ceteris paribus*).

2  If the price of the good changes then this is shown as a movement along the supply curve.

3  If any other factor changes then this is shown as a shift in the position of the supply curve.

*Observations from Figure 4.3*

☐ The response to a rise in price of the good produced from P1 to P2 is to increase the quantity supplied from Q1 to Q2.

☐ A change in some other factor, e.g. a rise in costs, means that the firm is only willing to supply quantity Q3 at price P4 rather

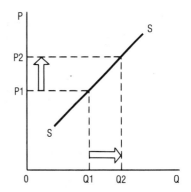

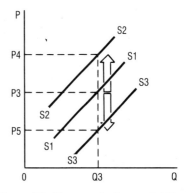

**Figure 4.3**  Movements along and shifts in supply curves

37

than at the original price P3 and shows a shift in the supply curve from S1 to S2 (upwards to the left). A fall in costs would shift the curve downwards to the right, i.e. from S1 to S3, and the firm would be willing to supply Q3 at price P5.

4 Factors that will cause a shift in a firm's supply curve include:
(a) *a change in the producer's objectives*—e.g. if a firm decides to lower prices in order to increase their market share,
(b) *a change in price of other goods*—e.g. a change in price of another good might encourage the firm to transfer production to the more profitable good,
(c) *a change in the price of factors of production*—e.g. a rise in wage rates or raw material import prices,
(d) *the imposition of a tax*—e.g. an increase in excise duty payable by the producer normally means that higher prices are charged to consumers,
(e) *a change in technology*—e.g. new techniques can cut costs and hence supply prices may fall,
(f) *a change in legal restrictions*—e.g. a change in rules and regulations about safety standards may involve increases in costs for the producer.

There are many other factors that influence firms' supply decisions that students can add to this list.

## Exercise 1

1 Two firms make bicycles on a Pacific island. They are willing to supply bicycles each week as shown (see left).
(a) What is the elasticity of supply of Penny Company?
(b) What is the elasticity of supply of Farthing Company between price $40 and $50?
(c) What is the total supply of bicycles per week on the island (assuming none are imported) at price level $30?
(d) What would be the increase in quantity supplied if prices rose to $50?
(e) List three situations that would cause the supply curve for bicycles on the island to shift to the right.

| Penny Company | |
|---|---|
| Price $ | Quantity |
| 10 | 5 |
| 20 | 10 |
| 30 | 15 |
| 40 | 20 |
| 50 | 25 |
| 60 | 30 |

| Farthing Company | |
|---|---|
| Price $ | Quantity |
| 10 | 0 |
| 20 | 0 |
| 30 | 20 |
| 40 | 25 |
| 50 | 30 |
| 60 | 35 |

2 The following separate circumstances influence the supply conditions for a High Street hamburger outlet. State how each would be represented on the outlet's supply curve, opting for one of:
    i) a shift upwards (to the left)
    ii) a shift downwards (to the right)
    iii) a movement along
(a) a rise in the price of beef
(b) an increase in indirect tax on take-away food
(c) a union agreement to raise wage rates
(d) the introduction of computerised cooking techniques
(e) an increase in the price of hamburgers
(f) an increased volume of sales
(g) an increase in the charges made by the franchise owners
(h) an increase in rates charged by the local council

# 4.6 Profit

**1 Profit**
The residue when total costs have been substracted from total revenue.
   So, Profit = Revenue – Costs

**2 Normal profit**
The amount of profit that a producer needs as reward for his efforts to make him prepared to stay in business. Less than normal profit will force a business to close eventually. More than normal profit will encourage other firms to enter the market.

**3 Abnormal profit**
Any profit over and above normal profit.

# 4.7 Revenue

**1** Firms receive revenue when they sell their products.

**2 Total revenue** is calculated by multiplying the price of a unit by the quantity sold.

**3 Average revenue** is total revenue divided by quantity of sales.

**4 Marginal revenue** is the extra revenue received as a result of selling one more unit of the good produced.

**5** The total revenue received by a firm depends on the nature of demand for the firm's product (see *Units 2 and 3*), which in turn depends on the market structure that the firm operates in (see *Unit 5*).

# 4.8 Costs

**1 Total cost** is calculated by multiplying the unit cost by the quantity produced.

**2** Total costs can be divided into fixed costs and variable costs.

**3 Fixed costs** do not vary as output varies.

**4 Variable costs** do vary as output varies.

**5** The distinction between fixed costs and variable costs depends on the time period under consideration. Economists define three time periods:
(a) *the short run*—during which fixed costs cannot be changed,
(b) *the long run*—during which fixed costs can be changed but no new technology introduced,
(c) *the very long run*—during which fixed costs can be changed and new technology introduced.

**6 Average costs** are total costs divided by quantity produced.

**7 Marginal cost** is the cost of producing one extra unit.

**8 Cost curves**
*Observations from Figure 4.4*
   □ ATC = average total cost—normally ATC curves are U-shaped.

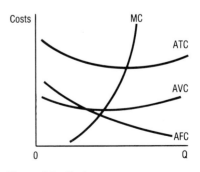

**Figure 4.4** Cost curves

☐ MC = marginal cost—MC must cut ATC at its lowest point.
☐ AFC = average fixed cost—AFC slopes down to the right as overheads are spread over greater levels of production.
☐ AVC = average variable cost—AVC is U-shaped due to the effect of economies and diseconomies of scale (see *Unit 4.9*).

9 **Short run and long run cost curves**
*Observations from Figure 4.5*
☐ SRAC = short run average cost curve. ·LRAC = long run average cost curve.
☐ In the short run fixed costs cannot be changed, so the firm has the option of only a limited volume of output.
☐ In the long run factors a production can be bought, or sold, thus changing the range of the firm's output.
·☐ Economies and diseconomies of scale (see *Unit 4.9*) will operate in both the short and long run situations.

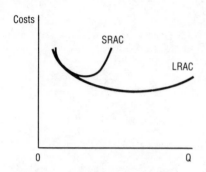

**Figure 4.5** Short run and long run cost curves

## Exercise 2

1 Which of the following would you consider were fixed costs and which variable costs in running a bed and breakfast boarding house, over a period of one month?
(a) electricity
(b) local authority rates
(c) depreciation of the kitchen
(d) expense incurred to meet fire regulations
(e) advertisements placed in tourist board brochures
(f) food

2 A family opened a bed and breakfast boarding house which had five double rooms. They estimated that fixed costs were £30 per week. Variable costs were £10 per week per occupied double room (see left).
(a) For each level of room occupancy calculate:
    i) average total cost
    ii) average fixed cost
    iii) average variable cost
(b) Draw a diagram to show how these (ATC, AFC and AVC) vary with the number of rooms occupied.

| Rooms occupied | Total fixed cost (£) | Total variable cost (£) |
|---|---|---|
| 0 | 30 | 0 |
| 1 | 30 | 10 |
| 2 | 30 | 20 |
| 3 | 30 | 30 |
| 4 | 30 | 40 |
| 5 | 30 | 50 |

3 A cake shop calculates its fixed and variable costs for making bakewell tarts, each day.

| Output | Total fixed cost (p) | Total variable cost (p) |
|---|---|---|
| 20 | 1000 | 800 |
| 40 | 1000 | 1800 |
| 60 | 1000 | 2600 |
| 80 | 1000 | 3000 |
| 100 | 1000 | 5000 |
| 140 | 1000 | 6700 |

   (a)  For each level or change in level of output calculate:
      i) total cost
      ii) average total cost
      iii) marginal cost per unit
   (b)  Draw a diagram to show how these (TC, ATC and MC) vary with the level of output of bakewell tarts. (N.B. MC should be plotted at the mid-point of each output range.)

**4  Essay**
What factors will cause a firm's supply curve to shift in the short run and in the long run?

# 4.9 Economies and diseconomies of scale

**1**  **Economies of scale** refer to a fall in unit cost as the quantity of output increases.

**2**  **Diseconomies of scale** refer to a rise in unit costs as the quantity of output increases.

**3**  **Internal economies and diseconomies of scale** arise from cost changes from within the firm itself.

**4**  **External economies and diseconomies** arise from cost changes outside the firm.
*Observations from Figure 4.6*
☐  Economies of scale are experienced up to quantity Q1.
☐  Quantity Q1 is the most efficient volume of output.
☐  After quantity Q1 diseconomies of scale are experienced.

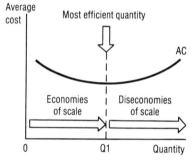

**Figure 4.6**  Economies and diseconomies of scale

**5**  **Internal economies of scale**
Sources of internal economies of scale include:
   (a)  *Purchasing economies*—e.g. bulk buying discounts.
   (b)  *Financial economies*—e.g. ability to raise money on the stock exchange.
   (c)  *Production economies* including:
      i) Learning economies, e.g. from specialisation,
      ii) linking of processes, e.g. where production of the final good involves several separate processes which each have different levels of optimum efficiency,
      iii) stochastic economies, e.g. where random events such as breakdowns occur more evenly, requiring less than a proportionate increase in maintenance staff,
      iv) increased dimensions, e.g. where doubling linear dimensions more than doubles capacity without requiring a doubling of attending labour,
      v) spreading fixed costs, e.g. where machinery is only available to make large volumes of output,
      vi) Law of Variable Proportions (see *Unit 1.10*)
   (d)  *Marketing economies*—e.g. through the control of channels of distribution.

**6**  **External economies of scale**
Sources of external economies of scale include:
   (a)  *Agglomeration*—i.e. the attraction of associated firms to provide raw materials, to process waste products or to offer specialist services.

(b) *Improved infrastructure*—e.g. quicker transport links to markets.

(c) *Development of skilled labour pool*—e.g. through previous experience or through courses operated at local further education colleges.

**7 Internal diseconomies of scale**
Sources of internal diseconomies of scale include:

(a) *Overspecialisation*—e.g. through the workforce becoming bored with their work, or through losing identity with the final product being made.

(b) *Loss of managerial control*—e.g. managers finding it difficult to adjust their style as the number of employees grows.

(c) *Decline in labour relations*—e.g. through workers being frustrated that they have lost channels of communication with the management.

(d) *Complacency through monopoly power*—i.e. firms with abnormal profits may not have the same pressures to control their costs.

**8 External diseconomies of scale**
Sources of external diseconomies of scale include:

(a) *Congestion*—e.g. transport costs rise if traffic flow becomes slower.

(b) *Shortage of skilled labour*—e.g. finding people with the necessary skills may become a problem as overall recruitment rises.

(c) *Rising land values*—e.g. more expensive housing as demand for a limited stock of houses increases.

## Exercise 3

1 An aircraft has research and development (R and D) costs of £100m. Production costs are constant at £1m per aircraft.
   (a) What is the break-even point of production if the selling price of the aircraft is: i) £1.25m ii) £3m
   (b) What is the manufacturer's profit or loss if at a selling price of £1.25m sales are: i) 50 ii) 200 iii) 500
   (c) What would be the break-even point of production at a selling price of £1.25m if:
      i) government paid 50% of R and D costs
      ii) inflation meant that R and D costs doubled
   (d) What are the opportunities for achieving economies of scale in the production of aircraft?

2 The manufacture of cans of soft drink involves four processes A,B,C and D. The most efficient volume of output for the four processes is 2, 6, 12 and 18 respectively, (hundreds of cans/hour).
   (a) What is the minimum volume of output that would ensure that all four processes were operating at their most efficient level?
   (b) Why would an output of 1500 cans/hour not be an optimal volume of output for the firm?
   (c) What source of internal economies of scale is illustrated by this question?

3  Size of firms in manufacturing industry, and days lost through strikes in 1979.

| Number of employees | Total number of firms (by size of firm) | Total number of workers (by size of firm) ('000s) | Total working days lost (by size of firm) ('000s) |
|---|---|---|---|
| 1–10 | 62,445 | 288.0 | |
| 11–20 | 18,476 | 265.7 | 302 |
| 21–49 | 16,847 | 515.8 | |
| 50–99 | 8,482 | 594.0 | |
| 100–199 | 5,821 | 814.7 | 1,382 |
| 200–499 | 4,339 | 1,330.1 | |
| 500–999 | 1,408 | 968.6 | 1,089 |
| 1000–2499 | | | 1,497 |
| 2500–4999 | 908 | 1,969.5 | 1,486 |
| 5000 + | | | 23,295 |
| | 118,726 | 6,746.5 | 29,051 |

(Based on information from *Annual Abstract of Statistics* 1984, HMSO)

(a) What can be inferred from this data regarding the relationship between strikes and stoppages and the size of firms?

(b) Does this data provide evidence of a potential diseconomy of scale?

(c) What factors might lead to a higher incidence of strikes in large firms than in small firms?

## 4  Project Erika

Ford aim to make more than 1m Escorts a year throughout the world. The development of the Escort (codenamed 'project Erika') cost £1500m and was the most expensive in the company's history.

To produce the Escort, Ford pooled its world-wide resources on an impressive scale, a project made possible partly by the sheer geographical spread of the Ford empire and partly by the use of the trans-national computer network.

Escorts are made in two main centres, Saarlouis in Belgium and at Britain's Halewood, into which Ford invested £135m in addition to the £207m invested there in 1978. A brand new engine plant was built at Bridgend, Wales.

In the United States, Ford has built a brand new engine plant for the Escort and completely re-tooled two of its manufacturing plants in Wayne and Metuchen, Michigan.

At the same time the Hiroshima based Toyo Kogyo, makers of Mazda, in which Ford have a 25% stake, built a plant to build the Japanese version of the Escort, the Mazda 323, which was sold throughout the Far East and Australasian markets.

The secret of the Erika project lay in the huge savings in research and development that can be achieved by building an international family of cars around a single concept. By pooled design, Ford claimed to have saved £75m and 15,000 engineering man-hours.

However the company could not afford to completely ignore the variations in national taste anymore than it can by-pass national government regulations which vary from country to country.

(a) What opportunities for economies of scale are indicated in the extract?

(b) Does the extract suggest there may be some diseconomies of scale associated with such a project?

(c) List three other economies of scale that are likely to arise in car production.

(d) Give one diseconomy of scale often associated with the car industry.

**5  Essay**

Why are conventional average cost curves assumed to be U-shaped? What is the relevance of the Law of Variable Proportions to this U-shape?

## Review

### Unit 4 will have helped provide answers to the following questions

1  What is the usual relationship between quantity supplied and price of the good?
2  What factors affect the elasticity of supply?
3  What factors will cause a shift in the position of a supply curve and the movement along a supply curve?
4  How is profit calculated when costs and revenue are known?
5  What do the typical family of cost curves look like?
6  What are the sources of economies and diseconomies of scale?

### Unit 4 has introduced the following terminology

Abnormal profit
Average cost
Average revenue
Diseconomies of scale
Economies of scal
Elasticity of supply
External economies (or diseconomies)
Fixed costs
Individual firm's supply
Internal economies (or diseconomies)
Long run
Marginal cost
Marginal revenue
Market supply
Normal profit
Revenue
Short run
Variable costs
Very long run

### Multiple choice questions

1  The table shows the quantity of a good the firm is willing to supply each month at the prices indicated.

| Quantity | Price (£) |
| --- | --- |
| 50 | 5 |
| 100 | 10 |
| 150 | 15 |
| 200 | 20 |

What is the elasticity of supply with respect to a rise in price from £10/unit to £15/unit?
(a) 0.2   (b) 0   (c) 1   (d) 5   (e) 25

2  A supply curve which is vertical indicates an elasticity of supply of:
(a) 0
(b) between 0 and 1
(c) 1
(d) infinity
(e) between 1 and infinity

Questions 3 and 4 refer to the following table which shows the level of short run total cost for a firm when it produces the quantity of output shown.

| Quantity | Short run total cost (£) |
| --- | --- |
| 0 | 100 |
| 10 | 120 |
| 20 | 140 |
| 30 | 160 |

**3** Total fixed cost at output 20 is:
  (a) £100
  (b) £360
  (c) £20
  (d) £7
  (e) cannot be calculated from the table

**4** Average total cost at output 20 is:
  (a) £360
  (b) £140
  (c) £7
  (d) £2
  (e) cannot be calculated from the table

**5** If, for a firm, total fixed costs are £1000, average total cost is £4 and average variable cost is £3, what is the volume of output of the firm?
  (a) 250  (b) 333  (c) 500  (d) 750  (e) 1000

**6** Which of the following would cause the supply curve of a firm to shift downwards (to the right)?
  (a) imposition of an indirect tax on the firm's product
  (b) a requirement by the firm for higher profit margins
  (c) a rise in wage rates
  (d) a fall in the cost of components
  (e) a rise in the cost of advertising for the firm

**7** Fixed costs are:
  (a) those costs which can vary in the short run,
  (b) those costs which can never change,
  (c) those costs which cannot be altered in the very long run,
  (d) those costs which do not vary with output in the short run,
  (e) those costs which are incurred by society.

**8**

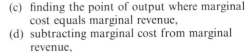

**Figure 4.7** Cost curves

Which of the cost curves in Figure 4.7 shows the typical shape of an average fixed cost curve?
  (a) A  (b) B  (c) C  (d) D  (e) E

**9** The marginal profit earned by a firm producing a good can be calculated by:
  (a) multiplying the price of the good by the quantity sold,
  (b) finding the extra revenue received when selling an additional unit of the good,

  (c) finding the point of output where marginal cost equals marginal revenue,
  (d) subtracting marginal cost from marginal revenue,
  (e) subtracting marginal revenue from average revenue.

**10** If average total cost is falling:
  (a) marginal cost must also be falling,
  (b) marginal cost must be rising,
  (c) marginal cost must equal average cost,
  (d) marginal cost must be greater than average cost,
  (e) marginal cost must be less than average cost.

**11** The Law of Variable Proportions will have an effect on the shape of the average cost curve of a firm in:
  (a) the short run
  (b) the long run
  (c) very long run
  (d) after two years
  (e) no circumstances at all

**12** Which of the following is not an example of an internal economy of scale for a holiday tour operator?
  (a) introduction of computerisation
  (b) national advertising compaigns
  (c) ability to raise additional finance from the general public
  (d) bulk booking of plane seats
  (e) an advantageous position in all UK airports

## Answers

### Exercise 1

**1** (a) 1—any straight line supply curve passing through the origin has a price elasticity of supply of 1.
  (b) 0.8. % change in quantity supplied is 20, % change in price is 25.
  (c) 35 (15 from Penny Company + 20 from Farthing Company).
  (d) 20 (total supply up from 35 to 55).
  (e) i) imports allowed ii) cut in cost iii) new island manufacturer iv) introduction of new technology, e.g. a robot v) cut in taxation.
**2** (a) shift upwards
  (b) shift upwards
  (c) shift upwards
  (d) shift downwards
  (e) movement along
  (f) shift downwards (assuming some economies of scale)
  (g) shift upwards
  (h) shift upwards

## Exercise 2

1  (a) variable
   (b) fixed
   (c) fixed
   (d) fixed
   (e) fixed
   (f) variable

2

| Rooms | TFC | AFC | TVC | AVC | ATC |
|-------|-----|-----|-----|-----|-----|
| 0 | 30 | — | 0 | — | — |
| 1 | 30 | 30 | 10 | 10 | 40 |
| 2 | 30 | 15 | 20 | 10 | 25 |
| 3 | 30 | 10 | 30 | 10 | 20 |
| 4 | 30 | 7.5 | 40 | 10 | 17.5 |
| 5 | 30 | 6 | 50 | 10 | 16 |

3

| Output | TFC | TVC | TTC | ATC | MC |
|--------|-----|-----|-----|-----|-----|
| 20 | 1000 | 800 | 1800 | 90 | — |
| 40 | 1000 | 1800 | 2800 | 70 | 50 |
| 60 | 1000 | 2600 | 3600 | 60 | 40 |
| 80 | 1000 | 3000 | 4000 | 50 | 20 |
| 100 | 1000 | 3500 | 4500 | 45 | 25 |
| 120 | 1000 | 5000 | 6000 | 50 | 75 |
| 140 | 1000 | 6700 | 7700 | 55 | 85 |

4  Suggested essay plan.
   Introduction:  Definition of terms i) short run ii)
      long run iii) very long run iv) supply curve
   Main paragraphs:  i) Diagrams to show shifts up-
      wards and downward ii) SR factors, e.g. change
      in objectives, change in variable costs iii) LR
      factors, e.g. bigger better machinery, economies
      of scale, technology, change in prices of other
      goods, removal of legal restrictions
   Conclusion.

## Exercise 3

1  (a) i) 400 (price exceeds variable cost by £0.25 per
         aircraft, fixed costs £100m). ii) 50 (price now
         exceeds variable cost by £2 m per aircraft fixed
         costs still £100m)
   (b) i) £87.5m loss ii) £50m loss iii) £25m profit
   (c) i) 200 ii) 800 (400 if they happened
         simultaneously)
   (d) Examples are: i) financial ii) research and
         development iii) spreading fixed costs. Clearly
         limited production economies if only small
         numbers are sold.

2  (a) 36. This is lowest common multiple of most
         efficient volume of output of each process. 18
         of A, 6 of B, 3 of C and 2 of D all working at
         most efficient level at this level of output.

   (b) None of the processes can be operating at their
         most efficient level.
   (c) Economies of linked processes (see *Unit 4.9*[5]).

3  (a) Majority of days lost from strikes occur in
         large organisations. 90% of days lost occurred
         in firms with more than 1000 workers, which
         constituted 30% of total workers and less than
         1% of total number of firms.
   (b) Larger firms are more susceptible to strikes.
         Strikes cause a rise in unit cost, e.g. because
         capital lies idle while the workers withdraw
         their labour.
   (c) Less communication between workers and
         management. Workers identifying less with
         products produced and the success of the firm.
         More opportunities for worker solidarity.

4  (a) i) spreading fixed costs, e.g. research and
             development ii) use of indivisible capital, e.g.
             central computerisation
   (b) Over-standardisation of a product
   (c) See *4.9* for ideas
   (d) Decline in labour relations

5  Suggested essay plan.
   Introduction:   Definition of terms i) Conventional
         cost curves are total, average and marginal
         cost curves ii) Difference between fixed and
         variable costs iii) Importance of the time
         period.
   Main Paragraphs:  i) Draw diagram of cost curves,
         and explain ii) Law of Variable Proportions
         relevant in the short run as fixed factors are
         fixed in short run only. Produces diminishing
         marginal product from extra factor input, i.e.
         causes rising unit costs after a certain point of
         output. Assume paid constant rates, all factor
         inputs are equally efficient iii) Other factors
         (See *Unit 4.9*)
   Conclusion.

## Multiple choice answers

1  (c) Supply curve is straight and passes through the
         origin.
2  (a) Perfectly inelastic supply.
3  (a) Fixed cost does not change with output in the
         short run.
4  (c) Total cost divided by quantity produced.
5  (e) AFC = £1 if ATC = £4 and AVC = £3.
6  (d) Fall in costs shifts supply curve downwards.
7  (d) By definition.
8  (a) See *Unit 4.8*.
9  (d) Profit is the difference between revenue and
         cost.
10 (e) If the average is falling, the marginal addition
         must be less than the average.
11 (a) Law of Variable Proportions only operates if
         other factors are fixed.
12 (e) This comes from outside the firm itself and is
         an external economy of scale.

# The theory of the firm

UNIT 5

## 5.1 Preview

1 In free market economies firms make goods and services in order to sell them for a profit.
2 Although traditional economic theory assumes that firms will aim to maximise profits; observations of business behaviour suggest that other objectives may also be important.
3 Decisions as to what price to charge and what quantity of output to produce will be affected by the nature of the market the firm operates in.
4 Theory suggests that firms who are unable to earn normal profits will close down in the long run.

## 5.2 Firms

1 There are many hundreds of firms producing goods and services in the British economy. Their diverse size and form of ownership mean that no single theory is likely to be able to explain all business behaviour.
2 Firms can be classified in a number of ways.
   (a) *Legal type of ownership*—e.g. as a sole proprietor, partnership, private company, PLC, co-operative or nationalised industry.
   (b) *Size*—e.g. through numbers of employees, or value of turnover or assets employed.
   (c) *Sector*—e.g. private (non-government controlled) or public.
   (d) *Market share*—e.g. as monopolists (see *Unit 5.8*), oligopolists (see *Unit 5.7*) or competitive (see *Unit 5.5 and 5.6*).

## 5.3 Objectives of firms

1 It is a key assumption of traditional economic theory (known as marginal analysis) that firms will seek to maximise short run profits.
2 Empirical (or behavioural) studies of firms suggest that other aims and objectives might be more important.
3 The concept of profit maximisation can be challenged because of:
   (a) *The time factor*—the way to achieve long run growth of profits may involve a sacrifice of short run profits e.g. cutting prices in the short term to force competitors out of the market.
   (b) *Lack of knowledge*—any maximising concept implies that all alternative courses of action are known and have been considered, whereas in practice firms do not have such information available to them.
   (c) *Variety of interested groups*—medium to large firms involve the co-operation of a variety of different interest groups e.g.

47

owners (shareholders), managers, workers, customers and central and local government. Their individual aims may clash with those of other groups, e.g. managers may support diversification of product ranges to secure their jobs which could involve initial expense and a fall in profits and dividends for the shareholders.

(d) *Control*—profit maximisation may suggest growth to a point where the present form of ownership is no longer possible, and retaining control (especially for a family operation) may be more important than increasing profits.

4 Alternative objectives suggested from behavioural studies include:

(a) *growth*—e.g. of market share, output, or through diversification,

(b) *survival*—the main purpose of a business is to stay in business,

(c) *satisficing*—reasonable profits (satis-factory) without undue risks (sacri-fice).

5 Profit is clearly important overall, but short run profit maximisation may not accurately explain business decisions.

## Exercise 1

1 Trusthouse Forte plc have business interests in the areas of catering, hotel operation, property and leisure. In their annual report and accounts they publish their company philosophy:

### The Company Philosophy

To increase profitability and earnings per share each year in order to encourage investment and to improve and expand the business.

To give complete customer satisfaction by efficient and courteous service, with value for money.

To support managers and their staff in using personal initiative to improve the profit and quality of their operations whilst observing the Company's policies.

To provide good working conditions and to maintain effective communications at all levels to develop better understanding and assist decision making.

To ensure no discrimination against sex, race, colour or creed and to train, develop and encourage promotion within the Company based on merit and ability.

To act with integrity at all times and to maintain a proper sense of responsibility towards the public.

To recognise the importance of each and every employee who contributes towards these aims.

(Source: THF plc Annual Accounts 1985.)

(a) Are Trusthouse Forte PLC aiming to maximise short run profits?

(b) Which interest groups within the company are likely to benefit from increasing profitability and earnings per share?

(c) How do Trusthouse Forte aim to satisfy the aims and objectives of their staff?

(d) Is it possible that growth and expansion of the business may not lead to an increase in profits?

(e) Does a policy of acting with integrity towards the public clash with an objective of increasing profits?

2 Tesco and Sainsbury operate large supermarket chains in the UK. Details of their turnover (sales) and profit levels for the period 1978 to 1983 are given in the table below.

| TESCO | | | SAINSBURY | | |
|---|---|---|---|---|---|
| Year | Sales £m | Profit £m | Year | Sales £m | Profit £m |
| 1978 | 953 | 28.5 | 1978 | 797 | 27.6 |
| 1979 | 1201 | 37.6 | 1979 | 988 | 32.6 |
| 1980 | 1530 | 36.5 | 1980 | 1190 | 43.8 |
| 1981 | 1820 | 35.6 | 1981 | 1531 | 62.0 |
| 1982 | 1994 | 42.7 | 1982 | 1875 | 83.3 |
| 1983 | 2276 | 53.5 | 1983 | 2383 | 107.9 |

(Based on information from Tesco and Sainsbury Reports and Accounts for 1983)

(a) Compare the experience of the two companies with respect to their profit performance during the growth of their businesses.

(b) Suggest reasons why firms in the same line of business may experience different levels of profits.

(c) If you have access to other company reports see whether growth tends to lead to increased or decreased levels of profit.

# 5.4 Marginal analysis of firms' behaviour

1 Traditional economic theories of the behaviour of firms aim to predict:
(a) the prices the firms will charge for their product,
(b) the volume of output they will produce in different circumstances.

2 The behaviour of a firm will vary according to the nature of the market the firm operates in. Economists refer to four main market types:
(a) perfect competition,
(b) imperfect competition (also known as monopolistic competition),
(c) oligopoly,
(d) monopoly.

3 These market types are based on specific assumptions about the products produced, the behaviour of consumers, the motivation

of the producers and the number of competing firms. The market types should be treated as a basis for the theoretical models rather than as mirror images of any particular product market.

4 Above all, marginal (i.e. economic) theories are based on the assumption of profit maximisation. Firms will maximise profits at the quantity of output where:

(a) total revenue exceeds total cost by the biggest amount, or

(b) where marginal cost equals marginal revenue.

*Observations from Figure 5.1*

☐ Output of quantity Q1 gives maximum profit. Distance between TC & TR is greatest at Q1.

☐ Output at quantity Q2 gives less profit than Q1 because there are still extra goods that can be made at a marginal profit.

☐ Output of quantity Q3 gives less profit than Q1 because at this level of output marginal cost is greater than marginal revenue so the producer is making a marginal loss on each additional unit of production.

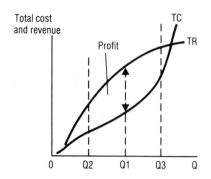

Total cost and revenue

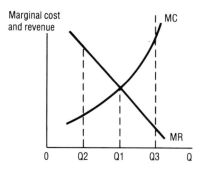

Marginal cost and revenue

**Figure 5.1** Maximum profit

## Exercise 2

1 A firm estimates that for its product total revenue and total cost vary with output as shown in the table.

| Quantity | Total revenue (£) | Total cost (£) |
|---|---|---|
| 1 | 30 | 21 |
| 2 | 37 | 26 |
| 3 | 43 | 30 |
| 4 | 48 | 33 |
| 5 | 52 | 37 |
| 6 | 55 | 42 |
| 7 | 57 | 48 |
| 8 | 58 | 56 |

(a) Calculate total profit at each level of output.

(b) What is the marginal revenue from the 3rd good?

(c) What is the marginal cost of the 3rd good?

(d) Is it profitable for the firm to make the 3rd good?

(e) Repeat (b), (c) and (d) for the 4th, 5th and 6th goods.

(f) When profit is at a maximum what is the relationship between marginal cost and marginal revenue?

## 5.5 Perfect competition

1 The following conditions are necessary for a market to be perfectly competitive.

(a) *Large numbers of buyers and sellers* No single firm or consumer is large enough to affect market price. Firms are therefore said to be price takers.

(b) *Homogeneity* The outputs of all firms selling goods for a market are exactly the same. Consumers therefore cannot express a preference for one firm's output.

(c) *Divisibility* Consumers can buy, and producers can make, exactly the quantity they wish.

(d) *Freedom of entry and exit* Firms can enter and leave the market in the long run without difficulty. There are therefore no barriers to entry.

(e) *Perfect mobility* There are no transport costs to deter consumers from trading wherever they want.

(f) *Perfect knowledge* Consumers and producers have perfect information about the price of other goods and of other business opportunities.

(g) *Rationality* Consumers will aim to maximise their satisfaction from spending their incomes. Producers will aim to maximise profits.

## 2 Equilibrium position in the long run for a firm in perfectly competitive markets

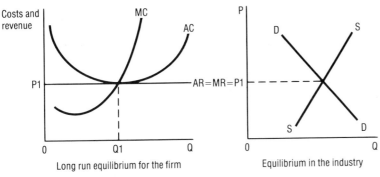

**Figure 5.2** Equilibrium in perfectly competitive markets

*Observations from Figure 5.2*

☐ Firms take the industry price P1 set by demand and supply conditions in the industry.

☐ The firm will get this price whatever quantity of output it decides to produce. The firm's AR and MR curves are therefore horizontal lines at price leave P1 (AR = MR = P1).

☐ Maximum profit will be earned at the level of output where MC cuts MR from below, i.e. quantity Q1 (MR = MC).

☐ Firms are earning normal profits.

## 3 A change in market conditions

(a) *A rise in market price*

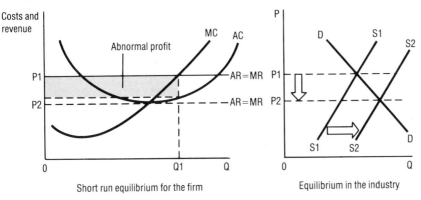

**Figure 5.3** Results of a rise in market price

*Observations from Figure 5.3*

☐ In the short run the firm can earn abnormal profits making quantity Q1 at P1, the quantity at which MC cuts MR from below.

☐ In the long run additional firms will enter the market to take advantage of the opportunities for abnormal profit, causing a shift in the industry supply curve to the right (S1 to S2), and a fall in the market price, P1 to P2, and erosion of the abnormal profit.

(b) *A fall in market price*

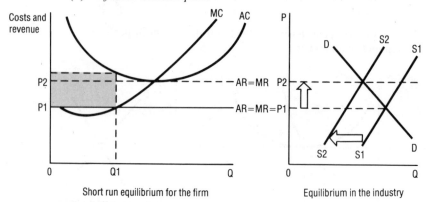

Short run equilibrium for the firm        Equilibrium in the industry

**Figure 5.4**   Results of a fall in market price

*Observations from Figure 5.4*

☐ In the short run firms will find themselves earning less than normal profits, even at the minimum loss (maximum profit) point of production Q1.

☐ Firms will leave the industry, causing the industry supply curve to shift to the left (S1 to S2), and market price to rise, P1 to P2. This results in removing the loss.

## 4   The supply curve for firms in perfectly competitive markets

In perfectly competitive markets the firm's supply curve coincides with the upward sloping part of the firm's marginal cost curve.

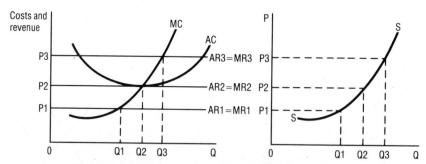

**Figure 5.5**   Supply curve in perfectly competitive markets

*Observations from Figure 5.5*

☐ At price P1 maximum profit point of production is Q1, found where MC cuts MR from below.

☐ At price P2 output will rise to Q2, and at price P3 to Q3.

☐ The supply curve (S), which shows the quantity supplied at different price levels, is therefore the same curve as the upward sloping part of the firm's marginal cost curve.

# Exercise 3

**1** A firm producing its product in a perfectly competitive market estimates its total costs at various levels of output as shown in the table (on the right).

(a) What quantity will the firm be prepared to produce in the short run if market price is:
  i) £49 per unit
  ii) £27 per unit
  iii) £16 per unit
  iv) £8 per unit
(b) From this information produce the supply curve for this firm.

| Quantity | Total cost (£) |
|----------|----------------|
| 1 | 6 |
| 2 | 10 |
| 3 | 12 |
| 4 | 12 |
| 5 | 20 |
| 6 | 36 |
| 7 | 63 |
| 8 | 112 |

**2** Mr Allen owns Easedale House Farm in the heart of Lakeland. His main source of income comes his dairy herd. He is bound to sell all his milk to the Milk Marketing Board at the price they fix. At present the price is £0.70p per gallon.

(a) Draw a graph to show the average and marginal revenue curves facing Mr Allen.

Mr Allen's son Jethro has been away at agricultural college and he has learnt about the different costs that affect the dairy producer and how these costs vary with output. He realises that a knowledge of the costs at the farm would help Mr Allen maximise his profits. (Mr Allen has had some ideas about this for years but he does not understand the terminology that Jethro now uses).

(b) Make a list of possible fixed and variable costs facing a dairy farmer over a six month time period.

A rigorous analysis of the cost situation at Easedale House Farm produces the results shown in the table.

| Output (galls) | Total fixed cost (£) | Total variable cost (£) |
|----------------|----------------------|-------------------------|
| 100 | 100 | 10 |
| 200 | 100 | 80 |
| 300 | 100 | 140 |
| 400 | 100 | 180 |
| 500 | 100 | 300 |

(c) Calculate average cost and marginal cost for each level of output from 200 gallons to 500 gallons. Add these figures to the graph drawn in part (a) of this question.
(d) What is the most profitable level of output for Mr. Allen?

Mr Allen is impressed with this analysis. However, the 400 gallons output figure suggested by the calculations is above what Mr Allen is used to producing. He considers he does about the right amount of work now (he likes time off to follow the hound trailing). Jethro wants to travel for a few years and Mr Allen wants to keep control of the farm until Jethro returns to take over.

(e) Is Mr Allen a profit maximiser? What are his likely business objectives?

## 5.6 Imperfect competition

1 The conditions in imperfectly competitive markets are the same as those in perfectly competitive markets except that consumers can differentiate one firm's output from another. This differentiation of products normally involves branding, e.g. one firm's red pullover is made distinct from another firm's red pullover by an embroidered trade mark.

2 Firms can influence the quantity of the product they sell by altering its price. The demand curve for their product will slope downwards to the right.

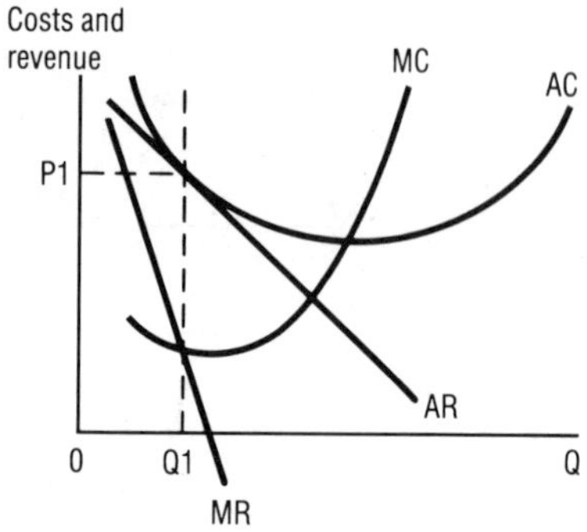

3 **Equilibrium position in the long run for a firm in an imperfectly competitive market**
*Observations from Figure 5.6*
□ The firm's demand curve (or average revenue curve) slopes downwards to the right (AR).
□ As average revenue is falling as quantity of output increases marginal revenue (MR) must be less then average revenue.
□ Average total cost (AC) and marginal cost (MC) are drawn conventionally.
□ The maximum profit point of production is found where MC cuts MR from below, i.e. at quantity Q1.
□ To sell quantity Q1 the firm must charge price P1.
□ In this position the firm is earning normal profit.

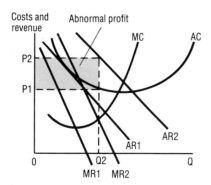

**Figure 5.6**  Long run equilibrium in imperfect competition

4 **A change in market conditions**
   (a) *An increase in demand for the firm's product*
      *Observations from Figure 5.7*
      □ The increase in demand is shown by a shift in the demand curve to AR2. MR2 is the associated marginal revenue curve.
      □ Maximum profit point of output is now Q2 (where MC cuts MR from below). To sell this output the firm can charge P2.
      □ This allows them abnormal profit in the short run, indicated by the shaded area.
      □ This abnormal profit encourages other firms to enter the market, and as they do so they push the firm's demand curve back towards the long run equilibrium position at AR1 and so abnormal profits are eroded.
   (b) *A fall in demand for the firm's product* will work in the opposite way to that outlined above. Short run losses will force firms to leave the market increasing the market share for the remaining firms until they are again back to the long run equilibrium position at AR1 in Figure 5.7

**Figure 5.7**  Results of an increase in demand (short run equilibrium in imperfect competition)

## 5.7 Oligopoly

1 An oligopoly is a market that is dominated by a few firms. There is no longer freedom of entry, or at least there are barriers to growth for smaller firms. A market dominated by two firms is called a duopoly.

2 The outcome of decisions taken by a firm in an oligopolistic situation will depend on the reaction of rival firms.

**3** If price changes are not followed then demand for a firm's product is likely to be relatively elastic, i.e. they will gain a lot of business if they cut their price, and lose a lot of business if they raise price.

**4** If price changes are followed, then between them the firms are acting like a single large firm, and demand for the products of each individual firm will be relatively inelastic.

**5** **The assumed kinked demand curve of the oligopolist**
*Observations from Figure 5.8*
☐ The price charged by the firm is originally at level P1.
☐ It is assumed that price rises by this firm will not be followed by the rival firms, giving section ab of the AR ( = D) curve.
☐ It is assumed that price cuts will be followed by the rivals so that they do not lose business. This gives section bc of the AR curve.
☐ The overall marginal revenue curve (MR) is made up the relevant sections of the separate marginal revenue curves, showing a discontinuity (jump) at quantity Q1.
☐ Maximum profit will be earned where MC cuts MR from below, i.e. at quantity Q1. To sell quantity Q1 the firm has to charge price P1.
☐ Abnormal profit can be earned in the long run.

**6** The significance of this analysis is that oligopolists stand to lose out if they change their prices. They will therefore have to compete in non-price ways, e.g. by product innovation, through marketing or through after-sales services.

**7** The kinked demand curve only exists if the firm thinks the rival firms will not follow price rises. However, if all firms have been faced with similar cost pressures then price rises by one firm (called the market leader) may very well be followed by the other firms.

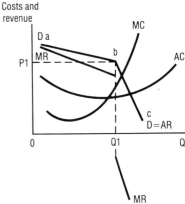

**Figure 5.8** Equilibrium for a oligopolist

---

## Exercise 4

**1** Two petrol stations compete for business on the main street of a small town. The present price of petrol in both garages is 50p/litre. Garage A estimates that if he lowers his price Garage B will cut his prices too, and between them they may get a little extra business. Garage A also estimates that if he raised price, Garage B would do nothing, so most of the customers would buy their petrol at the cheaper Garage B. Garage A imagines his demand schedule is as shown (see right).

| Price (p/litre) | Sales (litres/day) |
|---|---|
| 60 | 100 |
| 55 | 300 |
| 50 | 500 |
| 30 | 550 |
| 10 | 600 |

(a) Draw his imagined demand curve.
(b) What would his total revenue be if he charged:
  i) 50p/litre ii) 60p/litre iii) 30p/litre
(c) In what circumstances might Garage A consider lowering or raising his price?
(d) Would it be in the garages interests to form an agreement about pricing their petrol? What would be Garage A's revenue if both garages charged 60p/litre?
(e) How might Garage A compete with Garage B without getting involved in a price war?

2   Visit branches of banks in your locality. Find out what prices they charge for:
        (i)   operating private bank accounts,
        (ii)  lending money (base rate),
        (iii) the rate of interest they pay on deposit accounts.
    (a) Do these prices vary significantly?
    (b) How do the banks compete with each other?
    (c) What kind of market structure do you think applies to banking?

3   **Essay**
    Describe the problems involved in applying marginal analysis to oligopolistic markets.

## 5.8 Monopoly

1   A monopoly is a market where there is only one producer. The firm's output is therefore the industry's output.

2   **Equilibrium for a monopolist**
    *Observations from Figure 5.9*
    ☐ The elasticity of demand for the firm's product indicates the firm's degree of monopoly power.
    ☐ For maximum profit the firm produces at the point where MC cuts MR from below, i.e. at Q1.
    ☐ The abnormal profit is indicated by the shaded area and is $(AR - AC) \times$ quantity sold.
    ☐ New suppliers cannot enter the market because of the barriers to entry, so this is a short run and a long run equilibrium position.

3   **Price discrimination by monopolists**
    A monopolist will be able to raise his total revenue if he charges different prices to different customers. He can do this if:
    (a) he can isolate different groups of customers,
    (b) he can prevent resale from one group to another,
    (c) each group has a different elasticity of demand for the product.

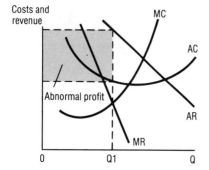

**Figure 5.9**   Equilibrium for a monopolist

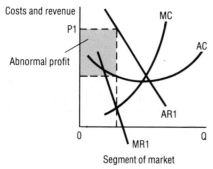

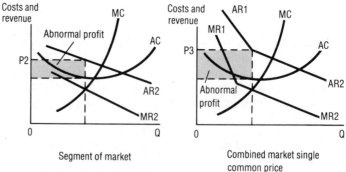

**Figure 5.10**   Price discrimination

*Observations from Figure 5.10*
☐ The combined revenue from charging separate prices P1 and P2 is greater than that obtained when a common price P3 is charged to all customers.
☐ This is only true if the elasticities of demand in each sector are different.

# Exercise 5

**1** Examine the three examples of pricing behaviour which follow.

## Dialled Calls
## Local

| | | | Approximate **Cost** to the customer including VAT | | | | | Time for one unit |
|---|---|---|---|---|---|---|---|---|
| | | | 1 min | 2 mins | 3 mins | 4 mins | 5 mins | |
| | | **Cheap** | 6p | 6p | 6p | 6p | 6p | **8 mins** |
| **Local** | L | Standard | 6p | 6p | 12p | 12p | 17p | 2 mins |
| | | Peak | 6p | 12p | 12p | 17p | 23p | 1 min 30 secs |

## All inland calls

| Charge rate period | Mon | Tue | Wed | Thu | Fri | Sat | Sun |
|---|---|---|---|---|---|---|---|
| 6.00 pm – 8.00 am | **Cheap rate** | | | | | | |
| 8.00 am – 9.00 am | **Standard rate** | | | | | | |
| 9.00 am – 1.00 pm | **Peak rate** | | | | | | |
| 1.00 pm – 6.00 pm | **Standard rate** | | | | | | |

## British
## TELECOM

Example 1 Telephone calls

Example 2 Watersmeet Theatre

| Apex return Period* | | | | | One year excursion Period* | | | | |
|---|---|---|---|---|---|---|---|---|---|
| 1 | 2 | 3 | 4 | 5 | 1 | 2 | 3 | 4 | 5 |
| £654 | £737 | £820 | £877 | £934 | £782 | £862 | £942 | £1,001 | £1,060 |

| Standard return fares (all times of the year) | | | |
|---|---|---|---|
| Luxury First | Business | Economy | Non-stop Economy |
| £3,796 | £2,004 | £1,822 | £1,462 |

Example 3 Air fares to Australia.
London to Sydney

*1 = May, June
2 = March, April, July.
3 = Jan, Feb, Aug, Sept, Dec 24–31
4 = Oct, Nov.
5 = Dec 1–23
(refers to time of outward travel)

(a) Explain how these operators can charge different prices to different groups of their customers.

(b) Why do these operators discriminate between groups of their customers?

## 5.9 The decision to close down

1 If a firm is earning less than normal profits it will close down in the long run.
2 However, in the short run it may continue to trade if it can earn some 'trading surplus' which it can use to pay for some of its fixed costs.
3 A trading surplus will be earned if, at the point of production, average revenue is greater than average variable cost.

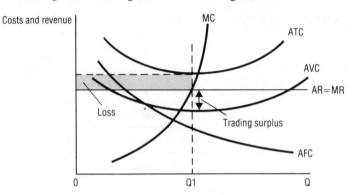

**Figure 5.11** Close-down point for a firm in perfect competition

*Observations from Figure 5.11*
□ Minimum loss quantity of output is Q1.
□ At Q1 AR is less than ATC so less than normal profit is being earned.
□ At Q1 AR is greater than AVC so a trading surplus is being earned which can be used to offset some of the fixed costs, which of course cannot be changed in the short run.

4 Firms may stay in business if they earn less than normal profits if:
(a) they think that demand for their product will increase again,
(b) they can reduce their overall costs, e.g. through the introduction of new technology.

## Exercise 6

1 Should Glenferrie Electricals (UK) cease trading?
Glenferrie Electricals (UK) manufacture one product, a measuring aid operated by computer for engineering industries.
   The managing director feels that the product is not making a satisfactory profit. On closer examination his accountants produce the data given in the table.

| Output/ month | Average revenue(£) | Total fixed costs/month(£) | Total variable costs/month(£) |
|---|---|---|---|
| 10 | 36 | 800 | 400 |
| 20 | 33 | 800 | 600 |
| 30 | 30 | 800 | 700 |
| 40 | 27 | 800 | 800 |
| 50 | 24 | 800 | 1500 |
| 60 | 21 | 800 | 2400 |

He has to take one of three decisions:
(a) close down immediately,
(b) carry on trading in the short run with the view to closing down when his fixed costs can be altered,
(c) carry on trading in the long run.
Which decision would you recommend the managing director take? Justify your decision with a detailed graphical presentation of the full cost situation facing him, and any other factors you think are relevant.

2   **Essay**
    How would an entrepreneur act when faced with a fall in the level of demand for his product?

# 5.10 Limitations of marginal analysis

Empirical (or behavioural) studies of firms' behaviour suggest that there are a number of reasons for believing firms do not behave as predicted in marginal analysis. Some of the reasons suggested for this are:
(a) firms do not seek to maximise short run profits (see *Unit 5.3*),
(b) firms do not have perfect knowledge, and hence may not know the nature of demand for their product,
(c) the average cost curve may not be smooth, or U-shaped, if the firm employs significant indivisible fixed factors,
(d) many firms produce more than one product so it is impossible to allocate fixed costs accurately for each individual product,
(e) 'normal profit' may change for an entrepreneur if economic circumstances change,
(f) oligopoly is the most common market structure and marginal analysis needs additional assumptions about behaviour to cope with it.

# 5.11 Alternative pricing procedures

1   Traditional theory suggests that firms first find the quantity of output that gives them maximum profit and then charge a price that will allow them to clear that quantity.
2   In practice, firms may well operate the other way round; fixing their price first and then selling what they can at this price.
3   Prices are often fixed by *mark-up or full-cost methods*, where standard percentages are added to variable costs to cover fixed costs and profits.
4   If there are already similar products on sale in the market prices will be set according to the competition, and the quality and design of the product amended if necessary.

## Exercise 7

1   The committee of St. Andrew's Youth Club have to decide what price to charge for coffee at their weekly meetings. The hire of the kitchen is £3 per night. A jar of coffee which makes 60 cups, costs £1.80p. Coffee whitener, enough for 60 cups, cost 90p. Sugar costs 50p per kg, enough for 50

spoonfuls. Plastic cups are sold in packets of 50 and cost 50p per packet. On average 60 members attend meetings.
(a) If you were on the committee what price would you recommend? State your reasons.
(b) Should cups without sugar or whitener be cheaper?
(c) At special monthly meetings up to 120 members attend. Would it be rational to change the price for these meetings? Explain your reasoning.

## Review

### Unit 5 will have helped provide answers to the following questions

1 According to marginal theories of the firm what is the chief motivation of businessmen?
2 What alternative objectives may they be aiming for in practice?
3 In traditional theory how is the maximum profit of output for a firm to be found?
4 What are the assumptions on which the four main market types are based?
5 What is the long run and short run equilibrium situation of the firm in each market structure?
6 In what circumstances can a firm sell the same product to different customers at different prices?
7 When will firms cease trading in the short run and the long run?
8 What are the limitations of the traditional marginal theories of the firm?

### Unit 5 has introduced the following terminology

Barriers to entry
Behavioural theories
Degree of monopoly
Discriminating monopolists
Duopoly
Empirical studies
Full-cost pricing
Imperfect competition
Kinked demand curve
Marginal analysis
Market leadership
Mark-up pricing
Monopolistic competition
Monopoly
Oligopoly
Perfect competition
Product differentiation
Satisficing

### Multiple choice questions

1 Which of the following is a true statement?
  (a) Firms in perfect competition cannot earn abnormal profit in the short run.
  (b) All firms earning less than normal profits in imperfectly competitive markets will cease trading in the short run.
  (c) Firms in monopolistically competitive markets cannot earn abnormal profits in the long run.
  (d) Oligopolists never change their prices.
  (e) Monopolists cannot earn normal profits in the short run.

2 According to traditional marginal analysis which of the following are assumed to make the key business decisions about pricing and quantity of output?
  (a) owners
  (b) workers
  (c) customers
  (d) government
  (e) all of the above

3 The maximum profit point of output occurs where:
  (a) average cost equals average revenue
  (b) average revenue equals price
  (c) total revenue equals total cost
  (d) marginal revenue equals marginal cost
  (e) average cost equals marginal cost

4 According to traditional theory firms aim to:
  (a) increase their market share
  (b) satisfy the ambitions of their managers
  (c) maximise profits
  (d) satisfice
  (e) survive in business

Questions 5 to 7 refer to the following market structures:
  (a) perfect competition
  (b) imperfect competition
  (c) oligopoly
  (d) duopoly
  (e) monopoly

5 To which market structure does the Covent Garden vegetable market most closely approximate?

6 Which market structure best describes a motorway service station which is 5 km away from a motorist who has 8 km of petrol left in his petrol tank?

7 Which market structure best describes the production of detergents for automatic washing machines in Britain?

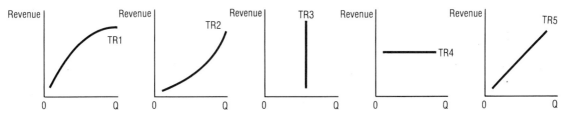

**Figure 5.12** Total revenue curves

**8** Which of the curves in Figure 5.12 illustrates the total revenue curve for a firm operating in an imperfectly competitive market?
(a) TR1 (b) TR2 (c) TR3 (d) TR4 (e) TR5

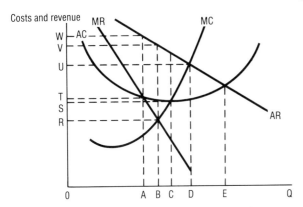

**Figure 5.13** The revenue and cost position of a firm

Questions 9 to 11 refer to Figure 5.13

**9** Maximum profit is earned at output:
(a) 0A (b) 0B (c) 0C (d) 0D (e) 0E

**10** Which rectangle shows the abnormal profit being earned by the firm?
(a) WT × 0A (b) RT × 0A (c) WR × 0A
(d) SV × 0B (e) SU × 0C

**11** For which market structure could Figure 5.13 be an equilibrium situation?
(a) perfect competition in the short run
(b) perfect competition in the long run
(c) imperfect competition in the short run
(d) imperfect competition in the long run
(e) monopolistic competition in the long run

**12** Which of the following would be a valid reason for disregarding traditional marginal analysis of the firm?
(a) Very few examples of perfect competition can be found in the real world.
(b) Producers do not have perfect knowledge of business opportunities.
(c) Customers are not always rational.
(d) Some firms seek to expand market share at the expense of profits.
(e) The conclusions from marginal analysis are misleading and unhelpful in explaining actual business behaviour.

## Answers

### Exercise 1

**1** (a) Profit is clearly important for THF, but the company probably has a medium term view of profit levels.
(b) Shareholders (through dividend payments), managers (through improved and expanded business opportunities), and possibly workers and customers generally.
(c) THF appears to provide job satisfaction by encouraging workers to use initiative, it offers good promotion opportunities, and good working conditions.
(d) Growth involves initial expenditure, and perhaps moves into less familiar areas and so may lower profits in the short run.
(e) All successful firms must be market orientated. Without customer support there are no sales or profits at all.

**2** (a) Tesco's profit fell £37.6m on sales of £1201m [3.1%] in 1979 to £35.6m on sales of £1820m [1.95%] in 1981, although restored to £53.5m on sales of £2276m [2.35%] by 1983. Sainsbury's profit grows steadily with increased sales at constantly higher profit margins.
(b) Tesco's were slow to set up superstores. Since 1981 they have closed over 300 smaller stores, itself a costly business. Tesco has opted for lower margins to attract custom (in its 'Checkout at Tesco' campaign). Sainsbury's own brand goods have a special reputation amongst shoppers.

### Exercise 2

**1** (a) to (e)

| Quantity | TR | MR | TC | MC | Total profit |
|---|---|---|---|---|---|
| 1 | 30 | — | 21 | — | 9 |
| 2 | 37 | 7 | 26 | 5 | 11 |
| 3 | 43 | 6 | 30 | 4 | 13 |
| 4 | 48 | 5 | 33 | 3 | 15 |
| 5 | 52 | 4 | 37 | 4 | 15 |
| 6 | 55 | 3 | 42 | 5 | 13 |
| 7 | 57 | 2 | 48 | 6 | 9 |
| 8 | 58 | 1 | 56 | 8 | 2 |

(f) When marginal cost equals marginal revenue.

## Exercise 3

**1** (a)

| Quantity | TC | MC |
|----------|-----|----|
| 1 | 6 | — |
| 2 | 10 | 4 |
| 3 | 12 | 2 |
| 4 | 12 | 0 |
| 5 | 20 | 8 |
| 6 | 36 | 16 |
| 7 | 63 | 27 |
| 8 | 112 | 49 |

In perfectly competitive markets $AR = MR = P$.
Maximum profit occurs where $MR = MC$.
So, at price £49 quantity will be 8
      at price £27 quantity will be 7
      at price £16 quantity will be 6
      at price £8 quantity will be 5
i.e. the supply curve is the upward sloping part of the marginal cost curve in perfectly competitive markets.

**2**

| Output | Total fixed cost | Total variable cost | Total cost | Average total cost | Marginal cost |
|--------|-------|-------|-----|-----|-----|
| 100 | 100 | 10 | 110 | 1.1 | — |
| 200 | 100 | 80 | 180 | 0.9 | 0.7 |
| 300 | 100 | 140 | 240 | 0.8 | 0.6 |
| 400 | 100 | 180 | 280 | 0.7 | 0.4 |
| 500 | 100 | 300 | 400 | 0.8 | 1.2 |

N.B. Marginal cost should be plotted at the mid-point position.
(d) Maximum profit output = 400 gallons.
(e) No. He wants to survive to hand on his farm to his son.

## Exercise 4

**1**

| Price (p) | Quantity | Total revenue (£) |
|-----------|----------|-------------------|
| 60 | 100 | 60 |
| 55 | 300 | 165 |
| 50 | 500 | 250 |
| 30 | 550 | 165 |
| 10 | 600 | 60 |

(c) If Garage A thought Garage B would follow, or if he made an agreement with Garage B. He may have sufficient reserves to try and drive Garage B out of business.
(d) Yes (if it is legal to do so). Demand curve would lose its kink, so total revenue would probably be $475 \times 60 = £285$.

(e) In non-price ways, e.g. service, free gifts, other facilities.

**2** Own research. Prices in oligopolies are unlikely to differ by much for any length of time. Banks compete in non-price ways, e.g. through branch location, advertising and services offered.

**3** Suggested essay plan.
  Introduction:  Definition of terms i) Marginal analysis (i.e. finding where $MR = MC$) ii) Oligopolistic markets
  Main paragraphs:  i) Kinked demand curves, based on assumptions of rivals' behaviour. ii) Generates discontinuous MR curve, so MC cuts it in this area, suggesting oligopolists should charge the price they are in fact already charging.
  Conclusion.

## Exercise 5

**1** (a)  Identify different groups (e.g. by their unemployment benefit cards, or pension books, or by imposing conditions on travelling, e.g. advance booking). Prevent resale from one group to another.
   (b)  Groups have different elasticities of demand. Producers are reducing consumer surplus.

## Exercise 6

**1**

| Quantity | AR | MR | TR | AFC | AVC | ATC | MC |
|----------|----|----|----|-----|-----|-----|-----|
| 10 | 36 | . | 360 | 80 | 40 | 120 | |
| 20 | 33 | 30 | 660 | 40 | 30 | 70 | 20 |
| 30 | 30 | 24 | 900 | 26.6 | 23.3 | 50 | 10 |
| 40 | 27 | 18 | 1080 | 20 | 20 | 40 | 10 |
| 50 | 24 | 12 | 1200 | 16 | 30 | 46 | 70 |
| 60 | 21 | 6 | 1260 | 13.3 | 40 | 53.3 | 90 |

He will carry on trading in short run if, at the maximum profit (minimum loss) point of output AVC is less than AR.
Maximum profit point of output is where MC cuts MR from below, about 37. At quantity 37, AR is about 28, AVC about 21. The firm is making a trading profit of about 7 on each item, which it can use to offset some of the fixed costs which have to be paid in the short run.

**2** Suggested essay plan.
  Introduction:  Definition of terms i) Entrepreneur ii) Fall in demand, i.e. a shift to the left of the firm's demand curve
  Main paragraphs:  i) Depends on which market structure, in particular whether abnormal profits were being earned ii) Identify different time periods iii) Identify fixed and variable costs iv) Outline close-down decision as in *Unit 5.9.*
  Conclusion.

## Exercise 7

1 (a) Do you want to make a profit out of your members?

(b) Do you want to deal only in round figures?

(c) What level of demand do you anticipate?

My students settled for 15p a cup, no change of price for variations or special meetings.

This illustrates full-cost or mark-up price fixing in practice.

## Multiple choice answers

1 (c) There are no barriers to entry so other firms enter to get a share of the profits.

2 (a) Owners are assumed to take decisions in order to maximise profits.

3 (d) By definition.

4 (c) See 2 above.

5 (b) Even vegetables can be branded through their packaging.

6 (e) Only possible producer or supplier in this circumstance, i.e. a local monopoly.

7 (c) The big three are Unilever, Colgate-Palmolive and Proctor and Gamble.

8 (a) Higher quantities can only be sold by lowering prices.

9 (b) Where MC cuts MR from below.

10 (d) Abnormal profit is (AR—AC) × quantity sold.

11 (c) In short run abnormal profit is possible in imperfectly competitive markets.

12 (e) It does not matter if the assumptions are unrealistic as long as they help understanding.

# UNIT 6 Prices

## 6.1 Preview

1 In free markets prices are determined by the interaction of supply and demand.
2 An equilibrium price is one at which quantity demanded in a given period equals the quantity supplied in that period.
3 Changes in prices cause producers and consumers to alter the quantities they supply and demand, and therefore leads to re-allocation of resources.
4 Not all prices are determined in free markets. Controlled prices may not coincide with equilibrium prices.

## 6.2 Free market equilibrium

1 **The equilibrium price**

The price in a market which results in equal quantities being supplied to a market and demanded in the market is called the equilibrium price.

*Observations from Figure 6.1*

☐ At price P1 quantity supplied equals quantity demanded (equilibrium price).

☐ At price P3 quantity supplied is Q3 but quantity demanded is only Q2. The excess supply will force prices down towards P1.

☐ At price P2 quantity supplied is only Q2 but quantity demanded is Q3. The shortage of supply will force price up towards P1.

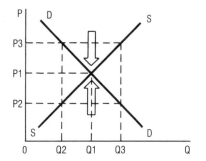

**Figure 6.1** Free market equilibrium

2 **Consumer and producer surplus**

In free markets all consumers and producers pay the equilibrium price. However, the demand and supply curves show that some consumers and producers would still be prepared to trade in the market at different prices.

*Observations from Figure 6.2*

☐ The equilibrium price is P1.

☐ Some consumers would have been willing to pay more for the product than price P1, e.g. at price P3 quantity Q2 would still have been demanded. These consumers are receiving the good for less than they would have been prepared to pay, i.e. they are receiving *consumer surplus*.

☐ Some producers would have been willing to supply goods to the market for less than price P1, e.g. at price P2 they would have been willing to supply quantity Q2. These producers are receiving more money than they needed, i.e. they are receiving *producer surplus*.

☐ Total consumer surplus is shown by area 'abc'. Total producer surplus is shown by area 'abd'.

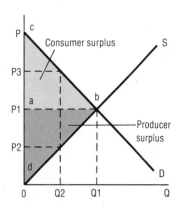

**Figure 6.2** Consumer and producer surplus

## Exercise 1

1 The information on page 65 (right) is produced by a shoe shop concerning sales of a particular design of shoe.

(a) Draw a diagram to illustrate the demand and supply situation for this shoe design.
(b) At a price of £15 per pair what would be the shortage of pairs of the shoes?
(c) At a price of £35 per pair what would be the surplus of pairs of shoes?
(d) What is the equilibrium price of these shoes?
(e) What is the level of consumer and producer surplus at this equilibrium price?

| Price (£) | Quantity demanded each week | Quantity supplied each week |
|---|---|---|
| 0 | 90 | 0 |
| 5 | 80 | 5 |
| 10 | 70 | 10 |
| 15 | 60 | 15 |
| 20 | 50 | 20 |
| 25 | 40 | 25 |
| 30 | 30 | 30 |
| 35 | 20 | 35 |
| 40 | 10 | 40 |
| 45 | 0 | 45 |

2 A stockbroker finds the demand and supply for shares in Carlton Brewery PLC is as in the table.

| Price (£) | Quantity supplied each day | Quantity demanded each day |
|---|---|---|
| 7.00 | 5000 | 0 |
| 6.60 | 4000 | 1000 |
| 6.20 | 3000 | 2000 |
| 5.80 | 2000 | 3000 |
| 5.40 | 1000 | 4000 |
| 5.20 | 0 | 5000 |

(a) Draw demand and supply curves for the shares.
(b) If the share price was £6.40 would there be more or less shares being bought than sold?
(c) What is the equilibrium share price?
(d) A take-over bid is made for Carlton Brewery PLC, increasing the demand for shares, at all prices, by 2000 each day. What will happen to the equilibrium share price?

3 In November 1983 a colour TV licence cost £46. All licence money went to the BBC. Commercial television is not 'free' as consumers pay higher prices for the goods that are advertised. The estimated cost per viewer of TV advertisements was 1.5p per viewing hour, which totals about £45 per year per set.

*Which?* asked viewers to imagine there were no advertisements or licence fees and to tell them what they would be prepared to pay on a weekly basis to receive each channel. The data obtained showed:

| | | | |
|---|---|---|---|
| BBC1 | 85p per week | £44.20 per year | |
| BBC2 | 60p per week | £31.20 per year | Total BBC £75.40 per year |
| ITVI | 70p per week | £36.40 per year | |
| Channel 4 | 16p per week | £8.32 per year | Total IBA £44.72 per year |

(Based on information from *Which?* November 1983, March 1984 Consumer's Association)

(a) Assuming that *Which?* figures are accurate, is it possible to infer anything from these figures about households' 'consumer surplus' for TV?

# 6.3 The price mechanism revisited

1 Changes in prices send signals to consumers and producers, e.g. a rise in price will lead to less being demanded but more being supplied in a market.

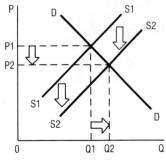

1 A fall in costs – a downwards
shift of the supply curve

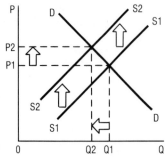

2 An increase in costs – an upwards
shift of the supply curve

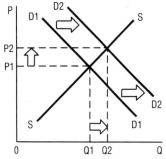

3 An increase in demand – a shift
to the right of the demand curve

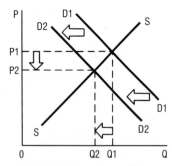

4 A decrease in demand – a shift
to the left of the demand curve

**Figure 6.3**  Effects on supply and
demand curves

2  Changing in the conditions of supply and demand will lead to a change in the level of equilibrium price.
3  Resources will be re-allocated according to the change in market conditions.
See Figure 6.3.

# Exercise 2

1  The following separate events influence the market for microwave ovens. Consider how each would affect:
  (i)  the supply curve
  (ii)  the demand curve
  (iii)  the equilibrium price
  (iv)  the quantity bought and sold
Show the effect by drawing a series of demand and supply curves for microwave ovens.
(a)  A fall in the costs of making microwave ovens.
(b)  A rise in the level of Value Added Tax (payable by producers) levied on all electrical goods.
(c)  A rise in the price of conventional gas and electric cookers.
(d)  Producers of microwave ovens wish to increase their profit margins.
(e)  A health scare causes a loss of consumer confidence in microwaves.
(f)  Producers mount a successful advertising campaign.
(g)  Governments introduce a subsidy to producers of microwave ovens.
(h)  There is a general increase in consumer incomes.

2  **Commodity prices**
(a)  Palm-oil prices are in the throes of a 'boom-bust' cycle, reaching record highs of nearly $1000 a tonne. Malaysia, the biggest producer, expanded its output by 30% in 1982 to 3.5m tonnes helped by the introduction of the pollinating weevil to increase yields. World prices slumped to $350 a tonne, so planters used less fertiliser. This together with the dry weather and exhausted trees, reduced Malaysia's output to only 3m tonnes in 1983 when demand for palm-oil was strong because of a shortage of soya bean oil.
  Describe and account for the movements in the price of palm-oil. Use demand and supply diagrams to show:
    (i)  situation 1—before 1982
    (ii)  situation 2—after the introduction of the weevil
    (iii)  situation 3—in 1983
(b)  Cobalt has a new lease of life. After drifting around $6 a lb for a year its price has rocketed to $11 a lb in a week. Free market prices peaked at $44 a lb in 1978 following the invasion of Zaire which produces half world's cobalt. Then substitution and recession hit consumption, producers' stocks piled up to 20,000 tonnes by the end of 1982 and prices fell to below $4 a lb. Zaire slashed output by 7000 tonnes between 1981 and 1983 and stocks fell to 12,000 tonnes.

Describe and account for the movements in the price of cobalt. Use demand and supply diagrams to show:
  (i) situation 1—before 1978
  (ii) situation 2—after the invasion of Zaire
  (iii) situation 3—at the end of 1982
  (iv) situation 4—in 1984 after the slashing of output

(c) Sugar prices have sunk to 5.5c a lb, the lowest for a year. Bad weather around the world last year initially pointed to a small deficit in the 1983–4 season after two years of surplus. But crops were sweeter than expected. Total production will be about 95m tonnes giving a small surplus.

Describe and account for the changes in sugar prices from the 1979–80 season to the 1983–84 season. Use demand and supply diagrams to show:
  (i) situation 1—summer 1979
  (ii) situation 2—summer 1980
  (iii) situation 3—summer 1982
  (iv) situation 4—summer 1983

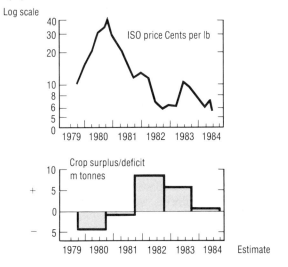

**Figure 6.4** Sugar (Based on information from *Economist*, Commodity Price Index: 10.3.84, 10.2.84, 12.5.84)

# 6.4 Problems of increasing supply

1 If producers find it difficult to adjust the level of supply to meet the new conditions in a market then market price may not move smoothly to the obvious new equilibrium price.
*Observations from Figure 6.5*
☐ Demand has increased from D1 to D2.
☐ Given that supply (S1) cannot be altered at all, i.e. supply is perfectly inelastic, the price rises to P4. Equilibrium quantity stays at Q1.
☐ In the short run supply (S2) can be increased a little, supply is less inelastic. Price falls back to P3. Equilibrium quantity increases to Q2.

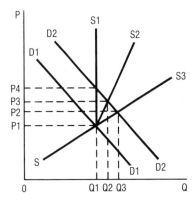

**Figure 6.5** Adjusting level of supply

☐ In the long run when factors of production can be changed, i.e. resources re-allocated, supply (S3) will be more elastic, and price will fall back to P2. Equilibrium quantity increases to Q3.

2 **Cobwebs**

In markets where it takes time to adjust the level of supply to changes in market conditions it is possible that prices will be observed to fluctuate. These fluctuations may tend towards the long tun equilibrium price (a convergent cobweb) or away from the long run equilibrium price (a divergent cobweb).

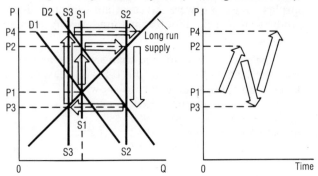

**Figure 6.6** Cobwebs

*Observations from Figure 6.6*
☐ Demand rises from D1 to D2.
☐ In the short run supply is fixed at S1. Price rises to P2.
☐ At price P2, however, producers will want to supply S2.
☐ When S2 reaches the market, price falls to P3.
☐ At this low price P3 producers will only plant to supply S3.
☐ When this fixed supply of S3 reaches the market, price will rise to P4 and so on.
☐ Price is diverging from the long run equilibrium price. If the gradient of the demand curve was less than the gradient of the supply curve the cobweb would converge on the long run equilibrium price.

---

## Exercise 3

1 There are two interesting features of the supply of houses. First, the number of houses cannot be increased quickly. Second, the market is supplied largely from the stock of existing houses. The construction industry tends to react to high prices today by having more houses for sale tomorrow. Home owners do not react to changing prices quickly either. There are legal and technical delays between the time they decide to sell or buy and the time they actually do so.
   (a) What is the shape of the short run supply curve for houses?
   (b) What is the nature of the price elasticity of demand for houses?
   (c) What would happen to the demand for houses if mortgages became more easily available?
   (d) What would be expected to happen to the supply of houses after a period of, say, two years?

(e) Are the conditions outlined above likely to lead to a cobweb situation?

(f) Prices of houses are rarely seen to fall in money terms in the UK. Does this mean that cobwebs do not occur in the UK housing market?

2 The following information (see table on the right) is known about the demand and supply of deep-sea divers in a country where immigration is prohibited.

(a) What is the original equilibrium wage?

(b) Supply is fixed in the short run at 40 divers, as it takes one year to train new divers. A discovery of precious stones in shell-fish causes demand for divers to rise by 20/month at each wage level. What will be the immediate effect on wages?

(c) How many people will plan to be divers at this new wage?

(d) When these people complete training what will happen to wages?

(e) At the new lower wage how many people will plan to be divers? In the short run they are all committed to year long contracts of employment.

(f) Is the wage level converging or diverging? Why didn't wages move directly to the new equilibrium level?

| Wage level ('000 $) | Demand/month | Supply/month |
|---|---|---|
| 20 | 55 | 17.5 |
| 30 | 50 | 25 |
| 40 | 45 | 32.5 |
| 50 | 40 | 40. |
| 60 | 35 | 47.5 |
| 70 | 30 | 55 |
| 80 | 25 | 62.5 |
| 90 | 20 | 70 |
| 100 | 15 | 77.5 |

## 6.5 Indirect taxation and subsidies

1 Producers who have to pay indirect taxes (either on the value added or on the quantity supplied) will count the tax as part of their costs of production.

2 An increase in tax will cause an upward shift (to the left) of the supply curve.

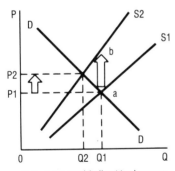

% (ad valorem) indirect tax increase

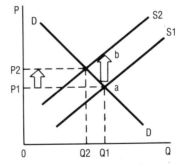

Flat rate (specific) indirect tax increase

**Figure 6.7** Types of indirect tax increases

*Observations from Figure 6.7*

☐ The imposition of a tax shifts the supply curve from S1 to S2.

☐ A percentage (or *ad valorem*) tax also changes the gradient of the supply curve, a fixed percentage of a higher price being more than a fixed percentage of a lower price.

☐ At price P1 tax increase is ab, but equilibrium price increases by less than this from P1 to P2 with equilibrium quantity falling from Q1 to Q2.

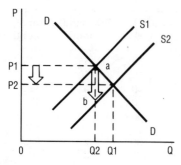

**Figure 6.8** Effect of a subsidy on supply

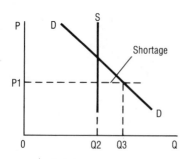

**Figure 6.9** Shortage in supply

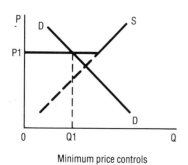

Minimum price controls

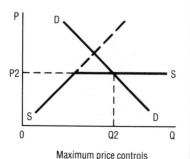

Maximum price controls

**Figure 6.10** Minimum and maximum price controls

☐ The extent to which producers pass the tax increase on to the consumer depends on the elasticity of demand for the product.

3 Subsidies will allow the producer to shift the supply curve downwards (to the right).

*Observations from Figure 6.8*

☐ The subsidy shifts the supply curve from S1 to S2.

☐ The extent of the subsidy at price P1 is ab. Equilibrium price falls from P1 to P2, i.e. by an amount less than the subsidy Equilibrium quantity increases from Q1 to Q2.

☐ The extent to which the subsidy is passed on to the consumer depends on the elasticity of demand for the product.

## 6.6 Restricted supply and black markets

1 If supply is restricted, and at a controlled price demand exceeds supply then goods will have to be rationed and a black market may develop.

*Observations from Figure 6.9*

☐ Price is fixed at P1.

☐ Supply cannot be increased, e.g. it is a concert hall with only limited capacity.

☐ At price P1 demand exceeds supply by Q3–Q2, giving the potential for the development of a black market.

## 6.7 Minimum and maximum prices

1 In some markets authorities may impose minimum or maximum price levels or controls.

*Observations from Figure 6.10*

☐ Goods cannot be supplied at less than minimum price P1, but they can be supplied at prices above P1 according to suppliers discretion, creating an effective supply curve P1–S.

☐ Goods cannot be supplied at more than maximum price P2, but they could be supplied at the discretion of the suppliers for less, creating an effective supply curve P2–S.

## Exercise 4

1 How much of an increase in indirect tax will be passed on to consumers if:
(a) price elasticity of demand is zero
(b) price elasticity of demand is infinite
(c) elasticity of supply is zero

2 Agricultural markets provide a number of interesting situations for the application of supply and demand analysis.
(a) Assume demand for food is price inelastic, and that the supply of food in the short run is perfectly inelastic. Draw a diagram to show the effect on food prices if in the long run there is an unexpectedly good harvest.
(b) In order to prevent fluctuations in farmers' incomes (as in part (a) above) the actual market demand curve can be distorted by government intervention, buying goods

for intervention stores, or releasing buffer stocks.

In Figure 6.11 D1 = Actual (non-government) demand curve

D2 = demand curve after government intervention

S1 = supply after a poor harvest

S2 = supply after a good harvest

i) What is the elasticity of demand of D2 if it means that farmers' incomes stay stable whatever the level of prices?

ii) What quantity will the government have to buy for intervention stores to stabilise incomes after the good harvest?

iii) What quantity will the government have to release from the buffer stock to stabilise incomes after the poor harvest?

(c) What features of agricultural markets make cobweb price fluctuations likely without government intervention?

(d) Assume that demand for food is income inelastic, and that over time technological progress has increased the supply of food significantly.

Draw a diagram to show what happens to farmers' incomes in the long run (over 20 years or so) as income levels elsewhere rise.

(e) Assume that the market price of tinned mushrooms is below the price the government thinks is reasonable for growers. The government guarantees a price higher than the existing market price, and achieves this by buying up all supplies over the level needed to generate the guaranteed price.

Draw a diagram to illustrate this situation, showing clearly the level of support buying undertaken by the government.

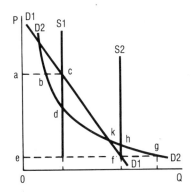

**Figure 6.11**  Intervention in agricultural markets

3  Nationalised industries have more freedom over the setting of prices than private sector firms.

In Figure 6.12 AC slopes downwards throughout because the nationalised industry faces high fixed costs.

(a) If it is decided the industry should aim to maximise profits, what price should it charge, and what quantity of output will be produced?

(b) If it is decided that the industry should merely break even, i.e. produce at a point where total revenue equals total cost, what price should it charge, and what quantity will be produced?

(c) If, in order to obtain a more efficient allocation of resources, the industry is instructed to set prices equal to marginal cost what will be the price level, what will be the quantity of output, and will the industry be making a profit or a loss?

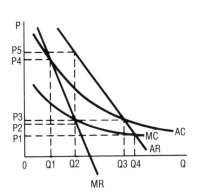

**Figure 6.12**  Pricing options for nationalised industry

4  **Essay**

'Market forces always operate to produce a stable equilibrium price.' Discuss.

# Review

## Unit 6 will have helped provide answers to the following questions

1 How are prices determined in free markets?
2 How does the operation of the price mechanism cause a re-allocation of resources?
3 Why do prices not always move towards a new stable equilibrium price when market conditions change?
4 How does supply and demand analysis help to highlight the particular problems of price and income in agriculture?

## Unit 6 has introduced the following terminology

Black market
Buffer stock
Cobwebs
Consumer surplus
Equilibrium price
Guaranteed price
Indirect taxation
Intervention store

Maximum price
Minimum price
Producer surplus
Rationing
Stable equilibrium price
Subsidies
Support buying
Unstable equilibrium price

## Multiple choice questions

1 If the supply of a good is perfectly elastic, and a subsidy is paid to the producers of the good, the price to consumers will fall by an amount dependent on:
(a) the price elasticity of demand for the good,
(b) the income elasticity of demand for the good,
(c) the size of the subsidy per unit as all will be passed on to the consumer,
(d) the size of the subsidy per unit as some of it will be passed on to the consumer,
(e) the level of indirect taxation levied on the good.

2

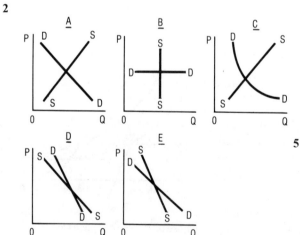

Figure 6.13   Market equilibrium positions

Which of the graphs in Figure 6.13 represents a position of unstable equilibrium?
(a) A   (b) B   (c) C   (d) D   (e) E

3

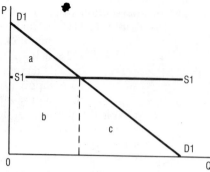

Figure 6.14   Consumer surplus

In Figure 6.14 S1 represents a perfectly elastic supply curve for a product, and D1 represents the demand curve for the product.
The area of consumer surplus is:
(a) a   (b) b + c   (c) b   (d) c   (e) a + b

4

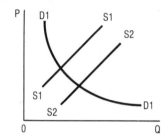

Figure 6.15   A shift in supply

In Figure 6.15 S1 is the original supply curve, S2 shows an increase in supply. D1 is a demand curve with unitary price elasticity.
Which observation is inconsistent with that shown in Figure 6.15?
(a) Total revenue received stays unchanged following the increase in supply.
(b) The quantity traded rises following the supply increase.
(c) The equilibrium price falls following the supply increase.
(d) Total outlay on the good falls following the supply increase.
(e) Average revenue for producers falls following the supply increase.

5

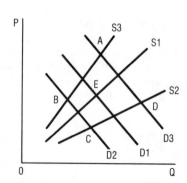

Figure 6.17   Shifts in supply and demand

In Figure 6.16 S1 represents the free market supply curve of labour. The union negotiates a minimum wage level of W1 for these workers. D1 represents the demand curve for these workers. Abolition of the minimum wage agreement would lead to:
(a) a rise in the wage rates of the workers,
(b) no change in the wage rate but a fall in the demand for workers,
(c) a rise in the demand for labour and a fall in wage rates,
(d) an increase in demand for labour but leave wage rates unchanged,
(e) a fall in the demand for labour and a fall in wage rates.

**6** If a nationalised industry wishes to set prices so that total revenue equals total cost it should produce at the point where:
(a) average cost equals average revenue
(b) marginal cost equals marginal revenue
(c) average cost equals marginal cost
(d) average revenue equals marginal cost
(e) average revenue equals marginal revenue

Questions 7 to 9 refer to the following data for a product.

| Price (£) | Quantity demanded/wk | Quantity supplied/wk |
|---|---|---|
| 1 | 20 | 10 |
| 2 | 20 | 15 |
| 3 | 20 | 20 |
| 4 | 20 | 25 |
| 5 | 20 | 30 |

**7** In this market equilibrium price is:
(a) £1  (b) £2  (c) £3  (d) £4  (e) £5

**8** At price £5 there is:
(a) a shortage of 10 units per week
(b) a surplus of 10 units per week
(c) a shortage of 30 units per week
(d) a surplus of 30 units per week
(e) equal supply and demand of the product

**9** If demand increases by 10 per week at each price level what will happen to the equilibrium price level?
(a) Increase to £4.
(b) Increase to £5.
(c) Remain unaltered until supply can be adjusted.
(d) Fall to £1.
(e) Cannot be determined from the information given.

**10** In Figure 6.17, D1 is the original demand curve, and S1 the original supply curve. Which point on the diagram is consistent with the imposition of an indirect tax on the good, and a general rise in consumers' incomes?
(a) A  (b) B  (c) C  (d) D  (e) E

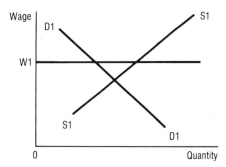

**Figure 6.16** A market for labour

# Answers

## Exercise 1

**1** (a) Diagram to have price on vertical axis, quantities on horizontal.
(b) 45 (60 demanded but only 15 supplied).
(c) 15 (35 supplied but only 20 demanded).
(d) £30 per pair. (Quantity demanded equals quantity supplied at 30).
(e) Consumer surplus = 225 (half of 15 × 30). Producer surplus = 450 (half of 30 × 30).

**2** (b) More sales (3500) than purchases (1500).
(c) £6.00.
(d) Rise to £6.40. Quantity demanded equals quantity supplied at 3500.

**3** (a) Overall 'cost' of TV is estimated at £101 per year. Consumers would be prepared to pay £120.12p, so there is some consumer surplus. Most of the surplus seems to come from BBC, but it is not possible to buy the channels separately.

## Exercise 2

**1** (a) Shifts supply curve downwards.
(b) Shifts supply curve upwards, and increases its gradient.
(c) Shifts demand curve to the right.
(d) Shifts supply curve upwards.
(e) Shifts demand curve to the left.
(f) Shifts demand curve to the right.
(g) Shifts supply curve downwards.
(h) Shifts demand curve to the right.

**2** (a)

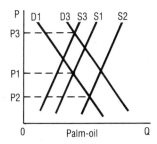

(b)                    (c)

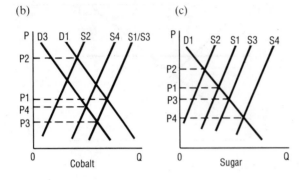

**Figure 6.18**  Changes in commodity prices

## Exercise 3

1  (a)  Almost vertical—relatively inelastic supply.
   (b)  In short run also price inelastic.
   (c)  Demand curve for houses would shift to the right.
   (d)  Rise as builders take advantage of the new profitable opportunities.
   (e)  Yes, increase in demand coupled with short run fixed supply.
   (f)  Cobwebs do occur. Prices fall in real if not money terms.

2  (a)  $50,000.
   (b)  Rise to $90,000—the level where new demand level equals the fixed supply.
   (c)  70—found from supply curve information
   (d)  fall to $30,000—the level where new demand equals this increased supply.
   (e)  only 25.
   (f)  Diverging—the wage level is not moving towards the expected equilibrium level of $66,666.

## Exercise 4

1  i) all of it  ii) none of it  iii) all of it
   Draw the diagrams to check.

2  (b)  i)  Price elasticity must be 1 if revenue stays constant with price changes.
       ii)  fg will have to be removed from the free market, i.e. the government will have to demand this amount.
      iii)  bc will have to be released to reduce effective demand from D1 to D2.

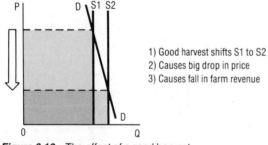

1) Good harvest shifts S1 to S2
2) Causes big drop in price
3) Causes fall in farm revenue

**Figure 6.19**  The effect of a good harvest

(c)  Fluctuating supply and demand conditions—supply time lags.

(d)

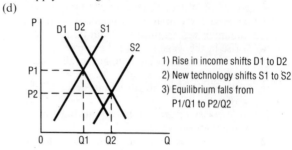

1) Rise in income shifts D1 to D2
2) New technology shifts S1 to S2
3) Equilibrium falls from P1/Q1 to P2/Q2

**Figure 6.20**  Falling agricultural incomes

(e)

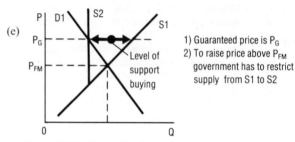

1) Guaranteed price is P$_G$
2) To raise price above P$_{FM}$ government has to restrict supply from S1 to S2

**Figure 6.21**  Support buying policy

3  (a)  Maximum profit point is where MC cuts MR, quantity Q2 price P5.
   (b)  Break even means total revenue equals total cost, i.e. at Q3, P3.
   (c)  Marginal cost pricing means setting prices (AR) equal to MC i.e. Q4, P1.

4  Suggested essay plan.
   Introduction:  Definition of terms i) Market forces, i.e. supply and demand ii) Stable equilibrium price
   Main paragraphs:  i) Show diagramatically stable position but ii) Cobwebs—when there are supply time lags iii) Market forces may be controlled e.g. wage rates
   Conclusion.

## Multiple choice answers

1  (c)  Supply curve moves downwards. Price falls by this amount whatever nature of demand.
2  (d)  A movement away will cause further movements away.
3  (a)  The difference between what consumers would pay and what they have to pay.
4  (d)  Total outlay stays the same when PED = 1.
5  (c)  Market moves back to where D1 and S1 intersect.
6  (a)  At this point total revenue equals total cost.
7  (c)  At this price quantity demanded equals quantity supplied = 20.
8  (b)  Supply exceeds demand by 10 at price £5.
9  (b)  At this price quantity supplied equals new quantity demanded = 30.
10  (a)  Where D3 meets $3.

# The size of firms

# UNIT 7

## 7.1 Preview

1 *Unit 4* introduced the concept of economies of scale. If there are opportunities for economies of scale, production will be more efficient if production stems from a large organisation.

2 *Unit 5*, however, introduced some of the consequences of market imperfections, particularly when associated with monopoly power.

3 Competition policy is the name given to a number of government measures that aim to strike a balance between producer and consumer interests in terms of business size and market structure.

4 Current legislation is based on a 1973 Act of Parliament. Recent interpretation of the Act has meant that greater emphasis is now placed on creating competition in markets.

## 7.2 Small firms

1 **Definition of small**
   (a) *Appropriate legal structure*—i.e. all non-listed companies (companies which cannot sell shares to the general public).
   (b) *Using set criteria* (as used in the Bolton Committee of Inquiry on Small Firms 1971), e.g. in manufacturing—less than 200 employees, in construction—less than 25 employees, in retailing—turnover of less than £50,000 p.a.
   (c) *Behaviour*—typical small firms have three characteristics:
      (i) they have a small share of the market,
      (ii) they are managed in a personalised way by their owners,
      (iii) they are independent of other organisations, e.g. merchant banks or pension funds.

2 **Importance of small firms**
   (a) Using set criteria to define 'small' there are between 1m and 1.5m small firms operating in the British economy. They are responsible for about 15% GNP, and 20% of total employment.
   (b) As they are typically labour intensive they are an important source of new jobs. Recent US research showed over 80% of new jobs were created in the small firms sector.
   (c) They have a record for technical innovation.
   (d) They provide an outlet for entrepreneurial talents, especially for those who dislike working in large organisations.
   (e) They can satisfy demand in restricted or specialised markets.
   (f) Small firms have good records for labour relations.

3 **Why do small firms stay small?**
   (a) They may be producing for a limited market.
   (b) There may be no cost advantages in increased size, e.g. where

personalised customer service is an essential part of the service offered.

(c) The ability, and/or ambition, of the entrepreneur may be limited.

(d) The small-business man may be too busy with day to day survival to undertake the planning necessary for expansion.

(c) Small firms may be unable to break down the barriers to growth (entry) established by existing large organisations in the market (see *Unit 7.2[4]*).

(f) Finance may be difficult at reasonable rates and for suitable time periods (see *Unit 7.3*).

**4 Barriers to growth for small firms**

(a) Shortage of the supply of key materials or components.

(b) High advertising and strong branding of the established products in the market.

(c) Larger firms are able to enjoy economies of scale and thus charge lower prices than the small, growing firm.

(d) The large firms may have abnormal profits or other reserves to finance short run price wars to choke off new competition.

(e) Established companies may control key channels of distribution.

(f) The position of the existing firms may be protected by patents or trade-mark legal restrictions.

# 7.3 Finance for small firms

1 A major problem for small firms is thought to be a shortage of suitable finance. Originally called the 'MacMillan Gap' after an investigation in the 1930s, more recent reports include the Bolton Committee Inquiry (1971) and the Wilson Committee Inquiry (1980). Both reports felt that more finance was needed for:

(a) risk capital,

(b) medium terms,

(c) without too much demand for security.

2 **Traditional sources of finance** for small firms include:

(a) owners own capital,

(b) borrowing from family and friends,

(c) borrowing from banks through loans or overdraft facilities,

(d) taking trade credit, i.e. altering cash flow by delaying payment of some bills.

(e) factoring, i.e. transferring the claim on the company's debts to a financial institution for an immediate cash payment.

3 There are a growing number of institutional agencies or special agencies run by banks, pension funds and assurance companies, e.g. Investment in Industry (3is) and its subsidiary Industrial and Commercial Finance Corporation (ICFC).

4 The government has taken a number of initiatives to expand the finance available to small businesses.

(a) The Business Start-up Scheme (1981)—which encourages investors to inject capital into small businesses by offering them tax advantages.

(b) The Loan Guarantee Scheme (1981)—where the government

provides 80% guarantees for loans where no other security is available.
(c) Venture Capital Scheme (1980)—where investors equity losses can be offset against income tax instead of capital gains tax.

## Exercise 1

1   Imagine you are the owner of a small firm specialising in roofing and guttering repairs.
  (a) What would be the advantages for you of running your own business?
  (b) What disadvantages would you have compared to larger firms?
  (c) If you required a relatively large cash injection, say £10,000, how might you set about raising it?
  (d) What other problems, apart from raising finance, might you encounter in trying to expand your business?

2   Look in a copy of *'Yellow Pages'* or another local directory.
  (a) How many separate firms are there offering the following goods or services?
     (i) Legal services—solicitors firms
     (ii) Plumbing services
     (iii) Landscape gardening
     (iv) Precision engineering
     (v) Telephone service and installation
  (b) Why are the markets for i) to iv) above dominated by small firms?

## 7.4 Growth of firms

1   Small firms can grow into large firms either through *internal* growth, i.e. from within the company itself, or through *external* growth, i.e. by merging with or taking over other firms.

2   Growth can be classified in four ways.
  (a) *Horizontal growth*—expansion within the same industry at the same stage of the production process.
  (b) *Vertical growth*—expansion within the same industry but at different stages of the production process.
  (c) *Conglomerate growth*—expansion in some other industry apparently unconnected with the original line of business.
  (d) *Lateral growth*—expansion into production of an allied good which is, however, neither an input nor an output of the firm.

## Exercise 2

1   Classify the following examples of business growth in two ways: first as to whether the growth is internal or external, and second as to whether it is horizontal, vertical, conglomerate or lateral.
  (a) McDonald's extend their franchise to more burger outlets.

(b) Horizon Travel purchases new Boeing 737 jets to fly its holiday makers to the continent.

(c) S & W Berisford (sugar manufacturers) take over British Sugar (sugar manufacturers).

(d) Herbert Morris (crane makers) are taken over by Babcock and Wilson (engineers).

(e) British American Tobacco take over Eagle Star insurance.

(f) S & L Ltd (ski clothes hire) open a plastic dry-ski slope.

(g) Trafalgar House (conglomerate owning Cunard liners) take over Scott-Lithgow (ship-repairers owned by British Shipbuilders).

(h) Take over of Stimpsons (estate agents) by Lloyds Bank to expand their Black Horse Agencies.

(i) Expansion of C.A.S.E. PLC to produce new lines of communications hardware.

(j) Decision by Servowarm (central heating installers) to manufacture their own central heating boilers.

(k) BBC development of microcomputers.

# 7.5 Finance for larger firms

1 There are additional sources of finance available for larger firms. These include:

(a) *Sale of shares to the public*—either through public listing on the Stock Exchange or, since 1980, through listing on the Unlisted Securities Market (USM).

(b) *Issue of loan stock or debentures*—fixed interest loans to companies which involve no participation in company ownership.

(c) *Retaining profits (plough-back)*—some 80% of investment expenditure is financed in this way. Small companies are less likely to be able to generate sufficient funds from this source.

## Exercise 3

1 (a) How might a public company set about raising £5m to finance expansion?

(b) What factors would it consider in reaching its decision?

2 (a) What is the economic role of the Stock Exchange?

(b) What role is played by the Unlisted Securities Market?

*Some references*

*A Guide to the British Financial System* (1984) (Banking Information Service) p18

*A Textbook of Economics* (1982) Livesey F. (Polytech. Publishers) p67

*The UK Economy—a Manual of Applied Economics* (1982, 9th edn.) Prest A.R., & Coppock D.J., eds., (Weidenfeld & Nicholson) p96

or, look up 'Stock Exchange' in the index at the back of any good textbook.

# 7.6 The impact of monopoly power

## 1 Measurement of monopoly power

Concentration Ratios (CRs) measure the proportion of output or sales from the largest firms in an industry, e.g. a statement that $CR_5 = 80\%$, means that the five biggest firms, between them, produce or sell 80% of goods in that market.

## 2 A comparison of long run equilibrium positions of firms in monopoly and perfect competition

*Observations from Figure 7.1*

□ AR(PC) shows the demand curve for the firm in a perfectly competitive market. AR(M) shows the demand curve for the monopolist, with the appropriate MR(M) curve below.

□ Costs, for now, are assumed to be the same for both firms.

□ The price charged by the monopolist P(M) is above that charged in perfect competition P(PC).

□ Quantity produced in perfect competition Q(PC) is greater that than produced in monopoly Q(M).

□ In perfect competition production is carried out at the most efficient point (AC is at a minimum) but this is not so for the monopolist.

□ The monopolist earns abnormal profit, whereas in perfect competition only normal profit is earned.

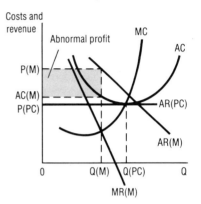

**Figure 7.1** The monopolist and a firm in perfect competition

## 3 The advantages and disadvantages of monopoly power.

| Disadvantages of monopoly power | Advantages of monopoly power |
|---|---|
| Abnormal profit means: Less incentive to be efficient and to develop new products. Resources available to protect market dominance. | Abnormal profit means: Finance for investment to maintain competitive edge. Reserves to overcome short term difficulties, giving stability to employment. Funds for research and development. |
| Monopoly power means: Higher prices and lower output for domestic consumers. | Monopoly power means: Countervailing power to match overseas large organisations. |
| Monopolists may waste resources by undertaking cross-subsidisation, using profits from one sector to finance losses in another sector. | Cross-subsidisation may lead to an increased range of goods or services available to the consumer. |
| Monopolists may undertake price discrimination to raise producer surplus and reduce consumer surplus. | Price discrimination may raise total revenue to a point which allows survival of a product or service. |
| Monopolists do not produce at the most efficient point of output. | Monopolists may be able to take advantage of economies of scale which means that unit costs may still be lower than the most efficient unit cost position of a competitive firm. |
| Monopolists can be complacent and develop inefficiencies. | There are few permanent monopolies and the abnormal profit opportunities act as an incentive to break down the monopoly through a process of creative destruction, i.e. breaking the monopoly by product development and innovation. |
| Monopolists lead to a misallocation of resources by setting prices above marginal cost, so that prices are above the opportunity cost of providing the good. | There are reservations about advocating marginal cost pricing especially where externalities are involved. Monopolists avoid undesirable duplication of services. |

Table 7.1. Monopoly power.

## 7.7 Competition policy

1 It is clear from the balance of arguments presented in the previous section that it cannot simply be claimed that monopoly or big business is bad, and competition or small business is good.
2 The government's response to dealing with the complexities of Competition Policy involves legislation and covers:
   (a) monopolies
   (b) mergers
   (c) restrictive practices
   (d) resale price maintenance
   (e) consumer protection
   (f) promotion of small firms
   (g) privatisation

## 7.8 Monopolies and merger legislation

1 Monopolies and mergers are controlled by the 1973 Fair Trading Act and the 1980 Competition Act.
2 Each situation is judged on its own. No generalisations are made about the desirability or otherwise of monopolies or mergers.
3 Investigations are carried out by the Monopolies and Mergers Commission (MMC). Industries can be investigated if:
   (a) one firm controls over 25% of the output,
   (b) two or more firms are involved in a complex monopoly controlling more than 25% of the output,
   (c) an efficiency audit in the public sector is called for.
   Additionally, the activities of a single firm can be examined if there is reason to believe it is involved in uncompetitive practices. Mergers can be referred to the MMC for examination if a transfer of more than £15m of assets is involved.
4 At present about 200 cases are referred to the MMC for a preliminary investigation each year. Of these, five or so will be extended to a detailed six month investigation, each costing the taxpayer some £0.5m. The MMC makes recommendations to the Secretary of State for Prices and Consumer Affairs, who normally, but not always, follows their advice.
5 MMC judgements are based on its interpretation of how the public interest is affected by the monopoly or merger proposal. Here are some of the factors which might be considered in this respect.
   (a) *Conduct indicators*—e.g. what pricing policy has been followed, has advertising been excessive, have there been many consumer and trade complaints.
   (b) *Performance indicators*—e.g. is the level of profit excessive, have costs been controlled.
   (c) *Macroeconomic factors*—e.g. will exports benefit, will jobs be secured, will investment in new products increase.
6 The operation of the MMC has, however, been criticised for a number of reasons.
   (a) MMC is slow to reach conclusions.
   (b) Members of the MMC (academics, civil servants etc.) lack expertise to investigate complex industrial matters.
   (c) MMC operates on a small scale—most monopoly situations and mergers pass uninvestigated.

(d) Judgements of the MMC have been inconsistent, e.g. over two merger proposals by Lonrho in 1980-1.

However, in defence of the MMC.

(a) The issues involved are complex.

(b) The MMC does provide a safety net against extreme abuse of monopoly power.

(c) The MMC acts as a deterrent against growth of monopoly power.

(d) Its flexible approach allows changes of emphasis within the existing legislation.

7   The Conservative government of Margaret Thatcher, aiming to promote competition has allowed the MMC to exert itself more, and rejections of mergers have become more common since 1980.

## Exercise 4

1   Read the outline details of three cases that have been examined by the MMC.

*Hoffman La Roche* (1973)—A Swiss firm, they controlled 99% of the market for Valium and Librium sleeping pills. The National Health Service was the single buyer of the drugs in the UK. They suspected exorbitant prices were being charged, way above the normal costs of production giving abnormal profit levels.

*European Ferries and Sealink UK* (1980)—European Ferries are a private company who own Townsend Thoren-sen ferries. Sealink UK was a government owned subsidiary of British Rail. In 1980, when the bid for Sealink was made, 2.6m tourist vehicles crossed the channel, of which 1m went with Townsend Thorensen and 0.8m went with Sealink. In 1980 ferry operators were involved in a price war and were subject to new competition from other shipping lines and hovercraft services. In 1980 Sealink lost £8m.

*Lonrho and House of Fraser* (1981)—Lonrho is a wide ranging conglomerate, led by a dynamic entrepreneur 'Tiny' Roland. The House of Fraser is the largest depart-ment store operator in the UK and includes among its 120 stores, Harrods. Lonrho has grown through a history of takeovers and had a reputation for ensuring that the newly acquired businesses were efficiently run. The merger posed no real threat to competition except in a minor way as Lonrho owned Brentford Nylons whose products were sold in the House of Fraser stores.

(Source of information: *Guardian*)

(a) What are the conditions for a reference to the MMC?

(b) Identify areas of the public interest that might have been harmed by the three cases.

(c) What lines of argument might the companies have used in their evidence to the MMC?

(d) What would your recommendations to the Secretary of State be if you were sitting on the MMC?

(e) Try to find out what actually was proposed by the MMC.

**2** For decades British Oxygen (BOC) has had no competition in supplying oxygen gas for medical purposes. In 1983 BOC had a turnover of £1700m, £20m of which was estimated as sales to the Department of Health and Social Security (DHSS). Overall, 30% of BOCs profit of £150m in 1983 came from health care (in 1979 it was only 10%) although most of this came from the US.

Thirty years ago, BOC was investigated by the then Monopolies and Restrictive Practices Commission which expressed worry about the lack of competition and the 'unjustifiably high profits'. BOC gave various undertakings to the Commission.

By 1983 BOC was facing competition in gas supplies from a small West Midlands firm, Medigas, whose turnover was £150,000 p.a. Having begun business buying oxygen from BOC to sell to divers, they expanded into selling gas for people needing oxygen at home, refilling ambulance cylinders and chemists supplies. Expansion meant that it became profitable to buy cheaper liquid oxygen supplies. BOC, allegedly, refused to supply them forcing Medigas to seek alternative supplies from the US.

A second firm, MGI (Medical Gas Installations) had set up a business to install gas equipment for the West Midlands Regional Health Authority, but were dependent on parts from BOC. BOC were, allegedly, slow to meet MGI orders despite undertakings BOC had given to the British Standards Institute about the 'neutrality' of their supply operations. MGI are further threatened by a contract signed by BOC and DHSS giving BOC monopoly rights to examine and change gas equipment in 850 hospitals.

(Source of information: *Guardian*)

(a) What are the sources of BOC's monopoly power?
(b) Is a rise in profits sufficient to suggest that 'profits were excessive'?
(c) On what grounds may BOC have felt justified in refusing to supply Medigas and MGI?
(d) On what grounds might the MMC have felt BOC were operating against the public interest?
(e) Why might the DHSS have felt justified in signing the contract with BOC?

**3** To what extent is the slowdown in the rate of concentration in British industry the result of government monopoly and merger legislation?

*Some references*
*British Economy Survey*, vol 11, no 2, Spring 1982 (Oxford University Press) p5
*Economist*, 5.2.83, p37
*A Textbook of Economics* (1982) Livesey F., (Polytech. Publishers) p280
or, look up 'Monopolies and Merger Policy' or 'Competition Policy' in the index at the back of any good textbook.

See Answer section for a suggested essay plan.

# 7.9 Restrictive Practices and Resale Price Maintenance

1 **Restrictive Practice**
An agreement between two or more firms to act together, e.g. to share a market or to fix prices.

2 **Resale Price Maintenance**
This occurs when producers can fix the price that their produce is sold for in shops.

3 Restrictive Practices are covered by 1956 and 1976 Acts of Parliament, and clauses 85 and 86 of the Treaty of Rome.

4 Restrictive Practices are assumed to be illegal unless they can be proved to be in the public interest by satisfying one or more of eight *gateway* clauses. They can then be registered with the Office of Fair Trading.

5 The gateways cover matters such as:
(a) safety and protection of the public against injury,
(b) protection of employment,
(c) protection of exports, or from imports,
(d) whether there has been any effective loss of competition,
(e) whether the public are being denied 'other specific and substantial benefits'.

6 The legislation is extremely effective, so much so that it may have encouraged some mergers, where the legislation is less severe.

7 Resale Price Maintenance (RPM) is governed by 1964 and 1976 Acts which outlaw RPM unless similar gateways can be passed to those of the Restrictive Practices situation. Only a few products are sold with RPM, e.g. pharmaceuticals and books. Many producers provide a Recommended Retail Price but this cannot be enforced.

# 7.10 Consumer protection

1 Consumers are protected through numerous Acts. Examples of these are the Trades Description Acts, Food and Hygiene Regulations, and Consumer Credit Acts.

2 The Office of Fair Trading establishes codes of conduct for various groups of traders, e.g. by registering second-hand car dealers.

3 Consumer bodies have been established to monitor the performance of nationalised industries.

# 7.11 Privatisation

1 **Nationalised industries** are thought by the Conservative government to exhibit undesirable features of monopoly power and big business. The policy of returning some of them to the private sector is known as privatisation.

2 In 1980, nationalised industries contributed about 10% of total output and employed about 11% of the workforce.

3  **Privatisation** is achieved by:
   (a) Selling all, or part of the company to the public through share issues, e.g. 100% of Amersham International, and 51% of British Telecom.
   (b) Selling control of the company to the workforce, e.g. as with the National Freight Corporation.
   (c) Disposal of assets, e.g. as with the sale by British Rail of their hotels, and Sealink.
   (d) Introduction of a secondary competitive force to weaken the public sector monopoly power, e.g. as with Mercury to compete with British Telecom, and private coaches to compete with the National Bus Company.

4  **Reasons for privatisation** include:
   (a) The introduction of more 'commercial judgement' into pricing and investment policy.
   (b) The removal of problems of interference in management of companies by politicians.
   (c) Weakening of the power of the public sector unions which was considerable due to:
      (i) the assumed 'bottomless pit of government funds',
      (ii) few competitive products,
      (iii) the ability of the government to raise prices to consumers,
      (iv) the ability of the unions to 'hold the country to ransom' in strikes.
   (d) Raising of finance through the sale of shares and assets, to help fund the public sector borrowing requirement.
   (e) Doctrinal and political reasons.

5  **Objections to privatisation** are based on the following points:
   (a) Not all industries are appropriate for the private sector, e.g.
      (i) basic utilities of gas, electricity and water,
      (ii) those considered to be of strategic importance like British Nuclear Fuels and the Bank of England,
      (iii) those required to operate services for broader social and economic considerations, e.g. rural bus routes, provision of telephone boxes.
   (b) Buyers will not be found for loss-making concerns, or where big debts or pension rights have accumulated.
   (c) It seems illogical to use taxpayers money to prop up industries in bad times, but not let them benefit from profits in good times.
   (d) Privatised firms are likely to inherit monopoly power which may be used against the public interest.

## Exercise 5

1  **Case 1**
   At the start the government was not very interested in privatising the Post Office. It has usually seemed more interested in nibbling at its monopoly. Until recently only the National Girobank was considered saleable. But now Norman Tebbit and his advisers want to sell a majority shareholding in a combined business consisting of Giro-

bank and Post Office counter services. Only the basic postal service would remain state owned.

That would create the oddest of privatised monopolies: the main role of the counters, apart from selling stamps, is doing the business of government departments under an agency agreement—making pension payments, selling road fund licences and so on. Either this monopoly would have to be so regulated that it would involve no risk of abuse—in which case why privatise it?—or else government departments might forever be complaining about the cost of doing business through the semi-private post office. Unless shops and banks could compete for these agency agreements?

(Based on information from *Economist* 31.3.1984)

**Case 2**

The privatisation of cleaning, catering and laundry services in hospitals is steaming ahead, isn't it? Well, not exactly. Though it is called 'competitive tendering' these days, some authorities are refusing to do it under any name.

Competitive tendering in the NHS has been around in a small way for some time. What is new is that everybody must try it. Sometimes it has led to savings when, in order to hand in a better tender than the private competition, NHS cleaners and launderers have shown that they themselves can cut their costs. So far, however, the competition (like the food) is not all that hot in hospital catering. The number of NHS hospitals using private caterers has dwindled from thirty-four in 1965 to two in 1983, partly because few companies are willing to handle the complicated diets or the unpredictable demands in hospitals as patients come and go. In 1981–2, 11% less was spent on hospital contract cleaning in NHS hospitals than in 1980–1. Of the so-called 'hotel services' only laundries showed a growth in the private sector in the period: £7.7m (out of a total of £65m) was contracted out in 1981–2.

(Based on information from *Economist* 3.3.84)

(a) What advantages might the government be seeking in attempting to privatise these areas of economic activity?
(b) Why is it not always possible to find buyers for services at present operated by the public sector?
(c) What disadvantages might there be from such policies of privatisation?

# 7.12   Multinational companies

1  **Multinational companies**

Those companies which undertake direct foreign investment, i.e. they produce goods or services in more than one country. These companies are responsible for the majority of world trade in manufactures.

2  Multinational companies have the following features:
(a) they have considerable marketing power,
(b) the vital functions of the company, e.g. decision making, are highly centralised,

(c) they can adopt financial strategies, e.g. transfer pricing, to ensure they avoid as much tax as possible,

(d) traditional multinationals adjusted their products to meet local conditions, e.g. companies such as ICI, IBM and Xerox. But increasingly, new style global corporations operate as if the whole world were a single market, selling the same product in the same way everywhere. Such companies include Sony, Seiko, Coca Cola, McDonalds and the big oil companies.

3 Multinationals pose special problems for governments because:

(a) production can be switched from one country to another without consideration of the social costs involved,

(b) workers in factories are divorced from decision making,

(c) the extent of intra-company trade across national borders can alter balance of payments positions and cause instability in currencies,

(d) companies may adopt uncompetitive practices, e.g. sharing out markets for its subsidiaries,

(e) the extent of their vast sources of finance make them impervious to national government monetary policies.

4 Despite the problems listed above, government still values the investment funds and job creation from multinationals.

## Exercise 6

1 On 1 February 1984 the Nissan Corporation of Japan announced plans to undertake direct foreign investment in Britain.

The project involved two stages. First, 24,000 cars would be assembled in its new UK plant from parts shipped in from Japan. Five hundred jobs would be created. The 24,000 cars would be included in the 11.6% market share voluntary export restraint by Japanese car makers. Second, 100,000 cars would be built a year in a new factory, involving about 80% local content, directly employing 2700 jobs in total.

The government was to provide Nissan with £35m in addition to the 22% regional development grants, Nissan would spend £50m initially and a further £300m for stage two.

Reaction to the announcement was mixed. Peter Shore, Labour Party spokesman, said the scheme did not mean a net increase in jobs or an improvement in the balance of trade. Ken Gill, secretary of the engineering union AUEW-TASS, said it was a body blow for British Leyland, and was likely to destroy more jobs than it created. Norman Tebbit, government minister for trade and industry, said that British Leyland would not suffer. Overall jobs would rise by 6000. The Nissan project represented an important opportunity to create fresh investment and jobs in the motor industry. It would introduce a major efficient new domestic customer for the UK components industry.

(a) Why do you think Nissan wants to undertake direct foreign investment in the UK?

(b) Why were the UK unions worried by the proposal?

(c) What do you imagine was the reaction of unions in Japan to the Nissan plans?

(d) Identify the possible effects of the project on employment in the UK.

(e) How might the project affect the UK balance of payments?

(f) Accepting Norman Tebbit's estimate of 6000 jobs created by the project, do you consider the government's money was wisely spent in encouraging Nissan to come to the UK?

# Review

## Unit 7 will have helped provide answers to the following questions

1 What is the importance of the small firms' sector to the economy?

2 What are advantages and disadvantages of operating a small firm?

3 What are the main sources of finance available to small and large firms?

4 What are the arguments for and against increasing the amount of competition in markets?

5 What are the main elements of government competition policy?

6 How effective has government policy been?

7 What are the main reasons for privatising nationalised industry?

8 What are the advantages and disadvantages for national governments of multinational companies?

## Unit 7 has introduced the following terminology

Barriers to growth (entry)
Competition Policy
Complex monopoly
Concentration ratios
Conduct indicators
Conglomerate growth
Consumer protection
Countervailing power
Creative destruction
Cross-subsidisation
Debentures
Gateways
Global corporations
Horizontal growth
Institutional agencies
Large firms
Lateral growth
MacMillan Gap
Marginal cost pricing
Mergers
Monopoly and Mergers Commission
Multinational corporation
Nationalised industries

Office of Fair Trading
Performance indicators
Plough-back (of profits)
Privatisation
Public interest
Resale Price Maintenance
Restrictive Practices
Small firms
Stock Exchange
Trade credit
Transfer pricing
Unlisted Securities Market (USM)
Vertical growth

## Multiple choice questions

1 If the cross-price elasticity of demand for a firm's product, with respect to price changes of all other goods, is zero or negative then the firm sells its product in:
   (a) a monopoly market
   (b) an oligopolistic market
   (c) an imperfectly competitive market
   (d) a monopolistically competitive market
   (e) a perfectly competitive market

2 Which of the following sources of finance is least likely to be available to a small firm?
   (a) selling shares to the general public
   (b) ploughing back past profits
   (c) taking additional trade credit
   (d) borrowing from a bank
   (e) factoring debts

3 Which of the following is untrue of small companies?
   (a) they have a good record of technical innovation
   (b) they are good sources of new jobs
   (c) they can benefit from economies of scale
   (d) they provide an outlet for entrepreneurial talents
   (e) they can satisfy demand in specialist markets

**4** If a company operated a merchant shipping fleet, and it took over a company that owned docks this would be an example of:
(a) vertical growth
(b) horizontal growth
(c) lateral growth
(d) conglomerate growth
(e) concentrated growth

**5** Shares in public companies (like Airship Industries, Virgin Records and Acorn Computers) which have chosen not to seek a share quotation and full membership of the Stock Exchange can be bought and sold:
(a) on the Unlisted Securities Market
(b) through the government broker
(c) directly through a jobber
(d) from a building society
(e) on the gilt-edged market

**6** Which of the following firms operates in the public sector of the economy?
(a) Co-operative Wholesale Society
(b) ICI
(c) British Caledonian
(d) National Bus Company
(e) Marks and Spencer

**7** An industrial concentration ratio of 80% indicates that:
(a) one firm produces 80% of the goods bought in a market
(b) 80% of a product is made in one standard region
(c) 80% of goods in a market are imported
(d) 80% of the output of a good is produced by a few firms
(e) 80% of goods produced are exported by a firm

**8** The largest source of finance for investment expenditure in Britain is:
(a) issuing new shares on the Stock Exchange
(b) government grants
(c) ploughing back past profits
(d) issue of new debenture loan stock
(e) issuing new shares through a scrip issue

**9** Traditional theory suggests that resources will be allocated in an optimal way if the prices of all goods are set equal to:
(a) marginal cost
(b) average total cost
(c) marginal revenue
(d) average revenue
(e) average fixed cost

**10** Monopolies may be considered to be acting against the public interest in which of the following situations?
(a) They use their monopoly or abnormal profit to finance new investment expenditure.
(b) They use their abnormal profit to overcome short term fluctuations in demand

(c) Their large size enables them to take advantage of economies of scale.
(d) They can compete effectively with overseas companies.
(e) They can raise their prices and restrict the quantity of goods on sale to the consumers.

**11** Multinational companies are those which:
(a) invest in overseas government stocks
(b) sell exports
(c) have shareholders living in more than one country
(d) undertake direct foreign investment
(e) sell goods in more than one country

**12** Government Competition Policy is generally assumed to include all but one of the following:
(a) investigation of monopoly situations
(b) investigation of merger proposals
(c) registration of Restrictive Practices
(d) tax allowances for firms to set up business in depressed regions
(e) legislating on Resale Price Maintenance

## Answers

### Exercise 1 .

**1** (a) Control of the business, being one's own boss, quick decision making, personal service to the customer, incentive to do well, good labour relations with employees.
(b) Limited finance, possible limited ability, limited scope for specialisation, limited ability to take advantage of economies of scale, owner carries all the risk.
(c) Borrow from relatives or friends, mortgage house, borrow from a bank.
(d) See (b) above plus competition from other firms, size of the market.

**2** (a) Many firms except for telephone services, which is a state monopoly.
(b) Personalised service, low start-up costs, small or limited market, limited opportunities for economies of scale, no significant barriers to entry.

### Exercise 2

**1**

| | | | |
|---|---|---|---|
| (a) | McDonalds | Internal | Horizontal |
| (b) | Horizon | Internal | Vertical |
| (c) | S&W Berisford | External | Horizontal |
| (d) | Babcock & Wilson | External | Vertical/Lateral |
| (e) | BAT | External | Conglomerate |
| (f) | S&L | Internal | Vertical |
| (g) | Trafalgar House | External | Conglomerate/Vertical |
| (h) | Lloyds Bank | External | Lateral? |
| (i) | CASE | Internal | Horizontal |
| (j) | Servowarm | Internal | Vertical |
| (k) | BBC | Internal | Lateral |

## Exercise 3

1 (a) Issue new shares either to general public or to existing shareholders (rights issue), issue debentures or loan stock, plough back past profits, borrow from merchant bank.

(b) Current pattern of share ownership, whether existing shareholders support the board; relationship between expected profit flows and interest dividend obligations; possibility of interference by creditors; relative costs of alternative sources; current share price, related to ratio of retained and distributed profits.

2 (a) i) Provides second-hand market for existing shares—makes them liquid.
ii) Imposes rules and regulations on quoted company to give investors confidence.
iii) Provides second-hand market for government securities (gilts).
iv) Allows for the quotation of unit trust prices.

(b) By the mid-1970s the flow of new companies coming onto the Stock Exchange had all but ceased. USM established in November 1980, offered a market place for shares in companies that could not or were not prepared to satisfy all the Stock Exchange rules, e.g. USM companies need only offer 10% of shares to the general public instead of the 25% figure for the Stock Exchange and who felt finance from banks was too expensive or involved too many restrictions. By November 1984, 325 companies had come to the USM involving companies from oil to computers and leisure to bloodstock. The USM has been successful in attracting capital to business and in providing attractive savings to investors.

## Exercise 4

1 (a) 25% of market, plus complex monopoly situations and uncompetitive practices by a single firm. Mergers that involve transfer of more than £15m. General concern about the effect of business behaviour on the public interest.

(b) Excessive cost to the taxpayer, money could have been spent elsewhere (drugs). Rise in prices and restricted services (ferries). Imposition of barrier to new entrants. Restriction of choice of products, loss of expert management (stores).

(c) Profit needed to finance research and development (drugs). Need to stabilise industry, to reduce over-capacity and reduce costs and prices. Offering superior service (ferries). Better management, more efficient use of resources (stores).

(d) Your opinion.

(e) Hoffman La Roche—ordered to cut prices on librium by 60% and valium by 75%, and to repay money to NHS. Challenged in courts. Similar cases in Holland and West Germany.

European Ferries—take over rejected by MMC. Argued that it would lead to high prices, a reduced service and the erection of barriers to entry. Rejected EF's proposal to allow government regulation of prices. Market forces thought to do a better job. Lonrho—take over rejected by MMC. Argued that it would upset the Fraser management and cause a loss of key board members. Said 'difficulties were inherent in a merger between two large companies with different histories'.

2 (a) Control of raw materials and components. Government contracts. Barriers to entry through large scale operation.

(b) No. Profit levels have to be related to, e.g. turnover, capital employed, risks taken.

(c) Safety. Secure long lasting supply requirements. Economics of scale for NHS.

(d) High costs to NHS. Restriction of competition.

(e) See (c) above.

3 Suggested essay plan.
Introduction:  Definition of terms i) Concentration ii) Monopoly and merger legislation
Main Paragraphs:  i) Statistics on concentration, e.g.% share of manufacturing net output of largest 100 enterprises is: 1953 27%, 1963 36%, 1973 40%, 1983 41%. Number of mergers peaked in 1972–3, involving about 1300 acquisitions and take overs. From 1975–82 down to between 300 and 450 ii) Main points of monopoly and merger legislation (see *Unit 7.8*) iii) Evaluation of MMC work iv) Attitude of Conservative Government to competition v) Other reasons for mergers, e.g. state of the economy, reduced opportunities for horizontal mergers.

Conclusion.

## Exercise 5

1 (a) Increase in competition and hence lowering of costs and prices. Improvements in managerial efficiency. Widening of consumer choice. Reduction of political influence in running areas of activity. Reduction of the size of the PSBR (government borrowing) at the time of sale of the assets. Reduced burden on the PSBR to finance expansion or development. Break-up of trade union power in the public sector.

(b) Not profitable. Large debts. High pension obligations (often index-linked).

(c) Creation of private sector monopolies. Loss of jobs. Reduction of wages. Operators less willing to provide the services associated with 'broader social and economic considerations'.

## Exercise 6

1 (a) Britain is inside EEC, allows tariff free access to EEC markets. Exports to Britain limited by 11% voluntary export restraint.

(b) Introduction of Japanese working practices.
Loss of jobs in other British car firms, e.g. BL.

(c) Initially it was hostile, they feared loss of jobs in Japan.

(d) 2700 jobs directly at Nissan. Extra jobs possible in component manufacture. Extra jobs from general multiplier effect. Possible job losses at BL.

(c) Inflow of capital, exports of cars to EEC, save Japanese imports. Outflow of interest, dividends and profits to Japan, imports of machinery and other components.

(f) Total government aid about £112m for 6000 jobs. Much of the cost is a one-off payment but hopefully jobs will last for several years. At around £5000 per job it is about the cost of unemployment benefit per person. Plus human and social advantages of job creation.

## Multiple choice answers

1 (a) If XED was + ve goods would be substitutes, i.e. there would be competition.

2 (a) only public companies (PLCs) can do this.

3 (c) Small scale of output for small firms means economies of scale are unlikely.

4 (c) Same industry, different stage of production.

5 (a) USM is an over-the-counter market for such shares.

6 (d) Public sector is owned by government.

7 (d) e.g. $CR_5 = 80\%$ of output from five biggest firms.

8 (c) About 80% finance comes from ploughed back profits.

9 (a) Marginal cost pricing (see *Unit 7.6[3]*).

10 (e) (a) to (d) are all advantages.

11 (d) By definition.

12 (d) This is a regional employment measure.

# Prices of resources
# UNIT 8

## 8.2 Factors of production

1  **Factors of production** (see *Unit 1.10[2]*)
    (a) Land—natural resources
    (b) Labour—human resources
    (c) Capital—artificial resources
    (d) Enterprise

## 8.3 Combinations of factors of production

1  **Isoquants (or equal-product or iso-product curves)**
    Isoquants show the combinations of two factors which are needed to produce a certain level of output of a product. They are drawn on the understanding that:
    (a) there is a given state of technology,
    (b) the product can be made in a number of different ways.

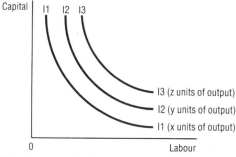

**Figure 8.1**  Isoquants for Good X

*Observations from Figure 8.1*

□ Each isoquant (I1, I2, I3) represents a different level of output of Good X (x,y,z).

□ Isoquants are shaped this way because it becomes increasingly difficult to substitute one factor for another.

□ The slope of the isoquant is determined by the ratio of marginal products of the two factors.

2 The addition of a budget or price line shows the quantities of the factors the producer will demand.

*Observations from Figure 8.2*

□ AB represents the budget line of the producer.

□ The gradient of the line is determined by the relative prices of the two factors (capital and labour).

□ At point C, the slope of the isoquant is equal to the gradient of the price line, so the ratio of marginal products from the two factors equals the ratio of prices of the two factors, or

$$\frac{MP(lab)}{MP(cap)} = \frac{P(lab)}{P(cap)} \quad \text{or} \quad \frac{MP(lab)}{P(lab)} = \frac{MP(cap)}{P(cap)}$$

where MP(lab) = marginal productivity of labour
MP(cap) = marginal productivity of capital
P(lab) = price of labour
P(cap) = price of capital

□ The best combination of factors for the producer is, then, OK capital with OL labour.

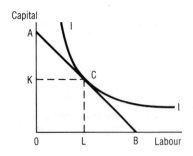

**Figure 8.2** Determination of the demand for a factor

## Exercise 1

1 A manufacturer is asked about the combinations of employees and machines that would be needed to produce two levels of output. The manufacturer gives the answers as shown in the table.

| Output level A | | Output level B | |
|---|---|---|---|
| Employees | Machines | Employees | Machines |
| 30 | 70 | 45 | 90 |
| 35 | 50 | 55 | 70 |
| 55 | 20 | 90 | 35 |
| 65 | 10 | 100 | 30 |
| | | 140 | 20 |

(a) If the annual cost of a machine is £500, estimate the number of employees the manufacturer will need to produce output level A if the annual wage is: i) £1,000, ii) £500.

(b) If the manufacturer wished to increase output to level B, and the cost of the machine stayed unchanged, estimate how many people would be employed if wage rates per year were i) £1000 ii) £500.

2 A farmer has an estate of 10 acres. It is split into three fields, two fields of three acres and one of four acres. He aims to maximise his profits.

He calculates the return he would get per year if his land was used in three different ways.

| Potatoes | | Wheat | | Caravans | |
|---|---|---|---|---|---|
| Acres | Total revenue (£) | Acres | Total revenue (£) | Acres | Total revenue (£) |
| 0 | 0 | 0 | 0 | 0 | 0 |
| 1 | 16 | 1 | 15 | 1 | 26 |
| 2 | 25 | 2 | 27 | 2 | 50 |
| 3 | 27 | 3 | 36 | 3 | 72 |
| 4 | 22 | 4 | 42 | 4 | 92 |
| 5 | 10 | 5 | 45 | 5 | 110 |
| | | 6 | 45 | 6 | 116 |
| | | | | 7 | 120 |

Cost per acre to the farmer of each form of use is:
i) Potatoes—£4.50 ii) Wheat—£4.50 iii) Caravans—£9.00
(a) In theory how much land should he allocate to each use?
(b) Would you recommend allocation of his land in this way?

# 8.4 Demand for factors of production

**1 Derived demand**
People do not employ resources as an end in itself. They use resources to make other goods or services. So the demand for factors of production is said to be derived from the demand for the final good or service produced with the resources.

**2 Profit maximisation**
It is assumed that producers employing resources will be aiming to maximise short run profits. They will, therefore, employ factors if the cost of employing them is less than the revenue generated by them.

**3 Revenue product**
The revenue generated by employing a factor of production will be the additional goods produced by the factor multiplied by the price that each unit of the good is sold for, i.e.

Marginal revenue product = marginal physical product × price of the final good

**4 Law of Variable Proportions**
As defined in *Unit 1.10(3)* the Law of Variable Proportions suggests that as additional units of a factor of production are added to a fixed set of other factors then the marginal product from each additional unit of the factor will at first rise but then begin to fall, and may even become negative. When marginal product increases the firm experiences increasing returns to scale. When marginal product falls the firm experiences decreasing returns to scale.
*Observations from Figure 8.3*
☐ Total physical product (TphyP) starts to decline at quantity Q1 of the factor.

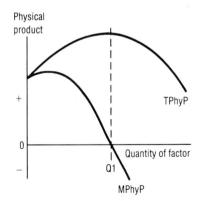

**Figure 8.3** Total and marginal physical product curves

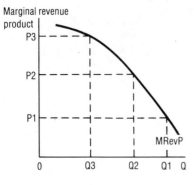

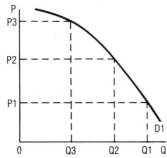

**Figure 8.4** Demand curve for a factor

☐ Marginal physical product (MphyP) becomes negative at quantity Q1 of the factor.

**5 The price of the final product**
The market structure in which the final good is sold will affect the relationship between the final price of the good, and the quantity of the good being sold on the market. In perfectly competitive markets any quantity of output from a firm will result in the same market price (see *Unit 5.5*) but in imperfectly competitive markets an increase in quantity supplied to a market will cause a fall in market price (see *Unit 5.6*).

**6 Derivation of the derived demand curve for a factor**
*Observations from Figure 8.4*
☐ MRevP = marginal revenue product curve, derived from the marginal physical product curve (see *Unit 8.4[4]*) and the price fetched by the final good (see *Unit 8.4[5]*).
☐ At factor price P1, demand for the factor will be Q1, as units of the factor in excess of Q1 are not profitable for the producer, i.e. cost per unit exceeds marginal revenue product.
☐ At factor price P2, demand for the factor will be Q2, at price P3 quantity demanded will be Q3, and so on.
☐ It is clear that the demand curve for the factor (D1) is the downward sloping part of the marginal revenue product curve.

# Exercise 2

1

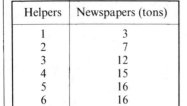

**Figure 8.5** An isoquant map

The isoquant map (Figure 8.5) shows the combinations of capital and labour required to produce various levels of output of Good X.
If the firm employs a fixed quantity of capital (K) what can be inferred from the diagram about the returns from additional units of labour?

2 A youth club collects old newspapers on a Friday evening. The table (left) shows the weight of newspapers collected with different numbers of helpers involved.
(a) Calculate the marginal physical product of each helper.
(b) Up to what number of helpers do they experience increasing returns to labour?
(c) If they can sell each ton of newspaper for £6, calculate the marginal revenue product of each helper.
(d) If each helper could earn £6 an evening delivering leaflets and the youth club wishes to maximise its

| Helpers | Newspapers (tons) |
|---------|-------------------|
| 1 | 3 |
| 2 | 7 |
| 3 | 12 |
| 4 | 15 |
| 5 | 16 |
| 6 | 16 |

revenue, how many helpers should be employed collecting newspapers?

3   The table (right) shows the number of sheep sheared by workers on a farm each day.

| Shearers | Sheep |
|----------|-------|
| 1 | 24 |
| 2 | 52 |
| 3 | 90 |
| 4 | 124 |
| 5 | 146 |

   (a) What is the marginal physical product of the fourth shearer?
   (b) If each fleece sells for £2, and the daily wage of shearers is £44, how many shearers will be employed?

4   **Essay**
    How would a profit maximising businessman decide how many workers to employ?

## 8.5 Supply of factors of production

1   In most situations the supply of a factor of production will increase as the price paid for it increases and decrease as the price paid for it decreases, e.g. the higher the market price of the oil the more oil will be extracted from the North Sea; fewer people will want to become teachers as the real wages of teachers decline.
    *Observations from Figure 8.6*
    ☐ At price P1, quantity of factor supplied is Q1.
    ☐ At higher price P2, more of the factor is supplied, at Q2.

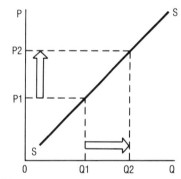

**Figure 8.6**   Supply of factors of production

### Exercise 3

1   List four factors which will influence the overall size of the population looking for work?
2   List four factors which will fix the supply of labour for the following situations.
    (a) Development electrical engineers for a firm making sophisticated information technology.
    (b) Policemen.
    (c) Construction workers on the Channel link.
3   List three factors that affect the supply of land?
4   List three factors that affect the supply of entrepreneurs?
5   List four factors that a firm might take into account in deciding whether to purchase a new machine?

## 8.6 Pricing of factors of production

1   **An equilibrium market price** for a factor can be determined from the supply curve and demand curve for that factor.
    *Observations from Figure 8.7*
    ☐ Equilibrium price of the factor is P1.
    ☐ At P1, quantity demanded equals quantity supplied, at Q1.

2   **Economic rent** is defined as any payment to a factor of production over and above what is necessary to secure its supply, i.e. it is income received over and above income obtainable in the next best occupation.

3   **Transfer earnings** are defined as the payments to factors that are necessary to secure the supply of the factor.

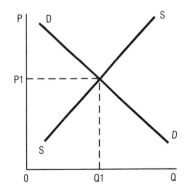

**Figure 8.7**   Equilibrium market price for a factor

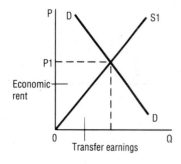

Economic rent

Transfer earnings

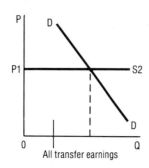

All transfer earnings

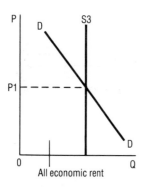

All economic rent

**Figure 8.8** Economic rent and transfer earnings

4 **Quasi-rent** is defined as temporary economic rent.

5 **Diagrammatic representation of economic rent and transfer earnings.**
   *Observations from Figure 8.8*
   ☐ All units of the factor are paid the equilibrium price P1.
   ☐ The supply curve, S1, shows that some units of the factor would have been supplied at lower prices than P1.
   ☐ Where elasticity of supply is between 0 and infinity earnings of factors will be partly economic rent and partly transfer earnings.
   ☐ If supply is perfectly elastic (S2) all payments are transfer earnings.
   ☐ If supply is perfectly inelastic (S3) all payments are economic rent.

## Exercise 4

1 In the early days of North Sea oil exploration, deep-sea divers could earn very high salaries. The high salaries encouraged other people to train for such work and to gain suitable experience for working in the North Sea. As the newly trained workers became available so the high salaries began to fall.
   (a) Explain the relevance of the concept of quasi-rent to the above example.

2 A tennis player earns £300/week. Alternatively, she could have managed a sports shop for £200/week, been a sales representative for a sports firm earning £175/week or been a shop assistant at £100/week.
   (a) What is her level of economic rent?
   (b) What is her level of transfer earnings?

3 A person has invested £30,000 in buying a house. Rent brings in £4000 per year, but repairs cost £1000 per year. Assuming he is a profit maximiser, what is his level of economic rent from the property if he could have received a return of (a) 5% and (b) 10%, by using the £30,000 elsewhere.

4 Silent Rage, a heavy metal band, are offered a recording contract for £50,000 for a year's work. Their manager, who arranged the contract takes 20%. There are four members of the band. The only alternative employment the band members will consider is working on the buses earning £100 per week each.
   (a) How much economic rent does the band earn between them?

5 If a factor of production cannot transfer to any other activity will it earn any transfer earnings? Explain your answer.

6 A firm operating in an imperfectly competitive market is earning normal profit. Is any of this profit economic rent? Explain your answer.

7 Jane got a job with a local electrical engineering firm on a Youth Training Scheme earning £30 per week. She could have got £45 per week in Social Security payments. Is Jane earning negative economic rent?

**8**  A taxi driver earns £250 per week, of which 20% comes from tips from the passengers. Without the tips he does not think it is worth being a taxi driver. What is the level of his economic rent?

# 8.7 Criticisms of traditional distribution theory

1  Employers of factors of production do not always seek to maximise short run profits (see *Unit 5.3*).
2  Firms may not be in a position to calculate marginal physical product because:
   (a) there may be no measurable output, e.g. in health care and education,
   (b) production involves the combination of a number of factors, each being essential to the production process. For example, does the marginal productivity of a dustman increase if he works with a faster dustcart?
3  Firms may not be able to calculate marginal revenue product because:
   (a) they cannot calculate marginal physical product (see above),
   (b) there is no marketed final product, e.g. traffic wardens do not sell anything but clearly reduce social costs.
4  Many factors are hired by firms in oligopoly situations where employers can only assume what the shape of their demand curve for the final product looks like.
5  The UK economic system is that of a mixed economy. Many factors are employed in markets where the free market does not operate.

# 8.8 Wage determination and distribution theory

1  **Productivity bargaining**
   *Observations from Figure 8.9*
   □ Productivity refers to output per unit of factor input.
   □ An increase of labour productivity will shift the marginal revenue product curve (or demand curve for labour) to the right (D1 to D2).
   □ Employers can afford to pay higher wage levels (W1 to W2) and employ more workers (Q1 to Q2).

2  **Trade unions' closed shop agreements**
   A closed shop refers to a situation where people have to belong to a trade union before they can apply for a job (pre-entry closed shop), or where they have to join a trade union when they get a job (post-entry closed shop).
   *Observations from Figure 8.10*
   □ D1 is the employer's demand curve for labour.
   □ S1 is the free market supply curve of labour.
   □ S2 is the closed shop supply curve of labour, labour supply is restricted and controlled by the union.
   □ Wages will increase (W1 to W2) but fewer people will be employed (Q2 to Q1).

3  **Trade union's influence on wage rates**
   Unions may succeed in pushing wage rates above the market

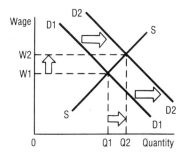

*Figure 8.9*  Result of increased labour productivity

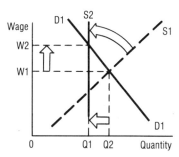

*Figure 8.10*  Result of a closed shop situation

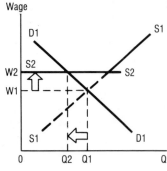

Competitive demand for labour

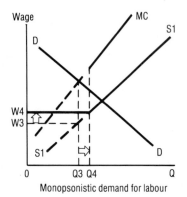

Monopsonistic demand for labour

**Figure 8.11**  Competitive and monopsonistic demand for labour

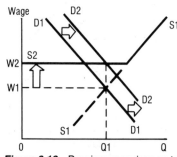

**Figure 8.12**  Passing wage rises on to the consumer

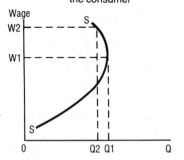

**Figure 8.13**  Backward sloping supply curve for labour

equilibrium level. No worker will work for less than the union rate, so the supply curve for labour becomes perfectly elastic at this wage rate.

*Observations from Figure 8.11*

☐ D1 is the employer's demand curve for labour.

☐ S1 is the market supply curve of labour.

☐ The free market equilibrium wage rate is W1, the quantity of labour demanded is Q1.

☐ The union wage rate is W2. Supply changes to S2. Fewer people are employed at level Q2.

☐ MC is the marginal cost curve for labour if purchased in a monopsonistic market, i.e. by a major employer. It is above S1 because all workers have to be paid extra wages.

☐ Employers buy labour to the point where MC = MR.

☐ If unions push up wages from W3 to W4, workers employed rises from Q3 to Q4.

**4  Passing wage rises on to customers in higher prices**

*Observations from Figure 8.12*

☐ D1 is the original demand curve for labour.

☐ S1 is the free market supply curve of labour, S2 shows the supply curve after union negotiation of wage rate W2.

☐ D2 shows the new demand curve for labour if employers are willing to increase the price of the final good to the consumer, i.e. if the marginal revenue product curve of labour can be shifted to the right in this way.

☐ Higher wages (W2) result in the same number of workers employed (Q1).

**5  The backward sloping supply curve for labour**

In unpleasant jobs, e.g. mining underground, a wage rise may lead to a reduced supply of labour. If this happens workers have apparently reached a satisfactory level of income, and additional income is insufficient to compensate for further reduction in leisure time.

*Observations from Figure 8.13*

☐ At wage rate W1, quantity of labour supplied is Q1.

☐ At higher wage rates (W2) less labour is supplied, at Q2.

## 8.9 Other factors influencing wage levels

**1  The rate of inflation**

Workers appear to have a long term ambition to achieve an increase in their real living standards. Inflation, a rise in the cost of living, frustrates this ambition. In the short run, erosion of living standards may be tolerated, but in the long run workers take steps to restore real living standards.

**2  The cost of a strike**

An employer, especially one who owns significant capital assets, may find fighting a pay claim is more expensive than conceding. If such a pay claim is combined with a requirement of no job losses the producer must raise prices or take a cut in profits.

**3  Ability of a union to 'hold the country to ransom'**

Strikes and stoppages involve social as well as private costs. It is a matter of debate whether upsetting the public helps or hinders a union's cause.

4 **Pay league tables**

Fairness of pay levels is often assessed by reference to the pay of other groups of workers. Differentials refer to pay relationships within a single negotiating unit; relativities refer to pay relationships between different negotiating units. An erosion of differentials will make groups of workers uneasy.

5 **Ability of employers to pay**

Workers naturally consider that company profits are related to their efforts. High profits should, therefore, be reflected with high pay increases.

6 **Incomes policies**

Government may place limits on wage increases. Incomes policies in the UK in the 1960s and 1970s imposed a mixture of flat rate and percentage ceilings on wage rises. The government is a major employer and can control public-sector wage levels directly.

## Exercise 5

1 Refer to a current or recent wage dispute reported in the media. What arguments are being used by the unions to support the pay claim. What are the management's counter arguments?

2 (a) Is it possible to estimate the marginal revenue product of your Economics teacher?

(b) Can distribution theory still be used to explain the reaction of your teacher's employers, who might well argue that any increase in pay would necessitate a reduction in the number of teachers employed?

(c) If you were engaged by a teachers' association or union to prepare a case to support a substantial pay claim for secondary school teachers,

i) What arguments would you employ?

ii) What evidence would you seek to back up your arguments?

iii) What counter arguments would you expect to hear from employers?

3 Explain why absenteeism among miners might increase if wage rates are increased.

## 8.10 Trade unions

1 Trade unions are voluntary associations of workers whose aims are to protect the interests of their members. In some circumstances it is necessary to belong to a trade union in order to obtain work in a particular industry, i.e. where closed shop agreements are in operation (see *Unit 8.8[2]*).

2 The objectives of trade unions are therefore:

(a) *Economic*—e.g. concerned with pay, job protection, conditions of employment, terms of contracts, hours of work, redundancy terms, pension rights, etc.

(b) *Macroeconomic*—i.e. to act as a pressure group on government to operate the economy in a way that they interpret will bring the most benefit to their members, e.g. planned growth, increased employment.

(c) *Political*—i.e. to support the election of governments that will introduce policies that they support.

(d) *Union*—i.e. to increase their own strength through increased membership and increased recognition by employers.

3   Trade union history involves a struggle against employers and governments to achieve privileges and recognition of rights, and then to defend their position. Areas of trade union activity that have attracted attention from governments since 1971 include:

(a) *Closed shop agreements*—i.e. compulsory membership of designated unions for workers in certain jobs. After 1982 these could only be enforced where 80% of workers in a place of work have voted for a closed shop. People who lose their job because they refuse to join the union can receive compensation from the government.

(b) *Secondary industrial action*—i.e. trade union activity involving firms with which the workers have no direct dispute, e.g. miners preventing the operation of coal trains or shipments of coal. After 1982 such secondary action was illegal. Unions could be sued for damages by the firms affected.

(c) *Trade union immunity*—i.e. trade unions being in a privileged position where they could not be held responsible for their actions and the effect of their actions in a court of law. This position was reaffirmed after the 1911 Taff Vale dispute and relinquished by unions that did not register under the 1971 Industrial Relations Act from 1971 to 1974. At present immunity has been removed for unlawful industrial activity, e.g. secondary picketing.

(d) *The right to strike*—at present denied to the Police and Armed Forces, but upheld for all others. In other countries those in the public sector, or in designated strategic industries are denied the right to strike. Between 1971 and 1974 the right to strike could be removed for up to 90 days during a so-called 'cooling-off' period.

(e) *Secret postal strike ballots*—i.e. making it compulsory for unions to hold a secret ballot by post for all workers before a strike decision can be made. In 1984 this was made compulsory with the government being prepared to provide funds for unions that organised such ballots.

(f) *The political levy*—some unions include in their basic affiliation fee a sum which is passed to the Labour Party. Workers can opt out if they wish to but the majority do not.

4   Trade unions are often blamed for most of the countries economic ills. Reformers either want to strengthen the union movement, e.g. by increasing the power and role of the Trade Union Congress (TUC), by increasing affiliation fees, by restructuring unions through mergers and rationalisation; or they want to weaken the movement, e.g. by removing some of their privileges and rights.

Some of these reforms may be desirable in their own right, but the unions could be seen to be merely reacting to events rather than causing them, e.g. do unions push for higher wages during periods of inflation to protect the living standards of their members, or to cause inflation?

# Exercise 6

**1** Table 1

|      | Number of unions | Number of members (m) |
|------|:----------------:|:---------------------:|
| 1977 | 481 | 12.8 |
| 1978 | 462 | 13.1 |
| 1979 | 456 | 13.2 |
| 1980 | 438 | 12.9 |
| 1981 | 421 | 12.2 |

The biggest 20 unions have two thirds of total membership of all unions.
About 50% of unions have less than 1000 members.

Table 2

| TU membership of ten largest unions ('000s) | 1979 | 1983 |
|---------------------------------------------|:----:|:----:|
| Transport workers (TGWU) | 2070 | 1633 |
| Engineers (AUEW) | 1200 | 1001 |
| Municipal workers (GMBWU) | 965 | 940 |
| Local government (NALGO) | 729 | 784 |
| Public employees (NUPE) | 712 | 702 |
| Shopworkers (USDAW) | 462 | 417 |
| Managerial staffs (ASTMS) | 471 | 410 |
| Electricians (EETPU) | 420 | 380 |
| Builders (UCATT) | 321 | 261 |
| Miners (NUM) | 255 | 245 |

(Based on information from *Economist*.)

(a) Describe what has happened to the number of unions, and to total union membership, between 1977 and 1983.

(b) What could have accounted for the fall in membership of trade unions after 1979?

(c) What factors might influence the membership levels of particular unions?

(d) Given that there were approximately 1,850,000 shopworkers, 940,000 local government workers and 260,000 miners in 1983, what can be inferred about the level of union membership in these work areas?

**Strikes and stoppages in the UK** (See table on right)

(a) Describe the changes in the level of strike activity in the UK since 1971.

(b) What factors are likely to have influenced the level of strike activity?

(c) What effects might such strike activity have on the performance of the economy?

(d) Should the trade union movement be blamed for the level of strike activity?

**3 The role of trade unions**

The purpose of a trade union is to attempt to achieve higher real wages and better working conditions for its members. Trade unions do this by playing the market game: by organising and disciplining their section of the labour force to attempt to fix the terms on which their particular category of labour is bought and sold. But the organisation of trade unions is not just an aspect of bargaining in the labour market. The mass organisation of labour is a necessary complement to modern factory production. It is virtually impossible to conceive of a sophisticated system of mass production without some form of organisation, acceptable to the workers, through which decisions and agreements can be made covering the broad majority of the industrial labour force—decisions not only on pay and

|      | Number of stoppages ('000s) | Working days lost (m) |
|------|:---------------------------:|:---------------------:|
| 1971 | 2.2 | 13.5 |
| 1972 | 2.4 | 23.9 |
| 1973 | 2.8 | 7.1 |
| 1974 | 2.9 | 14.8 |
| 1975 | 2.2 | 5.9 |
| 1976 | 2.0 | 3.5 |
| 1977 | 2.7 | 10.3 |
| 1978 | 2.4 | 9.4 |
| 1979 | 2.1 | 29.0 |
| 1980 | 1.3 | 11.9 |
| 1981 | 1.3 | 4.2 |
| 1982 | 1.5 | 4.2 |

(Based on information from *Annual Abstract of Statistics* 1984, HMSO)

hours, but also on the detailed organisation of work. The less representative trade unions are, the less effective they will be. If trade unions did not exist in a modern industrial economy, they would have to be invented.
(*Whatever Happened to Britain* (1982) Eatwell J., BBC/Duckworth)

(a) How could you show the effect of trade unions playing the market game through a diagram showing the demand and supply of labour in a given section of the labour market?

(b) Explain the sentence, 'The mass organisation of labour is necessary complement to modern factory production'.

(c) Give three examples of the substance of trade union agreements that might be considered to cover the 'detailed organisation of work'.

(d) What do you understand by the sentence, 'The less representative trade unions are, the less effective they will be'. Give an example of trade union activity that backs up your answer.

4 (a) Why might employers favour the establishment of a closed shop agreement in their firm or industry?

(b) Why would trade unions support a closed shop agreement?

(c) Why might some individuals be opposed to a closed shop agreement?

5 Is there any evidence to suggest that trade union legislation has led to an improvement in industrial relations, and hence an improvement in the performance of the economy as a whole?

## 8.11 Rent

1 In everyday usage rent refers to the payment made when people have the use of property belonging to someone else, e.g. the rent paid for a TV or for a room.

2 In economics, rent refers to payments made to the factor of production called land, which in turn is defined as natural resources which have no supply price. All payments to land, therefore, are in excess of the supply price, and are economic rent.

3 The rent paid for a particular piece of land will depend on the derived demand for it and the supply of it, as in the general findings of distribution theory.

## 8.12 Interest

1 Interest is the payment made for the use of money capital.

2 The interest rate may incorporate a number of elements.

(a) *Pure interest*—i.e. direct payment for the use of the funds as compensation to the creditor for his loss of liquidity.

(b) *Risk compensation*—i.e. additional payment to compensate the creditor for the possible loss of his loan.

(c) *Anticipated inflation cover*—i.e. additional payment to cover the creditor for the loss of the purchasing power of his loan if the value of money falls.

3  Although economists talk for convenience about the rate of interest, in practice there is a structure of rates of interest at any particular moment in time.

4  There are two main theories concerning the determination of the rate of interest.

(a) *Classical Theory*—which sees the rate of interest specifically as the price of loans, and hence fixed by the supply of loanable funds and the demand for loanable funds.

(b) *Liquidity Preference Theory*—which sees the rate of interest as the price of money, and hence is determined by the supply of money and the demand to hold money (see *Unit 16.5*).

5  The level of interest rates may be determined by the monetary authorities (i.e. the Treasury and the Bank of England) and may, therefore, not be the product of market forces at all (see *Unit 16.10*).

# 8.13 Profits

1  Profits are received by entrepreneurs. They are their rewards for organisation of the other factors of production, and for taking risks to produce goods and services for consumers.

2  According to standard distribution theory profit levels should be determined by the supply of entrepreneurs and the demand for entrepreneurs, which loosely translates to the number of firms and the level of demand for their goods and services.

3  Alternatively, profit can be seen as a residue, i.e. what is left from a firm's revenue after the other factors of production have been paid.

4  The level of profits received by a firm will depend on:

(a) the nature of competition in the market that the firm operates in, e.g. the fall in profits of US airlines following de-regulation which allowed for increased competition on all internal routes.

(b) the level of efficiency of the firm, e.g. the rise of profits of the National Freight Corporation after privatisation and better control of costs.

(c) the demand for the firm's product, e.g. the rise in profits of Times Newspapers following the introduction of the 'Portfolio' marketing game and the consequent increase in sales.

(d) the cost of finance for the firm, e.g. small haulage owners in debt to the banks have higher costs than those that finance truck purchases from ploughing back past profits.

# Review

## Unit 8 will have helped provide answers to the following questions

1 How does a firm decide the most profitable combination of factors for the production of a product?
2 What is meant by saying that demand for factors of production is derived from the demand for the final products made with the factors?
3 What influences the level of supply of the various factors of production?
4 In free markets how are the prices of factors of production fixed?
5 What are the shortcomings of traditional distribution theory?
6 What factors are involved in the determination of wage levels?
7 How can the theory of distribution be applied to the earnings of land, capital and enterprise?

## Unit 8 has introduced the following terminology

Classical theory (of determination of rate of interest)
Closed shop
Derived demand
Differentials
Economic rent
Interest
Isoquants
Liquidity preference theory
Marginal physical product
Marginal revenue product
Monopsonistic market
Pay league tables
Productivity
Productivity bargaining
Profits
Pure interest
Quasi-rent
Relativities
Rent
Salaries
Trade unions
Transfer earnings
Wages

## Multiple choice questions

1 Which of the following would cause a shift to the left of a marginal revenue product curve?
  (a) The firm raises the price of the final product.
  (b) The workforce increases productivity.
  (c) There is a rise in demand for the final product.
  (d) New, more efficient machinery is introduced by the firm.
  (e) The number of hours worked each week by employees is reduced.

2 Interest is the payment made for the use of:
  (a) land
  (b) human resources
  (c) capital
  (d) enterprise
  (e) natural resources

3 A line which shows that two factors have been combined to make a certain level of output of a product is called:
  (a) an indifference curve
  (b) a marginal revenue product curve
  (c) an equi-marginal curve
  (d) an isoquant
  (e) a liquidity preference curve

4 The marginal revenue product of any factor input can be calculated from knowledge of:
  (a) marginal physical product and the price per unit of the factor,
  (b) price per unit of output and marginal physical product of the factor,
  (c) total physical product and the number of units of the factor used,
  (d) quantity of factor inputs and marginal physical product,
  (e) total physical product and the number of units of the final product sold.

5 The demand for factors is described as derived demand because:
  (a) it is derived from the profit made by the firm,
  (b) it depends on the quantities of other factor inputs used,
  (c) it is derived from the demand for the final product,
  (d) it is derived from the costs of employing the factors,
  (e) it is derived from the Law of Variable Proportions.

6 The shape of the marginal revenue product curve for a firm in perfect competition is governed by:
  (a) the impact of diminishing marginal returns
  (b) the principle of derived demand
  (c) the law of diminishing marginal utility
  (d) the theory of comparative advantage
  (e) the shape of the firm's supply curve for the final product

7 Profit maximising firms will demand factors up to the point where:
  (a) marginal revenue product equals the price of the factor
  (b) marginal revenue product falls to zero
  (c) marginal physical product becomes negative
  (d) marginal physical product equals marginal revenue product
  (e) marginal physical product is zero

8 Demand for a factor of production has a value of price elasticity between two and five. Supply of the factor is perfectly elastic. Earnings of the factor are:
  (a) more economic rent than transfer earnings
  (b) more transfer earnings than economic rent

(c) all economic rent

(d) equally divided between economic rent and transfer earnings

(e) all transfer earnings

9 If a firm operating in a perfectly competitive market employs capital equipment to the point where the marginal returns from the capital is less than the cost of acquiring the equipment:

(a) the firm is maximising profits

(b) the firm should employ more capital in order to maximise profits

(c) the firm should employ less capital to maximise profits

(d) the firm must be benefiting from internal economies of scale

(e) the firm will be earning normal profits

10 Which of the following is a false statement?

(a) Abnormal profit in the short run in perfectly competitive markets is quasi-rent.

(b) Abnormal profit in the short run in monopoly is economic rent.

(c) Abnormal profit in the short run in oligopoly is economic rent.

(d) Normal profit in the short run in imperfectly competitive markets is transfer earnings.

(e) Normal profit in the short run in perfectly competitive markets is quast-rent.

# Answers

## Exercise 1

1 (a) Output A i) 50 machines + 35 people ii) 15 machines + 60 people

(b) Output B i) 80 machines + 50 people ii) 55 machines + 70 people

Method—Plot isoquant. Add price line (initially from 0 machines/60 people to 120 machines/0 people). Find point of tangency. Read off quantities. New price line (0 machines/75 people to 75 machines/0 people), added to find new point of tangency. Repeat for Output B.

2 Best allocation is where MRevP:P ratio for all uses is the same, i.e. 2 acres potatoes—9:4.5 = 2:1; 3 acres wheat—9:4.5 = 2:1; 5 acres caravans—18:9 = 2:1. This allocation unlikely in practice. Problems of caravaners in the crops perhaps.

## Exercise 2

1 Shows decreasing returns to scale, i.e. increasing numbers of extra workers for a given amount of extra output. This conforms to the concept of diminishing marginal returns or the Law of Variable Proportions.

2

| Helpers | Newspapers | MPhyP | MRevP | Opportunity cost/helper |
|---------|-----------|-------|-------|------------------------|
| 1 | 3 | 3 | 18 | 6 |
| 2 | 7 | 4 | 24 | 6 |
| 3 | 12 | 5 | 30 | 6 |
| 4 | 15 | 3 | 18 | 6 |
| 5 | 16 | 1 | 6 | 6 |
| 6 | 16 | 0 | 0 | 6 |

(a) They will use up to five helpers on newspaper collection.

3

| Shearers | Sheep | MPhyP | MRevP | Wage rate shearer |
|----------|-------|-------|-------|-------------------|
| 1 | 24 | 24 | 48 | 44 |
| 2 | 52 | 28 | 56 | 44 |
| 3 | 90 | 38 | 76 | 44 |
| 4 | 124 | 34 | 68 | 44 |
| 5 | 146 | 22 | 44 | 44 |

(b) They will employ up to five shearers.

4 Suggested essay plan.

Introduction: Definition of terms i) Profit maximisation ii) Labour (workers).

Main paragraphs: i) Demand curves for factors (*Unit 8.4[1 to 6]*) ii) Combinations of factors— need for equal MRevP:P ratios. iii) Labour may be linked to machinery, may be determined by demand for capital.

Conclusion.

## Exercise 3

1 Relationship between wage levels and unemployment benefit levels, size of population, age/sex structure of the population, tax levels, income levels, chances of finding work, retirement age, school leaving age.

2 Qualifications required and level of skill of workers, pay, company prospects, nature of the job, e.g. danger, hours, stress, alternative opportunities for work, geographical mobility of workers.

3 Rate of discovery, land reclamation, level of rent, tax levels.

4 Profit levels, tax regimes, custom and culture.

5 Return expected, risk involved, need for replacement machinery, tax levels, business objectives.

N.B. these are only some examples of factors for all resource supply levels.

## Exercise 4

1 Quasi-rent is temporary economic rent. Divers initially received a bonus payment through higher wages than those they had been paid when they decided to be divers. As supply of trained divers increased so the bonus disappeared.

2  (a) £100 (b) £200. Economic rent is income received over and above income obtainable in the next best occupation.

3  (a) £1500  (b) £0. Return from house = £3000/yr. Return from investment of £30,000 at 5% = £1500 Return from investment of £30,000 at 10% = £3000.

4  £19,200. Band gets £40,000 from contract. Earnings from the buses = $4 \times 100 \times 52 = £20,800$.

5  No, all economic rent. It will be supplied whatever is paid to it.

6  Normal profit is what is necessary to stay in business. If firms earn less than normal profit they will go out of business in the long run, so it is all transfer earnings.

7  She is concerned with long term income prospects, and the social and personal benefits from having a job.

8  Nil. He needs it all to stay driving his taxi.

## Exercise 5

1  Own research. Compare to points made in *Unit 8.8*.

2  (a) No. What is the marginal physical product? What is produced is not sold in a market.
   (b) Yes, see *Unit 8.8(3)*.
   (c)  i) Comparison with other workers (e.g. civil servants), comparison with changes in the cost of living, importance of education standards to long run health of society, ratepayers willing to provide money (!).
       ii) Inflation rates, pay league tables, national average wage levels.
      iii) Inability to pay more, need to curb costs for ratepayers, unproductive, supply of teachers exceeds demand at present time.

3  See *Unit 8.8(5)*, i.e. the concept of the backward sloping demand curve.

## Exercise 6

1  (a) Steady fall in number of unions, 481 to 421. Union membership peaked in 1979 at 13.2m. Fell back by over 1m since.
   (b) Rise in unemployment. Fall in inflation (less need to push for higher wages). Less role for trade unions to play with a Conservative government.
   (c) Success or otherwise in major disputes. History and tradition. Attitude and behaviour of management. Closed shop agreements.
   (d) Relatively high in mining and in local government. Low amongst shop workers.

2  (a) Number of strikes fluctuates less than days lost through strikes. There has been a drop in strike activity since 1979 and the 'winter of discontent'. Days lost figures distorted by major strikes, e.g. miners 1972, 1974; steel in 1980.
   (b) Levels of inflation. Levels of unemployment.

Attitude of government to pay settlements.
   (c) High strike activity leads to a loss of non-price competitiveness (unreliable delivery dates). It may deter direct investment from overseas as well as within the economy. Lowers profits in industry. Overall growth is threatened.
   (d) Over 90% of strikes are unofficial, i.e. not directly the responsibility of unions. Even official strikes can be viewed as responses to situations caused by management, government or other exogenous agencies.

3  (a) See *Unit 8.8(2,3)*.
   (b) Large scale production requires mass organisation of capital and management. Unions are a response to the need to balance the forces at work within the work situation.
   (c) E.g. pace of machinery, staffing levels, job descriptions, holiday arrangements.
   (d) Unrepresentative trade unions with low membership levels tend to become dominated by extremists. Unions with wider membership represent the views of the majority of workers.

4  (a) Simplified collective bargaining. Management knows who to deal with.
   (b) Membership leads to finance and more influence. Benefits gained by union activity are available to all workers, even to those who do not contribute to union finance through their membership subscription.
   (c) Loss of freedom. Transgresses the right 'not to belong' to a trade union.

5  Very little. Legislation has not been used in many cases. Other factors influence the level of strike activity, indeed some strikes might be political and aimed at the legislation itself. Strike activity is not the only element of industrial relations.

## Multiple choice answers

1  (e) All others would increase marginal revenue product.
2  (c) By definition.
3  (d) See *Unit 8.3(1)*.
4  (b) Marginal revenue product = marginal physical product × price of final good.
5  (c) People employ resources because they are used to make final goods and services.
6  (a) Alternative name for the Law of Variable Proportions.
7  (a) See *Unit 8.4(6)*.
8  (e) See *Unit 8.6(5)*.
9  (c) Marginal revenue product being less than cost of employing the capital means that profits are not being maximised. To raise MRevP less capital has to be used.
10  (e) Normal profit is needed by the firm to stay in business. It is transfer earnings.

# Introduction to macroeconomics UNIT 9

## 9.1 Preview

1 Macroeconomics is a study of the operation of the economy as a whole. It concerns itself, e.g. with the general level of prices, the aggregate level of output and employment, and the overall balance of payments position between Britain and the rest of the world.

2 Economies are normally regarded as operating satisfactorily if certain macroeconomic objectives are achieved.

3 The ability of the economy to achieve these objectives depends on the level of economic activity, i.e. the aggregate level of output, incomes or expenditure generated in the economy over a certain period of time.

4 The government has a number of policy weapons that it can use to influence the level of economic activity.

5 The government's ability to control the level of economic activity is hampered by a number of factors.

6 Further difficulties in operation of macroeconomic management stem from the theoretical differences between economists, and the political differences between the politicians who put the policies into operation.

## 9.2 Macroeconomic objectives

1 An ideal situation for an advanced economy would normally be considered to be one where there was:

(a) *Steady and sustainable economic growth*—i.e. a rate of growth of economic activity which would allow an increase in living standards without undue structural or environmental difficulties (see *Unit 20*).

(b) *Nearly full employment*—i.e. where allowing for structural and frictional problems those who wished to exercise their 'right to work' could do so (see *Unit 15*) without sacrificing price stability and external viability (see below).

(c) *Price stability*—i.e. where there is zero inflation (see *Unit 16*).

(d) *External viability*—i.e. where sufficient foreign currency is earned, or held in the reserves, to finance the desired level of imports (see *Unit 17*).

(e) *An acceptable distribution of wealth and incomes*—i.e. one that allows a more equitable distribution than would be the case in an entirely free market (see *Unit 14*).

## 9.3 The level of economic activity

1 The level of economic activity (measured through the National Income Accounts—see *Unit 10*) affects the extent to which these objectives can be realised. For example, a higher level of economic activity will lead to higher growth and more employment, possibly at the expense of price stability and external viability.

2 The level of economic activity is affected by key variables, some of which are directly connected with the objectives themselves.
3 These variables are:
   (a) savings (what is not spent on consumption expenditure from current income),
   (b) investment expenditure (the purchase of capital resources),
   (c) government expenditure,
   (d) taxation,
   (e) exports,
   (f) imports.
4 Savings, imports and taxation are withdrawals from the economy; investment expenditure, government expenditure and exports are injections into the economy (*see Unit 11*).

## 9.4 Government policy weapons

1 The government has the ability to influence the level of the macroeconomic variables, either directly or indirectly, through a variety of policy weapons. These can be categorised as follows:
   (a) *Fiscal policy*—i.e. policies concerned with government expenditure, taxation and borrowing (see *Unit 13*).
   (b) *Monetary policy*—i.e. policies concerned with the cost and availability of credit and the rate of growth of the money supply (see *Unit 16*).
   (c) *Trade policy*—i.e. policies concerned with the prices and volume of international trade, e.g. exchange rates, tariffs and quota arrangements (see *Units 17, 18*).
   (d) *Direct policy measures*—e.g. policies which control incomes and prices directly, planning controls (see *Units 15, 20*).
   (e) *Supply-side policies*—i.e. policies which are specifically concerned with the performance of producers in the economy, e.g. legislation about restrictive trade practices by trade unions, control over the development of monopoly power and anti-competitive practices (see *Units 5, 8*).

## 9.5 Problems of macroeconomic control

1 The government's ability to manage the economy has always been subject to a number of difficulties. These include:
   (a) *Exogenous shocks*—i.e. external factors beyond the control of the government, e.g. the impact of new technology on employment levels, demographic changes, the effect on the economy of the rise in world energy prices after the 1973 and 1979 OPEC price hikes.
   (b) *Unpredictable endogenous reactions*—i.e. as people cannot be relied on to react to a given change in economic circumstances in a predictable way the effect of policy changes is unpredictable, e.g. a cut in income tax might one year lead to a rise in consumer expenditure, but the next year might lead to a rise in savings.
   (c) *Speed of impact of policy measures*—some policy measures will lead to quick changes in economic behaviour while others have a more delayed effect. Some policy measures have a detrimental effect on the economy before having a longer-

term beneficial effect, e.g. raising VAT might increase inflation in the short run but help reduce it in the long run, a depreciation of the exchange rate may worsen the balance of trade in the short run but help it in the long run.

(d) *Forecasting difficulties*—it is not always possible for the government to know the exact state of the economy or the exact effect of policy measures that it has introduced. Indeed the whole operation of management of the economy has been likened to trying to drive a car by only looking out of the rear window. Information about the state of the economy is provided by indicators which can be categorised as:

    (i) lagging indicators—those which describe what *has* happened in the economy, e.g. monthly unemployment statistics, measures of inflation from the Retail Prices Index (RPI),

    (ii) leading indicators—those which anticipate what *is about to* happen in the economy, e.g. surveys of companies investment intentions, measures of inflation based on wholesale prices.

Naturally the government would like to have reliable leading indicators on which to operate but this is not always possible.

(e) *Incompatability of objectives*—the government may well have to set an order of priority for the pursuit of the macro-economic objectives as policies to improve the position on one objective, say inflation, may well cause a deterioration in the position of another, in this case unemployment (see *Units 15, 16*).

2   In addition to the problems outlined above there are *doctrinal differences of opinion* between politicians—the people who put economic policy into operation. For example, over the role of planning in the direction of finance to industry, over the position and contribution to the economy of nationalised industries (see *Unit 7*).

3   Also, there is considerable *difference of opinion amongst economists* as to the effects of certain economic strategies which has been stimulated by the apparent failure of 'Keynesian' demand management and the renewed interest in 'Monetarism'. For example, as to whether long run unemployment is better lowered by deflationary or reflationary strategies.

# Exercise 1

1   What would you regard as a satisfactory level for:
   (a) inflation
   (b) unemployment
   (c) growth
   (d) the balance of payments accounts
   Explain your answers.

2   Find up-to-date information about the levels of:
   (a) inflation
   (b) unemployment
   (c) growth of output
   (d) the balance of payments on current account

*References:* Teletext, *Ceefax 229.*
*Economist,* economic indicators at back of each edition.
*Economics Progress Reports,* published by the Treasury.
What are the trends in these areas of economic activity?
Are they moving towards or away from the desired level?

3  Find out the current levels of the following indicators of economic performance.
(a)  £:US$ exchange rate.
(b)  *Financial Times* ordinary share index or the FT-SE100 index of share prices.
(c)  Commercial bank base interest rates or mortgage rates of interest.

What information do these indicators convey about the state of the economy?

4  **US indicators confuse Wall Street**
The US Government measure designed to forecast activity ended an eighteen month rising streak with an unexpected 1.1% drop in March, officials said yesterday.

The decline in the leading indicators index confirmed Wall Street's belief that the rapid first quarter expansion pace has slowed dramatically.

The leading indicators measure is a composite of ten gauges designed to foreshadow economic changes by roughly 90 days. Commerce Secretary, Malcolm Baldridge, said the March 1.1% drop largely reflected the big declines in two of the ten measures—building permits and the average working week.

As a result, Mr Baldridge said, the 1.1% drop in the March index 'exaggerates the extent of the slowdown in economic activity', adding that the leading indicators ended the eighteen month rise with a dip 'normal at this stage of the economic expansion'.

(Based on information from *Daily Telegraph* 2.5.84)
(a)  Explain the following:
(i) leading indicators index (ii) Wall Street (iii) average working week
(b)  What can be inferred from the passage about the usefulness of this index as an aid to economic management?

5  Anticipated effect of budget changes.

| | Income tax basic rate from 30% to 27% | | VAT standard rate from 15% to 20% | | Public expenditure increased by £1b | |
|---|---|---|---|---|---|---|
| after 1 yr | | 4 yrs | 1 yr | 4 yrs | 1 yr | 4 yrs |
| GDP (%) | +0.4 | +0.9 | −0.7 | −0.8 | +0.3 | +0.4 |
| Unemployment ('000s) | −30 | −130 | +30 | +100 | −165 | −185 |
| Balance of trade (£b) | −0.5 | −3.9 | +1.5 | +4.0 | +0.3 | −1.5 |
| Price (%) | +0.1 | +1.1 | +2.1 | — | +0.6 | +0.8 |

(Based on information from *1984 Budget Analysis* Institute of Fiscal Studies)

(a) Into which category of policy weapons should the changes shown in the table be placed?

(b) Which of the basic macroeconomic objectives is improved by the cut in income tax from 30% to 27%?

(c) Of the three policy options shown which one has the quickest effect on the level of unemployment? Why might this be so?

(d) Which of the three policy options has the largest effect on the level of unemployment? Why might this be so?

(e) Which of the measures has the biggest effect on prices after one year? Why does it appear that all these options lead to higher inflation in the short run?

(f) Why is it important for the government to know the extent and speed of effect of its policy measures to control the level of economic activity?

# Review

## Unit 9 will have helped provide answers to the following questions

1 What is the difference between macro and micro economics?

2 What are the five main macroeconomic objectives?

3 What are the key variables that affect and are affected by the level of economic activity?

4 What are the main policy weapons available for government control of the economy?

5 What difficulties does the government experience in its control of the economy?

## Unit 9 has introduced the following terminology

| | |
|---|---|
| Endogenous variables | Lagging indicators |
| Exogenous variables | Leading indicators |
| Exports | Monetarism |
| External viability | Monetary policy |
| Fiscal policy | Planning |
| Full employment | Price stability |
| Government expenditure | Savings |
| Imports | Supply-side policies |
| Investment expenditure | Taxation |
| Keynesian economic policy | Trade policy |

## Multiple choice questions

1 Which of the following might be considered to be a cost associated with economic growth?

(a) A rise in the standard of living of the population.

(b) The creation of more tax revenue for the government.

(c) A rise in unemployment due to structural changes in the pattern of economic activity.

(d) A rise in competitiveness of industry in export markets.

(e) More investment by industry from increased profits.

2 Which is unlikely to be a consequence of increased unemployment?

(a) Increased government expenditure on social security payments.

(b) A fall in tax revenue for the government.

(c) A less equal distribution of incomes in the economy as a whole.

(d) A reduction in trade union influence and membership.

(e) A fall in illness and death rates.

3 Which of the following is least likely to benefit from a period of high inflation?

(a) Workers in an industry protected by a strong trade union.

(b) People in debt.

(c) The government.

(d) Pensioners living on the interest and dividends from past savings.

(e) Workers whose wages are linked to the retail prices index.

4 If a country has a surplus on its balance of trade (*ceteris paribus*) it can be deduced that:

(a) living standards are less in that country than would be the case if the balance of trade was in deficit,

(b) living standards would be higher if the balance of trade was in balance,

(c) living standards are lower in other countries,

(d) the government is spending less than it is receiving in taxation,

(e) the government will have to pay any surplus to people who have lent it money.

Questions 5 and 6 refer to the following policy instruments:

(a) controlling the level of bank lending

111

(b) management of the exchange rate

(c) changes in the rates of personal income tax

(d) controls on the method and manner of trade union activities

(e) imposition of limits to pay settlements in the private sector

**5** Which of the instruments listed above is an instrument of fiscal policy?
(a) a  (b) b  (c) c  (d) d  (e) e

**6** Which of the instruments listed above is an instrument of monetary policy?
(a) a  (b) b  (c) c  (d) d  (e) e

**7** A rise in the level of economic activity will lead to:
(a) higher unemployment
(b) higher inflation
(c) less imports of raw materials by industry
(d) less profits for industry
(e) reduced tax receipts for the government

**8** A fall in the level of economic activity will lead to:
(a) a rise in the level of savings
(b) an increase in consumption expenditure
(c) a rise in government expenditure on social security payments
(d) a rise in expenditure on imports
(e) a rise in Stock Exchange prices

**9** Which of the following should be considered to be the best example of a leading indicator of future levels of economic activity?
(a) The monthly official unemployment figures.
(b) The monthly changes in the level of retail prices.
(c) Surveys of investment intentions of industry.
(d) The monthly balance of trade accounts.
(e) The *Financial Times* 30 share index.

**10** Governments are likely to find the management of the economy difficult because:
(a) their objectives are incompatible,
(b) they find it difficult to obtain accurate information as to the actual state of the economy,
(c) it is not easy to predict the speed and extent of the effects of policy changes,
(d) the impact of external shocks to the economy cannot be predicted,
(e) all of the above.

## Answers

### Exercise 1

**1** (a) Zero inflation? A rate similar to those in the countries competing with Britain in world markets?

(b) 3% used to be considered 'the natural rate of unemployment' (see *Unit 15*). Work for all those that want it.

(c) Steady, sustainable growth of about 3% p.a.?

(d) A full employment, restriction free, medium

term balance. Not a surplus in the long run because this reduces living standards. Not a deficit in the long run because there will be insufficient reserves of foreign currency to finance the trade.

**2** Own research.

**3** (a) £: US$ exchange rate is less use as an indicator than the sterling effective exchange rate, which measures the value of sterling against a 'basket' of other currencies.

(b) The FT-SE 100 index was introduced in 1984 to be more representative of total moves on the market. Share prices react to dealers' interpretations of world economic events and to company performances.

(c) Base interest rates are a general indication of interest rate levels in the economy. Rising rates may reflect changing rates elsewhere in the world, or tighter money conditions in the economy which could cause a future downturn in the level of economic activity.

**4** (a)  (i) leading indicators attempt to predict future changes in the level of economic activity. An index of leading indicators is an average of several (ten in this example) indicators.

(ii) Wall Street is the US Stock Exchange.

(iii) Average working week reflects the hours people spend at work, and presumably varies according to the amount of short-time working or overtime worked. As such it is an indicator of economic activity.

(b) The Commerce Secretary seemed to be playing down the value of the index. As a measure of economic activity 90 days on it would not be expected to reflect the current state of economic activity.

**5** (a) Fiscal policy.

(b) Less unemployment, higher growth, at the expense of higher prices and a worse trade situation.

(c) Change in public expenditure. Direct creation of jobs by the government rather than indirect creation as a result of more consumer expenditure.

(d) Change in public expenditure. This involves a full multiplier effect, whereas some of the change in tax may result in a change in the level of savings.

(e) VAT increase. VAT causes costs to rise. The others increase demand in the economy.

(f) To hit its target the government has to get its timing and extent of policy changes accurate. Otherwise it will under or overshoot the target.

### Multiple choice answers

**1** (c) Growth inevitably involves change, and the loss of jobs in declining activities.

**2** (e) Unemployment causes stress and lack of status

for those unemployed, and can involve reduced standards of nutrition and well-being.

**3** (d) People living on relatively fixed incomes suffer from falling real incomes.

**4** (a) Standards of living depend on the levels of consumption, not the accumulations of surplus foreign currency.

**5** (c) By definition.

**6** (a) By definition.

**7** (b) Through higher wage claims, higher prices of imported materials if the recovery was world-wide, and perhaps because of increased growth of the money supply if the recovery had been orchestrated by the government in this way.

**8** (c) More people will be without paid employment.

**9** (c) Leading indicators look to the future, the others are based on past economic activity.

**10** (e) All the first four are probable difficulties.

# UNIT 10 Measurement of the level of economic activity

## 10.1 Preview

1 The data collected in measuring the level of economic activity is presented in the national income accounts.
2 There are three basic approaches to calculating the level of economic activity:
   (a) the output or production method,
   (b) the expenditure method, ·
   (c) the incomes method.
3 As all three methods are measuring the same thing, they should, when suitably defined, each give the same result.
4 The national income data is of use to the government, e.g. for formulating its macroeconomic strategy; and for businessmen, e.g. for planning new investment expenditure.

## 10.2 Definitions

1 There are several terms used in the national accounts which have precise meaning when used in this context.
   (a) *Gross*—refers to the fact that no allowance has been made for the wear and tear and obsolescence of assets used in production, e.g. buildings and machinery or in calculating the value of goods produced, i.e. for depreciation or capital consumption.
   (b) *Net*—indicates that an allowance has been made for depreciation or capital consumption.
   (c) *Domestic*—refers to economic activity resulting from productive units located in the UK regardless of the country of ownership.
   (d) *National*—refers to economic activity resulting from productive units owned by UK residents regardless of where the firm or plant is located.
   (e) *Market prices*—means that values are measured at the prices paid for the goods or services by the consumer, i.e. no allowance has been made for the effect of indirect taxes or subsidies.
   (f) *Factor cost*—means that values are measured in terms of the cost or producing them, i.e. ignoring the subsequent effect of indirect taxes and subsidies on the prices charged to the consumer.
   (g) *Constant prices*—means that values are taken at some selected base year so as to remove the effect of inflation.
   (h) *Current prices*—means that values are taken at the price levels which existed in the year or month in question, i.e. without making any allowance for the effect of inflation.
   (i) *National income*—in the UK it is taken to be net national product at factor cost.

# 10.3 The expenditure approach

1  The components of total final expenditure are:
   (a)  Consumption (C)
   (b)  Investment (I)
   (c)  Government Expenditure (G)
   (d)  Exports (X)
2  The accounts are presented as shown.

| |
|---|
| Consumers expenditure |
| +  General government final consumption |
| +  Gross fixed investment |
| +  Value of the physical increase in stocks |
| +  Exports of goods and services |
| =  **Total final expenditure at market prices** |
| −  Imports of goods and services |
| =  **Gross Domestic Product at market prices** |
| −  Indirect taxes |
| +  Subsidies |
| =  **Gross Domestic Product at factor cost** |
| +  Net property income from abroad |
| =  **Gross National Product at factor cost** |
| −  Capital Consumption |
| =  **Net National Product at factor cost (i.e. National Income)** |

3  Value of physical increase in stocks traces any increase in the level of stocks of finished goods or work-in-progress as this represents investment expenditure by the firm. A fall in stock levels (destocking) would cause this value to be negative.
4  Net property income from abroad involves the balance of dividends and profits flowing into and out of the UK during the time period.

# 10.4 The incomes approach

1  The chief source of income earned by factors as a result of economic activity are:
   (a)  wages and salaries
   (b)  rent
   (c)  profits
2  The accounts are presented as shown on page 116.
3  Stock appreciation means that stocks of raw materials or components have risen in value during the accounting period resulting in a rise in incomes which has not been directly caused by economic activity, i.e. in the process of actually producing something.
4  Imputed charge refers to a value added to incomes equal to an estimated value of the rent that owner occupiers of houses would have had to pay if they were tenants of the same properties.

```
  Income from empolyment
+ Income from self employment
+ Gross trading profits of companies
+ Gross trading surpluses of nationalised industries
+ Gross trading surpluses of general government enterprises
+ Rent
+ Imputed charge for the consumption of non-traded capital

= Total domestic income

− Stock appreciation
+ Residual error

= Gross Domestic Product at factor cost
```

5 Undistributed profits of companies are included in the accounts as they have been earned in the accounting period. It makes no difference what the firm does with the profits subsequently.

6 Residual error refers to a sum that is added to balance the accounts. Each approach to calculating national income involves thousands of figures collected from a variety of sources. It is not surprising that the totals are not, in practice, equal. The residual error appears in the income accounts purely for convenience of presentation.

# 10.5 The output method

1 National income based on output data is calculated by adding the sum of 'values added' by each firm in each industry. Industrial activity is conventionally classified according to the Standard Industrial Classification (revised in 1980).

2 Value added is the difference between the final value of the product and the cost of the inputs of raw materials and components, i.e. it is the rise in value of the product caused by the activities of the firm itself.

# 10.6 Problems associated with the measurement of economic activity

1 **Double counting**—the value of intermediate goods forms part of the value of final goods, and thus would be counted twice if the output of all industries was counted fully. This is avoided by counting only the 'values added'.

2 **Transfer payments**—these are incomes received other than from economic activity, e.g. as an entitlement from the state for a retirement pension or unemployment benefit. All transfer earnings are excluded from the accounts to avoid the income being counted twice, once when 'earned' and again when it was transferred.

3 **Non-marketed output**—the national accounts make no allowance for work done at home, e.g. for housework or home-grown vegetables, or charity or voluntary work.

4 **Black economy**—also referred to as hidden, unofficial, underground or twilight economic activity, this concerns unrecorded economic activity often associated with tax or insurance avoidance.

5 **Service industries**—in industries where there is no tangible product or where the product is not sold on the market it is difficult to value 'added value', e.g. in education and health. By convention the output of these industries is valued at cost.

# Exercise 1

1 The following data is known for a country (£m/year):
   (i) Gross domestic product at market prices = 52
   (ii) Gross national product at market prices = 50
   (iii) Gross domestic product at factor cost = 44
   (iv) Gross national product at factor cost = 42
   (v) National income = 37
  (a) What is the value of the allowance for indirect taxes and subsidies?
  (b) What is the value allowed for capital consumption?
  (c) What is the value of the allowance for net property income from abroad?

2 A country has a stock of factories and machines valued at £1000 b at the start of a year. Total output from these factories and machines during the year was £500 b. During the year the value of factories and machines fell by £200 b.
  (a) What is the value of depreciation during the year?
  (b) What was the value of net output during the year?

3 The following data refers to the 1982 UK National income accounts, measured at 1980 prices.

| | (£m) |
|---|---|
| Consumers' expenditure | 138,865 |
| General government final consumption | 49,011 |
| Gross domestic fixed capital formation | 37,614 |
| Value of physical increase in stocks and work-in-progress | − 1,031 |
| Exports of goods and services | 62,789 |
| Imports of goods and services | 57,997 |

(Based on information from *Annual Abstract of Statistics* HMSO)

  (a) Calculate the value of total final expenditure at market prices at 1980 prices.
  (b) Give an example of economic activity that would be included in gross domestic fixed capital formation.
  (c) What does it mean when value of physical increase in stocks and work-in-progress is shown as a negative value?
  (d) Would you expect the level of consumers' expenditure measured at current prices to be above or below £138,865 m?
  (e) Calculate the value of Gross Domestic Product at market prices?

(f) What adjustments would have to be made to this figure to calculate national income?

**4**

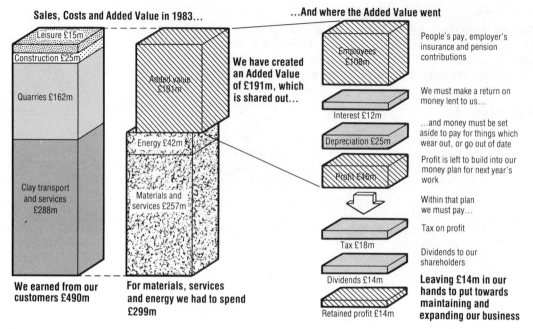

Sales, Costs and Added Value in 1983...   ...And where the Added Value went

Leisure £15m

Construction £25m

Quarries £162m

Clay transport and services £288m

Added value £191m

Energy £42m

Materials and services £257m

We have created an Added Value of £191m, which is shared out...

Employees £108m

Interest £12m

Depreciation £25m

Profit £46m

Tax £18m

Dividends £14m

Retained profit £14m

People's pay, employer's insurance and pension contributions

We must make a return on money lent to us...

...and money must be set aside to pay for things which wear out, or go out of date

Profit is left to build into our money plan for next year's work

Within that plan we must pay...

Tax on profit

Dividends to our shareholders

**Leaving £14m in our hands to put towards maintaining and expanding our business**

**We earned from our customers £490m**

**For materials, services and energy we had to spend £299m**

**Figure 10.1**   Source and application of finance by English China Clays PLC 1983

Figure 10.1 is taken from a report by the Chairman of the English China Clays Group to the employees.
(Source: English China Clays PLC. *Company Accounts* 1983)

(a) What was the value of the goods and services made by the firm in 1983 and sold to customers?

(b) What was the value of materials, services and energy that the firm bought in order to make this level of goods and services?

(c) What then was the 'value added' by the firm in 1983?

(d) What is the difference between 'value added' and 'profit'?

(e) How did the firm distribute its 'value added'?

(f) What did they intend doing with their profit of £46 m?

5   A firm produces microcomputers for £500 each. It buys in components and raw materials to the value of £150 per unit. Labour costs per unit are £100. Assuming there are no other costs what is the value added by the firm each month if the firm produces 500 computers each month?

6   A man is made redundant from a job that commanded a salary of £15,000 p.a. He decides to set up a small brewing company. He employs one full-time worker who was previously unemployed and receiving £3500 p.a. social security payments, and pays him £7000 p.a. He also takes on two school leavers on a government employment scheme. They are paid £25 per week, of which the government pays half. His wife helps out with the book-keeping but gets no direct salary. The company earned

£25,000 profit in the first year, of which £5000 was ploughed back into the business for expansion.
   (a) Assuming that other factors are constant what will be the change in national income as a result of this activity over the year?

7   For each of the items below state whether they should or should not be included in calculations of national income.
   (a) Interest received from deposits in the National Savings Bank.
   (b) Winnings at bingo.
   (c) Salaries of civil servants.
   (d) A value equivalent to the rent that would have been paid by owner occupiers to themselves.
   (e) Profits of a second-hand furniture shop.
   (f) Undistributed profits of private companies.
   (g) Unemployment benefits.
   (h) Gifts made by people to charities.
   (i) Profits of self-employed businessmen.
   (j) Rent paid by council tenants.

8   Why, in the UK national accounts, is the value of expenditure higher when measured at market prices than at factor cost?

9   Give an example of economic activity that would be included in;
   (a) net property income from abroad
   (b) residual error
   (c) general government final consumption

10   Which of the components in total final expenditure in the UK is the largest? Which do you think fluctuates the most?

11   **Which boom, which slump?**
In the second quarter of 1983 Britain's GDP slumped alarmingly by 1.8% compared with the first quarter. Right? Wrong: on another measure GDP slipped back only a trifling 0.09%. And on a third measure it was unchanged.
   GDP can be measured in three ways. In crude theory the results should be the same since output generates income which is then spent on consuming goods and services or saved for capital investment.
   Unfortunately the measures have been behaving very differently in Britain in the past year. The expenditure measure has been galloping ahead of the others, rising by 5.4% in the year to the first quarter of 1983. The other measures grew in the same period by a more sedate 2—3%.
   Optimists concluded from this that the black economy was booming.
                  (Based on information from *Economist* 24.9.83)
   (a) What are the three ways of measuring economic activity?
   (b) What are the four main components of total final expenditure?

(c) What is the 'black economy'?

(d) Why does the black economy mainly show up in the expenditure data?

(e) The treasury thinks that the output measure is the most accurate guide as to what is happening in the economy. Can you think of any reasons why this should be so?

(f) Apart from the effects of the black economy what else may have caused the different movements of the figures?

**12 Essay**

What are the three ways of measuring the level of economic activity? What problems will arise in calculating national income by any one of these methods?

# 10.7 Interpretation of the accounts

1 A rise in national income indicates some economic growth. This economic growth does not necessarily mean that welfare or the standard of living of the citizens has also increased by a corresponding amount.

2 There are several factors that need to be taken into account.

(a) *Inflation*—real economic growth can only be seen after an allowance has been made for any general rise in the level of prices—in the UK this allowance is made using the GDP deflators.

(b) *Population changes*—the standard of living of a citizen depends on each person's share of national income. Per capita (per head) figures give a better guide to this.

(c) *Distribution of income*—an increase in national income may not be distributed evenly to the population.

(d) *Goods and bads*—No allowance is made in the raw data for what is produced. If the goods and services produced do not benefit society (i.e. they are bads) then welfare will not be increased.

(e) *Conditions and hours of work*—greater output may be achieved as a result of people having to work harder or longer, a condition not normally associated with increased welfare. Work may become more pleasant with new technology representing an increase in welfare.

(f) *Opportunity cost of increased production*—extra output may result in some undesirable side products, i.e. externalities, e.g. pollution or illness.

(g) *Qualitative changes in consumer goods*—some goods can be produced more cheaply through technological advances, and at a higher quality, increasing welfare without increasing measured national income.

(h) *Valuation of public sector services*—individuals have no direct say in how taxes are spent, and whether this expenditure is increasing their welfare by an amount equal to their tax payments.

3 There are additional factors that are relevant to comparisons of living standards or welfare in different countries. These include:

(a) *Exchange rate levels*—for comparison, values in different currencies have to be converted to a common currency. The exchange rates chosen will clearly affect this comparison.

(b) *Difference in statistical processes*—different countries may use different accounting definitions and conventions. Like may not be compared with like if this is so.

(c) *The non-monetarised economy*—different countries have different customs and cultures. Lower or no production of goods does not necessarily mean a reduced standard of living for a particular group of people.

4 Long run comparisons of living standards through national income data may be misleading because of:

(a) *Change in role of women*—more women at work increases measured national income but may result in a deterioration of home and family care standards.

(b) *Growth of the public sector*—public services are not properly valued in the accounts so a change in the size of public sector will distort comparisons.

(c) *Exploitation of irreplaceable resources and damage to environment*—increases in the 'depreciation' of the environment are not reflected in the national accounts.

# Exercise 2

1 Consider each of the following situations in turn. For each state how the situation would have affected the national income accounts, and whether it could be reasonably assumed that the standard of living or welfare of the people concerned had changed correspondingly, e.g. expansion of cable TV in the UK would:

    (i) raise national income

    (ii) increase welfare especially if there were good programmes on the cable.

(a) The increased production in Britain during the Second World War.

(b) The effect in oil producing countries of large increases in oil export prices as in 1973 and 1979.

(c) The building and development of the Windscale/Sellafield processing plant for radioactive waste.

(d) A scheme to dam, and hence flood, the Franklin and Gordon river valleys in south-west Tasmania, Australia, to provide hydro-electric power which was to be exported to mainland Australia; but also involving the loss of wilderness considered to be of great environmental importance.

(e) Local authorities' sales of council houses to existing tenants.

(f) A hypothetical company develops a spray for controlling crop diseases but finds that workers exposed to the spray suffer health problems. This results in the need for increased expenditure on research and medical treatment.

(g) Previously unemployed school leavers establish a co-operative to provide a picture framing service financed by grants from local authorities.

2 A teacher employed in 1975 received a salary of £2000 p.a. In 1985 his salary had risen to £13,000 p.a. What key pieces of information would you need before you could say what had happened to his standard of living?

3 Assume that the following data is correct, for a given year.

| Country | GNP (market prices—$US) |
|---------|------------------------|
| United Arab Emirates | 12,000 |
| United Kingdom | 400,000 |
| South Africa | 60,000 |
| Zaire | 7,000 |

(a) From this data what can be inferred about the standard of living of the citizens in these countries?
(b) If the population is as follows: UAE 0.5 m, UK 56 m, SA 24 m and Zaire 24 m, what can now be inferred about the relative levels of the standard of living in these four countries?

4 **Essay**
Why may it be misleading to use changes in the level of national income as an indicator of changes in the welfare of citizens in a country over a certain period of time?

## Review

### Unit 10 will have helped provide answers to the following questions

1 What are the three basic approaches to measuring the level of economic activity?
2 What pitfalls are there to be overcome in each method?
3 To what extent should a change in the national income data be taken as evidence of a change in welfare of the citizens of a country?
4 What limitations are there in using national income data to compare standards of living of people of different countries?

### Unit 10 has introduced the following terminology

Bads
Black economy (underground economy)
Constant prices
Current prices
Depreciation (capital consumption)
Domestic (product)
Double counting
Factor cost
GDP

GDP deflators
GNP
Gross (product)
Imputed charge
Market prices
National income
National (product)
Net (product)
Net property income from abroad
Non-marketed output
Residual error
Service industries
Stock appreciation
Transfer payments
Value added

### Multiple choice questions

1 Adjusting Net National Product at factor cost to Gross National Product at market prices involves:
  (a) adding capital consumption and adding an inflation allowance,
  (b) adding depreciation and adding net property income from abroad,

(c) adding indirect taxes, subtracting subsidies and adding depreciation,
(d) adding net property income from abroad, adding subsidies and subtracting indirect taxes,
(e) adding an inflation allowance and adding net property income from abroad.

2  Which of the following would not be included in a measure of Gross Domestic Product at market prices?
(a) Production of a British owned firm operating in the Middle East.
(b) Production of nationalised industries in Britain.
(c) Production of a US owned company operating in Britain.
(d) Production of Japanese owned firms operating in Scotland.
(e) Production of local government services.

3

|         | National income |         | Population | Inflation |
|---------|--------|--------|------------|-----------|
| Country | year 1 | year 2 | rise (%)   | rise (%)  |
| A       | 100    | 120    | 10         | 10        |
| B       | 100    | 120    | 20         | 5         |
| C       | 100    | 110    | − 10       | 10        |
| D       | 100    | 100    | 0          | 5         |
| E       | 100    | 90     | 5          | − 5       |

In which country has there been a rise in real national income per head?
(a) A   (b) B   (c) C   (d) D   (e) E

4  Which of the following would not be included in measurements of national income?
(a) salaries of government ministers
(b) salaries of teachers
(c) imputed value for rent in owner-occupied houses
(d) income received for unemployment benefit
(e) salaries of army officers

Questions 5 and 6 refer to the following data.

| | |
|---|---|
| Net National Product at market prices | £30,000 m |
| Net National Product at factor cost | £25,000 m |
| Gross National Product at factor cost | £22,000 m |
| Gross Domestic Product at factor cost | £18,000 m |
| Residual error | £ 2,000 m |

5  What is the value of the allowance for net property income from abroad?
(a) £8000 m   (b) £5000 m   (c) £3000 m
(d) £4000 m   (e) £2000 m

6  What is the value of indirect taxes?
(a) £8000 m
(b) £5000 m

(c) £4000 m
(d) £2000 m
(e) impossible to calculate from the data given

7  Welfare is unlikely to be considered to have increased if a rise in measured national income involves:
(a) a reduction in working hours
(b) more goods being made available for consumption
(c) a rise in the level of employment
(d) better nutrition and health standards
(e) damage to the environment

8  A firm produces modems. All components cost the firm £100 per unit. Each modem sells at £200. Labour costs are £50 per unit. There are no other costs. Profit is therefore £50 per unit. What is the value added per unit by the firm?
(a) £350   (b) £200   (c) £150   (d) £100   (e) £50

9  Income which is not recorded because people do not declare the income received in their tax returns is known as:
(a) the non-marketed economy
(b) the consumption economy
(c) transfer payments
(d) the black economy
(e) the liquid economy

10  The 'value added' by British Nuclear Fuels is:
(a) included in the national accounts because processing nuclear waste involves economic activity,
(b) included in the national accounts because it helps preserve the environment,
(c) excluded from the national accounts because their product is an economic 'bad'.
(d) excluded from the national accounts because people do not buy nuclear waste,
(e) excluded from the national accounts because BNF's finances are provided by the government.

## Answers

### Exercise 1

1  (a) £8 m— the difference between values at market price and those at factor cost.
   (b) £5 m— National income is Net National Product at factor cost. Capital consumption is the difference between values measured as gross and those measured net.
   (c) £2 m— the difference between values concerned with domestic activity and those concerned with national activity.

2  (a) £200 b— depreciation is the fall in value of the capital stock.
   (b) £300 b— net output is total output (£500 b) less depreciation (£200 b).

**3** (a) £287,248 i.e $C + I + G + X$.

(b) GDFCF = building new factories, buying new machinery.

(c) Companies have been reducing the value of stocks and work-in-progress during the accounting period.

(d) Above—1982 prices would have been higher than 1980 prices.

(e) £229,251 i.e. $C + I + G + X - M$.

(f) GDP(MP) to NNP(FC) involves allowances for depreciation (G to N), indirect taxes and subsidies (MP to FC) and net property income from abroad (D to N).

**4** (a) £490 m—the company's sales or turnover. The value of its goods and services as they 'left the factory'.

(b) £299 m. This represents the value of materials, services and energy that the company used but which had been produced by other organisations.

(c) Value added is £191 m—the difference between values when they enter the firm and when they leave.

(d) Value added is difference between sales revenue and cost of bought in materials, services and energy. Profit is the difference between sales revenue and total costs.

(e) Wages and salaries (£108 m), interest payable on borrowed money (£12 m), depreciation allowance to replace worn out machinery (£25 m) leaving a profit before tax of £46 m.

(f) Corporation Tax took £18m, dividends paid to their shareholders accounted for £14 m, leaving £14 m to be added to the company reserves.

**5** £175,000 = 500 × 350. Value added per computer = £350. Labour costs are not deducted in the calculation of value added—they are part of the activity of the firm.

**6** + £18,300. Transfer payments should be ignored, i.e. the £3500 social security and the £1300 provided by the government for the training scheme. Undistributed profits should be included as the income was earned as a result of economic activity.

**7**

| Activity | Included in national income |
|---|---|
| (a) National Savings interest | No |
| (b) Winnings at bingo | No |
| (c) Salaries of civil servants | Yes |
| (d) Owner occupiers' 'rent' | Yes |
| (e) Furniture profits | Yes |
| (f) Undistributed profits | Yes |
| (g) Unemployment benefits | No |
| (h) Gifts to charities | No |
| (i) Profits of the self-employed | Yes |
| (j) Rent paid by council tenants | Yes |

**8** The value of indirect taxes is about x8 that of subsidies. In 1980 the difference amounted to £32 b in Britain.

**9** (a) Profits generated by British owned companies operating overseas.

(b) Not related to specific economic activity—it refers to activity that cannot be allocated elsewhere.

(c) Wages paid to civil servants.

**10** Consumption—about half. Exports and investment expenditure change the most.

**11** (a) Adding up (i) total value added output, (ii) total expenditure and (iii) total incomes.

(b) $C + I + G + X$.

(c) Unrecorded economic activity, e.g. a plumber doing a job and being paid in cash which will not be recorded in his accounts.

(d) Expenditure of income earned in the black economy will be traced, but the source of the income will not.

(e) Expenditure and incomes data suffers from short-term fluctuations (e.g. back-pay settlements and seasonal expenditure changes).

(f) An increase in the proportion of income that is saved.

**12** Suggested essay plan.

Introduction: Definition of terms (a) Economic activity. Three ways (i) output, (ii) expenditure, (iii) incomes. Seen with reference to simple diagram of circular flow. Brief outline of main items included.

Main paragraphs: (with examples from, say, incomes approach) (i) double counting—transfer earnings, (ii) black economy, (iii) imputed value for owner-occupiers' rent, (iv) undistributed profits of companies, (v) stock appreciation, (vi) non-marketed output—home production.

Conclusion.

## Exercise 2

**1**

| Situation | Raise national income | Standard of living or welfare change |
|---|---|---|
| (a) War | Rise | Limited by (i) extra work for women, (ii) longer hours of work, (iii) citizens suffering from 'human depreciation', e.g. through neglect of education, (iv) war profiteers, (v) blitz and evacuation. |
| (b) OPEC's oil | Rise | Limited by uneven distribution of incomes. |
| (c) Sellafield | Rise | Sellafield processes 'bads', i.e. radioactive waste, which arises from the production of goods valued by society e.g. electricity and hospital X-rays. |
| (d) Tasmania | Rise | Limited by subjective valuation of the externalities involved in such schemes. |
| (e) Council houses | Nil | Council house rent income replaced by 'imputed value' in accounts. Welfare increased if people value owner-occupancy, reduced for those on longer waiting lists. |
| (f) Crop spray | Rise | Limited by expenditure on health and medical research. |
| (g) New jobs | Rise | Outright increase in standards of living and welfare. |

**2** Information about inflation rates between 1975 and 1985. Information about changes in taxation and other direct deductions from pay.

**3** (a) Very little without information about population levels.
(b) Still not very much, although GNP/head measures a starting point (see *Unit 10.7*).

**4** Suggested essay plan.
Introduction:  Definition of terms (i) National income, (ii) Welfare (standard of living).
Main paragraphs:  See *Unit 10.7* with appropriate examples. Other methods e.g. quality of life indicators, goods/1000 of the population comparisons.
Conclusion.

## Multiple choice answers

**1** (c) See *10.2*.
**2** (a) Activity in (a) happens outside Britain, appears only in national measures.
**3** (c) Up 10% overall.
**4** (d) Unemployment benefit is a transfer payment, not received as a result of economic activity.
**5** (d) It is the difference between national and domestic measures.
**6** (e) MP to FC involves an allowance for indirect taxes and subsidies.
**7** (e) Pollution is a cost of growth.
**8** (d) Value added = sales value less cost of components.
**9** (d) Black economy refers to unrecorded economic activity.
**10** (a) All economic activity, whatever is being made, is included.

# UNIT 11 Determination of the level of economic activity

## 11.1 Preview

1 The level of national income depends on the level of expenditure, production or income in the economy over a certain period of time.
2 The components of expenditure, production and income were introduced in *Unit 10*.
3 The level of economic activity determines the extent to which the government will be able to achieve its major macroeconomic objectives.
4 A change in the level of economic activity will be caused by changes in the relationship of the various components of expenditure, production or income.

## 11.2 The circular flow of income

1 It is helpful to envisage economic activity as a circular flow of income and expenditure.
2 This circular flow concept is based on two relationships.
(a) One person's expenditure creates income for someone else.
(b) The receipt of income stimulates further expenditure.
So, Expenditure → Income → Expenditure → Income, and so on.
3 This situation is represented in Figure 11.1. For simplicity it is assumed initially that there is:
(a) no government activity
(b) no foreign trade
(c) just two sectors, namely households (consumers and providers of labour) and producers (employers of labour and producers of goods and services).

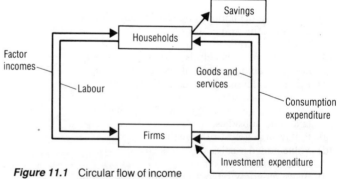

**Figure 11.1** Circular flow of income

*Observations from Figure 11.1*
☐ Households receive income from their employers. They can either spend their income on consumption goods or save it.
So Y = C + S
where Y = income, C = consumption, S = savings

☐ Expenditure in this system can arise either from consumption expenditure or from firms' investment expenditure which is financed out of past savings.

So Ex = C + I

where Ex = expenditure, C = consumption, I = investment

☐ As long as planned savings in the economy equal planned investment there will be no tendency for the level of economic activity to change.

4 **The velocity of circulation** in an economy is the number of times income is received and spent within a given time period.

## 11.3 Injections and withdrawals

1 In an open economy (one which participates in international trade) with government activity (i.e. government expenditure and taxation) producers and consumers have further alternatives for the allocation of their incomes and expenditure.

2 **Injections** into the circular flow arise when expenditure is undertaken that has not been generated by the receipt of current income. Injections can be:
   (a) *Investment expenditure* (I)—e.g. producers spending money on new factories and machinery.
   (b) *Export expenditure* (X)—e.g. foreigners' purchases of British produced medical supplies.
   (c) *Government expenditure* (G)—e.g. social security payments or defence expenditure.

3 **Withdrawals** from the circular flow (or leakages) arise when income received is not passed on as expenditure within the circular flow in the same time period. Withdrawals can be:
   (a) *Savings* (S)—e.g. deposits in Building Societies, contributions to pension or life assurance schemes.
   (b) *Imports* (M)—e.g. British purchases of Japanese made video-recorders.
   (c) *Taxes* (T)—e.g. income tax, value added tax.

*Observations from Figure 11.2*
   ☐ The lines represent money flows.
   ☐ Firms can be involved with all forms of withdrawals and injections but households rarely cause export earnings.
   ☐ The level of economic activity will clearly be influenced by the relative values of all withdrawals and injections in a given period of time.

4 Although there are clearly links between some of the components of withdrawals and injections it is fundamental to the theory of national income determination that they are seen as separate variables.

5 In practice, government spending tends to exceed taxation, the balance of payments rarely balances and current savings do not equal the level of current investment expenditure.

## 11.4 Equilibrium level of national income

1 **Equilibrium** occurs when there are no forces at work in the economy causing the level of economic activity to change.

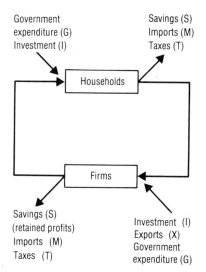

**Figure 11.2** Injections and withdrawals

2 This will occur in two circumstances:
   (a) *when total expenditure equals total income*
      i.e. Ex = Y
   (b) *when planned injections equals planned withdrawals*
      i.e. I + G + X = S + M + T

## Exercise 1

1 If in an economy:
  Exports = £100m, Imports = £50m, Investment = £200m,
  Savings = £150 m, Government spending = £100 m and
  Taxes = £150m (in a given period of time), would you
  expect the level of economic activity to be rising or falling?
  Explain your answer.

2 Find a copy of the latest National Income Accounts (e.g.
  from *CSO Annual Abstract of Statistics* or *Social Trends*)
  and find:
  (a) the difference between the level of government expendi-
      ture and taxation receipts,
  (b) the difference between exports and imports.
  And, much more difficult:
  (c) the level of savings and the level of investment
      expenditure,
  (d) what would these values suggest should be happening
      to the general level of economic activity? Is it
      happening?

3 For each of the following (*ceteris paribus*) state whether they
  should be considered to be:
      (i) injections
      (ii) withdrawals
      (iii) neither injections nor withdrawals
  (a) Increase in Value Added Tax.
  (b) The purchase in Britain of a Volkswagen Golf car.
  (c) Construction of the M25, London's orbital motorway.
  (d) Depositing £100 in a building society account.
  (e) The purchase of British made new machinery by a
      British firm.
  (f) American tourists visiting London.
  (g) Increase in the amount of tax paid by North Sea oil
      producers.
  (h) Firms increasing their reserves by retaining more of
      their profits.
  (i) A bank robbery, after which the money is taken out of
      the country.
  (j) The purchase of British made consumer goods by
      British households.
  (k) The sale of British made computer hardware to New
      Zealand.
  (l) Insurance premiums paid by foreign ship owners to
      Lloyds of London.

4 For each of the following (*ceteris paribus*) state what you
  think is the likely effect on the level of employment in a time
  period of one year.
  (a) British consumers buy more foreign cars in place of
      British made cars.

(b) The government lowers the level of income tax.
(c) Government plans to spend more on defence expenditure.
(d) The Bank of England lowers the rate of interest.

## 11.5 Diagrammatic representation of national income equilibrium

1 **Total final expenditure = National income (Ex = Y)**
*Observations from Figure 11.3*
☐ Total final expenditure comprises C + I + G + X.
☐ As income rises so will the level of total final expenditure, as indicated by the Ex function.
☐ A 45° line simply joins points where the values on either axis are equal, in this case points where Ex = Y.
☐ The equilibrium level of national income occurs where the Ex function crosses the 45° line, i.e. at Y1.

2 **Injections = withdrawals (J = W)**
*Observations from Figure 11.4*
☐ The level of injections rises as the level of national income rises as indicated by the J function.
☐ The level of withdrawals increases as national income increases as indicated by the W function. At low levels of income the level of withdrawals may be negative, e.g. if households are running down their savings to pay for current consumption.
☐ The equilibrium level of national income is found at the point where the two functions intersect, i.e. at income level Y1.

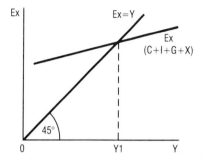

**Figure 11.3** National income equilibrium (Ex=Y)

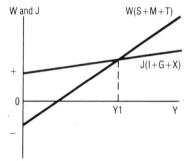

**Figure 11.4** National income equilibrium (J=W)

## Exercise 2

1 State what effect a rise in national income (*ceteris paribus*) would have on the following. Explain your answer.
(a) Government expenditure on social security payments.
(b) Government expenditure on health and education provision.
(c) Tax receipts from income tax.
(d) Tax receipts from Value Added Tax.
(e) Consumers' purchases of imports.
(f) Producers' purchases of imported raw materials.
(g) Producers' willingness and ability to export goods.
(h) Producers' willingness and ability to undertake investment expenditure. '
(i) The level of household savings.
(j) The level of consumption expenditure by households.
2 In the light of the answers produced in Question 1 do you think it was reasonable to draw the expenditure (Ex), Injections (J) and Withdrawals (W) functions as they are shown in Figures 11.3 and 11.4?

## 11.6 Changes in the level of economic activity

1 A change in the balance between planned total final expenditure and national income, and hence between planned injections and

planned withdrawals will destroy the equilibrium condition. There will be forces at work in the economy causing a change in the level of economic activity.

2

| Circumstance | National income |
|---|---|
| Total final expenditure rises | Rises |
| Total final expenditure falls | Falls |
| Injections exceed withdrawals | Rises |
| Withdrawals exceed injections | Falls |

## 11.7 The multiplier effect

1   A change in expenditure, or injections or withdrawals will cause a bigger change in the level of national income.
2   **The multiplier** is simply a number which relates the final change in national income to the expenditure change bringing it about. i.e. change in national income = multiplier × change in expenditure.
3   This multiple effect on the level of economic activity arises from the nature of the circular flow of income. For example, if local councils cut their expenditure on house building, incomes of firms building houses fall. They in turn employ fewer workers and buy fewer supplies from merchants so their incomes fall. They in turn undertake less expenditure and so on.

## 11.8 The size of the multiplier

1   The size of the multiplier depends on how much of any extra income that is received is passed on within the circular flow.
2   Specifically it is calculated as either:
    (a) the reciprocal of one minus the proportion of new income that is passed on as new expenditure within the circular flow, or
    (b) the reciprocal of the proportion of new income that is withdrawn from the circular flow.
3   **Marginal propensity** describes the proportion of new income that is allocated in a particular way, e.g. the *marginal propensity to consume* is the proportion of extra income that is spent on consumption expenditure. The *marginal propensity to save* is the proportion of extra income that is saved.
4   In a closed economy with no government activity the value of the multiplier will be:

$$\frac{1}{MPS} \quad \text{or} \quad \frac{1}{(1 - MPC)}$$

where   MPS = marginal propensity to save
MPC = marginal propensity to consume

5   In an open economy with government involvement the value of the multiplier will be:

$$\frac{1}{MPW} = \frac{1}{MPS + MPM + MPT}$$

or
$$\frac{1}{1 - MPC\,(1 - MPT_d) - MPM - MPT_i}$$

where MPW = marginal propensity to withdraw

MPS = marginal propensity to save

MPM = marginal propensity to buy imports

MPT = marginal propensity to pay taxes

MPC = marginal propensity to consume

$MPT_d$ = marginal propensity to pay direct taxes

$MPT_i$ = marginal propensity to pay indirect taxes

## Exercise 3

**1   British goods mean British jobs**

We continue to support British industry. More than 90% of 'St. Michael' clothing and home furnishing sold in Britain, Europe and other export markets is manufactured in the UK. More than 90% of our processed foodstuffs and those which can be grown in temperature climates is produced in the UK.

The BOC group, the National Freight consortium, Tibbett & Britten and Christian-Salvesen have developed for us exclusive transport systems that employ 2900 people.

Bovis construction, who have been building stores for us for nearly 60 years, employ 1500 people on our building sites.

In total Marks & Spencer and our suppliers employ 170,000 people in the UK producing, distributing and selling 'St. Michael' goods.

(Based on information from Marks & Spencer's *Annual Accounts 1983*)

(a) Identify any 'injections' to the circular flow from the passage.

(b) Why will more than the 170,000 people mentioned in the extract rely on the activities of Marks & Spencer for their employment?

**2   Essay**

Why will an increase in expenditure, whatever its source, cause an increase in national income that is greater than the original increase in expenditure?

## 11.9  Graphical representation of the multiplier

**1**   The multiplier in two examples (J = W)

*Observations from Figure 11.5*

☐ The original level of injections is J1.

☐ This gives an equilibrium level of national income of Y1, as at this level of income injections equals withdrawals.

☐ Injections rise to J2, the increase in injections being the distance between J1 and J2.

☐ Equilibrium national income increases to Y2.

☐ In both cases (1 and 2) the rise in national income is bigger

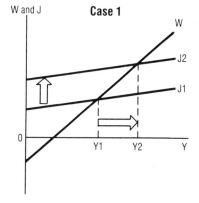

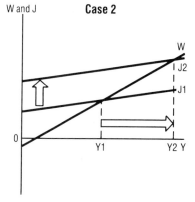

***Figure 11.5***  Graphical representation of multiplier effect using withdrawals and injections functions

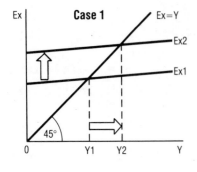

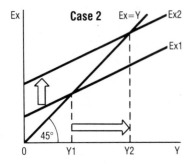

**Figure 11.6** Graphical representation of
multiplier effect using
expenditure functions

than the expenditure change bringing it about. In case 2 where the gradient of the withdrawals function is less, the value of the multiplier is larger.

2 The multiplier in two further examples (Ex = Y)
*Observations from Figure 11.6*
☐ The original expenditure function is Ex1. Equilibrium level of national income is Y1.
☐ If expenditure increases to Ex2, national income increases to Y2, the new equilibrium position.
☐ The rise in national income is bigger than the increase in expenditure bringing it about.
☐ In case 2 the multiplier is bigger than in case 1 as the gradient of the expenditure function is greater in case 2 than in case 1.

## Exercise 4

1 Assume you are dealing with a closed economy with no government intervention. The velocity of circulation within the economy is 1 per year. At the start of year 1 the economy is in equilibrium, planned savings equals planned investment at £20b per year. The marginal propensity to save is 0.5. At the start of year 2 planned investment rises by £8b.

| Time period | Planned I | Does S = I? | Is economy in equil.? | Cum.[1] rise in NY | Cum.[1] rise in S | Actual savings |
|---|---|---|---|---|---|---|
| 1 | 20 | Yes | Yes | — | — | 20 |
| 2 | 28 | No | No | 8 | — | 20 |
| 3 | 28 | No | No | 8 + 4 = 12 | 4 | 24 |
| 4 | 28 | | | | | |
| 5 | 28 | | | | | |
| 6 | 28 | | | | | |
| 7 | 28 | | | | | |

1 = cumulative

(a) Complete the table for the first seven years.
(b) *Ceteris paribus*, what will be the final cumulative rise in national income following the investment increase?
(c) When the multiplier process stops what will be the cumulative rise in actual savings?
(d) What is the value of the multiplier in this situation?

2 In the UK it is estimated that for an increase in national income of £1, firms save 18p, direct tax payments take 25p, personal savings take 6p, 10p is spent on imported goods and 10p is taken in indirect tax payments.
(a) On the basis of these figures what would be a reasonable estimate of the value of the multiplier in the real economy?

3 Assume a closed economy with no government intervention. Consumption is assumed to be a function of income and the level of consumption at different levels of income is found from the equation $C = 40 + (0.6)Y$ (where $C$ = consumption and $Y$ = income) Investment is assumed to be constant at all levels of income at £25m, so $I = 25$ (where $I$ = investment).
(a) What is the equilibrium level of national income?

(b) Show this situation on an income/expenditure diagram. Investment rises by £25m to £50m, so that I = 50.
(c) What is the new level of national income?
(d) Show the change in national income on your diagram.
(e) What is the value of the multiplier in this situation?

4 The original situation is as described in Question 3 above,

i.e. $$C = 40 + (0.6)Y$$
$$I = 25$$

(a) Draw the income/expenditure diagram again to show the equilibrium level of national income.
Savings now rise by £25m.
(b) What is now the equation of the consumption function?
(c) What is the new equilibrium level of national income?
(d) Draw this on the diagram to show the change in the level of national income.
(e) What is value of the multiplier in this situation?

5 **It looks like a billion dollar cup**
The bonanza from the 1986–87 America's Cup series is expected to be in the billion dollar range as the inflow of tourists swells to more than double its current level.

Research by the Western Australian Tourism Commission indicates that visitors during the Cup series could bring $600m to the State.

The multiplier effect associated with tourism is expected to boost this to more than $1.5b.

Seven major new hotels are being built, and other tourist developments are planned throughout the State. An additional 4000 jobs would be created from these developments.

(Based on information from *West Australian* 20.8.84)
(a) Explain what is meant by 'the multiplier effect associated with tourism'.
(b) What is the value of the tourism multiplier according to this article?
(c) What factors limit the size of the multiplier effect?

# 11.10 Deflationary and inflationary gaps

1 Deflationary and inflationary gaps describe the relationship between the actual level of national income, and the level of national income that would generate full employment, or more Generally achieve the government's macroeconomic objectives.

2 **A deflationary gap** refers to a situation where the actual level of economic activity is too low compared to the government target. The size of the gap is the shortfall of expenditure in the economy. A deflationary gap can be closed with reflationary policies.
*Observations from Figure 11.7*
☐ Ex 1 shows the actual expenditure function. Income is Y1 with this expenditure function.
☐ To reach the target level of income Y2, the expenditure function would have to rise to Ex2.
☐ This gap can be reduced with reflationary policies.

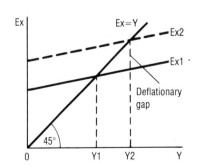

**Figure 11.7** A deflationary gap

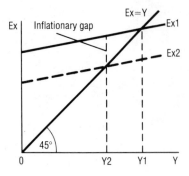

**Figure 11.8** An inflationary gap

3 **An inflationary gap** refers to a situation where the actual level of economic activity is too high compared to the government target. The size of the gap is the excess of expenditure in the economy. A deflationary or disinflationary policy will reduce an inflationary gap.

*Observations from Figure 11.8*

☐ Ex1 shows the actual level of expenditure. Income is Y1 at this level of expenditure.

☐ To reduce the level of income to the government target level of $\frac{1}{2}$, the expenditure function must be reduced to Ex2.

☐ This can be done with deflationary or disinflationary policies.

4 It is a mistake to view these gaps as static comparative positions. It may well be that a change in the level of economic activity will cause some change in the economy, e.g. a rise of economic activity might cause inflation, which in turn causes changes in the components of expenditure, e.g. savings, which changes the size of the gap. Thus, the gaps should be considered in a dynamic context and it is clear from this that government policy making is more complex than a simple analysis would suggest.

## 11.11 Additional concepts

1 **The savings/investment identity**

(a) In an equilibrium position, actual savings must equal actual investment (in a closed economy with no government activity).

$$Y = C + S \quad \text{(Income is either spent or saved)}$$
$$Ex = C + I \quad \text{(Expenditure is either consumption or investment)}$$

But in equilibrium

$$Ex = Y \quad \text{(Expenditure equals income in equilibrium)}$$

So $C + S = C + I$
So $\quad S = I$

(b) However, there is nothing to suggest that plans to invest will equal plans to save. Indeed, as investment expenditure and savings are done largely by different people for different reasons it would be coincidence if they were equal.

(c) So, if plans to invest differ from plans to save then the level of economic activity will move from one equilibrium position to another. At the original and final level of economic activity, actual investment will equal actual savings.

(d) It is clear that some plans are not fulfilled, e.g. firms may experience an unplanned increase in investment through stock increases if consumers save more than anticipated and sales are correspondingly lower than expected.

(e) The phrase *ex ante* is sometimes used to describe planned or intended activity, *ex post* to describe actual or realised activity.

2 **The paradox of thrift**

(a) The apparent contradiction of decisions to save more, causing the level of savings to fall, is an application of the concept of *ex ante* and *ex post* situations.

(b) If people plan to increase savings (*ceteris paribus*) the level of national income will fall. At the lower level of income people cannot afford to save as much as before.

*Observations from Figure 11.9*
- ☐ Planned savings rise from S1 to S2.
- ☐ As a result national income falls from Y1 to Y2.
- ☐ At the lower level of income Y2 the level of savings is only S3.
- ☐ Plans to save more lead to a reduction in actual savings.

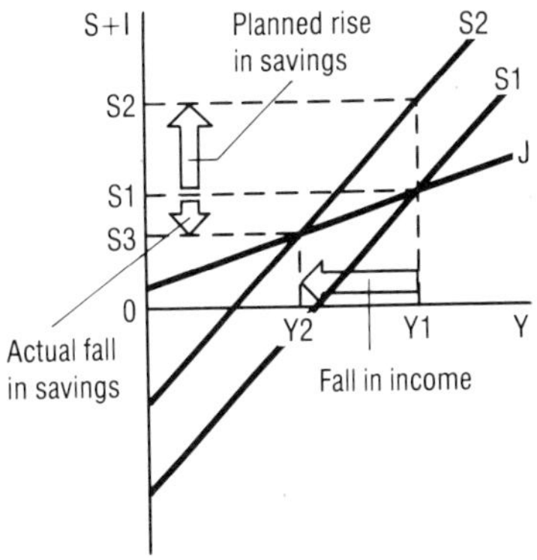

**3   The balanced budget multiplier**

(a) If the government changes the level of taxation and government expenditure by the same amount, the effect on the level of economic activity will not be neutral.

(b) An increase in government expenditure will, on its own, increase national income through a full multiplier effect. However, an increase in taxation will not reduce the level of national income by the same amount as some of the extra tax payments will be met out of savings, i.e. money that is already withdrawn from the circular flow.

(c) The combined effect of an equal change in tax and government expenditure is to change the level of economic activity by the size of the budget change, i.e. a £10b rise in government expenditure coupled with a £10b rise in taxation will lead to a £10b rise in national income.

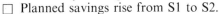

**Figure 11.9**   The paradox of thrift

## Exercise 5

1   If government expenditure rises by £Xm and the value of the multiplier is 4 (*ceteris paribus*) what will be the final change in the level of national income?

2   In an economy, for an extra pound of income received people save 20p, buy 20p of imports and have to pay 20p in taxes.
   (a) What is the marginal propensity to consume home produced goods?
   (b) What is the marginal propensity to withdraw?
   (c) What is the value of the multiplier?

3   In a closed economy with no government activity the marginal propensity to consume is 0.75. The equilibrium level of national income is £40b. By how much must expenditure rise if the equilibrium level of national income is to rise to £50b?

   A government feels that the level of national income is £6000b too low for its particular policy objectives. The marginal propensity to withdraw is 0.33. At cabinet, the Chancellor of the Exchequer suggests £2000b be injected into the economy, the Prime Minister suggests £3000b be injected, the Minister for Trade suggests £18,000b, and the Transport Secretary suggests £600b. Who, if anyone, was right?

   In an economy the marginal propensity to import is 0.2. If the level of national income rises by £200m what will happen to the level of imports?

6 In a closed economy, the marginal propensity to consume is 0.8.
  (a) If income tax is raised by £100m, what will happen to the level of consumption expenditure?
  (b) If the multiplier is 5 what will be the final fall in national income following this decrease in consumption expenditure?
  (c) If government expenditure was also raised by £100m and the multiplier was 5, what would be the rise in national income from this government expenditure increase alone?
  (d) If the tax increase and government spending increase happened at the same time, what would happen to the level of national income?

7 **Essay**
In a closed economy with no government involvement, savings always equal investment. How then, does the level of economic activity ever change?

## Review

### Unit 11 will have helped provide answers to the following questions

1 What are the two basic relationships that underpin the concept of a circular flow of income?
2 What are the injections and withdrawals that relate to the circular flow?
3 What are the two basic conditions for equilibrium in the circular flow?
4 Why will a change in expenditure cause a bigger change in the level of national income?
5 What are inflationary and deflationary gaps? What policies are appropriate for each type of gap?

### Unit 11 has introduced the following terminology
Balanced budget multiplier
Circular flow of income
Closed economy
Deflationary gap
Equilibrium (of national income)
*Ex ante*
*Ex post*
Inflationary gap
Injections
Marginal propensity
Multiplier
Open economy
Paradox of thrift
Savings/investment identity
Velocity of circulation
Withdrawals

### Multiple choice questions

1 In a closed economy with no government intervention, the level of consumption expenditure varies with output according to the equation $C = a + bY$ where C is the level of consumption, a is the level of consumption at zero income, b is the marginal propensity to consume, and Y is the level of income. If consumption at zero income is 100, and the value of the multiplier is 4 the consumption function will have an equation of:
  (a) $C = 100 + (0.75)Y$,
  (b) $C = 100 + (0.25)Y$,
  (c) $C = 100 + (0.5)Y$,
  (d) $C = 75 + Y$,
  (e) $C = 25 + Y$

Questions 2 and 3 refer to Figure 11.10 which shows the savings and investment functions in a closed economy with no government activity.

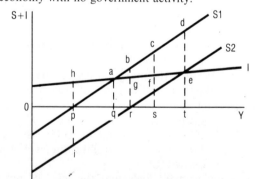

**Figure 11.10** Savings and investment functions

2 If the level of savings in the economy is S1, what is the equilibrium level of income?
  (a) Op  (b) Oq  (c) Or  (d) Os  (e) Ot

3 If savings fall from S1 to S2 the value of the multiplier can be found from:
  (a) rt/da  (b) qt/de  (c) pr/bc  (d) pq/pr  (e) de/qt

4 If the equilibrium level of national income in an economy is below the level of national income desired by the government to achieve its macro-

economic objective there is said to exist in the economy:
(a) a reflationary gap
(b) a deflationary gap
(c) an inflationary gap
(d) a devaluationary gap
(e) a Watford gap

5  The table shows the levels of investment, savings, taxation and government spending at various levels of income. There is no foreign trade (Figures in £b.)

| Income | Investment | Savings | Government spending | Taxation |
|--------|-----------|---------|---------------------|----------|
| 500 | 120 | 100 | 90 | 50 |
| 600 | 140 | 120 | 85 | 60 |
| 700 | 160 | 140 | 80 | 70 |
| 800 | 180 | 160 | 75 | 80 |
| 900 | 200 | 180 | 70 | 90 |

What is the equilibrium level of income?
(a) £500b  (b) £600b  (c) £700b  (d) £800b
(e) £900b

6  In a closed economy with no government activity there exists a deflationary gap of $4000m. If the marginal propensity to save is 0.2 what must be the change in investment expenditure to close the gap?
(a) + $800m  (b) − $800m  (c) + $400m
(d) − $400m  (e) + $400m

7  Which of the following is a withdrawal from the circular flow?
(a) taxation
(b) government expenditure
(c) exports
(d) investment expenditure
(e) consumption expenditure

8  In which of the following situations would the level of national income remain unchanged?
(a) when withdrawals exceeded injections
(b) when expenditure equals injections
(c) when withdrawals equal injections
(d) when expenditure is greater than income
(e) when withdrawals equal leakages

9  Which of the following is least likely to happen when the level of national income rises?
(a) savings will fall
(b) taxation receipts will rise
(c) exports will rise
(d) imports will rise
(e) government expenditure on social security will fall

10  If, in an economy, the marginal propensity to save is 0.1, the marginal propensity to buy imports is 0.2, and the marginal propensity to pay taxes is 0.1, what is the value of the multiplier?
(a) 0.4  (b) 0.5  (c) 2.5  (d) 2  (e) 10

# Answers

## Exercise 1

1  Rising. Injections $(I + G + X) = £400m$. Withdrawals $(S + M + T) = £350m$.

2  Own research.

3

| Activity | Injection/ withdrawal | Reasons |
|----------|----------------------|---------|
| (a) VAT | Withdrawal | Taxation |
| (b) VW car | Withdrawal | Import |
| (c) M25 | Injection | Government investment expenditure |
| (d) Deposit | Withdrawal | Saving |
| (e) Machine | Injection | Investment in fixed capital |
| (f) Tourist | Injection | 'Invisible' inflow from tourism |
| (g) Oil tax | Withdrawal | Taxation |
| (h) Retained profits | Withdrawal | Corporate savings |
| (i) Robbery | Neither | If the money was being saved in the banks, it has now gone out of the country |
| (j) Consumer purchases | Neither | Consumption expenditure is the basic element of the circular flow of income and expenditure |
| (k) NZ computer | Injection | Export |
| (l) Insurance premiums | Injection | 'Invisible' export earnings |

4

| | | |
|---|---|---|
| (a) Fall | Less employment in the British car industry plus multiplier effect. | |
| (b) Rise | Rise in disposable income increases expenditure and creates demand for goods and services. | |
| (c) Rise | Direct creation of jobs in appropriate industries plus multiplier effect. | |
| (d) Rise | Likely to lead to less savings, and greater investment expenditure, increasing the level of economic activity. | |

## Exercise 2

1

| | | |
|---|---|---|
| (a) Fall | Less employment, more earned incomes | |
| (b) Rise | More finance available | |
| (c) Rise | Higher incomes, more income tax receipts | |
| (d) Rise | More expenditure, more VAT receipts | |
| (e) Rise | Increased expenditure on all goods and services some of which will be imports | |
| (f) Rise | Increased production requires more imported raw materials | |
| (g) Unclear | Some products may switch out of exports to satisfy the buoyant home demand, others may be encouraged to export with their increased profits or more able to export because investment has made their goods competitive | |
| (h) Rise | Bigger profits provide increased finance for the expenditure, and more activity in the economy increases profitable opportunities. | |
| (i) Rise | See *Unit 12* | |
| (j) Rise | See *Unit 12* | |

2 (a) Expenditure $= C + I + G + X$ i.e a,b,g,h,i
above—overall rise with rise in incomes.
(b) Injections $= I + G + X$ i.e. a, b, g, h above—
overall rise with rise in incomes.
(c) Withdrawals $= S + M + T$ i.e. c,d,e,f,i above—
overall rise with rise in incomes.

## Exercise 3

1 (a) Exports and investment expenditure.
(b) Multiplier effect of M&S economic activity.

2 Suggested essay plan
Definition of terms: National Income—a measure
of the level of economic activity. Sources of
expenditure (i.e. $C + I + G + X$). Equilibrium
condition destroyed by an increase in
expenditure.
Main paragraphs: Multiplier effect based on:
i) circular flow ii) level of withdrawals from
circular flow. Size depends on 1/mpw $dNY = m$
$\times dEx$. Graphical representation.
Conclusion. Any injection leads to multiple
increase in national income.

## Exercise 4

1 (a)

| Time | Planned I | Does S = 1? | Equil? | Cum dNY | Cum dS | Actual S |
|------|-----------|-------------|--------|---------|--------|----------|
| 1 | 20 | Yes | Yes | — | — | 20 |
| 2 | 28 | No | No | 8 | — | 20 |
| 3 | 28 | No | No | 12 | 4 | 24 |
| 4 | 28 | No | No | 14 | 6 | 26 |
| 5 | 28 | No | No | 15 | 7 | 27 |
| 6 | 28 | No | No | 15.5 | 7.5 | 27.5 |
| 7 | 28 | No | No | 15.75 | 7.75 | 27.75 |
| END | 28 | Yes | Yes | 16 | 8 | 28 |

(b) 16
(c) 8 The multiplier stops when $S = I$ again.
(d) 2 Multiplier $= 1/mps = 1/0.5 = 2$

2 69% of extra income is withdrawn, giving a
multiplier (1/mpw) of 1.45. In advanced economies
with significant intervention from governments
multipliers tend to be between 1 and 2.

3 (a) $C = 40 + (0.6)Y$ $I = 25$
In equilibrium $Ex = Y$
$Ex = C + I$
So $Y = 40 + (0.6)Y + 25$
$(0.4)Y = 65$ Therefore $Y = 162.5$

(b)

| Y | C | C + I |
|-----|-----|-----|
| 0 | 40 | 65 |
| 100 | 100 | 125 |
| 200 | 160 | 185 |
| 300 | 220 | 245 |
| 400 | 280 | 305 |

Add 45° line (joining 0,0 to 400,400). Point of
intersection coincides with $Y = 162.5$

(c) 225. $dEx = 25$ Multiplier $= 2.5$ $dNY = 62.5$
(d) Expenditure function shifts 25 upwards at all
income levels
(e) 2.5.

4 (a) As in Question 3
(b) $C = 15 + (0.6)Y$
(c) 100
(d) Expenditure function shifts downwards by 25 at
each level of income.
(e) Still 2.5–mps still at 0.4.

5 (a) Tourists spend money which generates incomes
for people providing tourist services, who in
turn spend more and generate further incomes
and so on.
(b) 2.5—$1500m $\div$ $600m.
(c) The level of mpw i.e. proportion of extra
income saved, claimed in taxes, and spent
outside the economy.

## Exercise 5

1 $+ £4Xm$     $dNY = m \times dEx$     $dNY = 4 \times X$
2 (a) 0.4
(b) 0.6
(c) 1.66 Multiplier is 1/mps
3 £2.5b. Multiplier is 4. dNY needed is £10b.
4 Chancellor of the Exchequer. dNY required is
£6000m. Multiplier is 3.
5 $+ £40m$. Income up £200m, for each £ extra 20p
imports, i.e. £200m $\times 0.2 = £40m$
6 (a) Fall by £80m. $0.8 \times £100m$
(b) Fall by £400m. £80m $\times 5$
(c) Rise by £500m. £100m $\times 5$
(d) Rise by £100m. The balanced budget multiplier
at work (see Unit 11.11).
7 Suggested essay plan.
Definition of terms: Closed economy, no
government involvement leaves $C + I$
expenditure components, and income can only
be spent on C or saved. See Unit 11.11 for
identity.
Main paragraphs: Only identical ex-post. Plans
important. Will differ. $I > S$ then NY will rise.
$I < S$ then NY will fall. Incorporate multiplier
effect. Use paradox of thrift as example.
Conclusion.

## Multiple choice answers

1 (a) $C = a + bY$. $a = 100$. Multiplier $= 1/1 - b$.
2 (b) Oq is where $W = J$.
3 (b) Multiplier is dNY divided by dEx.
4 (b) Actual NY $<$ Target NY.
5 (e) At £900b     $S + T = I + G = £270b$.
6 (a) Multiplier is 5. Required $dNY = £4000m$.
7 (a) By definition.
8 (c) By definition.
9 (a) Savings rise with rises in national income.
10 (c) Multiplier is $1/mpw = 1/0.4 = 2.5$.

# Consumption, savings and investment

# UNIT 12

## 12.1 Preview

1  *Unit 11* explained that the relative values of components of expenditure and injections and withdrawals were important for the determination of the level of economic activity.
2  *Unit 12* investigates three of those variables: consumption expenditure, investment expenditure and savings.
3  Households are faced with a basic decision whether to spend or save their incomes. Savings are usually channelled through financial institutions to be available for the finance of investment expenditure.
4  Consumption expenditure is the biggest component of total final expenditure, but is relatively stable. Investment expenditure is subject to much greater fluctuations.

## 12.2 Definitions

1  **Consumption expenditure** is money spent on new goods and services which give immediate benefit, e.g. on food, clothes and leisure activities.

2  **Investment expenditure** is money spent on the purchase of capital goods which provide a flow of future benefits, e.g. on machinery and buildings.

3  **Saving occurs** when households refrain from spending some of their current incomes.

4  The distinction between some forms of consumption expenditure and investment expenditure is somewhat arbitrary, e.g. a washing machine is expected to provide a flow of future benefits to a household but is classified as a consumer good (or more accurately as a consumer durable good).

## Exercise 1

1  Classify the following activities as either:
  i) savings
  ii) consumption expenditure
  iii) investment expenditure

  (a) £100 deposited by an individual in a building society account.
  (b) The purchase of a new house by a household.
  (c) The purchase of a new colour TV set by a household.
  (d) The purchase of raw materials for increasing stock levels by a firm.
  (e) The purchase by a firm of a new machine.

(f) Employees contributions to their pension fund.
(g) Expenditure by the government on wages for civil servants.
(h) Retained profits by a firm which are added to its reserves.
(i) Purchase by an individual of Premium Bonds.
(j) Expenditure by a firm on training apprentices.

## 12.3 The consumption function

**1   The consumption function**
This shows how the level of consumption expenditure varies according to the level of income. The level of income is clearly an important factor in determining the level of consumption expenditure.

**2   A linear consumption function**
*Observations from Figure 12.1*
☐ The 45° line shows points of equal consumption and income $(C = Y)$.
☐ If the consumption function (C1) is above the 45° line, this indicates consumption expenditure is greater than income, i.e. households are using up past savings or borrowing. They are said to be dis-saving.
☐ If the consumption function (C1) is below the 45° line, not all income is being spent on consumption expenditure, i.e. households are saving.
☐ Such a consumption function will have an equation of
$$C = a + bY$$
where C = the level of consumption
a = the level of consumption at zero income
b = the marginal propensity to consume
Y = the level of income.

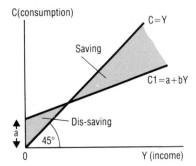

**Figure 12.1**   Linear consumption function

**3   The propensities to consume**
(a) *Marginal propensity to consume (MPC)* is defined as the extra consumption undertaken as a result of receiving an extra £1 of income. It is therefore equal to the gradient of the consumption function.
(b) *Average propensity to consume (APC)* is the proportion of income spent on consumption, and is calculated as:
$$\frac{\text{total consumption}}{\text{total income}}$$
It is equal to the gradient of a line from the origin to the relevant point on a consumption function indicating the level of consumption at a particular level of income.
*Observations from Figure 12.2*
☐ APC at income level Y1 is the gradient of line OP.
☐ APC at income level Y2 is the gradient of line OQ.
☐ MPC at all levels of income is the gradient of the consumption function, i.e. MPC = b(C = a + bY).

**4   Short run and long run consumption functions**
(a) In the short run households will allow the level of consumption to be affected by many factors. The consumption will be

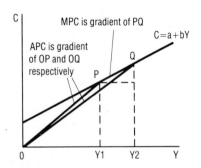

**Figure 12.2**   MPC and APC

less closely related to changes in income, i.e. it will be flatter.
(b) In the long run the consumption function will be closer to the 45° line, as households find they have run out of past savings or sources of borrowing, or have built up sufficient pools of savings.

*Observations from Figure 12.3*
☐ C1 indicates a short run consumption function.
☐ C2 indicates a long run consumption function.

**5 What measurement of income is most appropriate?**
(a) *Real or money income?*
If money incomes rise, people may, in the short run, feel better off even if prices rise at the same time. Such people are said to suffer from *money illusion*, i.e. they have changed their habits on the basis of a change in money income even though real income has not changed.
(b) *Actual versus permanent income?*
Friedman suggested that people have a long term view of income changes over their lifetime, and are, therefore, slow to react to changes in actual income levels. A view of permanent income levels would explain the behaviour of typical households who spend a lot when they are young, save more in middle age to allow them to maintain their living standards when income drops when they retire.
(c) *Gross or disposable income?*
Disposable income (take-home pay) is likely to be less than gross income because of deductions for taxation and national insurance contributions. Long term expenditure plans have to be based on disposable income levels.

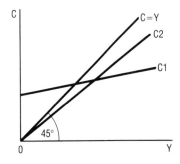

**Figure 12.3** Short run and long run consumption functions

# 12.4 The savings function

**1** As household income can either be spent or saved the savings function can be determined from the consumption function.

**2 The consumption and savings functions**

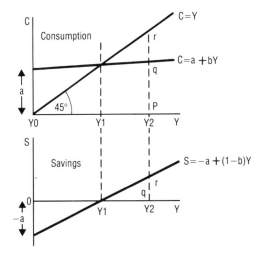

**Figure 12.4** Consumption and savings

*Observations from Figure 12.4*
☐ Where consumption crosses the 45° line, savings = zero.
☐ At income level Y0 consumption is 'a' and savings '− a'.
☐ At income level Y2 consumption is 'pq', savings 'qr'.
☐ The gradient of the savings function is $(1 − b)$. Adding the savings and consumption functions would produce the 45° line.

---

## Exercise 2

| Income | Consumption |
|--------|-------------|
| 0      | 100         |
| 50     | 125         |
| 100    | 150         |
| 150    | 175         |
| 200    | 200         |
| 250    | 240         |
| 300    | 280         |
| 350    | 305         |
| 400    | 330         |

1 The information (see left) refers to a household's consumption at various levels of income (£/month).
(a) Plot the consumption function. Add a 45° line.
(b) What is the level of saving at income levels £0, £100, £200, £300, £400?
(c) Draw the savings function.
(d) What is the level of average propensity to consume at income levels £200, £300, £400.
(e) What is the level of marginal propensity to consume at income levels £150, £250, £350?

---

## 12.5 Shifts in the consumption function

1 The level of income is not the only factor that influences the level of consumption expenditure.
2 These other factors include:
(a) *Time of year*—e.g. before Christmas and in summer holiday time.
(b) *Change in climate*—e.g. more expenditure on fuel in cold weather.
(c) *Expectations of price increases*—e.g. in the period shortly before the budget.
(d) *Lack of availability of goods*—e.g. in wartime consumer goods are in short supply as resources are concentrated on weapons.
(e) *A change in credit terms*—e.g. a reduction of rates of interest would be expected to lead to more bank borrowing to finance consumption expenditure.
(f) *A change in savings habits* (see *Unit 12.6*).
3 A change in any of these factors would cause a shift in the position of the consumption function.

## 12.6 Shifts in the savings function

1 Saving can be divided into:
(a) *Contractual saving*—i.e. saving that involves regular contributions or payments, e.g. pension schemes or life assurance policies.
(b) *Discretionary saving*—i.e. saving based on the household's judgement of current economic circumstances.
2 Further types of saving are:
(a) *Transactions motive savings*—i.e. savings to finance known future transactions or purchases, e.g. expenditure later on in the week following pay receipt on a Friday.
(b) *Precautionary motive savings*—i.e. savings to cover unknown

future transactions or purchases, e.g. money to meet accidents or emergencies.

(c) *Speculative motive savings*—i.e. savings to generate income through interest, dividends or capital gains.

3   Of these contractual and transactions motive savings tend to be relatively stable. The others are influenced by a number of factors which include:

(a) *Changes in the rate of interest*—e.g. cuts in the rate of interest reduce the incentive for people to save.

(b) *Inflation:*
   i) inflation may be taken as an indication of general economic uncertainty and thus cause people to raise their precautionary motive savings,
   ii) inflation may cause money rates of interest to rise and thus cause people to save more,
   iii) inflation lowers the real rate of return on savings making it more of a sacrifice to postpone consumption expenditure.

(c) *The general view of economic circumstances*—e.g. rising unemployment may cause a rise in savings as people become more unsettled about the future.

4   A change in any of these factors will cause a shift in the savings function.

# Exercise 3

1   Levels of consumption expenditure and personal disposable income between 1972 and 1982 in Britain.

| Year | Consumption expenditure (£m) | Personal disposable income (£m) | Inflation (% change in RPI) | Unemployment (%) |
|------|------------------------------|----------------------------------|------------------------------|-------------------|
| 1972 | 40,500 | 44,830 | 7.1 | 3.6 |
| 1973 | 46,150 | 51,980 | 9.2 | 2.6 |
| 1974 | 53,087 | 60,343 | 16.1 | 2.5 |
| 1975 | 65,339 | 74,659 | 24.9 | 3.9 |
| 1976 | 75,792 | 85,814 | 15.1 | 5.2 |
| 1977 | 86,712 | 96,919 | 12.1 | 5.2 |
| 1978 | 99,596 | 113,319 | 8.4 | 5.6 |
| 1979 | 118,383 | 135,928 | 17.2 | 5.3 |
| 1980 | 136,890 | 160,620 | 18.1 | 6.8 |
| 1981 | 152,239 | 173,973 | 12.0 | 10.3 |
| 1982 | 167,128 | 187,302 | 5.4 | 12.1 |

(Based on information from *Annual Abstract of Statistics* 1984, HMSO)

(a) Does the data support the view that changes in personal disposable income lead to changes in consumption expenditure?

(b) Calculate the level of savings in 1972, 1975, 1977, 1980 and 1982.

(c) For each of these years calculate the savings ratio, i.e. the level of savings divided by the level of personal disposable income.

> (d) Does there appear to be a relationship between the savings ratio and the level of inflation?
>
> (e) How might the black economy distort these figures?

## 12.7 Investment expenditure

1  Investment expenditure involves the purchase of:
   (a) *Fixed capital*—e.g. machinery, buildings, vehicles,
   (b) *Working capital*—e.g. stocks and work-in-progress,
   (c) *Financial capital*—e.g. government bills or bonds,
   (d) *Non-material capital*—e.g. training and apprenticeships.

2  Investment expenditure is carried out by groups within the economy. For example in 1982 total gross domestic fixed capital formation was £42,172m of which:

   £9963m spent by *personal sector*, e.g. on house purchases.

   £14,723m spent by *industrial and commercial companies*, e.g. on new machinery.

   £5805m spent by *financial companies* including financial institutions, e.g. on new businesses.

   £7221m spent by *public corporations and nationalised industry*, e.g. in opening new coal mines.

   £2134m spent by *central government*, e.g. on motorway construction.

   £2326m spent by *local authorities*, e.g. on council housing.

   (Based on information from *Annual Abstract of Statistics* 1984 Table 14.6 HMSO)

3  Investment expenditure on fixed capital is either:
   (a) *Net*, i.e. new or additional expenditure.
   (b) *Replacement*, i.e. to cover the depreciation of the existing capital stock.
   Therefore, gross investment is net investment plus replacement investment.

4  With such a variety of investment types being undertaken by a range of agencies within the economy it is unlikely that any single theory will be able to explain all this investment behaviour.

## 12.8 Economic theory and the level of investment expenditure

1  **Keynesian Theory**
   (a) If firms are interested in profitable opportunities then they will undertake investment expenditure if the returns from the project exceed the costs of undertaking the project.
   (b) Costs can be envisaged as being determined by the current market rate of interest, either because the firm will have had to pay interest on any borrowed funds being used to finance the project, or because the rate of interest respresents the opportunity cost of spending the money on the project rather than investing it elsewhere.

(c) Returns from the project will be determined by the extra production generated by the investment and the price charged for the product produced in the final market. Calculation of the rate of return from an investment project involves consideration of a number of factors.

   (i) *Timing of the cash flow.* Present money is worth more to a business than future money for two reasons. Present money can be used to generate benefit or utility, i.e. there is an opportunity cost involved in waiting for the arrival of future money and inflation reduces the purchasing power of future money. In order to take this into account firms need to discount future cash flows to an equivalent present value. This is known as Discounted Cash Flow (DCF) appraisal.

   (ii) *Externalities.* In some projects externalities, social benefits and costs are significant and can change the balance of private benefits and costs. Techniques for including the values of the externalities are called Cost Benefit Analysis (CBA).

   (iii) *Risk and uncertainty.* Investment expenditure provides a flow of benefits in the future, but the longer the time horizons are the more uncertainty there will be about the level of returns from a project. Some business decisions are based on incomplete information or depend for their success on the actions and reactions of other businesses.

   (iv) *Shared resources.* Very little can be produced by capital alone. The extra production from an investment project may depend as much on additional labour productivity as on the new machinery installed.

   (v) *Service industries.* From some projects the output may be intangible (e.g. from some medical equipment) or the output may not be sold on the open market (e.g. state education).

(d) If it can be assumed that the problems of calculating the return from an investment project can be overcome then the rates of return at various levels of investment expenditure are likely to be subject to the law of diminishing marginal returns or Law of Variable Proportions, i.e. returns from additional projects will fall as the quantity of investment expenditure rises.

*Observations from Figure 12.5*

   ☐ MEI = marginal efficiency of investment, which measures the rate of return from additional investment projects at various levels of investment expenditure.

   ☐ Rof I = rate of interest, the cost of undertaking investment expenditure.

   ☐ If all firms are aiming to maximise profits the level of investment expenditure will be I1; at the point where the MEI curve falls to equal the Rof I curve.

**2 Accelerator Theory**

(a) This states that the level of investment expenditure is determined by the rate of change of output (or income in the economy).

      i.e. $I = a(Y_{t+1} - Y_t)$

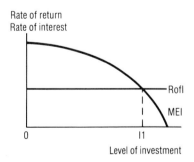

**Figure 12.5** Determination of level of investment

where I = the level of investment expenditure

a = the accelerator

$Y_{t+1}$ = the level of income at time period t + 1

$Y_t$ = the level of income one time period earlier, i.e. time period t

(b) The accelerator theory assumes that:
   i) firms have a *fixed capital:output ratio*, e.g. if capital(K):Output(O) = 4 it always takes £4 worth of capital to make £1 worth of output,
   ii) firms have *no stocks of finished goods* ready to push onto the market,
   iii) firms have *no spare capacity*, i.e. they cannot use their existing capital stock more to increase output,
   iv) firms experience *no difficulty in increasing supply*, e.g. there are no financial difficulties or bottlenecks in the supply of capital goods,
   v) firms consider that any *change in demand for their product is permanent*,
   vi) firms existing *machinery depreciates at a constant rate*.

(c) In such circumstances an increase in demand will result in an increase in output, which will require additional capital equipment and hence will involve investment expenditure. If the assumptions listed above do not hold the accelerator effect will be dampened. The assumptions are less likely to hold at certain stages of the business cycle than others, e.g. in a recession firms will have spare capacity and may have involuntarily built up stocks of finished goods.

## Exercise 4

1 According to Keynesian theory what will be the effect on the level of investment expenditure of the following? Check your answer by drawing a series of diagrams (as in Figure 12.5) with appropriate shifts in either the MEI or Rof I curves.
   (a) Expansion of the level of economic activity by general government reflationary policies.
   (b) A fall in the market rate of interest.
   (c) Increased competitiveness of British goods in export markets.
   (d) A rise in the cost of borrowing money.
   (e) The development of new technology.
   (f) A fall in the level of business expectations.

2 A football team with ambitions to win the Football League Championship have, at the start of a new season, the chance of buying a player for £250,000. It is estimated that, barring injury, he will play for five years and then retire. Each year that he plays it is estimated that he will bring in to the club an extra £75,000 profit, e.g. through extra gate receipts, European Cup competitions, etc.
   (a) Using the discount table provided (left), calculate whether it would be profitable for the club to buy the player if the rate of discount was i) 10% and ii) 20%.

| | Present value of £1 | |
| --- | --- | --- |
| Years hence | at 10% rate of discount | at 20% rate of discount |
| 1 | 0.909 | 0.833 |
| 2 | 0.826 | 0.694 |
| 3 | 0.751 | 0.579 |
| 4 | 0.693 | 0.482 |
| 5 | 0.621 | 0.402 |

i.e. £1 in two years' time discount at 10% is worth an equivalent present value of only 82p.

(b) How, in the real world, would the decision be taken?

3 A man has £4000 redundancy pay with which to start up a business. He has two projects available, each costing £4000. The net returns each year from each project are as given in the table (right).

| Year | Project A | Project B |
|------|-----------|-----------|
| 1 | 1000 | 3000 |
| 2 | 1000 | 2000 |
| 3 | 5000 | 1000 |

    (a) Which is the better project option for him if the rate of discount is i) 10% and ii) 20%.

    (b) Should he go ahead with the better option or look for something else to do with his money if the market rate of interest is 10%?

4 What factors would a private enterprise company take into account when deciding whether to invest money in establishing a STOLport (Short take off and landing airport) in London's dockland? What additional factors might be considered by a planning or development agency before allocating the company an investment grant?

5 A firm has a fixed capital:output ratio of 2, i.e. it takes £2 of capital to produce £1 output. Depreciation is constant at 20 units of capital each year. In year 1 output is 100 units, and the capital stock equals the desired capital stock of 200 units. The table shows the change in output in years 2 to 9 inclusive.

| Year (1) | Total output (2) | % change in output (3) | Desired capital (4) | Net Invest[1] (5) | Replace Invest[1] (6) | Total Invest[1] (7) |
|------|------|------|------|------|------|------|
| 1 | 100 | — | 200 | — | 20 | 20 |
| 2 | 120 | 20 | 240 | 40 | 20 | 60 |
| 3 | 130 | | | | 20 | |
| 4 | 135 | | | | 20 | |
| 5 | 138 | | | | 20 | |
| 6 | 140 | | | | 20 | |
| 7 | 140 | | | | 20 | |
| 8 | 130 | | | | 20 | |
| 9 | 130 | | | | 20 | |

[1] = investment expenditure

    (a) Complete columns 3, 4, 5 and 7 in the table.

    (b) Draw a diagram to show:
       i) total investment each year
       ii) the level of output each year
       iii) the % change in output each year

    (c) Which of ii) or iii) above shows the closest correlation to the level of total investment? Is this what would be expected from the accelerator theory of investment determination?

**6 The accelerator may not respond**

The main hope for continued economic growth at the start of 1984 is that the buoyant consumer demand would fuel a revival in the investment cycle.

There is a broad consensus amongst economists that one of the most important influences on industrial investment is the level of change of industrial output, usually with a time-lag of up to two years.

Because each unit of output requires 3 or 4 units of capital, changes in output usually bring about changes in investment expenditure several times greater than the output change. Recent output rises, according to this theory, are taken by industrialists as a guide to future levels of demand, and provide the profit increases to help finance higher investment expenditure.

The link could also be termed the decelerator as much as an accelerator, since the falls in both investment and output, particularly in manufacturing, have been bigger than the rises, notably between 1979 and 1982.

Table 1. Changes in investment expenditure and output between peaks and troughs in the business cycle.

| Time of peak or trough | Change in manf. invest- ment (1980 prices) [%] | Time of peak or trough | Change in output (1980 prices) [%] |
|---|---|---|---|
| Q1 1971 to | | Q3 1970 to | |
| Q3 1972 | − 24.2 | Q1 1972 | − 4.7 |
| Q4 1974 | + 21.3 | Q2 1974 | + 17.1 |
| Q1 1976 | − 17.4 | Q3 1975 | − 11.8 |
| Q1 1979 | + 21.0 | Q2 1979 | + 9.5 |
| Q1 1983 | − 45.2 | Q1 1981 | − 14.5 |
| | | Q2 1983 | + 3.4 |

Table 2. Changes in investment and output in selected industries 1979–82 (at constant 1980 prices).

| | % change in investment expenditure (GDFCF) | % change in net output |
|---|---|---|
| Coal and coke | + 11.8 | − 4.5 |
| Metals | − 58.6 | − 21.5 |
| Chemicals | − 50.3 | − 11.1 |
| Vehicles | − 41.8 | − 13.7 |
| Textiles and clothing | − 37.5 | − 25.4 |
| Construction | − 48.5 | − 13.4 |
| Communications | + 29.5 | + 7.7 |
| Business and financial services | + 31.4 | + 13.4 |

(*Lloyds Bank Economic Bulletin*, No 61, January 1984)

(a) According to the accelerator theory what determines the level of investment expenditure?

(b) From the data given what would seem to be a reasonable value for the accelerator in Britain?

(c) Why does the value of the accelerator vary from cycle to cycle and from industry to industry?

(d) What is meant by saying the accelerator works with a time-lag? How long does the time-lag appear to be?

(e) From Q1 1981 output was rising, but investment expenditure went on falling. Had the accelerator stopped working?

(f) What other theories of investment determination are there? Are these consistent with the operation of the time-lagged accelerator in periods of recovery?

# Review

## Unit 12 will have helped provide answers to the following questions

1 What information is shown on a consumption function?
2 What circumstances may cause the consumption function to shift its position?
3 How is the savings function related to the consumption function?
4 Is there a link between the level of savings and the level of investment expenditure?
5 What economic theories explain the level of investment expenditure?
6 What difficulties might be experienced in calculating the rate of return from an investment project?
7 Why does investment respond to changes in national income after a time-lag?

## Unit 12 has introduced the following terminology

Accelerator
Average propensity to consume
Consumption expenditure
Consumption function
Contractual savings
Cost benefit analysis
Discounted cash flow
Discretionary savings
Disposable income
Dis-saving
Financial capital
Fixed capital
Gross income
Investment expenditure
Marginal efficiency of investment
Marginal propensity to consume
Money illusion
Non-material capital
Permanent income hypothesis
Precautionary motive savings
Savings
Speculative motive savings
Transactions motive savings
Working capital

## Essays

1 Examine the relationship between the level of national income and the level of investment expenditure.
2 What is the importance of consumption expenditure in determining the level and changes in the level of national income?

## Multiple choice questions

1 A person earns £12,000 a year. Each year she pays £2000 in income tax, £1000 in national insurance contributions and other deductions. During the year she estimates she will pay a further £2000 in indirect taxes, like Value Added Tax and Excise Duty. Her disposable income each year is:

(a) £7000   (b) £9000   (c) £10,000   (d) 11,000
(e) £12,000

2 Which of the following is not an example of investment expenditure?
(a) Purchase of new machinery by a firm
(b) Purchase of a new house by a household
(c) Purchase of a new factory by a firm
(d) Addition to stocks of finished goods by a firm
(e) Purchase of national savings certificates by a household

Questions 3,4, and 5 refer to the following consumption function:

| Income | Consumption |
|--------|-------------|
| 1000 | 1250 |
| 2000 | 2000 |
| 3000 | 2750 |
| 4000 | 3500 |
| 5000 | 4250 |

3 What is the value of the marginal propensity to consume in the situation described in the table?
(a) 0.25   (b) 0.5   (c) 0.75   (d) 1.25   (e) 2

4 What is the value of the average propensity to consume at income level £2000?
(a) 0.25   (b) 0.5   (c) 0.75   (d) 1   (e) 0

5 What is the level of dis-saving at income level £1000?
(a) 0   (b) 250   (c) 500   (d) 750   (e) 1250

6 According to the accelerator theory of investment expenditure the level of investment is a function of:
(a) the rate of interest
(b) the rate of interest and the marginal efficiency of investment
(c) the level of national income
(d) the rate of change of the rate of interest
(e) the rate of change of national income

7 The table shows the level of national income at different time periods.

| Time period | Level of national income |
|-------------|--------------------------|
| 1 | 150 |
| 2 | 200 |
| 3 | 250 |
| 4 | 275 |

If the level of investment is determined by the following formula:

$$I = a(Y_{t+1} - Y_t)$$

where $I$ = the level of investment, $a$ = the accelerator, $Y_t + 1$ = the level of income in time period $t + 1$, and $Y_t$ = the level of income at one time period earlier than time period $t + 1$, i.e. in time period $t$, and the level of investment in time period 2 was 100 what was the value of the accelerator?

(a) 0   (b) 0.5   (c) 1   (d) 2   (e) 200

**8** The present value of £1 is higher than that of £1 in the future because:
  (a) inflation raises the purchasing power of money in the future
  (b) people incur an opportunity cost in waiting for the money
  (c) the future is threatened by risk and uncertainty
  (d) governments may increase the rate of interest
  (e) all of the above

**9** Which of the following is likely to cause an increase in investment expenditure?
  (a) a fall in the rate of increase in national income
  (b) the development of a large number of new products
  (c) a slowdown in the rate of depreciation of capital
  (d) a fall of incomes of people in export markets
  (e) an increase in the cost of borrowing money

**10** Cost Benefit Analysis attempts to evaluate investment projects by taking into account:
  (a) only private costs and benefits
  (b) only social costs and benefits
  (c) the timing of cash flows
  (d) the opportunity cost of investment expenditure
  (e) both private and social costs and benefits

**11** Which of the following will dampen the accelerator?
  (a) Producers have no spare capacity.
  (b) Producers have no stocks of finished goods.
  (c) Producers have no difficulty in raising appropriate finance.
  (d) Producers feel the change in demand is lasting.
  (e) Producers can reduce their capital:output ratio.

**12** What form of savings will be influenced by a change in the arrangements for paying for goods and for the receipt of wages and salaries?
  (a) Precautionary savings.
  (b) Transactions motive savings.
  (c) Discretionary savings.
  (d) Speculative motive savings.
  (e) Contractual motive savings.

# Answers

## Exercise 1

**1**

| | | |
|---|---|---|
| (a) | Building society deposit | Saving |
| (b) | New house purchase | Investment |
| (c) | New TV purchase | Consumption |
| (d) | Increasing stocks | Investment |
| (e) | Purchase of new machine | Investment |
| (f) | Pension contributions | Saving |
| (g) | Wages of civil servants | Consumption |
| (h) | Retained profits | Saving |
| (i) | Premium Bonds | Saving |
| (j) | Training expenditure | Investment |

## Exercise 2

**1**

| Y | C | S | APC | MPC |
|---|---|---|---|---|
| 0 | 100 | −100 | | |
| 50 | 125 | | | |
| 100 | 150 | −50 | | |
| 150 | 175 | | | 0.5 |
| 200 | 200 | 0 | 1 | |
| 250 | 240 | | | 0.8 |
| 300 | 280 | 20 | 0.93 | |
| 350 | 305 | | | 0.5 |
| 400 | 330 | 70 | 0.825 | |

## Exercise 3

**1** (a) Despite limited data, in general the relationship appears to hold, although there are some exceptional years and other short term factors.

(b), (c)

| | Level of savings | Savings ratio |
|---|---|---|
| 1972 | 4,330 | 9.6 |
| 1975 | 9,320 | 12.4 |
| 1977 | 10,207 | 10.5 |
| 1980 | 23,730 | 14.7 |
| 1982 | 20,174 | 10.8 |

(d) In general savings ratio rises with inflation, and falls back when inflation falls, but there are other factors affecting both savings levels and inflation levels.

(e) Black economy incomes will be excluded, but expenditure included, so savings could rise with a rise in the extent of the black economy.

## Exercise 4

**1** (a) Shift of MEI to the right—more investment expenditure.
  (b) Fall of Rof I line—more investment expenditure.
  (c) Shift of MEI to the right—more investment expenditure.
  (d) Rise of Rof I line—less investment expenditure.
  (e) Shift of MEI to the right—more investment expenditure.
  (f) Shift of MEI to the left—less investment expenditure.

**2** (a)

| Year | Cash flow | Present value at 10% discount | Present value | Present value at 20% discount | Present value |
|---|---|---|---|---|---|
| 1 | 75,000 | 0.909 | 68,175 | 0.833 | 62,475 |
| 2 | 75,000 | 0.826 | 61,950 | 0.694 | 52,050 |
| 3 | 75,000 | 0.751 | 56,325 | 0.529 | 43,425 |
| 4 | 75,000 | 0.693 | 51,975 | 0.482 | 36,150 |
| 5 | 75,000 | 0.621 | 46,575 | 0.402 | 30,150 |
| TOTAL | | | 285,000 | | 224,250 |

Compared to cost equivalent present value is higher at 10% rate of dicount, but lower at 20% rate of discount. Buy at 10% circumstances but not at 20%.

(b) Are football chairmen profit maximisers? There is so much uncertainty in professional football that these calculations could not be relied on.

**3** (a)

| Project A | | Project B | |
|---|---|---|---|
| 10% rate | 20% rate | 10% rate | 20% rate |
| 909 | 833 | 2727 | 2499 |
| 286 | 694 | 1652 | 1388 |
| 3755 | 2895 | 751 | 579 |
| 5490 | 4422 | 5130 | 4466 |

Project A is better if the rate of discount is 10%, project B better if the rate of discount is 20%.

(b) He gets about 10% return on his investment over three years at 20% rate of discount, but almost 29% return at 10% rate of discount. It depends what rate of return he could get from alternative investments.

**4** The company would be concerned with private costs and benefits (e.g. construction costs, landing fees, etc.). The planning authorities would be more interested in externalities (e.g. extra job creation, noise pollution and danger).

**5**

| Year | Total output | % change in output | Desired capital | Net invest | Replace-ment invest | Gross invest |
|---|---|---|---|---|---|---|
| 1 | 100 | | 200 | | 20 | 20 |
| 2 | 120 | + 20 | 240 | 40 | 20 | 60 |
| 3 | 130 | + 8.3 | 260 | 20 | 20 | 40 |
| 4 | 135 | + 3.8 | 270 | 10 | 20 | 30 |
| 5 | 138 | + 2.2 | 276 | 6 | 20 | 26 |
| 6 | 140 | + 1.4 | 280 | 4 | 20 | 24 |
| 7 | 140 | 0 | 280 | 0 | 20 | 20 |
| 8 | 130 | − 7.1 | 260 | − 20 | 20 | 0 |
| 9 | 130 | 0 | 260 | 0 | 20 | 20 |

There is a close correlation between gross investment and % change in output, a relationship predicted by the accelerator theory.

**6** (a) The rate of change of output (income).

(b) As $I = A(dNY)$ value of A appears to be between 5 and 1.5 from the data.

(c) Varies because the degree to which the assumptions are valid varies (e.g. there may exist some spare capacity) and because there are different capital: output ratios in different industries.

(d) Investment responds to previous changes in the rate of change of national income, the time-lag is between six and eighteen months (fifteen months on the Treasury's model).

(e) Bigger time-lag than usual because:
  i) firms waiting to see if demand change was permanent
  ii) difficulties were experienced over financing

expansion because profits levels were low
  iii) still spare capacity and stocks in industry

(f) Keynesian (see *Unit 12.8*). Yes. A rise in income and output gives better opportunities for profit, which shifts the position of the MEI curve indicating more investment will take place.

## Suggested essay plans
### Essay 1
Definition of terms:  i) Investment expenditure ii) National income iii) Relationship can be two way, i.e. investment affects national income, and changes in national income affects investment.

Main paragraphs:  NY → I Keynesian approach (limitation and difficulties of application of analysis). Accelerator theory with time-lag (limitations of analysis). Other empirical observations from British economy, e.g. need for profits in the financing of investment expenditure. I → NY Multiplier effect. Investment as an injection in the circular flow.

Conclusion.

### Essay 2
Definition of terms:  (i) Consumption, (ii) Consumption function, (iii) Equilibrium level of national income

Main paragraphs:  Consumption biggest component of Total Final Expenditure. Directly related to the level of income (especially in long run). Show equilibrium with Keynesian income/expenditure diagrams. Link with savings (a withdrawal from the circular flow), and evidence of shifts in the functions in the short run. Importance of other components of expenditure (i.e. X + M + I). Short run instability of marginal propensities alters the short run value of the multiplier.

Conclusion.

## Multiple choice answers
**1** (b) £12,000, £3000 indirect taxes not relevant to calculation of disposable income.

**2** (e) This is saving.

**3** (c) $dC = £750$ $dY = £1000$ $mpc = dC/dY$

**4** (d) $C = £2000$ $Y = £2000$ $apc = C/Y$

**5** (b) Dis-saving is negative savings. At $Y = £1000$ $C = £1250$.

**6** (e) By definition.

**7** (d) $I = a (dY)$, i.e. $100 = a (50)$ $a = 2$

**8** (b) Future £1 has to be discounted to find an equivalent present value.

**9** (b) More profitable opportunities, shifts MEI to the right.

**10** (e) Answer (b) would give just as misleading results as answer (a).

**11** (e) More output can be produced from using existing capital more efficiently.

**12** (b) e.g. from people switching to payment of wages by cheques reduces holdings of cash.

# UNIT 13 Fiscal policy

## 13.1 Preview

1 Fiscal policy involves the areas of taxation, government expenditure and borrowing.

2 Changes in the level of taxation and government expenditure can be used to manipulate the level of economic activity, as taxation is a withdrawal from the circular flow, and government expenditure an injection.

3 The overall level of taxation and government expenditure is also thought to be important for the general health of the economy, e.g. too much government expenditure may harm growth by denying resources to the wealth-creating private sector.

4 Taxes and areas of expenditure can have specific effects on sectors of the economy, e.g. the level of excise duty on tobacco causes loss of sales and jobs in the cigarette industry.

5 Fiscal policy both affects the economy and is affected by the economy, e.g. a rise in taxation may cause a rise in unemployment which in turn causes a rise in government expenditure on social security payments.

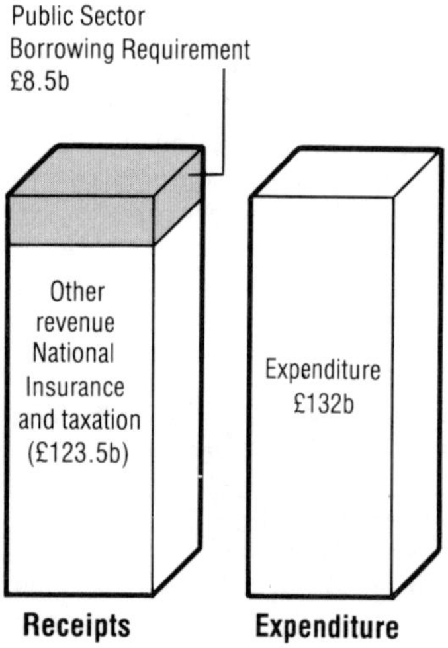

Public Sector
Borrowing Requirement
£8.5b

Other
revenue
National
Insurance
and taxation
(£123.5b)

Expenditure
£132b

**Receipts**     **Expenditure**

*Figure 13.1* Expenditure, revenue and borrowing

## 13.2 The relationship between government expenditure, taxation and the public sector borrowing requirement

1 Planned government expenditure in 1985–6 was £132b.

2 Government revenue from taxation, other revenue such as royalties and interest receipts and national insurance contributions leave a sum of £8.5b to be borrowed in order to finance this level of expenditure.

3 **The Public Sector Borrowing Requirement (PSBR)** is the difference between public sector expenditure and revenue in a given year.

4 **The National Debt** is the accumulated PSBR. It stood at £103.9b in 1982.

## 13.3 The need for government expenditure

1 Governments need to spend money for several reasons.
   (a) *Provision of public goods*—e.g. defence, law and order (see *Unit 1.4 [4]*).
   (b) *Provision of merit goods*—e.g. fire services, recreation areas (see *Unit 1.4 [5]*).
   (c) *Macroeconomic management*—e.g. to create employment, to promote exports.

(d) *Microeconomic management*—e.g. to encourage the growth of small firms, to expand food production.

(e) *Transfer payments*—e.g. to redistribute income and wealth from the relatively well off to those not so well off through benefits and pensions.

(f) *Interest on the national debt*—e.g. interest payments on gilts, prizes for Premium Bonds.

(g) *Expenditure by nationalised industries*—e.g. subsidies for the National Coal Board and British Rail.

(h) *Contribution to the European Economic Community*—(see Unit 19.3).

## 13.4 The need for taxation

1  The main reasons why governments levy taxes are:

(a) *Raise revenue*—to finance the expenditure needs mentioned in 13.3.

(b) *Discouragement of the consumption of de-merit goods*—taxes raise prices and hence discourage consumption of goods that the government feels people should not consume, e.g. cigarettes.

(c) *Redistribution of income*—more taxation is raised from the relatively rich than the relatively poor to help bring about a more equitable distribution of income and wealth (see Unit 14).

(d) *Undesirability of raising revenue in other ways*—e.g. excessive borrowing may cause interest rates to rise and cause a rise in the growth of the money supply, hitting growth and causing inflation.

## 13.5 Government expenditure in the UK

1  Government expenditure can be classified according to who is undertaking the expenditure; i.e.

(a) *central government* (approx. 65%)

(b) *local government* (approx. 25%)

(c) *nationalised industry* (approx. 10%),

or, according to the type of expenditure involved; i.e.

(a) *current expenditure on goods and services*, e.g. school books, civil servants pay (approx. 45%)

(b) *current expenditure on transfer payments*, e.g. pensions and benefits (approx. 30%)

(c) *capital expenditure*, e.g. on prison building, on unemployment offices and motorways (approx. 25%).

2  There are four major spending departments within the government.

(a) *Social Security* (approx. 30% by 1986–7).

(b) *Defence* (approx. 14% by 1986–7).

(c) *Health* (approx. 12.5% by 1986–7).

(d) *Education* (approx. 10% by 1986–7).

3  Although the Conservative government of Margaret Thatcher wanted to cut down government expenditure during 1979–84 this proved to be difficult for several reasons.

(a) Rise of unemployment benefits.

(b) High rates of interest raising payments on the national debt.
(c) Losses of nationalised industries in the recession.
(d) Pay rises in the public service sectors.
(e) Continued demand for defence, health and education expenditure.

## Exercise 1

### 1 Total public expenditure

| | 1978/9 (out-turn) (£m) | 1983/4 (estimated out-turn) (£m) | 1984/5 (plans) (£m) | 1986/7 (plans) (£m) |
|---|---|---|---|---|
| Defence | 7,497 | 15,716 | 17,031 | 18,660 |
| Housing | 3,467 | 2,733 | 2,411 | 2,750 |
| Education | 7,755 | 13,339 | 13,052 | 13,750 |
| Social Security | 16,175 | 32,821 | 34,729 | 38,960 |
| Health | 7,425 | 14,688 | 15,421 | 17,250 |
| Trade/industry/ employment | 3,747 | 6,296 | 6,211 | 4,450 |
| Nationalised industry borrowing | 442 | −248 | −836 | −930 |
| Sale of assets | 0 | −1,200 | −1,900 | −2,000 |
| Law and order | 2,035 | 4,861 | 4,901 | 5,300 |
| Total central govt. | 46,860 | 88,782 | 93,737 | 100,750 |
| Total local govt. | 17,995 | 32,780 | 32,127 | 33,760 |
| Planning total | 65,752 | 120,328 | 126,353 | 136,680 |

(Based on information from *1984 Expenditure* White *Paper*)

(a) Give three examples of government expenditure on social security.
(b) What happened to the proportion of government expenditure on social security between 1978–9 and 1986–7? Why?
(c) Given that there are about 56m people in Britain, how much is planned to be spent per head of population on defence expenditure by 1986–7?
(d) What was planned to happen to expenditure on health between 1983–4 and 1984–5:
   (i) in money terms
   (ii) in real terms, given the rate of inflation was about 5%
(e) What were the plans for spending on education in the same time period:
   (i) in real terms
   (ii) in money terms
(f) Is there any evidence of a squeeze on local authority spending in the data presented?
(g) Explain what negative borrowing by the nationalised industries means?
(h) What name is given to the government's policy of 'sale of assets'? Should these figures be included here?
(i) Why is the government so keen to control the growth of government expenditure?

(j) What are the short term prospects for employment levels with such a programme of government expenditure?

# 13.6 Taxation

**1 Principles of taxation**

Although first outlined in the *Wealth of Nations* in 1776, Adam Smith's *Principles of Taxation* are still relevant as a basis for examining forms of taxation.

The basic principles of taxation are:

(a) *Certainty*—tax rates should be clear and known to the taxpayer. There should be no arbitrary taxation.

(b) *Economy*—taxes should be relatively cheap to collect.

(c) *Convenience*—taxes should be levied at a time when it is convenient for the taxpayer to raise the revenue.

(d) *Equity*—taxes should be levied according to peoples' ability to pay.

**2** Judgement about the principle of equity involves three terms:

(a) *Progressive taxes*—taxes where the proportion of income going in tax rises as income rises, e.g. as with personal income tax.

(b) *Proportional taxes*—taxes where the proportion of income going in tax stays the same at all levels of income, e.g. as with some forms of Value Added Tax.

(c) *Regressive taxes*—taxes where the proportion of income going in tax falls as income rises, e.g. as with excise duties on petrol, alcohol and tobacco.

**3** Taxes can be categorised as either:

(a) *Direct*—those levied directly on incomes or wealth, e.g. personal income tax, company corporation tax, capital transfer tax.

(b) *Indirect*—those levied when expenditure is undertaken, e.g. Value Added Tax and excise duty.

**4** Indirect taxes can either be:

(a) *Ad valorem*—the amount of tax being a percentage of the value of the good or service bought, e.g. in 1984 the rate of VAT was 15%.

(b) *Specific*—the amount of tax being a set sum of money per unit of the good or service bought, e.g. vehicle excise duty was £90 per car in 1984.

**5** The level of direct taxation involves a distinction between:

(a) *the average rate of taxation*—calculated as the total tax paid divided by the total income received,

(b) *the marginal rate of taxation*—which is the rate of tax paid on the last unit of income received.

## Exercise 2

**1** A country operates a system of personal income tax as shown in the table (right).

Individuals have a tax free income allowance dependent on their status and personal circumstances.

| Tax rate | Band of taxable income (£) |
|----------|----------------------------|
| 30% | 1–15,000 |
| 40% | 15,000–20,000 |
| 50% | 20,000 and above |

(a) Person A earns £10,000 p.a. He has a tax free income allowance of £2000.
   (i) What is the marginal rate of taxation for Person A?
   (ii) What is his average rate of taxation?

(b) Person B earns £25,000 p.a. She has a tax free income allowance of £3000.
   (i) What is her marginal rate of taxation?
   (ii) What is her average rate of taxation?

(c) Assume in the next year there is inflation of 10%, and both Persons A & B get a 10% pay rise to compensate for this. The government leaves the tax rates, tax bands and personal allowances unaltered.
   (i) Calculate the increase in tax payment by both people.
   (ii) What could the government have done to prevent an increase in the tax burden?

2   A person has lived in three countries, each of which operated a system of personal income tax. The table shows the amount of tax he would have had to pay at different levels of income in the three countries.

| Income level | Tax paid | | |
|---|---|---|---|
| | in country A | in country B | in country C |
| 16,000 | 1,600 | 1,200 | 1,200 |
| 18,000 | 1,800 | 1,400 | 1,200 |
| 20,000 | 2,000 | 1,600 | 1,200 |

State whether the incidence of tax is progressive, proportional or regressive in each country.

3   A restaurant sells £500 worth of meals each evening (before tax). Value Added Tax is levied at 15%.

(a)  How much VAT is paid by the restaurant each evening?
A year later the average price of meals has risen by 10% and the restaurant still attracts the same number of customers.

(b)  How much VAT is now paid by the restaurant each evening.

(c)  If inflation in the country is generally 10% what will have happened to the real value of the government's VAT tax receipts?

4   An off-licence sells 100 bottles of wine a week, at an average price of £3 a bottle. Excise duty on each bottle is £1.50 regardless of the price of the bottle. All the excise duty is passed on to the customers.
A year later sales have stayed the same, but the price of wine has, in general, risen by 10%. The level of excise duty has stayed the same at £1.50 a bottle.

(a) What was the value of excise duty paid on the wine sales:
   (i) before the price rise
   (ii) after the price rise

(b) If inflation had been generally 10% during the year, what would have happened to the real value of this tax revenue for the government?

(c) What could the government do to maintain a stable real level of tax revenue from excise duties?

5 Assume that a bottle of whisky costs £5, £4 of which is duty. An off-licence sells fifty bottles a week at this price. In the budget duty is raised to £5 a bottle and the price charged to the customer rises to £6.

Price elasticity of demand for whisky is found to be 2.

(a) What will happen to the sales of whisky in the off-licence?

(b) What will happen to the amount of duty paid to the government from the change in the level of sales?

6 The following data refers to the trading of Spinney Software for January.

| Purchases | 1. Raw materials (excluding tax) | 5000 |
| | 2. Tax paid on raw materials | 1000 |
| | 3. Other purchases | 1000 |
| | 4. Tax paid on other purchases | 200 |
| Sales | 1. Sales (excluding tax) | 8000 |
| | 2. Tax paid on sales | 1600 |

(a) What is the 'value added' by Spinney Software in January?

(b) What is the net tax paid by Spinney Software in January?

(c) What rate of VAT is being applied in this example?

# 13.7 Taxation in the UK

The main forms of taxation in the UK are:

**1 Direct taxes on income**

(a) *Personal income tax*—levied at rising rates from 30% to 60% over set income bands, with tax free allowances dependent on status and personal circumstances.

(b) *Corporation Tax*—companies' profits tax (being reduced to 35% of taxable profits by 1987).

(c) *National Insurance contributions*—part paid by employers and part by employees.

**2 Direct taxes on wealth**

(a) *Capital Gains Tax*—a tax levied on any realised gain in the value of an owned capital asset, e.g. from shares or from property dealings.

(b) *Capital Transfer Tax*—a tax levied when wealth is transferred from one person to another, often on the death of one of the parties involved.

**3 Indirect taxes**

(a) *Value Added Tax*—levied at a standard rate of 15% but with some goods zero rated, e.g. food and children's clothing.

(b) *Excise Duty*—levied as a specific sum per volume on sales of alcohol, tobacco and petrol.

(c) *Local authority rates*—levied at a rate/£ on the rateable value of property owned.

(d) *Other user taxes*—paid when a good or service is used, e.g. vehicle excise duty.

## Exercise 3

**1**

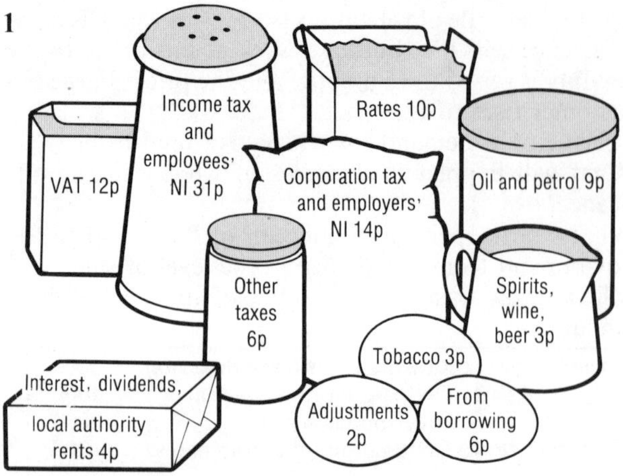

**Figure 13.2** How the government raises every pound (Source: *Daily Mail* 14.3.84)

(a) Which of the taxes shown in Figure 13.2 are direct taxes? What proportion of government revenue comes from direct taxation?

(b) Taxes on capital raised in 1983–4 only £1.5 b out of total government revenue receipts of £125.9 b. What taxes are levied on capital in the UK? Why are the receipts from them so small?

(c) What taxes are levied on tobacco, spirits, wine and beer?

(d) What two taxes are levied on petrol sales?

(e) Which of the items shown in Figure 13.2 would not normally be considered to be taxation receipts?

(f) Which is the chief source of finance for local authorities? What are the problems normally associated with this source of revenue?

**2 Fillip for wine trade, but beer drinkers and smokers suffer**
Sales of beer, spirits and tobacco are expected to shrink, at least for a time, in the wake of the Chancellor's excise duty changes (in the 1984 budget). There are now fears that sales declines could bring a further wave of job losses particularly in tobacco manufacturing, with a threat to tobacconists.

The Chancellor's 18p price cut on a bottle of table wine is expected to create a new surge in wine drinking.

The addition of 10p to a bottle of scotch with comparable increases for other spirits is seen as an inevitable threat to sales, particularly as trade increases are expected shortly. Distillers have been expected to add 15p to 20p a bottle at the shop counter. But the tax increase on spirits is much smaller than had been anticipated: indexation for inflation would have meant adding almost 28p a bottle.

Health lobbyists had urged the Chancellor to add 20p to a packet of cigarettes. Instead the impost was 10p on a packet of 20. A rise to have taken account only of inflation would have meant adding 3.5p.

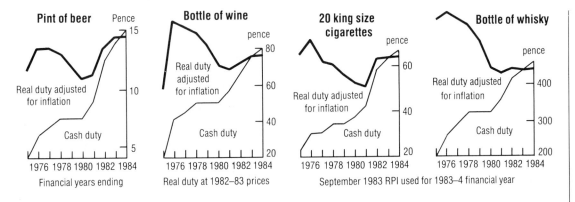

**Figure 13.3** The cash and real duty burden (Source: *Times* 14.3.84)

(a) Given that in 1984 the average price of a pint of beer was 70p, a bottle of wine £2.50, 20 king size cigarettes £1.10p and a bottle of whisky £6.50p, which of these goods' market prices contained the largest proportion of indirect taxation?

(b) What is the name given to the indirect tax imposed on these goods?

(c) Is this indirect tax a specific or *ad valorem* tax?

(d) Why is it important for the Chancellor to anticipate changes in the level of sales of these goods following his tax adjustments?

(e) Explain the difference between 'cash duty' and 'real duty'. Has the burden of duty risen in real terms on these goods over the time period shown?

## 13.8 Some problems associated with the operation of fiscal policy

### 1 High borrowing

(a) *Financial crowding-out.* One school of thought maintains that if the government has to borrow money to finance its expenditure from the savings of the private sector these savings will not then be available for the so called 'wealth creating' private sector. Additional demand for these funds will push up interest rates and discourage borrowing for investment expenditure.

However:

(i) Wealth creation is not exclusive to the private sector. For example, nationalised industry investment, and in the longer term educational investment, clearly create wealth.

(ii) Rates of interest may be determined by monetary factors rather than the loans market, and additionally are influenced by comparative international interest rates, e.g. those in US.

(iii) There is little evidence to suggest that investment is hit by a shortage of funds, but rather by a shortage of good projects.

(b) *Inflation.* If the government borrows from the banking system, or through the Bank of England, creating more liquidity, this will raise the money supply which in turn, after a time-lag, will cause prices to rise.

(c) *Debt interest.* Interest on the national debt amounts to some 10% of total government expenditure, imposing a burden on future generations. Where expenditure involves a project that provides a flow of benefits for the future this may seem quite reasonable, but not if the expenditure is financing consumption expenditure.

2   **High government expenditure**

(a) *Resource crowding-out.* If the government spends money on the expansion of non-marketed goods and services, e.g. health and education, resources are pulled away from the wealth-creating sectors.

However:

(i) Wealth creation does occur in the public sector (see above).

(ii) Public and private sectors of the economy are linked not separate, expenditure cuts in the public sector cause loss of demand in the private sector rather than generating extra production from the private sector, e.g. if British Rail is prevented from electrifying railway routes orders are lost by private sector contractors and cable suppliers.

(iii) If there is already spare capacity in the economy (e.g. 3m unemployed) some resources are not in short supply anyway.

(b) *Disincentive traps.* High levels of social security benefits may lead to a situation where someone is content to stay out of work rather than take a job and loose some benefits.

However, the trap could be removed by increasing disposable incomes rather than reducing benefit levels.

3   **High taxation**

(a) *Disincentive to work.* High rates of personal income tax and profits tax remove the incentive to work hard which would increase efficiency and profits.

However:

(i) Pay is not necessarily the only, or indeed the most important, reason for working.

(ii) Profits tax should aim to tax away economic rent (see *Unit 8.6*) but clearly not transfer earnings.

(b) *Inflation.* Indirect tax increases can be directly inflationary even though they are taking money out of the circular flow. By increasing costs they may cause pressure to increase wages and thus generate a cost/wage inflation spiral.

(c) *Disincentive traps*

(i) Poverty traps occur when people find that after a pay rise their take home pay is reduced following tax payments and loss of benefits, i.e. their effective marginal rate of taxation is over 100%. Raising the tax threshold for starting income tax, introducing a lower starting rate for income tax, or an inter-linking tax and benefits system would reduce the poverty trap.

(ii) Unemployment traps occur when people find disposable

income is reduced by undertaking employment rather than staying unemployed. Again this trap could be reduced through strategies outlined above.

## 4 Inflation and taxation

Exercise 2 introduced problems connected with inflation and tax revenue. If inflation causes tax revenue to rise this is called *fiscal drag*, e.g. as with personal income tax if rates are left unchanged; but if inflation causes the real value of tax payments to fall this is called *fiscal boost*, as with excise duty payments.

# Exercise 4

1  (a) Explain the terms:
(i) Public Sector Borrowing Requirement
(ii) debt interest
(iii) GDP
(a) What problems for the economy may have been generated by the rise in PSBR in the mid-1970s?
(b) What may have caused the rise in government expenditure as a proportion of GDP:
(i) from 1965 to 1975
(ii) from 1979 to 1981
(d) What sources of new revenue were available to the government after 1980?
(e) What benefits do you imagine would be felt by the economy from such a economic strategy, aiming to cut government expenditure, taxation and borrowing as a proportion of GDP?

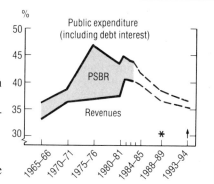

* Assuming 2¼% annual GDP growth and constant real public expenditure

† Assuming 1½% annual GDP growth and 1½% annual real public expenditure growth

**Figure 13.4**  Public sector expenditure, receipts and borrowing, as % GDP (Source: *Economist* 17.3.84)

## 2  Taxation and Growth

| Country | Taxes as % GNP 1971 | 1981 | Social Security contributions as % of total taxes in 1981 | Rate of growth (annual % 1970–79) GDP | GDP/head |
|---|---|---|---|---|---|
| Sweden | 50 | 57 | 29 | 2.0 | 1.6 |
| Norway | 51 | 55 | 24 | 4.4 | 3.9 |
| Holland | 47 | 50 | 41 | 3.1 | 2.3 |
| France | 40 | 47 | 44 | 3.9 | 3.3 |
| West Germany | 41 | 44 | 39 | 2.9 | 2.8 |
| Britain | 40 | 43 | 17 | 2.2 | 2.1 |
| Italy | 31 | 38 | 35 | 3.0 | 2.4 |
| Canada | 37 | 38 | 7 | 4.4 | 3.2 |
| Australia | 29 | 34 | 0 | 4.0 | na |
| United States | 32 | 33 | 26 | 2.4 | 3.2 |
| Switzerland | 25 | 29 | 30 | na | na |
| Japan | 22 | 28 | 30 | 5.4 | 4.1 |

(Based on information from *Economist* 28.4.84, *The UK Economy, A Manual of Applied Economics* (9th edn. 1982) Prest A.R. & Coppock D.S., (Weidenfeld & Nicholson p.54).

(a) What has happened to the proportion of GNP paid in taxes in all industrialised countries over the period 1971–81? Can you account for this change?

(b) What are social security contributions? Would ignoring the social security contributions alter the ranking of countries according to their tax levels?

(c) Does it appear from this data that Britain is a heavily taxed country?

(d) Does there appear to be any correlation between tax levels and the rate of economic growth achieved by a country?

## Review

### Unit 13 will have helped to provide answers to the following questions

1 What are the three main elements of fiscal policy?
2 Why does the government need to spend money?
3 On what principles should a tax system be based?
4 What are the main items of expenditure and tax revenue for the British government?
5 What are the problems associated with too high government spending, taxation and borrowing?
6 How can fiscal policy be used to control the level of economic activity?

### Unit 13 has introduced the following terminology

*Ad valorem* (indirect tax)　　Principles of taxation
Debt interest　　　　　　　　Progressive tax
Direct taxation　　　　　　　Proportional tax
Disincentive traps　　　　　　Public Sector Borrowing
Financial crowding-out　　　　　Requirement (PSBR)
Fiscal boost　　　　　　　　Regressive tax
Fiscal drag　　　　　　　　Resource crowding-out
Indirect taxation　　　　　　Specific (indirect tax)
Marginal rate of taxation　　　Transfer payments
National debt　　　　　　　Unemployment trap
Poverty trap

### Essay

What are the main principles of taxation? To what extent do any two of Britain's taxes conform to these principles?

### Multiple choice questions

1 Which of the following is not a measure to redistribute incomes through fiscal policy?
(a) unemployment benefits
(b) old-age pensions
(c) rent and rate rebates
(d) capital transfer tax
(e) child benefits

2

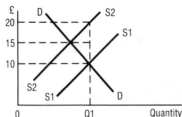

**Figure 13.5**

The imposition of an indirect tax

In Figure 13.5, S1 represents a firm's supply curve before the imposition of an indirect tax. S2 represents the supply curve after tax.

The level of specific tax/unit is:
(a) £0
(b) £5
(c) between £0 and £4.99
(d) between £5.01p and £9.99
(e) £10

3 In which of the cases below would the level of Public Sector Borrowing rise?

|   | Change in tax revenues | Change in govt. spending |
|---|---|---|
| A | +100 | +100 |
| B | +100 | +70 |
| C | −50 | −50 |
| D | −130 | −100 |
| E | +50 | −50 |

(a) A　(b) B　(c) C　(d) D　(e) E

4 The national debt is most likely to be considered a burden to future generations if:
(a) part of the borrowing is financed by the banking sector
(b) interest rates are falling
(c) it was incurred in order to finance consumption expenditure
(d) the debt is short term rather than long term
(e) it is financed out of increased direct taxation

5 A tax is regressive if:
(a) a high income earner pays more of the tax than a low income earner
(b) the tax is a direct tax rather than an indirect tax
(c) the average rate of tax increases as income increases
(d) the same amount of the tax is paid at all income levels
(e) the marginal rate of taxation is constant at all income levels

6 Figure 13.6 shows:
(a) the imposition of an *ad valorem* tax on a commodity for which demand is perfectly elastic,

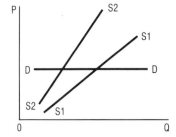

**Figure 13.6**

The imposition of
an indirect tax

(b) the imposition of a specific tax on a
commodity for which demand is perfectly
elastic,

(c) the imposition of an *ad valorem* tax on a
commodity for which the supply is perfectly
inelastic,

(d) the imposition of a specific tax on a
commodity for which demand has unitary
elasticity,

(e) the imposition of an *ad valorem* tax for which
supply is perfectly elastic.

7 For which of the following would you expect
inflation to cause a fall in the real value of tax
payments (assuming tax rates are left unaltered)?
(a) Value Added Tax.
(b) Excise duty on tobacco.
(c) Progressive income tax.
(d) Capital Gains Tax.
(e) Proportional income tax.

8 An increase in the level of PSBR will be expected
to lead to:
(a) a fall in the market rate of interest
(b) a slowdown in the growth of the money supply
(c) a shortage of finance for the private sector
(d) a fall in the national debt
(e) reduced need for government borrowing from
the general public

9 Which of the following is an instrument of fiscal
policy?
(a) Limits on wage increases in the private sector.
(b) Management of the exchange rate.
(c) Direction of private investment finance to
industry.
(d) Changes in the level of government
expenditure.
(e) Directly raising the level of growth of the
money supply.

10 Which of the following might be thought to
discredit the theory of resource crowding-out?
(a) Public sector expenditure generates demand
and activity within the private sector.
(b) Rates of interest are determined by other
factors such as rates of interest in the United
States.
(c) There has never been an observed shortage of
skilled labour.
(d) Not all the private sector can be considered to
be wealth creating.
(e) The PSBR has been falling as a percentage of
GNP since 1981.

# Answers

## Exercise 1
(a) (i) retirement pension
    (ii) Family Income Supplement
    (iii) unemployment benefits
(b) Increased from 24% to 28% of the planning total.
    More expenditure needed due to:
    (i) more old people, (ii) more unemployed,
    (iii) index-linked benefits
(c) £300/hd
(d) 5.5% increase, zero in real terms, i.e. after
    allowing for inflation of 5.3%.
(e) Drop of 25%, equivalent to a drop of 7% in real
    terms.
(f) Fall 1983–1984, then controlled rise of only 3%
    over four years.
(g) Requiring them to make profits, which then pass
    to the Treasury.
(h) Privatisation. It saves the government from
    borrowing in the year of the sale of assets but the
    money is not part of their revenue. If the PSBR is
    being used to measure the extent of financial
    crowding-out this money is merely being diverted
    from other sources of savings.
(i) Less borrowing allows better control of the money
    supply, and supposedly releases resources for the
    'wealth-creating' private sector.
(j) Unemployment will rise in the short run, e.g. from
    the loss of jobs in the public sector, and from
    complementary jobs in the private sector. The
    policy is basically deflationary.

## Exercise 2
1 (a) (i) 30%
      (ii) 24% Total tax paid is £8000 × 0.30 =
           £2400
  (b) (i) 50%
      (ii) 30% Total tax paid is £15,000 × 0.30
           + £5000 × 0.40 + £2000 × 0.50 = £7500.
  (c) Income rises by £1000, tax payments increase
      by £300, for Person A. Income rises by £2500,
      tax payments increase by £1250 for Person B.
      Bands of income could be index-linked (i.e.
      increased in this case by 10%) or the rate of
      tax applied in each band could have been
      reduced.

2

| Income level | % of income going in tax | | |
|---|---|---|---|
| | in country A | in country B | in country C |
| 16,000 | 10 | 7.5 | 7.5 |
| 18,000 | 10 | 7.8 | 6.7 |
| 20,000 | 10 | 8.0 | 6.0 |
| | Proportional | Progressive | Regressive |

3 (a) £75
  (b) £82.5  (15% of £550)
  (c) No change—money tax has risen by 10%, but
      inflation for the government is 10% as well.

**4** (a) (i) £150 (ii) £150
(b) Fall in real terms of 10%.
(c) Index-linked rates of duty (valorising duties).

**5** (a) Sales will fall by 40%, to 30 bottles.
(b) Fall by £50 from £200 to £150.
If the Chancellor wishes to increase revenue it's no good putting extra duty on goods where the price elasticity of demand is elastic.

**6** (a) £2000
(b) £400. Paid £1600, reclaimed £1200.
(c) 20%.

## Exercise 3

**1** (a) Corporation tax, personal income tax.
(b) Capital Gains Tax, Capital Transfer Tax. There are no proper wealth taxes in the UK.
(c) Excise duty.
(d) VAT and excise duty.
(e) Interest and dividends, and borrowing.
(f) Rates: They are regressive (the value of property is not directly linked with incomes and the ability to pay), they have limited capacity to raise money in poorer areas (often the areas in need of local authority expenditure), they act as a disincentive to local businesses, and some people avoid paying them.

**2** (a) Beer approx. 25%, wine 32%, cigarettes 60%, whisky 70%.
(b) Excise duty.
(c) Specific tax.
(d) Loss of revenue if demand for the good is price elastic. May fear further rise in unemployment. May be aiming to cut down the sales of de-merit goods, like cigarettes.
(e) Real duty refers to the level of cash duty adjusted for inflation. Real levels of duty have to be maintained to protect the purchasing power of the tax revenue collected from these sources.

## Exercise 4

**1** (a) (i) The difference between government expenditure and tax receipts in a given period of time.
(ii) Interest paid out by the government to holders of the national debt, e.g. National Savings Certificates and Treasury Bills.
(iii) Total output in UK.
(b) Crowding-out, slow growth. Difficulties of controlling the money supply, high inflation.
(c) (i) Index-linked pay settlements, increased scope of government activity, demographic trends, increased level of rate of interest.
(ii) Rise in unemployment, fall in the contribution to the exchequer of nationalised industries, fall in the level of GDP.

(d) Oil revenues.
(e) More resources available for growth, increased incentives, control of inflation, greater price competitiveness of British goods, fall in savings and corresponding rise in consumption expenditure, which in turn might encourage increased investment expenditure.

**2** (a) Tax has risen as a percentage of GNP. Caused by (i) ageing populations (ii) increased intervention by governments (iii) rising unemployment (iv) fall in the level of GNP.
(b) Payments by individuals as premiums for National Insurance schemes, e.g. for retirement pensions and unemployment benefits. Yes—tax burden in Australia would rise, and in France fall, for example.
(c) Not especially. Complaints about high tax in Britain valid if specifically referring to the low threshold for starting to pay income tax, and the high marginal rate at which income tax starts.
(d) No.

| | | |
|---|---|---|
| Norway | High growth | High tax |
| Sweden | Low growth | High tax |
| Japan | High growth | Low tax |
| United States | Low growth | Low tax |

## Suggested essay plan

Definition of terms:   Principles of taxation (after Adam Smith), See *Unit 13.6*. Outline of UK tax system, highlighting chosen two taxes (see *Unit 13.7*).
Main paragraphs:   e.g. examination of income tax + VAT with reference to four principles.
Conclusion.

## Multiple choice answers

**1** (d) CTT redistributes wealth (which admittedly might redistribute incomes in the long run as well).
**2** (e) The producers will only be willing to produce quantity Q1 at a market price £10 higher.
**3** (d) T has fallen by 130, G by 100, so PSBR has risen by 30.
**4** (c) Consumption expenditure gives immediate benefit, but the interest payments will be paid by following generations unable to receive any benefit from the expenditure.
**5** (c) By definition.
**6** (a) *Ad valorem* tax shifts supply curve and changes its gradient, perfectly elastic demand curve is a horizontal line.
**7** (b) For specific taxes money tax revenue stays the same but falls in real terms.
**8** (c) An example of financial crowding-out.
**9** (d) By definition.
**10** (a) It is difficult to imagine the public sector isolated from the private sector.

# The distribution of wealth and income UNIT 14

## 14.1 Preview

1 The level of a household's income determines how many goods and services the members of the household can enjoy.
2 Uncontrolled market economies tend to generate considerable inequalities of income and wealth.
3 Governments reduce the level of inequality through taxation and transfer payments.

## 14.2 Distribution of wealth

1 **Information about household wealth** can be gathered from three main sources:
   (a) surveys of assets and liabilities (calculating their net worth),
   (b) an analysis of investment income, e.g. dividends,
   (c) data provided for capital transfer tax purposes.

2 **Wealth is accumulated through savings out of:**
   (a) income,
   (b) inheritance, e.g. being left money in a will,
   (c) entrepreneurial fortunes, e.g. through business success,
   (d) capital gains, e.g. through rising share values,
   (e) windfalls, e.g. pools wins.

3 **Wealth can be classified as:**
   (a) marketable wealth, e.g. houses, land, shares, building society deposits,
   (b) non-marketable wealth, e.g. pension rights, future returns from life insurance schemes.

4 During the twentieth century inequalities in wealth in Britain have been reduced, e.g. in 1923 the wealthiest 1% held over 60% of the total marketable wealth but by 1979 the total had fallen to 24%. This reduction can be attributed to :
   (a) the introduction of capital transfer tax,
   (b) changes in the relative values of the different forms in which wealth is held, e.g. house values have risen faster than share values in general.
   The data presented in Exercise 1 shows that inequalities remain, however.

## Exercise 1

1 See tables overleaf.
   (a) Illustrate the distribution of wealth and income in the UK by drawing a Lorenz curve, i.e. plotting cumulative % of total wealth and income on the vertical axis against cumulative % of population on the horizontal axis.

| % of wealth owned by most wealthy | Marketable wealth | Non-marketable wealth | % of total income received by top 1% of population = 5.3 | |
|---|---|---|---|---|
| 1% | 24 | 13 | | |
| 2% | 32 | 18 | 5% | 16.0 |
| 5% | 45 | 27 | 10% | 26.1 |
| 10% | 59 | 37 | 25% | 49.6 |
| 25% | 82 | 60 | 50% | 76.5 |
| 50% | 95 | 81 | | |

(Based on information from *Social Trends* 1979 data)

(b) If the lines drawn had been straight lines what would this have indicated about the distribution of wealth and income?

(c) Is wealth or income more evenly distributed?

(d) What do you think is the chief source of wealth for the least wealthy 50%?

(e) What taxes are levied on wealth in the UK? What proportion of total tax revenue do they generate?

(f) What taxes are levied on incomes in the UK? What proportion of total tax revenue do they generate?

2 State whether you would expect the following to make the distribution of income more or less even. Explain your answers.

(a) An increase in the number of old people as a percentage of the population.

(b) An increase in the level of unemployment.

(c) An increase in divorce rates.

(d) Index-linked rates of benefits for social security payments and other government transfer payments.

(e) Reduction in the highest marginal rate of income tax from 83% to 60%.

(f) A more even wealth distribution.

## 14.3 Distribution of income

1 Household income comprises:
(a) wages and salaries (68% in 1981),
(b) income from self-employment (6% in 1981),
(c) income from investments (4% in 1981),
(d) annuities and pensions (other than from social security) (3% in 1981),
(e) social security benefits (13% in 1981),
(f) other (6% in 1981).

2 Income data presented in Exercise 1 included no allowance for:
(a) imputed values for owner-occupation of houses,
(b) fringe benefits received during employment,
(c) home production of goods and services,
(d) capital gains,
(e) undisclosed incomes received through the black economy,
(f) other aspects of welfare, e.g. opportunities for leisure and the level of job satisfaction.

3 Many households that appear in the lower half of the income league in any particular year may well expect to be in the other half at some other time of their lives, e.g. the low income groups

may include pensioners and students who have had, or will have, higher incomes in other years.

# Exercise 2

**1**

| Lower limit of income range | Number of households ('000s) | |
|---|---|---|
| | before tax | after tax |
| 1,350 | 300 | 419 |
| 1,500 | 1,290 | 1,700 |
| 2,000 | 1,300 | 1,880 |
| 2,500 | 7,290 | 9,750 |
| 5,000 | 5,780 | 4,580 |
| 10,000 | 2,174 | 889 |
| 15,000 | 530 | 136 |
| 20,000 | 222 | |
| 50,000 | 19 | 61 |
| 100,000 | 4 | |

Total households 22,200,000.
No data is provided for households with income less than £1350.
Data for 1981.
(Based on information from *Family Expenditure Survey*, HMSO)
(a) What % of households earned less than £2500 before tax and after tax in 1981 according to this data?
(b) What adjustments to this figure might be necessary to get a more accurate measure?
(c) Explain the terms:
   (i) fringe benefits
   (ii) capital gains
   (iii) imputed value for owner occupation.
(d) Which income groups tend to benefit from the sources of income mentioned in (c) above?
(e) Is there evidence from this data that income tax does succeed in redistributing income from the relatively rich to the relatively poor?

**2**  Sources of household income as a proportion of household income.

| | 1971 | 1973 | 1975 | 1977 | 1979 | 1981 |
|---|---|---|---|---|---|---|
| Wages and salaries | 73.9 | 73.5 | 74.8 | 72.0 | 71.6 | 68.1 |
| Self employment | 7.3 | 6.8 | 5.5 | 5.9 | 4.7 | 6.1 |
| Investment | 3.6 | 3.4 | 3.5 | 3.0 | 2.7 | 3.8 |
| Social security | 8.9 | 9.0 | 9.6 | 11.4 | 12.4 | 13.1 |

(Based on information from *Family Expenditure Survey*, HMSO)

(a) Describe and account for the changes in the sources of household income shown in the data above.
(b) Would such changes have tended to make the distribution of income more or less even over the period shown?

## 14.4 Poverty

1 Poverty can be considered in two ways.
   (a) *Absolute terms*, i.e. whether or not a household can purchase sufficient goods and services to maintain a necessary or prescribed standard of living.
   (b) *Relative terms*, i.e. through a comparison of one household's standard of living with that enjoyed by others.

2 In the UK, poverty is usually defined with reference to the government's Supplementary Benefit Scales, which are themselves linked to an average measure of standards of living in the economy.

3 Poverty is not just a function of low earnings. It is related to:
   (a) necessary expenditure,
   (b) social factors.
   Poverty is associated with such things as age, health, disablement, family size, family composition and unemployment.

4 Government provisions to alleviate poverty involve five main areas.
   (a) *National Insurance Benefits*, e.g. state retirement pensions, unemployment benefits.
   (b) *Child and Mobility Allowances* payable without a means test to families with children and to those who are disabled.
   (c) *Supplementary Benefits*—payable to those over sixteen and not in work, based on tables related to the consumption of necessities.
   (d) *Family Income Supplement (FIS)*—payable to those in work but on low pay.
   (e) *Other means-tested benefits*—e.g. free school meals, free dental care, rent and rate rebates.

5 There are several criticisms of the present system.
   (a) The numbers receiving Supplementary Benefits has been increasing, and includes groups of pensioners, single parent families and the unemployed who were supposed to be catered for by the original national insurance scheme.
   (b) It is estimated that there are over 2m below the official poverty line despite the benefits system, mostly because people do not claim the benefits to which they are entitled.
   (c) Incomes related benefits when withdrawn give rise to disincentive trap (see *Unit 13*).
   (d) FIS is calculated on income levels over a short period, but paid to the families for a long period, even if their circumstances have improved.
   (e) Non means-tested benefits, e.g. national insurance receipts and child benefits are paid to everybody qualifying, and not just to those in need.
   (f) The system is expensive to administer, costs ranging from 10p in the £ (in 1984) for the provision of Supplementary Benefits down to 1.5p in the £ for retirement pensions.
   (g) There is a low take-up of benefits due to the complications of claiming, and the multiplicity of benefits available.

6 Reforms that have been suggested involve three main ideas.
   (a) *Reform of the existing national insurance scheme* so it can cater for all pensioners, unemployed and single parent families.

(b) *Payment of a social dividend,* i.e. payment of a lump sum to everybody to provide for basic subsistence, the social dividend and any income received would all be subject to a proportional income tax.

(c) *Negative income tax,* i.e. setting for each household a bench-mark income related to status, family size etc., charging tax to those whose income exceeded the bench-mark, and repaying money to those whose income fell below the bench-mark.

## Exercise 3

1  Explain these terms.
   (a)  Means test
   (b)  Social dividend
   (c)  Poverty trap
   (d)  Negative income tax
2  Is it possible to eradicate poverty if income inequalities remain?
3  Go to the main Post Office in your area.
   Pick up copies of the forms explaining people's entitlements to various benefits. Would you consider them easy or difficult to fill in? Suggest other reasons why people might not claim for benefits to which they are entitled.
4  In 1984 there were about 3.5m full-time workers earning less than £100 per week. If part-time workers were included then some 6.5m were being paid less than £2.50 per hour.

   There were two forms of government intervention in this area of low pay. First there were forty separate Wages Councils to fix minimum wage rates in their particular area of concern; and second, Family Income Supplement (FIS) introduced in 1971, which paid to families half the difference between their actual pay and a prescribed level of income (around £90 per week in 1984).

   When the Wages Councils were set up by Winston Churchill (in 1909, and then called Trades Boards) he said 'it is a serious national evil that any class of his majesty's subjects should receive less than a living wage for their utmost exertions. It was formally supposed that the workings of the laws of supply and demand would naturally regulate and eliminate that evil .... whereas in sweated trades you had no parity of bargaining between employers and employees.'

   This view can be contrasted with that of the Conservative government of 1984 who thought that Wages Councils were an impediment to economic revival. Norman Tebbit (a Cabinet Minister) said in Parliament at this time, 'Is there really a case for imposing minimum wages which frustrate market forces? The answer to put it mildly would appear to be no.'

   (a)  What kinds of jobs are low paid?
   (b)  What are the characteristics of these jobs?
   (c)  What are the laws of supply and demand referred to by Winston Churchill and Norman Tebbit? Do they work satisfactorily in the labour market?

(d) What are Wages Councils?

(e) What is the Family Income Supplement?

(f) What would be the effect on the economy and on peoples' wages if the minimum wage regulation were abolished?

(g) How would you set about trying to calculate a 'living wage'?

5

| Social security payments | |
| --- | --- |
| | Estimated cost (£m) 1983–4 |
| *Total payments* | 33,752 |
| of which contributory benefits | 19,755 |
| non-contributory benefits | 13,997 |
| *Selected payments* | |
| Retirement pensions | 14,791 |
| Unemployment benefits | 1,528 |
| Invalidity benefits | 1,798 |
| Supplementary benefits | 5,693 |
| Child benefit | 4,011 |
| Housing benefit (including rent and rate rebates) | 2,478 . |
| Family Income Supplement (FIS) | 125 |

(Based on information from *Public Expenditure White Paper 1984*)

(a) In 1984 what proportion of social security payments involved
(i) pension payments,
(ii) Supplementary benefit payments?

(b) Which of the selected benefits listed above are paid to everybody qualifying for them, regardless of their income level?

(c) In what circumstances could someone claim
(i) Family Income Supplement,
(ii) Supplementary benefit?

(d) What arguments could be put forward in favour of making all benefits subject to a means test? What counter-arguments could be presented in favour of universal benefit payments?

(e) What trends in the levels of payments given above could be anticipated for the next decade?

6  **Essay**

Why does the UK social security system fail to eradicate poverty? How could the system be reformed?

## Review

### Unit 14 will have helped provide answers to the following questions

1 Why do free market economic systems tend to produce significant inequalities of income and wealth?

2 How would you attempt to define poverty?

3 What does the government do in the UK to reduce poverty?

4 What criticisms can be levelled at the present social security system?

## Unit 14 has introduced the following terminology

| | |
|---|---|
| Disincentive trap | National Insurance |
| Family Income Supplement | Negative income tax |
| (FIS) | Non-marketable wealth |
| Fringe benefits | Poverty |
| Marketable wealth | Social dividend |
| Means test | Supplementary benefits |
| Minimum wage | Wages Councils |

## Multiple choice questions

**1** Which of the following might form part of a household's current income?
(a) savings in a current (non-interest bearing) account in a bank
(b) their car
(c) the value of their house
(d) transfer payments from the government
(e) pension entitlement in the future when retirement age is reached

**2** Which of the following constitutes non-marketable wealth?
(a) houses
(b) land
(c) life assurance policies
(d) building society deposits
(e) shares in overseas companies

**3** In 1979 the most wealthy 1% in Britain were estimated to own what % of total marketable wealth?
(a) 5%   (b) 10%   (c) 15%   (d) 20%   (e) 25%

**4** Which of the following situations would tend to make the distribution of income in an economy more even?
(a) an increase in the level of unemployment
(b) an increase in the proportion of retired people
(c) a decrease in the rate of a progressive income tax system
(d) a more even distribution of wealth
(e) a reduction in the general level of social security payments

**5** Which of the following would not have the effect of raising a household's disposable income?
(a) ownership of their own house
(b) receipt of fringe benefits from employers
(c) an allowance from employers of a reduced rate of interest on a mortgage loan
(d) payment by the employer of a person's train season ticket
(e) an increase in the level of national insurance contributions

**6** Family Income Supplement is paid, in Britain, to:
(a) families with a large number of children
(b) workers on low pay
(c) unemployed people
(d) those forced to live on interest and dividends from past savings
(e) retired people

**7** Which of the following ways of redistributing income and wealth could not be replaced by the introduction of a system of negative income tax?
(a) Supplementary benefit payments
(b) Family Income Supplement payments
(c) retirement pension payments
(d) Capital Transfer Tax
(e) provision of free school meals for those on low incomes

**8** At the start of a year a person buys shares at a cost of £1000. During the year he receives £100 of dividends from these shares. At the end of the year he sells the shares for £1250. His capital gain on the shares during year was:
(a) £150   (b) £250   (c) £350   (d) £1000   (e) £1250

**9** Inequalities of incomes are necessary in market economies because:
  i) they stimulate people to try to increase their standard of living by working harder,
  ii) they attract labour to different occupations,
  iii) they reward people who have special talents.
(a) i) only
(b) ii) and iii) only
(c) i), ii) and iii)
(d) iii) only
(e) i) and ii) only

**10** Which of the following would not result in an increase in necessary or essential expenditure by a household, and hence contribute to possible hardship?
(a) a large family
(b) long illness
(c) a cut in wage rates
(d) disablement
(e) increasing age

## Answers

### Exercise 1

**1** (b) An equal distribution of income and wealth amongst the population.
(c) Incomes.
(d) House ownership, pension rights and life assurance policies.
(e) Capital Transfer Tax (CTT) and Capital Gains Tax (CGT). Less than 1%.
(f) Personal income tax and National Insurance contributions. 31% (see *Unit 13*).

**2** (a) Less even—pensioners have low incomes.
(b) Less even—unemployment benefit is less than income at work.
(c) Less even—more single parent families.
(d) Same—*ceteris paribus*, index-linked benefits keep those in receipt of benefits at the same level of real income.
(e) Less even—the well-off keep more of their high incomes.

(f) More even—wealth generates income for its holders.

## Exercise 2

1 (a) 45.8% before tax, 61.9% after tax (plus those below £1350 p.a.).
(b) See *Unit 14.3 (2)*.
(c) (i) payment in non-money form, e.g. company car, rent-free housing, cheap mortgages.
(ii) the rise in value of a capital asset, e.g. a house or shares.
(iii) the rent that would have been payed and received by owner-occupiers if they did indeed pay themselves rent.
(d) The relatively well-off.
(e) There is a fall in the number of households with incomes above £20,000 after tax, from 245,000 to 61,000.
2 (a) Rise in social security incomes (higher unemployment, demographic changes). Increased incomes from self-employment since 1979 (success of Conservative economic policy (?)).
Squeeze on public sector pay, and general recession effects on wages and salaries.
(b) Less even—unemployment benefit less than pay in work, although groups within the unemployed will have received large redundancy payments.

## Exercise 3

1 (a) Assessment of income and savings to determine the level of benefits to be paid.
(b) Lump sum payment to all, to cover for a basic level of subsistence.
(c) A situation where people on low incomes suffer a reduction in disposable income after a pay increase (experiencing an effective marginal rate of taxation over 100%).
(d) A system where income levels below a set figure would entitle a person to payments from the government.
2 In absolute terms, yes. In relative terms, no.
3 The forms are plentiful and difficult to fill in. People may not wish to rely on state 'charity'. They may have their own savings.
4 (a) and (b) Unskilled jobs, largely done by women, no unions involved, and where there may be ignorance of the laws, e.g. in textile manufacturing, cleaning, home workers.
(c) Demand for labour is derived from the demand for the products involved. The supply of labour is the number of people who are prepared to offer their employment in the industry at various levels of payment. No—market forces ignore the social aspect of wage levels.
(d) Forty councils which fix minimum wages for groups of low-paid workers.
(e) FIS is paid to people in work whose income is below Supplementary benefit level.

(f) Raise employment levels, reduce pay levels in already low paid areas.
(g) Calculate what is necessary to purchase the essentials for a family, after having argued about what is, and what is not, essential.

5 (a) (i) 44%    (ii) 17%
(b) Retirement pensions, unemployment benefits, invalidity benefits, child benefits.
(c) (i) FIS paid to people in work whose pay falls below official poverty levels
(ii) Supplementary benefits paid to people whose benefits from other sources do not reach minimum poverty levels
(d) For selectivity: benefits only paid to those that need them. Higher payments can be made to those in need. For universality: payments based on the insurance principle, people who have contributed to the National Insurance Fund should get benefits as a right. Completing a means test might be degrading and unpleasant. Avoids some of the disincentive trap problems that would be caused if all payments were means tested.
(e) Pensions will increase as average age of the population increases. Unemployment levels may not fall from their present levels. FIS may become more important if Wages Councils are abolished as proposed.

## 6 Suggested essay plan

Definition of terms:   (i) Poverty, (ii) Social security system.
Main paragraphs:   Problems (i) people don't claim all their entitlements, (ii) complicated system, (iii) cost, benefits don't always go to those in need, (iv) narrow gap between pay in work, and benefits received from social security (the disincentive trap), (v) the low personal income tax threshold.
Solutions: see *Unit 14.4 (6)*
Conclusion:   Original aims of Beveridge not achieved. Fowler review announced in 1984.

## Multiple choice answers

1 (d) The others are examples of wealth.
2 (c) This cannot be converted into money by selling it to someone else.
3 (e) See statistics in Exercise 1, question 1.
4 (d) Ownership of wealth allows the generation of some income.
5 (e) National Insurance contributions are paid out by households, not received.
6 (b) FIS is paid to people at work, whose income is below poverty levels.
7 (d) NIT is designed to replace all the various payments in the social security system.
8 (b) £1250 less £1000.
9 (c) All three are to do with the provision of incentives and the operation of market forces allocating resources.
10 (c) This cuts income, not essential expenditure.

# Unemployment

## 15.1 Preview

1 Since the experience of the 1930s, and the developments in macroeconomic understanding associated with the work of J.M.Keynes, governments have considered it an important objective to achieve high and stable levels of employment.

2 The re-emergence of high unemployment by 1980 showed that either governments had abandoned the objective of high and stable levels of employment, or that the economics of Keynes was no longer appropriate.

3 Many of the newly unemployed had previously been working in manufacturing industry. The term 'deindustrialisation' is used to describe the absolute job losses experienced in manufacturing industry.

4 In the present conditions Keynesian and Monetarist economists, and those that listen to them, propose very different solutions to the problem of unemployment.

5 Unemployment poses a problem to society: on economic, social and political grounds.

## 15.2 Measurement of the level of unemployment

1 In the UK the official unemployment figures are a count of people between sixteen and sixty registered as unemployed with the DHSS, and who are eligible for benefit. The count is taken on the second Thursday in each month. A separate total is produced for unemployed school leavers.

2 There are several reasons for believing that the offical figures *underestimate* the true level of unemployment.

(a) Some people, because of pride or the nature of the benefits system, *do not bother to register* as unemployed.

(b) Some people, when faced with difficulties in the job market, drop out of the labour market, e.g. women who decide to stay at home, students who stay on at college. This would be indicated in a drop in the *activity ratio* which measures the proportion of the potential working population who are at work or seeking work.

(c) Some people will be occupied in *government training or work opportunities schemes* with no prospect of permanent work when their schemes have been completed.

(d) Some people are forced on to *short-time working*.

3 There are also arguments put forward to suggest that the official figures may *overestimate* the true level of unemployment.

(a) *The existence of the black economy,* which means that some people may be registered as unemployed but are actually working within the unofficial economy.

(b) At any moment in time there is a certain *level of vacancies* about to be filled from the ranks of the unemployed, so some allowance for this should be made in stating the accurate excess supply of labour over the demand for labour.

(c) The official figures count those temporarily out of work, who for example, may be moving from one job to another, i.e. those described as *frictionally unemployed*.

4 Some countries estimate the level of unemployment by carrying out household surveys in addition to official counts. These surveys suggest that the monthly count system used in the UK, on balance, underestimates the level of unemployment.

## 15.3 Causes and types of unemployment

1 It is useful to separate the unemployed into categories according to the most likely cause of their unemployment. These groupings are not exclusive, e.g. a shipbuilder from the North East of England may be unemployed for structural, regional and general demand deficiency reasons.

2 There are several types of unemployment.

(a) *Demand deficiency or cyclical*—where total final expenditure $(C + I + G + X)$ in the economy is lower than the level needed to generate work for the total working population. As the level of aggregate demand tends to fluctuate this is also called cyclical unemployment.

(b) *Structural*—where a change in the pattern of demand in the economy causes job losses in certain industries, and where the unemployed are geographically or occupationally immobile and cannot move to areas of economic expansion.

(c) *Regional*—where economic activity tends to be lower than the national average because of undesirable location factors, e.g. large distances to the markets or poor infrastructure. Where a declining industry is concentrated in particular areas structural and regional factors are clearly interlinked.

(d) *Frictional*—where people who are moving from job to job are temporarily out of work.

(e) *Technological*—where jobs are lost, in the short term, through the introduction of new machinery. New technology invariably creates new jobs as well, but these are not always of relevance to the displaced workers.

(f) *Seasonal*—where demand for goods and services is affected by the time of year, and workers cannot find complementary work during the rest of the year.

(g) *Residual or hard-core*—where people cannot, or do not want to, work.

(h) *Youth*—where additional factors combine to reduce jobs available for young people, e.g. union minimum wage rate agreements, the lack of experience in work, the less stable life-style of young people.

## Exercise 1

1 For each of the following situations, from the list provided in *Unit 15.3*, state in which category the unemployed people could most appropriately be placed. There may be more than one category for each situation.

(a) Ex-workers from shipbuilding yards on the Clyde.

(b) Unemployed bricklayers in the winter months.

(c) White collar office workers made redundant through the introduction of computerised data processing.

(d) Unemployed graduates taking a holiday before starting work.

(e) Young people unable to find work at the end of a Youth Training Scheme project.

(f) Redundant local government employees following a cut back in services.

(g) Unemployed car workers due to a drop in demand connected with a general downturn in the level of economic activity.

(h) Unemployed workers from a textile factory in Liverpool, where the firm concentrated its reduced level of output in factories in the south-east of England.

(i) A disabled person unable to find suitable employment.

(j) Workers in a computer manufacturing firm who are replaced by computer controlled production processes.

(k) Job losses at factories of British American Tobacco due to a fall in the demand for cigarettes.

(l) Unemployed miners following the loss of pits after a strike.

2   **Surprise leap in jobless an aberration**

Unemployment in January (1984) rose by 120,300 to 3,199,678. The unexpectedly sharp increase compares to a normal seasonal increase for January of 93,000.

A fall of 1317 in the number of workless school leavers to 117,000 was attributed to the effects of the Youth Training Scheme on which 320,000 had been registered by the end of January.

Vacancies (unadjusted) fell by 6993 to 132,838.

Between December and January the number of people registering for benefit was 326,000, the number leaving the register was 231,000. The working population, excluding the unemployed, stood at 23,845,000. Government unemployment measures were assisting 663,000 in December keeping an estimated 470,000 people off the register.

(Based on information from *Daily Telegraph* 3.2.84)

(a) Why does unemployment normally rise in January?

(b) What is the principle behind the Youth Training Scheme? Do you think the extra 1317 jobs found for school leavers might have been offset by less employment for other groups?

(c) Why do you think there were so many unfilled vacancies?

(d) What can be inferred from the data provided concerning those joining and leaving the register in the month under examination?

(e) How literally should the 3,199,678 figure for unemployment be taken?

(f) What measures other than the YTS courses have the government been operating? Why cannot the government employ policies to achieve the objective of a 'high and stable' level of employment?

3 Unemployment in developed economies, October 1984 (% of population)

| OECD* average | 8.1% | Australia | 8.6% |
|---|---|---|---|
| EEC average | 9.9% | USA | 7.1% |
| UK | 13.4% | Canada | 11.0% |
| Belgium | 18.6% | Italy | 12.8% |
| Holland | 17.5% | Ireland | 16.7% |
| Japan | 2.6% | Spain | 20.5% |
| Sweden | 3.4% | West Germany | 8.6% |

* Organisation for Economic Co-operation and Development.

(a) From this data what can be inferred about the general level of unemployment in the UK compared to other developed countries?

(b) What do the generally high levels of unemployment in industrialised economies suggest about the causes of unemployment?

(c) Which countries have avoided high unemployment? Have they anything in common?

4 UK unemployment. Average of monthly counts during the years indicated.

| | Total working population (m) | Number of unemployed (m) | % rate of unemployment |
|---|---|---|---|
| 1972 | 25,267 | 837 | 3.7 |
| 1973 | 25,614 | 596 | 2.6 |
| 1974 | 25,658 | 599 | 2.6 |
| 1975 | 25,878 | 942 | 4.0 |
| 1976 | 26,093 | 1,301 | 5.5 |
| 1977 | 26,209 | 1,403 | 5.8 |
| 1978 | 26,342 | 1,383 | 5.7 |
| 1979 | 26,553 | 1,296 | 5.3 |
| 1980 | 26,700 | 1,666 | 6.8 |
| 1981 | 26,548 | 2,520 | 10.5 |
| 1982 | 26,535 | 2,917 | 12.2 |
| 1983 | 26,704 | 2,984 | 12.8 |
| 1984 | 26,687 | 3,224 | 13.4 |

(a) Draw a diagram to illustrate the changes in unemployment between 1972 and 1984.

(b) Highlight the key movements in the rate of unemployment during this period.

(c) Can you think of any reasons why unemployment rose so quickly after 1979?

# 15.4 Introduction to the reasons for the growth of unemployment

1 **Growth of the working population**

Until 1980 the size of the population seeking work was rising, e.g. in 1972 it stood at 25.2m but by 1980 had grown to 26.7m.

2 **World recession**

The rise of oil prices in 1973 and 1979 caused countries with balance of payments problems to deflate their economies, which became transmitted to other countries through the corresponding downturn in international trade flows.

**3  High exchange rate**

The discovery and exploitation of North Sea oil made sterling an attractive international currency. Capital inflows caused a rise in the effective exchange rate from 81 in 1977 to 102 in 1981 (compared to a value of 100 in 1975). Britain was described as suffering from the 'Dutch disease', a situation where the exchange rate is fixed by one successful industry (gas in the Dutch case, oil in the British case) but at a level too high for the other industries to remain price competitive.

**4  Medium Term Financial Strategy**

The Conservative government after 1979 embarked on a policy, codenamed the Medium Term Financial Strategy, which had at its root a desire to reduce the level of inflation through control of the money supply, and through control of government expenditure. This was so as to create, in the longer run, conditions in which steady and sustainable economic growth could occur. In the shorter run, however, the MTFS resulted in a reduction in aggregate demand and a rise in unemployment.

**5  New technology**

The late 1970s saw the first major impact of micro-electronic technological advances, and in the short run this had the effect of destroying more jobs than it created.

**6  Deindustrialisation**

Since 1966 British manufacturing industry had been growing less competitive. The factors outlined above accelerated the process of manufacturing decline in the UK (see *Unit 15.5*).

# 15.5  Deindustrialisation

1  The term deindustrialisation is used to refer to the decline in the number of jobs in absolute terms in manufacturing industries.

2  It does not specifically refer to the situation common in all maturing economics where the emphasis of employment moves from agriculture to manufacturing and on to service employment.

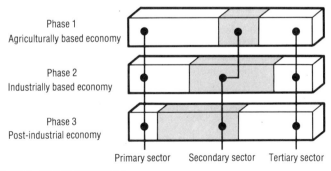

*Figure 15.1*  Deindustrialisation

3  Symptoms of deindustrialisation in the UK include:

(a)  *A deficit in manufactured trade.* In the UK, manufactured exports as a percentage of manufactured imports has fallen as follows:

| 1963 | 225% |
| 1970 | 150% |
| 1983 | 98% |

i.e. in the course of 1983 there were more imports of manufactured goods than exports of manufactured goods for the first time ever.

(b) *Imports penetration ratios.* As a percentage of the sales of goods in the UK, manufactured imports took a bigger share, e.g. in 1973 23% of vehicles were imports but by 1982 the figure was 45%.

(c) *Share of manufacturing jobs in the total of UK jobs.* In 1960 36% of jobs were in manufacturing industry, in 1970 only 34%, and by 1980 27%.

(d) *Absolute job losses in manufacturing industry.* Between 1966 and 1981 manufacturing jobs fell by 34%, a total of over 3m jobs.

(e) *Fall in the UK's share of world manufacturing exports.* Britain's share of world exports of manufactured goods has fallen from 25% in 1950, to 11% in 1970 and to 8% in 1983.

# Exercise 2

**1**

| Employees in industry ('000 s) | 1973 | 1983 | % change |
| --- | --- | --- | --- |
| Metal manufacturing | 518 | 259 | − 50 |
| Textiles/clothing | 1,017 | 566 | − 45 |
| Vehicles | 789 | 516 | − 35 |
| Mechanical engineering | 956 | 666 | − 30 |
| Metal goods | 563 | 397 | − 29 |
| Construction | 1,338 | 961 | − 28 |
| Electrical engineering | 955 | 753 | − 22 |
| Chemicals | 425 | 365 | − 15 |
| Mining and quarrying | 361 | 312 | − 14 |
| Transport and communications | 1,501 | 1,324 | − 12 |
| Public administration | 1,544 | 1,487 | − 3 |
| Gas, water and electricity | 335 | 323 | − 2 |
| Distributive | 2,691 | 2,612 | − 2 |
| Professional and scientific | 3,171 | 3,667 | + 16 |
| Insurance, banking and finance | 1,043 | 1,302 | + 23 |
| TOTAL | 22,182 | 20,069 | − 8 |

(Based on information from Department of Employment)

**2** (a) Pick an industry from those listed above in:
    (i) the primary sector
    (ii) the secondary sector
    (iii) the tertiary sector
    and explain what has happened to employment levels in these industries.

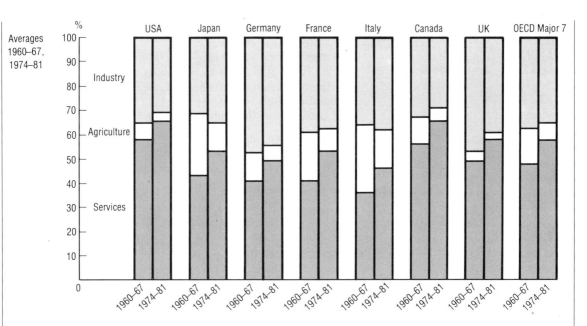

**Figure 15.2**
Distribution of employees

(Source: *Economic Progress Report*, No 165, Feb. 84, from OECD Historical Statistics.)

(a) Describe what has happened to the share of total output accounted for by agriculture, industry and services in the countries shown in Figure 15.2 since 1960.

(b) From this information, can it be seen which countries have been suffering from deindustrialisation?

(c) The demand for services has increased for a number of reasons. For each reason given below provide an example of a service that is associated with it.
  (i) Relatively high income elasticity of demand for leisure services.
  (ii) Change in the methods of payment of wages.
  (iii) Increase in the extent of home ownership.
  (iv) Increase in the average age of the population.
  (v) A shorter working week.
  (vi) Changes in technology.

(d) The growth of employment in services is linked to growth of employment in industry. Provide two examples to illustrate this.

(e) The growth in service sector employment has recently been concentrated in private sector provision of financial, business and personal sevices, in contrast to earlier expansion in public sector provision of distribution, transport and communication. Can you explain why this should be so?

## 15.6 Explanations for deindustrialisation

**1 Crowding-out**

As outlined in *Unit 13*, crowding-out can refer to:

(a) *Resource crowding-out*—which was thought to occur through the rise of government expenditure on non-marketed goods and services, e.g. health and education, which was pulling resources away from the wealth creating private sector of the economy.

(b) *Financial crowding-out*—which was allied to high government expenditure and borrowing which in turn restricted financial resources available to the private sector, and caused interest rates to rise.

For criticisms of these ideas see *Unit 13.*

2 **Lack of investment expenditure**

Investment is vital to the health of industry as:

(a) *it is an injection into the circular flow* and therefore stimulates general economic activity,

(b) *it allows technological advances* to be incorporated in production processes,

(c) *it promotes price and non-price competitiveness* through improving the efficiency of industry and the quality and reliability of their products.

Reasons for the lack of investment expenditure could include:

(a) *financial crowding-out* (see above),

(b) *lack of central financial planning*, as in Japan through the Ministry for International Trade and Industry (MITI) or in France through the Commissariat General du Plan,

(c) *lack of involvement of financial institutions with industry*, as in West Germany through their industrial banks,

(d) *removal of exchange controls* in 1979 which has allowed capital to flow overseas,

(e) *fall in profits of manufacturing industry* due to lack of demand for their products.

3 **Lack of competitiveness of UK manufacturing industry**

Deindustrialisation can be seen as a situation where the level of exports of a country is insufficient to pay for the volume of imports that a country would buy at a level of full employment. Competitiveness involves:

(a) *price factors*—e.g. wages costs, profit margins, exchange rates,

(b) *non-price factors*—e.g. quality, design, delivery dates, after sales service.

Both forms of competitiveness are clearly linked with the level of investment expenditure. Other causes of poor performance could include:

(a) *poor management*, e.g. lack of aggressive marketing, failure to control costs,

(b) *trade union activities*, e.g. restrictive practices agreements about manning levels and demarkation.

4 **Manufacturing industry as the engine of growth**

From what has been outlined above it is clear that once a process of deindustrialisation becomes established it is difficult to reverse, e.g. lack of profit leads to low investment which leads to uncompetitive goods which leads to lack of profits. There are important reasons for believing that manufacturing industry is important for growth in the economy.

(a) There is a *high income elasticity of demand* for manufactured goods, giving a virtually unlimited demand for the products of the secondary sector.

(b) There is considerable scope for the *introduction of technological developments* in the production of manufactured goods which increases efficiency and stimulates further investment expenditure.

(c) There are major opportunities for achieving *economies of scale* in most manufacturing processes.

(d) Growth in the secondary sector creates *demands for the services* of the tertiary sector.

## Exercise 3

1    1983 saw the end of an historic 200 year period during which Britain paid her way as an industrial nation. The balance of trade in manufactured goods, a surplus of £15b as recently as 1977, changed from a small surplus of £233m in 1982 to a thumping deficit of about £5b in 1983.

For the first three quarters of 1983 the UK trade in manufactures was £5.3b in deficit with EEC countries, but in surplus to the tune of £3.6b with the rest of the world. Since the period immediately before Britain joined the EEC, the position has changed from a small surplus with the EEC (£531m in 1970, £331m in 1971) to the present deficit of £5.3b in nine months of 1983. A steadily worsening trend was punctuated only in 1980 when the depth of the recession temporarily checked the remorseless growth of imports. During the same period the surplus of trade with the rest of the world expanded from £2b in 1970 to £3.6b in the first nine months of 1983.

It is worth emphasising that these figures refer only to trade in manufactured goods. They do not include oil or food, trade in which has been subject to special factors over the past decade because of the EEC's agricultural policies and the discovery of North Sea oil.

(a) What was the extent of the decline in the manufacturing trade balance from 1977 to 1983?

(b) What, if any, are the links between this decline in manufacturing trade performance and:
 (i) membership of the common market,
 (ii) the exploitation of North Sea oil.

(c) Why would the recession 'temporarily check the remoreless growth of imports'?

(d) What would be the likely effects on the economy of such a turn round in the manufacturing trade position?

## 15.7  Problems associated with high levels of unemployment

### 1   Economic

(a) *Cost to the exchequer.* It was estimated that each unemployed person cost the exchequer, on average, £100 per week in 1984. This figure would include allowances for:
 (i) unemployment benefits payments
 (ii) loss of tax revenue from the unemployed

(iii) cost of special schemes for the unemployed

(iv) administration

(b) *Waste of scarce resources.* Labour, unlike some raw materials, cannot be stored for later use. Unused labour resources are lost for all time.

(c) *Inequalities of income distribution.* Although in the short run unemployment benefits are linked to past wage levels, as time goes on the wage related element is reduced and the gap in the level of standard of living between those out of work and those in work widens. These inequalities may, in practice, be reduced through the payment of high redundancy payments and through incomes earned in the black economy.

**2 Social**

(a) *Work ethic.* While it is generally accepted that people should work those unable to work are bound to become frustrated and alienated from society.

(b) *Loss of status.* People are often accorded status in society according to the job they do. A jobless person, obviously, lacks status.

(c) *Crime and vandalism.* In a society that values the acquisition of material goods those denied the opportunity to buy such goods are bound to be tempted to get them illegally. Although work might be boring, being out of work may be more boring. Mindless vandalism is a possible release from boredom.

(d) *Health and suicide.* Unemployment leads to a fall in living standards and possibly of nutrition levels. Frustration and alienation cause depression. It has been suggested that there are 10,000 extra deaths a year for every 1m of unemployed in the country.

**3 Political**

Unemployment has risen through several politically sensitive thresholds without major political upheavals. Indeed the Conservative government was re-elected in 1983 with a landslide majority with the level of unemployment standing at over 3m. But government in the 1930s fared less well.

## 15.8 Policies for reducing the level of unemployment

**1 Demand management**

Keynesian economists argue that there is nothing automatic at work in the economy ensuring the level of aggregate demand will be at the level necessary to ensure full employment.

Governments have the responsibility to manage the level of aggregate demand, i.e.

(a) consumption +

(b) investment +

(c) government expenditure +

(d) exports

to an appropriate level through a mixture of:

(a) fiscal policy measures (tax, government expenditure and borrowing),

(b) monetary policy measures (rate of interest changes, control of the money supply and credit levels),
(c) direct policy measures (prices and incomes policies),
(d) trade policy measures (exchange rate changes, tariffs and quotas),
(e) supply side measures (monopoly control, regional policy, trade union legislation)

to close any deflationary gap that existed.

## 2 Controlling inflation

Monetarist economists stressed the key importance of inflation expectations in policies to lower the level of unemployment. This can be understood with reference to three concepts.

(a) *The natural rate of unemployment.* This is defined as the level of unemployment that is associated with a constant rate of inflation. It is fixed by factors such as labour mobility, job information channels, the relationship between social security pay and pay from employment, direct tax levels and minimum wage agreements. The natural rate of unemployment cannot be reduced by simple demand management in the long run without causing inflationary pressures.

(b) *The simple Phillips Curve.* This shows a statistical relationship between levels of unemployment and the rate of change of wages (wage inflation).

*Observations from Figure 15.3*
□ $U_n$ is the natural rate of unemployment. It has been estimated at 3% for the United Kingdom.
□ There appears to be simple trade-off between less inflation but more unemployment, and vice-versa.
□ The Phillips Curve seemed to be successful in predicting combinations of unemployment and inflation until 1967. Thereafter the relationship was broken. Between 1969 and 1975 there was both rising unemployment and rising wage inflation, leading to what economists called stagflation.

(c) *Expectations augmented Phillips Curves.* The explanation for the apparent breakdown of the Phillips Curve came from an emphasis on the role of expectations. If workers, for example, judge future inflation from present levels of inflation, they will demand increased wages to maintin real wage levels. So each level of unemployment becomes associated with a higher level of wage inflation.

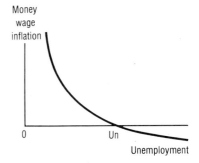

**Figure 15.3**  Phillips Curve

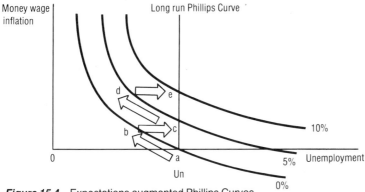

**Figure 15.4**  Expectations augmented Phillips Curves

*Observations from Figure 15.4*

☐ Each Phillips Curve is associated with a separate rate of wage inflation, e.g. 0%, 5%, 10% on the figure.

☐ If at point 'a' the government reflates the economy through demand management policies, the economy may move to point 'b' as employers demand more labour.

☐ Prices will rise, say to 5%, and hence workers will increase their money wage demands to maintain their real income levels.

☐ In pushing for higher wages, employees will cause employers to reduce their demand for labour again, recreating a level of unemployment at the natural rate (point 'c') but this time with an inflation rate of 5%.

☐ Further reflation would simply push the economy through points 'd' and 'e' respectively.

☐ Such movements of the economy suggest that the long run Phillips Curve is therefore a vertical line through the natural rate of unemployment.

### 3  Import controls and planning

(a) Reflation will not only cause inflation, but for an economy suffering from deindustrialisation, it will also push the balance of trade deeper into deficit.

(b) Some economists, notably from the Cambridge Economic Policy Group, believe therefore that in the short run import controls will be necessary if reflationary programmes are not to be curtailed by trade difficulties.

(c) During this protected phase, reflation will increase profits in domestic industry. With the appropriate channelling of finance into growth industries it is argued that the process of deindustrialisation can be reversed.

## Exercise 4

1  (a) What is a deflationary gap? Draw a diagram to illustrate a deflationary gap.

(b) For each of the following state whether the change indicated would (*ceteris paribus*) widen or close a deflationary gap.

   (i) An increase in government expenditure.

   (ii) An increase in export earnings.

   (iii) A decrease in company investment expenditure.

   (iv) A decrease in personal savings.

   (v) An increase in consumption of goods produced domestically.

   (vi) An increase in the size of the working population.

(c) Why is the change in expenditure that is necessary to close a deflationary gap smaller than the change in national income that it brings about?

(d) What might be expected to happen, as expenditure was increased to close the deflationary gap to:

   (i) the rate of inflation

   (ii) the balance of trade (exports less imports)

   (iii) the rate of growth

(e) What effect might the changes to inflation, the balance

of trade and growth noted in (d) above have on the level of aggregate expenditure and hence on the size of the deflationary gap?

2 State for each of the following the effect they would have on the natural rate of unemployment.
   (a) Widening the income difference between those in work and those in receipt of Social Security benefits.
   (b) Lowering the level of redundancy payments.
   (c) Introduction of a national minimum wage.
   (d) The closure of several small-town job centres.
   (e) Increasing the opportunities for job retraining.
   (f) Raising the threshold at which people start to pay income tax.
   (g) A reduction in the rate of inflation.

3 (a) What is meant by the term 'stagflation'?
   (b) How could a government, faced with an economy at position 'c' in Figure 15.4, argue that they had to introduce policies which would cause unemployment to rise in the short run so that unemployment could be reduced in the long run?
   (c) Is there a connection between the Conservative government post-1979's Medium Term Financial Strategy and the concept of expectations augmented Phillips Curves?

# 15.9 Regional policy measures

1 The level of economic activity within the UK is uneven. Measurements of this unevenness can be seen from:
   (a) levels of income or output per head of the population in each region,
   (b) a comparison of unemployment levels in different regions,
   (c) migration levels from the regions,
   (d) quality of life indicators for each area, e.g. numbers of cars per thousand of the population.

2 Regions can be categorised as:
   (a) congested, i.e. too high a level of economic activity,
   (b) normal,
   (c) underdeveloped, i.e. those where there is little economic activity,
   (d) depressed, i.e. those where traditional industry is in decline and new jobs are scarce.

3 Policy measures can be categorised as either:
   (a) taking work to the workers, i.e. trying to create jobs in the areas where unemployment is highest,
   (b) taking the workers to the work, i.e. making workers more occupationally and geographically mobile.

4 Most attention has been focused on taking work to depressed regions. Depressed regions have several characteristics.
   (a) A mix of economic activity that is dominated by low income generating industry, e.g. agriculture, or industry that is suffering from declining demand, e.g. because of overseas competition.
   (b) Undesirable location factors, e.g. large distances from the major markets.

(c) A distance apart from the financial centralisation within the City of London.

(d) Stereotyped images that deter businessmen and their families.

5 Regional policies have been operated by governments since 1934. Current measures include:

(a) The designation of areas as either Development Areas, Intermediate Areas, Inner City Areas and Enterprise Zones. Grants and tax allowances are available at varying levels according to area status.

(b) Investment grants for capital expenditure, e.g. up to 15% of the project cost for firms in Development Areas.

(c) Tax allowances which allow firms to depreciate their capital stock at rates which reduce their overall tax liability.

(d) Specific subsidies to industries that are concentrated in the depressed regions, e.g. shipbuilding and coal.

(e) Infrastructure development, e.g. motorway network development, regional airports.

(f) Advance built factories, available rent free for given periods of time.

(g) Retraining programmes, e.g. through subsidies to Industrial Training Boards.

(h) Job information services, e.g. Job Centres.

(i) Diversification of government employment, e.g. relocating the Driver and Vehicle Licensing Centre in Swansea.

(j) Building and planning controls in congested areas, e.g. by refusal of planning permission.

(k) Provision of area information, e.g. through the Scottish Development Agency.

6 Regional aid cost the government some £20b from 1963 to 1983. Between 1973 and 1983 it was estimated that 500,000 new jobs were created by regional measures at a cost of £35,000 per job. The high cost per job created must however be qualified because other jobs may have been saved, and jobs created are long lasting whereas the cost is a one-off payment.

7 Other aspects of any assessment of regional policy would include:

(a) Ideally the industry attracted to the regions by the incentives would be labour intensive, complementary, growth industries—but there are not many of these about.

(b) The incentives to November 1984 concentrated on manufacturing industry and therefore ignored the labour intensive service sector of the economy.

(c) Until November 1984 industry qualified for grants regardless of the number and cost of jobs created, but from 1985 grants were to be based on a sum related to the number of jobs created.

(d) Regional aid may not create jobs at all overall, but merely transfer them from elsewhere. Indeed some jobs may be destroyed by imposition of controls on expansion in the congested areas.

(e) The measures of regional aid were applied inconsistently during the 1960s and 1970s as Conservative and Labour governments changed the emphasis of their policies.

(f) Area status has depended on actual levels of unemployment rather that trend of unemployment, so, for example, until

November 1984 the West Midlands received no help as unemployment levels rose.

(g) The amount of footloose industry is anyway limited, so much regional aid will be ineffective.

(h) Much of the aid has gone to projects that would have taken place anyway.

# Exercise 5

1   Analysis of unemployment rates by standard regions.

|  | 1974 | 1975 | 1976 | 1977 | 1978 | 1979 | 1980 | 1981 | 1982 | 1983 |
|---|---|---|---|---|---|---|---|---|---|---|
| North | 4.6 | 5.8 | 7.2 | 8.0 | 8.6 | 8.3 | 10.4 | 14.6 | 16.5 | 17.5 |
| Yorks and Humberside | 2.5 | 3.8 | 5.3 | 5.5 | 5.7 | 5.4 | 7.3 | 11.5 | 13.4 | 14.6 |
| East Midlands | 2.2 | 3.5 | 4.5 | 4.8 | 4.7 | 4.4 | 6.1 | 9.6 | 11.0 | 11.9 |
| East Anglia | 1.9 | 3.3 | 4.7 | 5.1 | 4.8 | 4.2 | 5.3 | 8.4 | 9.9 | 10.6 |
| South East | 1.5 | 2.6 | 4.0 | 4.3 | 3.9 | 3.4 | 4.2 | 7.1 | 8.7 | 9.5 |
| South West | 2.6 | 4.6 | 6.2 | 6.5 | 6.2 | 5.4 | 6.4 | 9.3 | 10.8 | 11.7 |
| West Midlands | 2.1 | 3.9 | 5.5 | 5.5 | 5.3 | 5.2 | 7.3 | 12.7 | 14.9 | 15.3 |
| North West | 3.4 | 5.2 | 6.7 | 7.0 | 6.9 | 6.5 | 8.5 | 12.6 | 14.7 | 15.0 |
| Wales | 3.7 | 5.5 | 7.1 | 7.6 | •7.7 | 7.3 | 9.4 | 13.6 | 15.6 | 16.0 |
| Scotland | 3.8 | 5.0 | 6.7 | 7.7 | 7.7 | 7.4 | 9.1 | 12.6 | 14.2 | 14.9 |
| N. Ireland | 5.4 | 7.4 | 9.5 | 10.5 | 11.0 | 10.8 | 13.0 | 17.3 | 19.4 | 20.4 |
| United Kingdom | 2.6 | 4.0 | 5.5 | 5.8 | 5.7 | 5.3 | 6.8 | 10.5 | 12.2 | 13.8 |

(Based on information from *Annual Abstract of Statistics 1984*, HMSO)

(a) In 1982 which regions had unemployment levels greater than the UK average?

(b) Describe the level of unemployment in the West Midlands relative to the UK average level. What has caused this change?

(c) Has the inequality of unemployment rates, in general, narrowed or widened during the period shown? Explain your answer.

(d) Select any region and explain the factors you think determine its level of unemployment.

2   **Doubts greet £300m cut in aid for regions**

The government's new cut-price job-creating industrial package, announced at the end of November 1984, included for the first time the previously prosperous West Midlands, Sheffield and parts of Manchester. The scheme is designed to cut regional spending of nearly £300m to £350m by 1987–88.

Some service sectors previously excluded from grants will qualify. Capital grants will be limited to a cost per job of £10,000 or companies can opt for a jobs grant of £3,000 per job.

The far reaching changes are aimed at simplifying the systems of Special Development, Development and Intermediate Areas with a new assistance map and aid concentrated on selective rather than automatic grants. After the changes there would be only two tiers, Development Areas, where companies will qualify for automatic 15% grants, and Intermediate Areas which will qualify for selective assistance.

The boundaries for assistance were still to be 'travel to work areas'. Development Areas covered 15% of the working population, Intermediate Areas a further 20%.

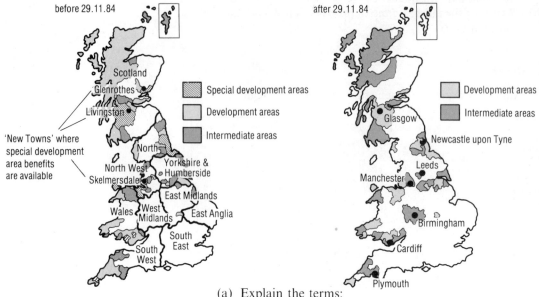

**Figure 15.5** Assisted areas (Based on information from *Times* 28.11.84)

(a) Explain the terms:
 (i) Development Area,
 (ii) Intermediate Area,
 (iii) Travel to work areas.
(b) Identify the areas with Development Area status after November 1984. Have the areas anything in common?
(c) What were the main changes in regional policy introduced in November 1984?
(d) To what extent did these changes attempt to overcome the weaknesses of the previous regional policy package?

3 **Sunderland settles for the dole**
It is nearly 20 years since the wretched economic condition of North-East England became a subject for national political concern. Then unemployment in the North-East stood at 6% compared to a national average of $2\frac{1}{2}$%. Practically every one of the government of the day's proposals for ending the 'grave social evil' has been implemented; roads built, dereliction cleared up, ports and railways refurbished, colleges expanded, golf courses and arts festivals inaugurated. Result? Of the would-be working population, 16% are now registered as unemployed, against the national average of $12\frac{1}{2}$%.

The relative disadvantage of the north has statistically diminished. That is small consolation for those that actually live there. The cost of trying to set the damaged region on its feet again has been immense, with public expenditure per head of the population running well ahead of the national level. The material quality of life has undoubtedly been much improved. But the economic return on the investment in the region is tiny.

The wrong things have been saved in the old mining-and-shipbuilding town of Sunderland, on the mouth of the river Wear. Just two mines now survive in the town, tapping rich seams out under the North Sea. Two shipyards survive also, thanks to massive government subsidies, great technical ingenuity and good labour relations. But the river is so narrow that sizeable ships have to be built in two halves and stitched together when afloat. The industry is dying a slow and merciful death.

Yet Sunderland is the only one of Britain's big urban settlements to have increased its population between the two censuses of 1971 and 1981, an unexpected development in one of the country's least successful places. It was massive public spending that caused the population to grow. Within the boundaries of the enlarged town the new town of Washington began in 1964.

The point of the place was to create an environment where private production could thrive. About 4200 residents of Washington, 17% of the workforce, are unemployed. At least another 1500 people, mostly women, who had jobs before moving to Washington, have not bothered to register. In Sunderland itself unemployment is much higher; well over a quarter of the potential workers registered at one employment exchange have no jobs. There are big housing estates especially down by the barely used docks where over half the adults have no work.

There is no particular social unrest as a result of this economic disaster. People dress respectably. There are fewer graffiti on the high rise flats that one would expect in a prosperous London suburb. Social workers report some real distress among their clients but it does not show. In the summer of 1981 when most of Britain's big cities rioted North-East England stayed calm. In the North-East a culture seems to be appearing of dependence on government handouts (plus, no doubt, some small earnings from the 'black economy'). Stolidly, the people seem to be settling in for a long period of freedom from the ambition to be employed.

(Based on information from *Economist* 10.7.82)

(a) Why is unemployment in the North-East described in the passage as 'this economic disaster', and as a 'grave social evil'?

(b) What benefits were expected from the policy measures outlined in the first paragraph?

(c) Explain the phrase at the start of the third paragraph which states that 'the wrong things have been saved'. What kind of industry would the North-East wished to have attracted?

(d) Why was Washington New Town created? Has it been a success?

(e) What evidence is there in the article of a fall in the activity ratio in the North-East?

(f) Why might some social unrest have been expected? Why do you think the political reaction to the high levels of unemployment has been so restrained?

## Review

### Unit 15 will have helped provide answers to the following questions

1 How accurate are the official measurements of unemployment levels?
2 What separate categories of unemployment can be identified?
3 Why did unemployment rise so fast in Britain between 1975 and 1981?
4 What do you understand by the term 'deindustrialisation'?
5 What are the basic ideas behind the theory of 'crowding-out'? What importance do you attach to these ideas?
6 What other explanations have been put forward for the poor performance of British manufacturing industry?
7 What is wrong with high levels of unemployment?
8 What can governments do to lower the levels of unemployment?
9 Why do regional differences in unemployment rates exist? Why do they continue to exist after government regional policy programmes?
10 How, and why, has the pattern of employment within Britain changed since 1970?

### Unit 15 has introduced the following terminology

Activity ratios
Deindustrialisation
Demand deficiency (unemployment)
Development Areas
Enterprise Zones
Expectations augmented Philips Curve
Financial crowding-out
Frictional (unemployment)
Import penetration ratios
Intermediate Areas
Medium Term Financial Strategy (MTFS)
Natural rate of unemployment
Phillips Curve
Regional (unemployment)
Residual, or hard-core (unemployment)
Resource crowding-out
Seasonal (unemployment)
Special Development Areas
Structural (unemployment)
Technological (unemployment)
Work ethic
Youth unemployment

### Essays

1 Define the term deindustrialisation. What caused the large drop in manufacturing industry between 1979 and 1983?
2 What are the consequences for the economy of deindustrialisation?
3 Discuss the statement that in the end new technology always creates more jobs than it destroys.
4 What are the main elements of regional policy in the UK? How successful have the policies been in reducing regional inequalities?

## Multiple choice questions

1 Which of Britain's standard regions showed the biggest rise of unemployment in the period 1975 to 1985?
(a) West Midlands (b) Scotland (c) East Anglia
(d) Wales (e) West Midlands

2 Which of the following is necessary for the development of structural unemployment?
(i) a change in the pattern of demand
(ii) immobility of labour
(iii) a fall in the level of total final expenditure
(a) (i) only
(b) (ii) only
(c) (i) and (ii) only
(d) (iii) only
(e) all three

3 Which of the following is the most reasonable explanation of high levels of unemployment in the North East?
(a) Lack of skills amongst the workforce.
(b) Un-cooperative trade unions.
(c) Lack of suitable transport infrastructure.
(d) Decline in the traditional employment industries.
(e) Lack of government grants available for the area.

4 Which of the following is not presented by economists as a description or explanation of deindustrialisation in the UK?
(a) The inability to export sufficient to pay for the full employment level of imports.
(b) The rise in government spending on non-marketed goods, hence crowding-out the wealth creating private sector.
(c) A fall in the relative numbers of jobs in manufacturing industry.
(d) High government borrowing crowding-out financial markets.
(e) A fall in the absolute number of jobs in manufacturing industry.

5 In which of the following industries would there have been a rise in jobs during the period 1975 to 1985?
(a) shipbuilding
(b) financial services
(c) textile manufacture
(d) agriculture
(e) mining

6 Unemployment, caused by the general low level of aggregate demand, is called:
(a) structural

(b) regional
(c) frictional
(d) cyclical
(e) residual

**7** Which of the following causes the official unemployment figures to overstate the actual level of unemployment?
 (a) The existence of the black economy.
 (b) People who have found employment since the count was taken.
 (c) A lack of any allowance for the level of notified vacancies.
 (d) People who 'cheat' the system.
 (e) All of the above.

**8** Which of the following is not a direct cost to the exchequer of high unemployment?
 (a) Loss of export earnings.
 (b) Loss of income tax payments from the unemployed.
 (c) The cost of administration of unemployment exchanges.
 (d) The provision of special schemes for the unemployed.
 (e) The unemployment benefit payments.

**9** Which of the following measures would tend to reduce the level of frictional unemployment?
 (a) Lowering the level of wages paid to young people.
 (b) Improving the infrastructure of the regions.
 (c) Increasing the level of aggregate demand.
 (d) Encouragement of retraining schemes.
 (e) Restrictions on the introduction of new technology.

**10** Which of the following will cause a drop in the activity ratio in an area of the country faced with high unemployment?
 (a) Less people stay on at school and college in full time education.
 (b) Women drop out of the labour market.
 (c) People move out of the area to seek better job prospects elsewhere.
 (d) More people lose their jobs as more factories close down.
 (e) There is an increase in birth rate in the region.

**2** (a) Seasonal unemployment increases, e.g. in construction and agriculture.
 (b) YTS gives training and work experience to young people. Some people think that employers recruit people on YTS rather than offering permanent jobs to other people.
 (c) Frictional unemployment, and structural difficulties concerning lack of labour mobility and information about the opportunities.
 (d) The unemployed do not comprise a stable group of people, people are leaving and joining the register each month, the change in the official figures is the net effect of the two. Longer-term unemployment is rising with the continuing high level of unemployment.
 (e) As an indication only (see *Unit 15.2*)
 (f) (i) There are some schemes to share out the existing work to more people, e.g. through early retirement, job sharing, redundancy pay provision.
 (ii) General macroeconomic management strategies highlight differences in economic philosophy. Some economists advocate standard Keynesian reflation to generate more economic activity, others insist that the initial strategy must be to eliminate inflation, and to deal with structural difficulties in the labour markets (trade union agreements, social security payments levels, Wages Councils) before 'high and stable' employment conditions can be created.

**3** (a) UK unemployment higher than EEC and OECD averages (at 12.7% compared to 9.9% or 8.1% respectively).
 (b) The causes of some of the unemployment are international, i.e. they involve the levels and balances involved with international trade.
 (c) Japan (2.6%) Sweden (3.5%). Not too much in common, apart from competitive industries.

**4** (b) Fluctuations of unemployment levels until the general onset of rising unemployment in 1975. A slight drop in 1978–9 was followed by a rapid rise in 1979–82 (from 1.3m to 2.9m).
 (c) See *Units 15.4 and 15.5.*

# Answers

## Exercise 1

**1**

| | Workers | Type of unemployment | | Workers | Type of unemployment |
|---|---|---|---|---|---|
| (a) | Shipbuilders | Structural/regional | (g) | Car workers | Demand deficiency |
| (b) | Bricklayers | Seasonal | (h) | Manufacturing | |
| (c) | Office workers | Technological | | workers | Regional |
| (d) | Graduates | Frictional | (i) | Disabled persons | Hard-core/residual |
| (e) | Young people | Youth/demand deficiency | (j) | Computer operators | Technological |
| | | | (k) | Tobacco workers | Structural |
| (f) | Local government employees | Demand deficiency (?) | (l) | Miners | Unclassifiable? |

## Exercise 2

**1**

| (a) (i) | Mining and quarrying | −14% | Introduction of new technology, new fuel, cheaper coal available from elsewhere. |
|---|---|---|---|
| (ii) | Textiles | −45% | Imports from low wage paying countries, uncompetitive British products, slow introduction of new technology. |
| (iii) | Insurance, banking and finance | +23% | Competitive internationally, growing demand for services, expansion of services offered. |

**2** (a) Services have grown in all countries, agriculture has declined in all countries. Industry has expanded in Japan and Italy.

(b) No—this shows relative shares, deindustrialisation refers to a fall in absolute number of jobs in manufacturing. Between 1973 and 1979 manufacturing employment fell in Japan, Germany, France and the UK of the countries shown.

(c) (i) hotels, sports centres
(ii) banking services
(iii) estate agents and solicitors
(iv) medical services
(v) recreational services
(vi) computer shops, video shops

(d) Services like financial, professional and scientific services are essential to industry, while industry is essential to distributive services.

(e) Curb on spending by government, high income elasticity of demand for 'new' services, introduction of new technology, e.g. in communications.

## Exercise 3

**1** (a) A turnround of £20b, from a surplus of £15b to a deficit of £5b.

(b) (i) EEC membership involves the removal of tariff barriers and encourages trade, but this has equal effect on imports and exports. Since membership, exports of manufactured goods to the EEC have risen faster than imports from the EEC.

(ii) The North Sea oil discoveries have hampered exports by:
(a) forcing up the rate of exchange of sterling by 41% in real terms between 1979–81.
(b) causing deficits in other countries which has reduced their ability to purchase our exports.

(c) Recession lowers incomes and hence the demand for imports. The effect on import levels depends on the value of the marginal propensity to import.

(d) Slow growth, loss of employment, underlying trade difficulties. In Britain the effect has been cushioned by the exports and revenue generated by North Sea oil.

## Exercise 4

**1** (a) Situations where the actual equilibrium level of national income is below the level that would generate full employment.

(b) (i) close
(ii) close
(iii) widen
(iv) close (less savings implies more consumption expenditure)
(v) close
(vi) widen (the level of national income required to generate full employment would have increased).

(c) The multiplier effect.

(d) (i) Inflation would increase (higher wage claims, pockets of excess demand, possible rise in the money supply through government reflationary policy).

(ii) The balance of trade would deteriorate (more imports purchased, some potential exports switched to the home market although extra demand might generate extra profits and investment expenditure and hence promote exports in the longer term).

(iii) The rate of growth would increase (more demand leads to more profits, more incentive to invest, need for increased capacity via accelerator effect).

(e) Increased inflation tends to increase savings and reduce consumption, and hit the price competitiveness of exports. Investment is encouraged through growth. The point of the question is to reinforce the point that the deflationary is a dynamic (i.e. moving) concept.

**2** (a) Lower. It would reduce the disincentive trap, encourage some people to find work.

(b) Lower. Unemployed people could not remain unemployed for as long without financial hardship.

(c) Raise. Fewer jobs would be offered by employers if low wages were increased.

(d) Raise. Less job information raises the level of people unable to find work.

(e) Lower. This would lower structural unemployment levels.

(f) Lower. It would lessen the extent of the poverty trap.

(g) Lower. More jobs from increased competitiveness of goods, and increased competitiveness of labour relative to capital.

**3** (a) High unemployment combined with high inflation.

(b) They have to deflate to get inflation out of the economy before permanent jobs can be created.

(c) The MTFS has the concept at its heart.

## Exercise 5

**1** (a) Northern Ireland. North Wales, West Midlands,

North West, Scotland, Yorkshire and Humberside.

(b) In 1974 unemployment in the West Midlands was below the national average (2.1% compared to 2.6%) but by 1982 it was above (14.9% to 12.2%).

This was caused by loss of jobs in, e.g. car manufacturing and engineering, and from the consequent multiplier effect. The area is at the heart of Britain's deindustrialisation.

(c) In absolute terms the difference between the highest unemployment and the lowest has widened from 2.9% (5.4% − 1.5%) to 10.7% (19.4% − 8.7%). In relative terms the highest to lowest ratio has narrowed from 2.82 (5.4%/1.5%) to 2.23 (19.4%/8.7%).

(d) Own research.

2 (a) (i) Area where 15% of project costs automatically paid by government grant.
 (ii) Area where selective assistance from the government available.
 (iii) The area within which people tend to travel to work.

(b) Dundee, Stathclyde, North Cumbria, Tyneside, Wearside and Teesside, Anglesey, Liverpool and parts of Cheshire, Corby, parts of South Wales, parts of Cornwall. High unemployment, declining industry, few positive factors for the location of industry.

(c) Cost per job figure introduced for grants, changes of area status, reduction of types of area to two, introduction of aid for service industries.

(d) See *Unit 15.9 (5)*.

3 (a) See *Unit 15.7*.

(b) Improved infrastructure reduces costs for business. Better social capital encourages management mobility. New facilities foster new attitudes.

(c) Ideally regional aid supports labour intensive, complementary, growth industries. Industries without a comparative advantage in an area will not be able to offer lasting employment opportunities.

(d) A new centre for the expansion of industrial activity. Some success, e.g. the attraction of Nissan to build cars there, but unemployment levels are still high.

(c) The mention of 1500 workers who have not registered as unemployed.

(f) Rejection by society, denial of the right to work. Financial consequences of unemployment may have been reduced by earnings from the black economy and from high redundancy payments.

## Suggested Essay Plans

### Essay 1

Definition of terms: Deindustrialisation (i) absolute loss of jobs in manufacturing better than (ii) situation where governments increase their spending on non-marketed output or (iii) a situation where a country exports insufficient to pay for its full employment level of imports as these pre-judge the cause of deindustrialisation.

Main paragraphs: See *Unit 15.6*.
Conclusion.

### Essay 2

Definition of terms: Deindustrialisation. Economic consequences involve: employment levels, growth rates, balance of payments problems, inflation.

Main paragraphs: Growth—manufacturing industry as the 'engine of growth'. Loss of traditional jobs—structural difficulties—new industries more capital intensive—shift to service sector employment. Balance of payments—decline in manufacturing balance, but overall effect cushioned by oil.

Conclusion.

### Essay 3

Definition of terms: Job creation. Job destruction.

Main paragraphs: Examples to illustrate job destruction, e.g. through introduction of robots in manufacturing processes, or data processing in white collar areas, and job creation, e.g. video retailing shops, microcomputer manufacture, retailing and applications.

Conclusion. Short term destruction versus long term creation.

### Essay 4

Definition of terms: Regional policy. Measurement of regional inequalities.

Main paragraphs: See *Unit 15.9* and data from Exercise 5.

Conclusion.

## Multiple choice answers

1 (a) See data in Exercise 5.
2 (c) Combination of changes in pattern of demand and resource immobility.
3 (d) Loss of jobs in shipbuilding, coal and steel industries.
4 (c) This happens in all economies as the level of real income increases.
5 (b) Rise of jobs has been concentrated in the tertiary or service sector.
6 (d) Or known as demand deficiency unemployment.
7 (a) Some people who are registered as unemployed are economically active.
8 (a) Loss of exports is not a direct cost to the exchequer.
9 (d) Better training enables people to move to new job opportunities sooner.
10 (b) Fewer people out of the potentially economically active population are seeking work.

# UNIT 16 — Money and inflation

## 16.1 Preview

1 Money is used in all advanced economies to overcome some difficulties associated with trade and exchange.
2 Money can take many different forms. Anything that performs the main functions of money can be considered to be money. The majority of effective money is created by the banking system.
3 If there is a general rise in the price level then the real value, or purchasing power, of money will fall.
4 Monetarist economists have restated the existence of a link between inflation and the growth of the money supply.
5 Control of inflation has been an essential ingredient of the Medium Term Financial Strategy, and is seen as a prerequisite for the long run reduction in the levels of unemployment.

## 16.2 Money

1 Money is used to overcome the difficulties experienced in barter.
   (a) Establishing a double coincidence of wants—finding someone who has what you want and also wants what you have.
   (b) Agreeing on a measure of value.
   (c) Wanting to store some of the value of a good for later use, i.e. the need to be able to store wealth.
   (d) Problems associated with transporting goods to an agreed market place.
2 Money is therefore required to fulfil four main functions.
   (a) *Medium of exchange*—a half way stage in the process of exchange. e.g. a worker exchanges his labour first for money (his wages) and then exchanges this money for goods and services.
   (b) *Unit of account*—a measuring rod of value, e.g. it is usual to talk of a *Toblerone* costing 2 Swiss Francs or 65 pence rather than 2 loaves of bread.
   (c) *Store of wealth*—money allows some of the value of a good which has been traded to be stored for later use, e.g. a worker does not have to spend all his income immediately, some can be saved and used at a later date.
   (d) *Standard for deferred payments*—money allows contracts to be signed and for payments to be made at some agreed later date.

## Exercise 1

1 Imagine you are the owners of a holiday resort where people come to stay in your villas, shop at your store, and take part in various sport and leisure activities within the resort.

You wish to establish your own money which will be used exclusively within the resort. What characteristics would your money supply have?

2  What is meant by the expression 'payment in kind'? Why are some people prepared, and able, to undertake trade or exchange without the use of money?

3  Countertrade is a generic name for international trade arrangements that avoid the need to use money. Countertrade may involve a simple swap of goods or services that are wanted by each partner, it may involve a 'buy-back' agreement where goods or materials may be provided by one country and the goods subsequently produced from these resources are bought back by the supplying country, or more likely involve a 'third-party' trading house. A typical countertrade arrangement might be as follows.

> The Government of Indonesia wants machinery, and has plywood to sell.
> A trading house agrees to buy plywood and sells the plywood to a furniture manufacturer.
> The trading house uses the money from the sale to sign a contract with the manufacturer of machines for delivery to Indonesia.
> The machine producer will normally pay a subsidy to the trading house.

Over 80 countries are believed to have been involved in countertrade in recent years, and although it is difficult to monitor, estimates suggest that trade to the value of $500 b is annually conducted under these type of arrangements. (Based on information from *Barclays Bank Briefing No 64*, August 1984)

(a)  What circumstances might have led to an increase in the level of countertrade arrangements?

(b)  Why, in the example above, might the Indonesian government have been unable to pay for the machinery they wanted directly?

(c)  Why would the exporting machinery company be prepared to pay a subsidy to the trading company?

(d)  Explain how the use of a 'third party' overcomes the basic problem of barter, i.e. the need to establish a 'double coincidence of wants'?

# 16.3  Some definitions

1  **Legal tender**

Money that the government has declared must be accepted if offered as settlement of debt.

2  **Fiat money**

Money that the government stipulates is money.

3  **Fiduciary issue**

Money that has no direct backing, e.g. with gold. The holders accept the money on trust that they will be able to exchange it for goods and services.

**4  Liquidity**
Refers to assets which can be turned immediately into a known amount of money. The longer it takes, or the more uncertain the value, the less liquid is the asset.

**5  Near money**
Refers to assets that perform only the function of a medium of exchange.

**6  Money substitutes**
Refers to assets which perform only the function of being a store of wealth.

## 16.4 Measurement of the money supply

1  There are many assets that perform some or all of the functions of money to a greater or lesser degree. Any definition of what actually does constitute the money supply at a particular moment is bound to be somewhat arbitrary.

2  A basic distinction can be made between:
  (a) *narrow measures*—which concentrate on money being a medium of exchange,
  (b) *broad measures*—which include those assets which may be both a store of wealth and a potential medium of exchange.

3  Narrow measures of the money supply include:
  (a) M0 (i.e. M zero)—alternatively known as the monetary base, which measures the value of notes and coins and the deposits of banks with the Bank of England.
  (b) NIBM1 (non-interest bearing M one)—which measures the value of notes and coins and non-interest bearing current account deposits in banks.

4  Broad measures of the money supply include:
  (a) £M3 (sterling M three)—which measures the value of M1 plus deposit or time deposits plus interest-bearing current account deposits, as long as the account is held in sterling.
  (b) PSL2 (private sector liquidity two)—which is basically M3 plus assets of a liquid nature held by the private sector outside the banks, e.g. in building societies, or in government securities like Treasury Bills.
  (c) DCE (domestic credit expansion)—which broadly speaking is £M3 plus a deficit, or minus a surplus, in the balance of payments accounts.

5  Experience has shown that the various forms of money, and hence the various measures of the money supply, do not always move together or to the same degree, e.g. M1 may fall at the same time as £M3 rises. In order to understand the overall nature of the money supply position the government monitors a number of the measures of the money supply.

## Exercise 2

1  State for each of the following whether they should be regarded as:
  (i) money
  (ii) near money
  (iii) money substitutes

(a) a current account held at the Midland Bank

(b) a Barclaycard with a £1000 credit limit

(c) an Abbey National Building Society Share Account deposit

(d) National Savings Certificates

(e) a £20 note

(f) ordinary shares held in ICI

2 Produce a suitable chart to show whether the following perform the functions of being:

      (i) a medium of exchange

     (ii) a store of wealth

    (iii) a unit of account

(a) a £50 note

(b) a guinea

(c) ordinary shares in Trusthouse Forte PLC

(d) Unit Trust holdings in Henderson's Japanese Trust

(e) an unused, valid, air ticket to Singapore

(f) an old master (i.e. painting)

(g) 1,000,000 peso note in Argentina

(h) cigarettes

(i) deposits held in the National Savings Bank

(j) a Scottish pound note in England

3 Place the following on a simple 'liquidity spectrum', i.e. with the most liquid assets on the left, and the least liquid assets on the right.

(a) Physical assets, e.g. a house.

(b) Long dated government securities, e.g. Consols dated 1990.

(c) Cash.

(d) Deposits in a building society with requirement for seven days' notice of withdrawal.

(e) Current account bank deposit.

(f) Treasury Bill, a 90 day loan to the government.

4 What promise is written on English bank notes? Does this mean that the English notes are not a fiduciary issue?

5 **Extract from the budget speech 13.3.84**

Monetary policy will continue to play a central role in pursuit of the government's policy objectives. Further restrictions are needed to achieve still lower inflation.

The growth of £M3 has been well within the 7–11% target range, with M1 at the top end of the range and PSL2 a little above it. The effective exchange rate has remained fairly stable despite international uncertainties.

One important development has been to give a more explicit role to the narrow measures of money. £M3 and the other broad aggregates give a good indication of the growth of liquidity. But a large proportion of this money is in reality a form of savings, invested for the interest it can earn. In defining policy it is helpful to make specific reference to measures of money which relate more narrowly to balances held for current spending.

It was for this reason that M1 was introduced as a target aggregate but it has not proved entirely satisfactory for that purpose. With the rapid growth of interest-bearing sight deposits M1 has become as increasingly poor measure of money held to finance current spending. Other measures of the money supply have not been distorted to the same extent. In particular M0, which consists mainly of currency, is likely to be a better indicator of financial conditions than M1.

The target range for £M3 will be set at 6–10%. The target range for narrow money will apply to M0 and for the next year will be set at 4–8%.

*(Hansard,* HMSO)

(a) What do you think were the government's objectives in 1984?

(b) What do you think is the link between control of the growth of the money supply and inflation control?

(c) What is the essential difference between narrow and broad definitions of the money supply?

(d) What do you understand by the terms
   (i) liquidity
   (ii) interest-bearing sight deposits
   (iii) target range for £M3

(e) Why is £M3 not considered to be a good measure of money held for current spending?

(f) In 1984 growth was expected to be about 3.5%, and inflation 4.5%. What relevance is this information to the setting of the target ranges for the growth of the money supply?

## 16.5 The rate of interest—The price of money

1 The monetary or liquidity preference theory of the determination of the rate of interest sees the rate of interest as the price of money.

2 In markets, prices are determined by the interaction of supply and demand.

3 The supply of money is assumed, for the time being, to be determined by the authorities (Bank of England and Treasury) and to be independent of the rate of interest.

4 The demand for money refers to people's desire to hold on to money or cash rather than spend it, or save it by investing in some less liquid security like a Government Bond.
People will demand money for two purposes.

(a) *Active balances*—(i) transactions motive balances to have liquid assets available to pay for known expenditures, (ii) precautionary motive balances to have liquid assets available to pay for unforeseen transactions.

(b) *Passive balances*—speculative motive balances because they did not wish to be holding a security because the real return from the security was low or because it could lose value if there was a change in the market rate of interest.

*Observations from Figure 16.1*

☐ The level of transactions (T) and precautionary motive (P) balances are unrelated to changes in the rate of interest. They are determined by institutional arrangements for receiving pay and making payments and people's general view of economic circumstances. Speculative motive balances (S) vary inversely with the rate of interest.

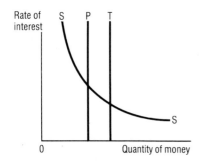

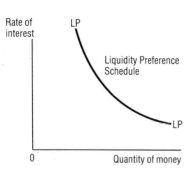

**Figure 16.1** Demand for money

□ The market value of a fixed interest security and the market rate of interest are inversely related. If the market rate of interest rises fewer people are going to be satisfied with an existing security offering them a less favourable return. Their sales of the security will force its market price down.

□ The sum of the separate transactions, precautionary and speculative motive balances creates the demand curve for money which is called the liquidity preference schedule (LP).

5   Determination of the rate of interest.

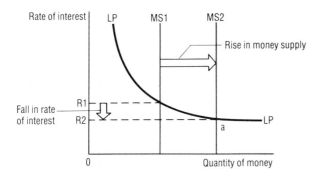

**Figure 16.2**   The rate of interest

*Observations from Figure 16.2*

□ The rate of interest (R1) is determined by the interaction of the money supply (MS) and demand (LP) curves for money.

□ If the money supply rises (MS1 to MS2) the rate of interest will fall (R1 to R2), until the liquidity preference schedule becomes totally interest-elastic after point 'a'.

□ An increase in the demand for money will cause a shift of the liquidity preference curve to the right, and a rise in the rate of interest.

---

# Exercise 3

1   A long-dated Government Bond is issued at a nominal price of £100, paying 10% p.a. (i.e. £10 per year) to the holder.
   (a) If the market price of the bond subsequently rose to £200 what would be the rate of return to the holder if the bond had been acquired at this higher price?
   (b) If the market rate of interest rose to 20%, at what market price would the bond again become a reasonable investment?
   (c) What is the general relationship between the market price of a fixed interest security and the market rate of interest?

2   On the 16 February 1984 the prices on the right were quoted for government stocks.
   (a) What was the market rate of interest?

3   What effect would the following have on the position of the liquidity preference curve?
   (a) A fall in the level of transactions motive balances.

> Exchequer, 13%, 1987, £106.56
> Treasury, 10%, 1992, £96.00
> War Loan, 3.5%, undated, £36.38

| Rate of interest | Speculative balance (£m) |
|---|---|
| 8 | 1,000 |
| 7 | 1,500 |
| 6 | 2,000 |
| 5 | 3,000 |
| 4 | 4,500 |
| 3 | 7,000 |
| 2 | 10,000 |

(b) A rise in the rate of interest.

(c) A rise in the level of precautionary motive balances.

(d) A rise in the market price of fixed interest securities.

4   At the current level of national income in an economy transactions motive balances equal £1000m, and precautionary motive balances £1500m.

Speculative motive balances vary with the rate of interest as in the table (left).

(a) What would be the rate of interest in the economy if the money supply was : (i) £3500m, (ii) £6000m

## 16.6 Credit creation by the banking system

1   It is apparent from the measures of the money supply outlined in *Unit 16.4* that deposits held in commercial (High Street or clearing) banks form an important part of the money supply.

2   The banking system has the ability to create credit on top of the amount of money deposited with it. This arises because experience has shown that banks have only to keep a fraction of their total deposits in cash form to meet the demands for cash from their customers. The remainder can be employed by the banks to earn a profit, and one profitable form of business is to lend money to people who wish to borrow.

3   People borrow to undertake expenditure. This expenditure generates further bank deposits and allows banks to undertake further lending. There is at work a credit creation multiplier effect, the size of which is determined by the amount of cash that banks feel they have to keep in cash form.

4   Banks arrange their assets so as to strike a balance between the need for liquidity and the desire to make a profit.

A simplified bank balance sheet will include the items shown in Table 16.1, below.

| ASSETS | LIABILITIES |
|---|---|
| Cash in tills | Shareholders funds |
| Cash on deposit at the Bank of England | Current account (sight) deposits |
| Money at call with the Discount Houses | Deposit account (time) deposits |
| Bills discounted | Other borrowing e.g. from the money market |
| Advances | |
| Investments | |

☐ *Discount Houses* are institutions at work in the City of London which take deposits for short periods of time from commercial banks (often overnight) and lend on this money to holders of bills who wish to exchange these bills for cash.

☐ *Bills* are essentially short term IOUs. Commercial Bills are issued by companies to confirm payment of an appropriate sum to the holder of the Bill at some future time. Treasury Bills are notes issued by the government as receipt for lending by the holder to the government of a sum of money for 90 days.

☐ *Bills discounted* refers to the banks activities in discounting bills along the lines described for the Discount Houses.

☐ *Advances* are loans made to customers, e.g. in the form of personal loans or overdrafts. It is the level of advances that is the key component in the creation of credit and hence in contributing to the growth of the money supply.

# Exercise 4

1  In an economy there is only one bank. The bank keeps 25% of all deposits in cash, and lends out the remaining 75%. A company within the economy sells exports valued at £1000 and deposits payment for these in the bank. Assuming there is sufficient demand for borrowing in the economy what will be the final rise of the money supply after the full credit creation multiplier effect has worked through?

2  Place the following assets of a commercial bank in order of liquidity, with the most liquid first and the least liquid last.
(a) Cash in the tills.
(b) Bills discounted.
(c) Investments with over two years to maturity.
(d) Advances to borrowers.
(e) Money on deposit with the Bank of England.

3  Place the assets listed above in the order of profitability for the bank, the least profitable first and the most profitable last.

4  In an economy what limits the ability of the banking system to create credit?

# 16.7 Inflation

1  *Inflation* is a general rise of the price level of an economy. Alternatively it can be seen as a general fall in the value of money within an economy.

2  *Hyper-inflation* refers to a situation where prices are rising so fast that money ceases to be able to fulfil its main functions. Inflation measured at several hundred per cent per annum would normally be considered to be hyper-inflation.

3  The consequences of moderate inflation (say a rate of less than 10% per annum) are significantly less than the consequences of more rapid inflation (say at a rate of around 25% per annum).

4  Inflation is measured by the production of an index number which monitors the rate of price increases. A number of separate indices are produced in Britain. These include:
(a) *The Retail Prices Index*—which attempts to trace the rise in the cost of an average family's expenditure over a given period of time. It involves establishing:
  (i) a regimen—i.e. a 'basket of goods' which represents the expenditure of an average family,
  (ii) weights—i.e. giving more prominence to items which form a large proportion of family expenditure and less to those which are less important,
  (iii) a base year—i.e. a year with which to compare subsequent changes, a year in which the value is fixed at 100,

(iv) a system of monitoring price changes.
(b) *The Tax and Price Index* which includes an allowance for direct tax changes on the level of the household's disposable income. For example, if the Retail Prices Index had risen by 10%, but direct tax cuts had increased disposable income by 10% there would be no change in the Tax and Price Index.
(c) *GDP deflators* which are calculated for various industries to monitor how price changes have affected the value of output in those industries. The deflators are used in the production of the National Income Accounts.

## Exercise 5

1  A household divides its expenditure as shown.

| Food | Clothing | Leisure |
|------|----------|---------|
| 50%  | 40%      | 10%     |

The price index for each item of expenditure changes as shown (year 0 = 100).

|        | Food | Clothing | Leisure |
|--------|------|----------|---------|
| Year 1 | 120  | 100      | 150     |
| Year 2 | 170  | 120      | 240     |

If the family was typical of all families in the economy what would be the rise in the Retail Prices Index from year 1 to year 2?

2  If in year 1 the Retail Prices Index equals the Tax and Price Index and by year 2 there have been no changes in prices but direct tax payments have increased by 5%, what will have happened to the relative levels of the RPI and TPI?

3  The table (left) shows the change in RPI and TPI in the UK in the twelve months before January of the year shown (1978 = 100).

| Year | Change in RPI | Change in TPI |
|------|---------------|---------------|
| 1975 | 19.9          | 25.5          |
| 1976 | 23.4          | 27.6          |
| 1977 | 16.6          | 18.5          |
| 1978 | 9.9           | 4.9           |
| 1979 | 9.3           | 6.1           |
| 1980 | 18.4          | 16.1          |
| 1981 | 13.0          | 14.0          |
| 1982 | 12.0          | 15.6          |
| 1983 | 4.9           | 5.2           |

(a) Illustrate the changes in RPI and TPI for the period 1975 to 1983.
(b) If you were a worker seeking to restore the real value of your disposable income in January 1979 what level of pay rise would you be seeking?
(c) If you wished to restore the real value of your gross pay in January 1979 what level of pay rise would you be seeking?
(d) What factors could have contributed to the change in the level of the Retail Prices Index?
(e) What factors could have contributed to the different movements of the Tax and Price Index and the Retail Price Index?

## 16.8 Causes of inflation

1  A number of separate factors contributing to inflation in an economy can be identified.

(a) *Cost-push factors*—i.e. a rise in the costs of industry, e.g. wage rates, imported raw materials, change in the volume of output or an increase in required profit margins, may cause price increases for the consumer.

(b) *Demand-pull factors*—i.e. an increase in demand relative to the available supply of goods and services will cause prices to rise, e.g. a general rise in the level of economic activity in the world normally causes the prices of raw materials (or commodities) to increase.

(c) *Excess growth of the money supply*—observations of some economists suggest that rises in the money supply over and above the level necessary to finance increased growth and the existing rate of price increases cause an increase in the rate of inflation after a time-lag of around twelve to eighteen months.

The monetarist theory of inflation is based on the *Quantity Theory of Money* which stated that:

$$M.V \equiv P.T$$

where  $M$ = the money stock,

     $V$ = the velocity of circulating of that money in a given time

     $P$ = the average level of prices

     $T$ = the number of transactions carried out in a given time

So $M.V$ was a measure of the overall availability of money and $P.T$ was a measure of the uses to which that money was put. If $V$ and $T$ were considered to be stable ($V$ being fixed by institutional factors and $T$ by the tendency for the level of economic activity to tend to full employment levels) then changes in $M$ led directly to changes in $P$.

Refinements to the theory have led to it being rewritten as

$$M = k(P.Y)$$

where  $M$ = the money stock

     $k$ = a constant, based on the inverse of the income velocity of circulation

     $P$ = the general level of prices

     $Y$ = the level of real national income

to highlight the fact that changes in money national income are seen to be directly proportional to changes in the money supply.

(d) *Inflation causes more inflation*

    (i) the effect of inflation expectations has already been noted with reference to expectations augmented Phillips Curves in *Unit 15*.

    (ii) Past price increases are seen to be an important factor in the pitching of pay claims. Workers may be able to accept a fall in their living standards in the short term, but after a time they will make attempts to restore or bring about a moderate increase in their real living standards.

2  Although it is helpful to isolate the separate factors contributing to inflation in practice any inflationary process is likely to involve an inter-mix of several factors.

## 16.9 Problems associated with inflation

1 Hyper-inflation would clearly have far-reaching effects on an economy as it would involve a breakdown of the monetary and banking systems of that country.

2 Moderate inflation may have several consequences.

(a) *Price uncompetitiveness of domestically produced goods*—so that exports fall and imports rise, pushing the balance of trade into deficit, or if measures are taken to control the trade situation, causing unemployment. These consequences assume a rate of inflation higher than that experienced by the major trading rivals.

(b) *Redistributive effects*:

(i) harming those living on relatively fixed incomes, e.g. people living on interest from past savings, relative to those in a position to adjust their money incomes,

(ii) harming workers in industries where unions are powerful relative to workers whose industries are less organised,

(iii) harming taxpayers by increasing the tax revenue of government through fiscal drag,

(iv) harming savers and creditors relative to borrowers and debtors as the real value of the money paid back falls with inflation.

(c) *Unemployment*—inflation forces up wage rates which makes labour less competitive relative to other factors of production, notably capital machinery.

(d) *Distortion of money values*—inflation changes the value of the measuring rod of value, i.e money. People become confused by price changes, and in changing their behaviour because of price changes, may suffer from money illusion.

## Exercise 6

1 Israel's annual rate of inflation reached 1000% in November 1984. Economists feared it would reach 2000% by early 1985. When inflation reaches these levels it accelerates quickly into hyper-inflation as everybody flees from the local currency into goods or foreign exchange.

It is pointless to save. Some Israelis are frantically buying consumer durables. One Jerusalem couple had a row of washing machines, dishwashers, a freezer and a refrigerator in their bedroom. None were plugged in, they were being kept as a dowry for their children.

The effect of 1000% inflation can be seen throughout Israel. Supermarket prices increase so often that goods are no longer marked in shekels but in a code which is translated into the shekel rate of the day by a computer at the cash desk. Most housewives have no idea how much they are paying and few care.

Spanish-made Seat cars were among the cheapest in Israel. Their price rises every day according to the dollar exchange rate. Wages are index-linked to the official inflation rate and are adjusted every six weeks.

The lessons of the twentieth century on how to cure hyper-inflation are clear. In August 1922 the Seipel government in Austria, faced with an annual inflation rate of 627,192% fixed the growth of the money supply to external indicators. In November 1923, the Weimar Government in Germany confronted with inflation of 3,450,000,000,000,000,000% issued a new currency altogether, the new Retenmark. In both cases prices started falling by the following week.

(Based on information from *Sunday Times* 28.10.84 and *Economist* 3.11.84)

(a) Explain the terms:
    (i) hyper-inflation,
    (ii) index-linked.
(b) Why is it pointless to save at such inflation rates?
(c) What might be the expected consequences of 1000% inflation for:
    (i) consumers,
    (ii) workers,
    (iii) the government.
(d) Why does inflation at these levels normally accelerate into hyper-inflation?
(e) What does the experience of Austria in 1922, and Germany in 1923, suggest might be the cause of hyper-inflation?

# 16.10 Policies for dealing with inflation

**1 Dealing with the symptoms of inflation**

(a) *Indexation*—i.e. linking money values, e.g. wage rates and rates of interest, to the level of inflation. By keeping real values, as opposed to money values, constant indexation reduces some of the redistributive effects of inflation. In Britain most government benefits are index-linked, as are the personal income tax thresholds (through the Rooker-Wise amendment).

(b) *Incomes policies*—by imposing limits on pay rises, either as flat rate or a percentage increase, incomes policies can, in the short run, prevent groups of workers moving ahead in the pay league at the expense of others.

(c) *Floating exchange rates*—by maintaining the price competitiveness of exports and home produced goods relative to imports, floating exchange rates can prevent a deterioration in the balance of trade. There may be other effects, however (see *Unit 18*).

**2 Dealing with the causes of inflation**

(a) *Deflation*—i.e. reducing the aggregate level of demand in the economy to:
    (i) eliminate demand pull factors,
    (ii) reduce wage demands through the fear of increased possibility of unemployment,
    (iii) lowering expectations of inflation,
    (iv) allowing the government stricter control of the growth of the money supply (see *Unit 16.10(2b)*).

(b) *Control of the growth of the money supply.* The monetary authorities (the Bank of England and the Treasury) have a number of policy options which can be used to control the growth of the money supply. These include:

(i) Open market operations—i.e. dealings in the market of the existing supply of government bills and bonds, e.g. if the Bank of England sells securities to the private sector then money will be withdrawn from banks and passed to the government, reducing, in turn, commercial banks' ability to create credit.

(ii) Funding operations by the Bank of England lengthen the average date to maturity of the national debt, i.e. they reduce the number of liquid securities in the financial markets and increase the number of illiquid securities.

(iii) Changing the level of interest rates, e.g. by open market operations which affect the demand and supply of securities and hence their market rate of interest. Or, through changing the rate of interest charged to commercial banks and other financial institutions by the Bank of England in operating as the lender of the last resort to the banking system.

(iv) Reduction of new borrowing requirements lowers the rate of interest through a reduced effect of financial crowding-out, and lessens the Bank of England's need to maintain liquidity in the financial system.

(v) Special Deposits or other direct controls on bank behaviour, in order to force liquid assets out of the commercial banks or to prevent them from increasing their liabilities by borrowing on the money market.

(vi) Directives are issued from time to time when the Bank of England feels that, e.g. lending levels should be frozen at a particular level or the direction of bank lending should be changed, e.g. away from property dealings.

(vii) The Bank of England has imposed cash, liquidity and 'Reserve Assets' *ratios* on the banks, where banks have to keep a certain proportion of their assets in a prescribed form. Lending can be forced down if assets can be withdrawn from within the prescribed area as banks have to cut down their advances in order to restore the ratio desired.

(c) *Difficulties in controlling the money supply* have been experienced by the Bank of England, and the growth of the money supply has tended to exceed the upper value of the target ranges prescribed for growth of the money supply since 1976.

The problems experienced included:

(i) The need for the government, and hence the Bank of England, to finance the Public Sector Borrowing Requirement and the national debt. There may be a clash, for example, between the need to raise finance for the government by the issue of Treasury Bills and the need to control the level of liquidity in the commercial banks.

(ii) The rate of interest required to control the money supply by causing a reduction in the demand for borrowing may also deter industrial investment, cause a rise in the cost of living for those with mortgages, increase the costs of industry already in debt to banks, and cause an inflow of short term capital from overseas.

(iii) Financial institutions may be able to avoid controls by undertaking what is known as *'round tripping'* i.e. swapping one form of asset for another.

(iv) Direct controls force banks to stop specific kinds of business but tend to force customers into other sources of finance—a process known as *disintermediation*.

(v) Banks may be able to readjust their assets without involving other institutions, e.g. selling investments to generate more liquidity. This is known as *liquidity management*.

(d) *Incomes policies.* Direct controls can be placed on wage rises to control the level of unit wage costs for industry. Incomes policies involve:

(i) setting some form of norm or target for pay settlements,

(ii) establishing some system for enforcement of the policy which could include legal backing, voluntary co-operation, fiscal back-up in the form of extra income tax for groups breaking the limits, and threats of withdrawal of government orders from offending firms.

Incomes policies are likely to be more effective, at least in the short term, if there is a clear justification for the policy, e.g. a crisis that can be seen and understood by most people.

Incomes policies have encountered a number of problems when applied in the British economy in the 1960s and 1970s. These problems included:

(i) A clash with market forces after a period of time of about two to three years, e.g. where a shortage of labour could not be ended without increasing wage rates beyond the limits set by the policy.

(ii) Any norms or target pay rise levels tended to become minimum levels, no one was willing to settle at a rate below the published norm.

(iii) The type of norm established affected wage differentials and relativities, e.g. % norms tended to increase differentials in absolute terms, but flat rate norms tended to reduce differentials in relative terms.

(iv) Some groups were able to evade the policy, e.g. by coming to bogus productivity deals or through the payment of perks.

(v) After policies are relaxed to allow more flexibility for wage bargaining all groups try to make up for lost time, opening the floodgates of wage push inflationary pressures.

(vi) After a time every group seems to have a special case for breaking the guidelines so that the policy becomes too flexible to be effective.

## Exercise 7

1 In his speech (to bankers and merchants at the Lord Mayor's banquet) Nigel Lawson said that the surge in narrow aggregates during 1977 had been followed by a surge in inflation in 1979, and the deceleration of narrow

money in 1979 and 1980 preceded by about eight quarters the decline of inflation in 1983–4.

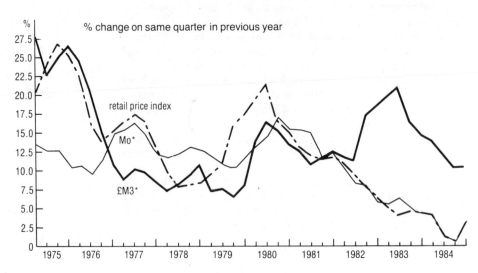

% change on same quarter in previous year

*plotted 8 quarters in advance

**Figure 16.3**   Money supply and inflation

However, the correlation is less satisfactory for 1975 and 1978. Retrospectively a measure of money supply can probably always be found that gives a good correlation with the rate of inflation if sufficiently lagged.

The Bank of England noted that the massive rise in energy prices in 1973, whose effect was aggravated by the partial indexation of wages, was a very important contributory factor to the rise in inflation in 1974–5 that had nothing to do with the British money supply in the preceding period. In the same way it could be argued that some of the rise in inflation in 1979, cited by Nigel Lawson, was due to the raising of VAT to 15% in the June 1979 budget as much as to antecedent money supply changes, and that the slow growth of M0 in recent years has been partly due to structural changes within the payments system, i.e. a switch to wages being paid by cheque rather than in cash, while the slowdown in inflation has been an effect of the tightened fiscal stance.

(Based on information from *Midland Bank Review*, Winter 1983.)

(a) Explain what is meant by the expressions:
    (i) surge in narrow aggregates
    (ii) good correlation...if sufficiently lagged
    (iii) partial indexation of wages
    (iv) tightened fiscal stance
(b) Does Figure 16.3 suggest that there is a close link between changes in inflation and changes in the money supply?
(c) Is the close relationship between inflation and lagged money supply changes proof that it was changes in the money supply that led to the slower rise in prices?
(d) What other causes of inflation were important during the period covered by Figure 16.3?

2  What are the main costs or trade-offs associated with government policies to control the rate of inflation by:
   (a) deflation
   (b) raising the rate of interest
   (c) incomes policies which limit the level of pay rises
   (d) controlling bank credit creation
   (e) raising the exchange rate

3  **Essay**
   Why might a government choose to set a target for the rate of growth of the money supply? What factors would it take into account in fixing such a target? What problems might be experienced in trying to achieve the targets set?

## Review

### Unit 16 will have helped provide answers to the following questions

1  What are the functions performed by money in an economy?
2  What characteristics does money need to be able to perform these functions?
3  Why are there several measures of the money supply?
4  What is the liquidity preference theory of the determination of the rate of interest?
5  What role do commercial banks play in the creation of credit?
6  How is inflation measured in Britain?
7  What are the main causes of inflation?
8  Why does inflation matter?
9  How can inflation be controlled?
10 What problems are associated with the various policy options for controlling inflation?

### Unit 16 has introduced the following terminology

Active balances
Bills discounted
Broad measures (of the money supply)
Commercial bills of exchange
Cost-push inflation
Current accounts (sight deposits)
Demand-pull inflation
Deposit accounts (time deposits)
Discount Houses
Disintermediation
Domestic Credit Expansion (DCE)
Fiat money
Fiduciary issue
Funding
GDP deflators
Hyper-inflation
Incomes policy
Indexation
Legal tender
Liquid assets
Liquidity management
Liquidity Preference Schedule
Medium of exchange
M0
M1
Money at call
Money substitutes
Narrow measures (of the money supply)
Near money
Open market operations
Passive balances
Precautionary motive balances
Private Sector Liquidity (PSL)
Quantity Theory of Money
Retail Prices Index (RPI)
Round tripping
Special deposits
Speculative motive demand for money
Standard for deferred payments
£M3
Store of wealth
Tax and Price Index
Transactions motive demand for money
Treasury Bill
Unit of account

### Multiple choice questions

1  Which of the following is not an asset of the commercial banks?
   (a) current account deposits
   (b) cash in their tills
   (c) money at call with the Discount Houses
   (d) advances made to customers
   (e) investments in government securities

2  Given the modified Quantity Theory of Money equation $M = kPY$ and that k is constant and there is full employment in an economy a rise in the money supply will lead to:
   (a) a fall in prices
   (b) a rise in prices
   (c) a fall in incomes

(d) a rise in incomes

(e) a rise in both prices and incomes

**3** Which of the following will affect the speculative demand for money?

(a) the expected future level of the rate of interest

(b) the value of transactions undertaken

(c) the value of the marginal propensity to consume

(d) the income velocity of circulation

(e) the level of money kept for unforeseen expenditures.

**4** If the Bank of England wishes to increase liquidity in commercial banks through open market operations it will:

(a) sell securities to the general public

(b) buy securities from the general public

(c) put up the market price of securities

(d) lower the minimum rate of interest of the Bank of England

(e) refuse to lend to the Discount Houses

**5** In arranging the exchange of goods, which of the following would not be helped by the introduction of money?

(a) Establishing the value of the items to be traded.

(b) Overcoming problems of storing some of the value of the good to be traded.

(c) Overcoming the difficulties in establishing a double coincidence of wants.

(d) Allowing payment for the goods to be delayed through some form of IOU.

(e) Arranging credit to help pay for part of the good.

**6** Which group would tend to do best during a period of inflation?

(a) people living on interest from past savings

(b) members of unions with strong bargaining power

(c) creditors

(d) taxpayers

(e) pensioners

**7** If the price of each of the following items rose by 10% in a year which would affect the Retail Prices Index the most?

(a) petrol

(b) tobacco

(c) wines and spirits

(d) food

(e) all would cause an equal change in the RPI

**8** The Tax and Price Index is a measure of inflation which includes an allowance for:

(a) the change of the value of money

(b) the changes in the level of direct taxation

(c) the changes in the total expenditure of consumers

(d) changes in the pattern of expenditure by consumers

(e) changes in the cost of production of industry

**9** Which of the following government policies is most likely to cause a rise in the rate of inflation?

(a) a revaluation upwards of the exchange rate

(b) a reduction in the level of aggregate demand

(c) the imposition of an incomes policy in the public sector

(d) an increase in liquidity in the banking sector

(e) a reduction in the level of Value Added Tax

**10** Which of the following is not a cause of cost-push inflation?

(a) a rise in the level of indirect taxation

(b) a rise in the demand for consumer goods

(c) a rise in the rate of interest paid on borrowed funds

(d) a rise in the price of imported raw materials

(e) a rise in union wage rates

## Answers

### Exercise 1

**1** Money should be

(i) convenient (portable, divisible, have high value for weight)

(ii) certain (difficult to forge, controllable supply)

(iii) liquid, i.e. acceptable

**2** A part or all of income or payment is made in non-money form, e.g. through the provision of free housing, a car, or even a firm's produce. It can be done where there is no difficulty in establishing a 'double coincidence of wants', and no difficulties in placing value on the exchanged items.

**3** (a) A shortage of foreign exchange for many Third World countries. The need for newly industrialised countries to find an outlet for their products. The world recession and the shortage of money acceptable as payments for international trade.

(b) Insufficient foreign currency.

(c) Without the services of the trading company no deal would have been possible.

(d) The 'double coincidence of wants' notion suggests that for barter to take place not only has the trader to find someone who has got what he wants to buy, but also one who is willing to buy what he has to sell. The trading company neither wanted the plywood nor had machinery to sell, but could bring together the parties who had.

## Exercise 2

**1**

| | Item | Money, Near money or Money substitute |
|---|---|---|
| (a) | Current bank account | Money |
| (b) | Credit card | Near money (up to credit limit) |
| (c) | Building Society deposit | Money substitute (for a payment to be made the 'money' in the account is first turned into a cheque or into cash). |
| (d) | National Savings | Money substitute |
| (e) | £20 note | Money |
| (f) | Shares in ICI | Money substitute |

**2**

| | Item | Medium of exchange | Store of wealth | Unit of account |
|---|---|---|---|---|
| (a) | £50 note | Yes | Yes | Yes |
| (b) | A guinea | No | No | Yes |
| (c) | THF shares | No | Yes | No |
| (d) | Unit trusts | No | Yes | No |
| (e) | Air tickets | Sometimes | Yes | No |
| (f) | Old master | No | Yes | No |
| (g) | 1m peso note | Yes | No | Yes |
| (h) | Cigarettes | No | No | No |
| (i) | National Savings | No | Yes | No |
| (j) | Scottish note | Yes | Yes | Yes |

**3** Liquidity spectrum

| Cash | Current Account | 7-day Deposit | Treasury Bill | Long dated securities | Physical assets |
|---|---|---|---|---|---|

**4** The promise is 'I promise to pay the bearer on demand the sum of X pounds'. It has no meaning as money in Britain is not directly backed by gold; it is a fiduciary issue.

**5** (a) Achieve price stability (in order to promote the competitiveness of British industry and long term employment through the achievement of sustainable economic growth).

(b) Changes in the money supply appear to be reflected in changes in the price level after a time-lag of between one and two years, as predicted by Quantity Theory of Money equation $M = kPY$. But there are other causes of inflation.

(c) Narrow measures concentrate on assets held to finance transactions, broader measures include assets held for savings purposes.

(d) (i) Assets which can be turned immediately into a known amount of money are liquid.

(ii) Interest-bearing sight deposits are current accounts where the depositor is paid interest.

(iii) Target range for £M3 refers to the upper and lower limits of growth of the money supply measure known as £M3 which have been set by the government.

(e) A large proportion of the assets included in £M3 are not held to finance transactions, but are part of people's savings.

(f) In such circumstances 8% growth of the money supply would be neutral, i.e. just enough to finance the expected increase in money national income. Money supply growth would have to be less than 8% if money was to become relatively scarce.

## Exercise 3

**1** (a) 5% using formula $\dfrac{\text{Issue price}}{\text{Market price}} \times$ rate of interest = yield

(b) £50.

(c) Rate of interest and market price of fixed interest securities are inversely related.

**2** Just under 10%. Bonds become more valuable to the holder the nearer they get to maturity.

**3** (a) Shift left.

(b) None—movement along.

(c) Shift right.

(d) None—movement along.

**4** (a) (i) 8% (the rate of interest where the money supply is equal to the sum of transactions, precautionary and speculative motive demands for money).

(ii) 4%.

## Exercise 4

**1** £4000 The credit creation multiplier

$$= \frac{1}{\text{cash ratio}} = 4$$

**2 and 3** Cash in tills/Money at the Bank of England/Bills discounted/Advances/Investments with over two years to maturity.

**4** Need to keep sufficient liquidity, activities of the monetary authorities, level of demands for loans.

## Exercise 5

**1** 42. Index numbers can be calculated by:

$$\frac{\text{sum of (changes in price} \times \text{weight)}}{\text{sum of weights}}$$

**2** RPI steady. TPI rise of 5%.

**3** (b) 6.1%.

(c) 9.3%.

(d) (i) rising costs (e.g. imported commodities, oil prices)

(ii) wage settlements (e.g. public sector pay review in 1978–9)

(iii) VAT changes (e.g. in the 1979 budget)

(iv) changes in the rate of growth of the money supply (e.g. after 1973–4 and 1979–80)

(v) previous levels, and expectations of, inflation rates

(e) Changes in the level of direct tax and national insurance contributions, e.g. lowering of income tax rates in 1979 budget.

## Exercise 6

1 (a) (i) The level of inflation at which money ceases to perform any of its main functions.

(ii) The adjustment of money values, e.g. wage levels, to changes in a given index of price increases.

(b) Money loses its purchasing power so quickly. People have to store their wealth in a form where value is maintained.

(c) (i) Need to shop early in the day. Loss of knowledge of values.

(ii) Falling real values of incomes leads to constant need to re-negotiate pay levels, circumstances which are likely to generate industrial unrest.

(iii) Distortion of tax revenues. Overall loss of support for the government.

(d) People anticipate increasing rates of inflation. Growing loss of confidence in the currency.

(e) Excess growth of the money supply. Loss of confidence in the currency.

## Exercise 7

1 (a) (i) Big rise in narrow measures of money supply (e.g. M0, NIBM1).

(ii) Close link between two variables, after allowing for a time gap.

(iii) Wages are linked to a proportion of any increase in prices.

(iv) Reduction in PSBR, reduction in government expenditure.

(b) Yes, between M0 and RPI lagged by 8 quarters (but not in 1975 and 1978).

(c) NO. The correlation could be a coincidence, e.g. the fall in inflation due to deflation, and the fall in M0 due to institutional changes in payments systems like moves to payment of wages by cheques away from the use of cash.

(d) See answer for Exercise 5, answer 3(d).

2 (a) Unemployment—slow growth—loss of competitiveness.

(b) Loss of investment expenditure. Higher costs for existing borrowers (e.g. businesses and people buying their houses through a mortgage loan).

(c) Strangulation of the labour market. Unfair treatment for those who can by-pass the regulations.

(d) Shortage of finance for investment expenditure, reduction of consumer credit, loss of employment.

(e) After a time period there will be a deterioration in the balance of trade.

## Suggested essay plan

Definitions of terms: Money supply. Target ranges.

Main paragraphs: Effect of excess growth of the money supply on inflation. Take into account real growth of national income, and existing level of inflation. Problems of control (see *Unit 16.10(2c)*).

Conclusion.

## Multiple choice answers

1 (a) Deposits are liabilities.

2 (b) Y cannot increase if there is full employment.

3 (a) See *Unit 16.5(4)*.

4 (b) This provides more money for the general public who deposit some of it in the banks.

5 (e) Money does not create credit.

6 (b) Real incomes can be maintained.

7 (d) Food has a bigger weight in the RPI calculation.

8 (b) See *Unit 16.7(4)*.

9 (d) Rise of growth of money supply leads to inflation after a time-lag of about twelve to eighteen months.

10 (b) This is initially demand-pull inflation.

# International trade and the balance of payments

## 17.1 Preview

1 International trade occurs because countries have different resources, and these resources are relatively immobile between countries, so countries are able to produce goods with different levels of efficiency.

2 Economic theory, through the Theory of Comparative Advantage, suggests that overall production can be increased if countries specialise in the production of goods in which they are relatively efficient, i.e. where the opportunity cost of making a good is relatively low.

3 Both parties to the trade will only benefit if suitable trading arrangements can be made, and no domestic or strategic considerations are damaged by the specialisation.

4 Few countries in the world allow free market forces to determine their trading patterns. Since the world recession of the late 1970s there have been increased pressures for protectionist policies.

5 The financial transactions between a country and the rest of the world are shown on the Balance of Payments Accounts.

6 Balance of Payments difficulties caused problems for the management of the British economy throughout the 1960s and 1970s, but with the emergence of North Sea oil the problems, at least on the surface, had diminished by the mid-1980s.

## 17.2 The theoretical basis for international trade

1 Countries have different allocations of resources, i.e. of land, labour, capital and enterprise.

2 These resources are relatively immobile between countries, so countries will have different levels of efficiency in making specific goods or services, i.e. the opportunity cost of making specific goods and services will vary from country to country.

3 A country that can make more units of a good with a given input of resources, or one that incurs a lower opportunity cost in making a unit of a good, is said to have an *absolute advantage* in the production of that good. The country that is not as efficient is said to have an *absolute disadvantage* in the production of that good.

4 If countries specialise according to *comparative advantages*, i.e. in the production of goods in which they are relatively efficient and where their absolute advantage is greatest, then total production can be increased.

5  Even if a country has an absolute advantage in all goods, the theory shows that if countries specialise according to comparative advantage then an increase in total production can be achieved.

6  Specialising countries will only gain from this increased production if suitable trade can be arranged, e.g. rates of exchange are beneficial to both parties, and transport costs do not erode the possible benefits.

7  The theory assumes that returns to scale will be constant, i.e. that resources within each country are mobile and that no economies or diseconomies of scale can be introduced.

## Exercise 1

N.B.  In all questions in this exercise it is assumed that resources are mobile within each country, that there are constant returns to scale, that the demand for the goods is stable, that there are no barriers to trade or transport costs. There are two countries involved, each capable of making two goods.

1  With X units of resources the production possible in two countries, A and NZ, of products wool and cars is as shown in the table (left).

|  | Wool (tons) | Cars |
|---|---|---|
| Country A | 100 or | 60 |
| Country NZ | 60 or | 50 |

   (a) In which goods has country A an absolute advantage?
   (b) In which goods has country NZ an absolute disadvantage?
   (c) In which good has country A a comparative advantage?

2  The table (left) shows the units of resources needed to make 1 kg of coffee or 1 dozen shirts in countries PNG and Ind.

|  | 1 dozen shirts | 1 kg coffee |
|---|---|---|
| Country PNG | 20 | 40 |
| Country Ind | 40 | 60 |

   (a) In which good(s) has country PNG an absolute advantage?
   (b) In which good has country PNG a comparative advantage?

3  The table (left) shows the production possible in two countries, WG and Sw, if two units of resources are used evenly to produce two products, washing machines (WM) and furniture (F).

|  | WM | | F |
|---|---|---|---|
| Country WG | 150 | and | 100 |
| Country Sw | 100 | and | 200 |

   (a) If WG and Sw specialise completely in the production of the product in which they have a comparative advantage what would be the total production of the two goods?
   (b) (i) If the terms of exchange are 3WM = 2F, and WG imports 100F from Sw, what will be the final availability of the two goods in each country?
       (ii) At these terms of trade which of the two countries will benefit?
   (c) (i) If the terms of trade are 1WM = 2F, and country WG imports 200F from Sw, what would be the final situation in each country?
       (ii) At these terms of trade which of the two countries will benefit?
   (d) (i) If the terms of trade are 1WM = 1F, and country WG imports 125F from Sw, what would the final situation be in each country?
       (ii) At these terms of trade which country will benefit?

4   Two countries, US and Can, make chemicals (C) and
    machines (M). If each uses two units of resources evenly
    between both products production is as in the table (right).
    (a) According to the theory of comparative advantage
        which country should specialise in the production of
        which product?
    (b) If specialisation does take place what will be the
        increase in total production of chemicals and machines
        from pre-specialisation days?

|            | C   |     | M  |
|------------|-----|-----|----|
| Country US | 100 | and | 60 |
| Country Can | 75 | and | 90 |

5   Two countries, J and GB produce two goods, videos (V) and
    medicine (M). The production that is possible in each
    country if one unit of resources is allocated to each product
    is as shown in the table (right).
    (a) If these countries both employ two units of resources on
        making the product in which they have a comparative
        advantage what will be the maximum number of extra
        videos that can be produced?

|            | V  | M  |
|------------|----|----|
| Country J  | 60 | 30 |
| Country GB | 40 | 10 |

6   Two countries, Br and Arg, have the production possi-
    bilities (shown in the table on the right) from the allocation
    of one unit of resources on producing meat and coffee.
    (a) If two units of resources were allocated to making the
        product in which each country has a comparative
        advantage what would be the gain in total production?
    (b) Does this mean that trade between the two countries
        can never be beneficial?

|             | Meat | Coffee |
|-------------|------|--------|
| Country Br  | 100  | 50     |
| Country Arg | 50   | 25     |

# 17.3  Trade liberalisation and protectionism

1   In the 1930s and during World War II trade flows between
    countries were severely restricted.
2   At the end of the war attempts were made to recreate conditions in
    which international trade could develop, led by the institutions of
    the International Monetary Fund (IMF), the International Bank
    for Reconstruction and Development (World Bank) and the
    General Agreement on Tariffs and Trade (GATT).
3   In general, convertible currencies, stable exchange rates, support
    for countries with short term balance of payments difficulties and
    the reduction of quotas and tariffs on manufactured goods
    allowed international trade to develop and the parties involved in
    it to benefit.
4   Some areas of economic activity remained protected, especially
    agriculture and service industries. There were also special ar-
    rangements made for trade in particular products, e.g. textiles
    (the Multi-Fibre Agreement-MFA) and steel.
5   Moves towards a return to protectionist policies have been made
    by:
    (a) *developing countries,*
        (i) experiencing balance of payments difficulties after the
            collapse of export earnings from raw materials and the
            rise of imported oil costs,
        (ii) wishing to protect their new and developing industrial
            base,
        (iii) feeling that present terms of trade mean that free trade
            benefits only the rich and powerful.

(b) *developed countries,*
  (i) experiencing stagflation, i.e. high unemployment with high rates of inflation,
  (ii) experiencing balance of payments difficulties,
  (iii) experiencing structural changes due to competition from other developed countries, e.g. Japan, and from newly industrialised countries, e.g. Taiwan, Korea and the Philippines.

6 Protectionism has taken the form of:
  (i) exempting 'sensitive' industries from the free trade arrangements,
  (ii) the introduction of new, non-tariff, barriers to trade (see *Unit 17.5*),
  (iii) bilateral agreements between countries rather than multi-lateral agreements through GATT.

## 17.4 Theoretical reasons for protectionism

1 Simple comparative advantage analysis is based on assumptions that do not hold in real life, that is:
  (a) There are *unlikely to be constant returns to scale* in the industries in which countries are supposed to specialise.
  (b) *Resources will not be mobile within each country,* and some will remain structurally unemployed after specialisation.
  (c) *Transport costs do exist,* and may erode any benefits gained from specialisation.

2 There are a number of other reasons why governments may be keen to protect certain industries.
  (a) *Short term macroeconomic considerations*—e.g. protection of employment, or export earnings, at the expense of higher long term growth and living standards.
  (b) *Infant industries*—i.e. new industries which have long term potential but in the short run are still relatively inefficient in world terms, e.g. microcomputing in Britain.
  (c) *Basic instability of markets*—e.g. agriculture, where governments are guaranteeing prices and incomes to farmers, imports must also be controlled.
  (d) *Strategic industries*—i.e. industries that are vital to a country and where withdrawal of international trade supplies would present significant problems, e.g. chemicals, banking.
  (e) *Prestige industries*—i.e. industries that governments feel should exist within a country, e.g. national airlines in developing countries.
  (f) *Dumping protection*—i.e. where a country is faced with imports from another country with a short run surplus selling its goods at less than cost price, e.g. as it is alleged Japan is doing with its semi-conductors (microchips) in the United States.
  (g) *Retaliation*—trade restrictions tend to become infectious as one country responds to controls imposed by others.
  (h) *Fluctuations in exchange rates*—which cause changes in the terms of trade, which in turn determines where the benefits of trade go. So countries will be unwilling to specialise in the production of a good which may become unsatisfactory for them if exchange rates change.

# 17.5 Forms of protectionism

**1**

|  | Indirect | Direct |
|---|---|---|
| Quantitative | Embargo | Quantitative restriction<br>Voluntary Export Restraints (VERs)<br>Orderly Marketing Agreements (OMAs)<br>Quotas<br>Local content laws<br>Tariffs |
| Fiscal | Subsidies to regions and public corporations | Subsidies on exports<br>Export credits<br>Discretionary government procurement |
| Administrative | Health and safety<br>Environmental<br>Customs procedures<br>Technical standards<br>Marks of origin | Import licensing |

(*Lloyds Bank Review* January 1984 No 151 p 33)

**2** **Indirect protection** means that all goods are generally protected by these measures, whereas **direct protection** means that specific goods are protected by these measures.

**3** **Embargoes** prevent all trade with one country and another.

**4** **Quotas** and other quantitative restrictions reduce imports by placing numerical limits on the volume of goods imported, or through restricting imports to a certain percentage market share of domestic demand.

**Voluntary export restraints** are limits placed on imports through the voluntary agreement of the exporters. **Orderly marketing agreements** are also informal ways of restricting competition in markets by limiting the volume of exports to certain areas.

**6** **Local content laws** prescribe a particular proportion of a good that has to involve locally produced components or assembly by domestic workers.

**7** **Discretionary government procurement** involves governments, who are major consumers in economies, allocating their expenditure to domestic producers even though foreign products may be cheaper or of superior quality.

**8** **The variety of health, safety and design regulations** imposed by governments can be used to reduce imports by imposing standards that imports do not conform with.

## Exercise 2

**1** The following are recent examples of protectionist measures. For each example state:
  (i) What type of protectionism is involved, e.g. from the list provided in *Unit 17.5(1)*.
  (ii) For what reason you think the protection has been provided.
  (iii) What costs, if any, are incurred by the protecting country.

(a) The European Economic Community restricts the imports of food from outside by the imposition of a variable levy, which varies according to the relationship between the level of EEC guaranteed prices and world food prices.

(b) The British government has to place a significant order for replacement of the RAF's jet trainer, and has short-listed firms which are British or who have an arrangement for a British manufacturer to assemble the plane on their behalf.

(c) Japan has ensured success for its micro-electronics industry by using the Ministry for International Trade and Industry (MITI) to channel investment capital to these firms at the expense of other areas of economic activity.

(d) Japanese car manufacturers have agreed to a voluntary limit of 11.6% market share of the British car market for their products.

(e) Australia insists that 40% of her trade is transported in Australian ships.

(f) The British government has provided financial support for Chrysler UK (now Peugeot-Talbot) and for British Leyland to ensure their continued production of cars in Britain.

(g) Many Third World countries give their own insurance companies sole rights to any domestic insurance business.

(h) Most countries operate their own national airline, supported by state subsidies and through pricing agreements with other national airlines.

(i) For short periods in 1983–4 Britain rejected imports of French long life milk because the water content of the milk was 'too high', and France rejected British pork exports because the animals had been fed with artificial hormones.

(j) The EEC countries each have their own array of quotas for the importation of textiles and clothing from twenty-five developing countries, which are co-ordinated through the Multi-Fibre Agreement.

**2  Essay**

What is the General Agreement on Tariffs and Trade? How does it operate? Why have the number of complaints to GATT increased in the 1980s?

*Further reading*

*Taking the New Protectionism Seriously* Hindley, B. and Nicolaides, E., (Trade Policy Research Centre), 1983.

*Multilateral Trade Policy in the 1980s* Greenaway, D., in the *Lloyds Bank Review* No 151 January 1984.

## 17.6 The balance of payments accounts

1 The balance of payments accounts of a country attempt to trace all financial transactions that take place between a country and the rest of the world over a given period of time.

2   The financial flows are divided into separate categories, and the accounts are presented as a compilation of these separate flows.

3   The balance of payments accounts are conventionally presented as shown in the table (right).

4   **Visible Trade** involves the import and export of goods, e.g. food, vehicles, machinery. The difference between the two is known as the trade gap, or the balance of trade.

5   **Invisible Trade** involves:
    (a) *Import and export of services*, e.g. financial, insurance, transport.
    (b) *Inflows and outflows from tourism.*
    (c) *Inflows and outflows of interest, dividends and profits* which result from previous capital flows.
    (d) *Governments' overseas spending*, e.g. on military bases, diplomatic activity.
    (e) *Private and government transfers*, e.g. for Britain's Common Market Budget contribution.

6   **The Capital Account** chiefly involves three types of flows.
    (a) *Short term capital*, moving around the world seeking advantageous interest rates and exchange rate movements and known as hot money.
    (b) *Portfolio capital*, invested, for example, in stocks and shares seeking income and capital growth over the medium term.
    (c) *Fixed or direct capital*, involved in the purchase of capital goods, e.g. factories, machinery.

7   **The Balancing Item** is akin to the residual error in the national income accounts, showing the value of flows that are known by the authorities to have taken place but which cannot be identified or allocated to a particular section of the accounts.

8   **The Balance for Official Financing** is generally taken to be the overall balance of payments position of a country.

9   **Official Financing** shows where any surplus on the Balance for Official Financing is placed, or where the foreign currency to meet any deficit comes from. There are two main options:
    (a) changing the level of gold and foreign currency reserves,
    (b) borrowing (or lending) from:
        (i) other governments,
        (ii) from official institutions like the International Monetary Fund.
    Additional money acceptable as settlement for international debts is created from time to time by the IMF in the form of additional Special Drawing Rights (SDRs) (see *Unit 18*).

10  **The Terms of Trade** should not be confused with the balance of payments accounts. The Terms of Trade specifically refer to the ratio of export prices to import prices.

|  |
|---|
| Visible trade |
| + Invisible trade |
| = **Current account** |
| + Capital account |
| + Balancing item |
| = **Balance for official financing** |
| (which must equal) **Official financing** |

# Exercise 3

1   In which section of the balance of payments accounts, if any, would you expect the following transactions to appear?
    (a) The purchase of a Volkswagen car in Britain.
    (b) An English family spending a holiday in France.

(c) The payment to staff in the British Embassy in Rome.
(d) Repayments of past loans from the International Monetary Fund by the British government.
(e) An inflow to Britain of 'hot money' seeking advantageous interest rates.
(f) The sale of North Sea oil to France.
(g) Receipts by British farmers of financial support from the Common Agricultural Policy commissioners in Brussels.
(h) The purchase by a British resident of Scottish whisky in London.
(i) The building of a new factory on Teesside by a Japanese car firm.
(j) The revenue earned by British Airways from foreign travellers.
(k) Additional foreign currency placed in the reserves by the Bank of England.
(l) American citizens buying shares on the London Stock Exchange.
(m) Profits repatriated by ICI from the operations of their overseas subsidiaries.
(n) Unrecorded transactions in foreign currencies.

2  The table (left) shows a summary of a country's balance of payments for a particular year. The items are presented in a random order.

| | |
|---|---|
| Visible exports | 100 ($m) |
| Net private investment | + 80 |
| Repayment of IMF loan | 25 |
| Visible imports | 120 |
| Balancing item | + 30 |
| Invisible imports | 50 |
| Changes in reserves | ?? |
| Invisible exports | 60 |

(a) Calculate the balance of trade.
(b) Calculate the balance on current account.
(c) Calculate the balance for official financing.
(d) What will be the change in reserves as a result of these flows?

# 17.7 Policy options for the balance of payments

1  Ideally countries will seek a long term balance on the balance of payments without the need to employ special restrictions or to reduce the domestic level of economic activity, thereby causing unemployment.

2  A surplus in the long run is undesirable as this means that the standard of living is being unnecessarily restricted. Standards of living are based on the consumption of goods and services not on the accumulation of money.

3  A deficit in the long run may be impossible as reserves and sources of borrowing foreign currency will be exhausted.

4  Governments may have specific objectives for different sections of the balance of payments consistent with the overall objective of a full employment, restriction free, balance. For example, a surplus on current account may be welcomed to allow fixed capital outflows in order to generate invisible inflows of interest, dividends and profits in the future.

5  In the shorter term governments have a basic policy option of:
(a) *financing the imbalance*, i.e. merely providing the necessary foreign currency or allocating it to reserves.
(b) *correcting the imbalance*.

6 The method of correction will depend on the section of the accounts where the imbalance is detected. Visible Account imbalances can be corrected through various means.

(a) *Deflation/reflation*—i.e. changing the level of economic activity within the economy. Lowering economic activity lowers national income, which in turn lowers demand for imports by an amount dependent on the level of marginal propensity to import in the economy, or the level of income elasticity of demand for imported goods.

(b) *Revaluation of the exchange rate*—a revaluation upwards raises export prices to foreigners and lowers import prices. A devaluation lowers export prices to foreigners and raises import prices. The effect of this on import and export revenues will depend on the values of the import and export price elasticities of demand. For a devaluation to improve the balance of trade situation the sum of the price elasticities of demand for imports and exports must add up to more than one. This is known as the Marshall–Lerner condition, (see *Unit 18.7(2)* for a fuller explanation).

(c) *Direct controls*—through the imposition of tariffs, quotas or other impediments to trade.

(d) *Improved efficiency within the domestic economy*—improvements in the price and non-price competitiveness of goods will lead to more exports and to import substitution.

7 The Capital Account can also be improved through various means.

(a) *Rate of interest changes*—with particular effect on the short term capital account.

(b) *Exchange controls*—limiting the availability of foreign exchange for those wishing to invest overseas.

## 17.8 Some drawbacks in the policy options

1 **Financing** through borrowing involves agreeing to interest rate payments and a debt repayment schedule. Borrowing from the IMF may involve additional restrictions on the operation of domestic economic policy (see *Unit 18*).

2 **Deflation** involves the creation of unemployment. In less developed economies reduction in incomes may reduce standards of living already close to primary poverty levels. In developed economies deflation will reduce profits and firms' ability to invest and protect the price and non-price competitiveness of their products.

3 **Devaluation** will only improve the overall balance of trade if the sum of the price elasticities for imports and exports adds up to more than one (see *Unit 18.7(2)*). In the short run this is unlikely to be so, and the consequent deterioration in the balance of trade position could lead to short term capital outflows and the rise in import prices could cause inflation. Exporting firms may take the opportunity of devaluation to raise profit margins rather than lower prices to foreigners, thereby negating the hoped for expenditure switching effect of the devaluation.

4 **Direct measures** provoke retaliation. A general move towards trade restrictions would lead to an overall fall in living standards.

5 **Raising the rate of interest** would deter industry from undertaking investment expenditure, which in turn would harm the level of non-price competitiveness of goods produced.

## Exercise 4

1 The government, through deflationary policies, lowers income levels by £20b. If the marginal propensity to import within the economy is 0.25 what will be the drop in the value of imports?

2 If there is general world recovery, and the income elasticity of demand for a country's exports is twice that of its income elasticity of demand for imports, what would be expected to happen to that country's balance of trade?

3 A British firm produces a computer which sells for £4000 in the UK. The initial rate of exchange for £:DM is 1:4. The price elasticity of demand for imported computers in West Germany is 0.8. Sales of the computer to West Germany are initially 100 per month.
   (a) What is the initial price of the computer in West Germany in Deutschmarks?
   (b) What is the revenue, in £s, received by the British firm from its sales of computers in West Germany?
   The rate of exchange of £:DM now changes to 1:3.
   (c) Does this represent a devaluation or revaluation upwards of the value of £ relative to the value of DMs?
   (d) What is the new price of the computer in West Germany assuming the firm does not change its profit margins?
   (e) What will be the new level of sales of computers in West Germany following this change in price?
   (f) What will be the revenue, in £s, for the firm now?

4 A country exports $500m and imports $1000m in a month. The government decides to devalue its $ value by 10%.
   (a) What will happen to the value of imports and value of exports, and hence the balance of trade, in each of the situations shown in the table.

|  | Price elasticity of demand for exported goods | Price elasticity of demand for imports |
|---|---|---|
| Situation 1 | 0.2 | 0.3 |
| Situation 2 | 0.4 | 0.4 |
| Situation 3 | 0.5 | 0.8 |

   (b) What is the sum of the price elasticities of demand for imports and exports when the devaluation improves the balance of trade position?
   (c) How would the devaluation affect the balance of trade in the situations above if:
       (i) exporters did not lower prices to foreigners,
       (ii) the devaluation caused 5% inflation in the domestic economy,
       (iii) devaluation caused a $50m capital outflow if the balance of trade position worsened.

## 5 The composition of UK visible trade, 1972 and 1982

| SIC (Series 2) | DESCRIPTION | EXPORTS (fob) | | | IMPORTS (cif) | | Values in £m |
| | | 1972 | 1982 | of which in 1982 | 1972 | 1982 | of which in 1982 |
|---|---|---|---|---|---|---|---|
| 0 | Food | 345 | 2,496 | Cereals 773 Meat 346 | 2,100 | 6,413 | Veg. and fruit 1,608 Meat 1,370 |
| 1 | Beverages and tobacco | 314 | 1,450 | Beverages 1,059 | 255 | 836 | Beverages 517 |
| 3 | Fuels | 241 | 11,193 | Petroleum products 10,641 | 1,247 | 7,401 | Petroleum products 6,274 |
| 2,4 | Raw materials | 302 | 1,341 | Ores 346, Textile fibres 315 | 1,252 | 3,929 | Ores 977, Wood 673 |
| 5 | Chemicals | 950 | 6,119 | Medical supplies 978 Plastics 875 Organic and Inorg. Chemicals 2,286 | 630 | 4,181 | Plastics 1,107 Organic and Inorg. Chemicals 1,712 |
| 6 | Semi-manufactured goods | 2,191 | 7,941 | Non-metallic mineral manf. 1,611 | 2,197 | 9,861 | Paper 1,678 Textiles 1,927 |
| 7 | Machinery and Transport | 4,090 | 18,097 | Road vehicles 3,108 | 2,287 | 16,357 | Road vehicles 4,496 |
| 8 | Misc. manufactured goods | 881 | 5,157 | Scientific instruments 1,255—Clothes 840 | 867 | 6,683 | Scientific instruments 1,053—Clothes 1,500 |
| 6–8 | Total manufacturing | 8,113 | 37,316 | | 5,983 | 37,083 | |
| 9 | Other | 284 | 1,700 | | 144 | 1,275 | |
| | TOTAL | 9,602 | 55,538 | | 11,072 | 56,940 | |
| | TOTAL on balance of payments basis | 9,437 | 55,546 | | 10,185 | 53,427 | |

(Based on information from *Annual Abstract of Statistics* Table 12.4 HMSO)

(a) Explain the terms:
   (i) fob
   (ii) cif
   (iii) SIC (Series 2)
(b) What was the balance of trade in Britain (on the balance of payments basis) in 1972 and 1982?
(c) Identify the key changes in the composition of British imports and exports from 1972 to 1982.
(d) What does the theory of comparative advantage suggest should dominate the pattern of world trade? Do these figures discredit the theory?
(e) To what extent is it true to say that British trade composition can be described as exporting manufactured goods to pay for imports of food and raw materials?

## 6 Direction of UK visible trade, 1972 and 1982 (see table overleaf)

| COUNTRIES | EXPORTS (fob) | | | IMPORTS (cif) | | Values in £m |
| | 1972 | 1982 | of which in 1982 | 1972 | 1982 | of which in 1982 |
|---|---|---|---|---|---|---|
| European Community | 2,934 | 23,117 | West Germany 5,414 France 4,486 | 3,524 | 25,252 | West Germany 7,414 Netherlands 4,474 |
| Rest of Europe | 1,567 | 6,713 | Sweden 1,935 Switzerland 1,196 | 1,794 | 8,346 | Sweden 1,674 Norway 2,023 |
| North America | 1,600 | 8,335 | United States 7,451 | 1,805 | 8,112 | United States 6,638 |
| Other developed | 946 | 3,241 | South Africa 1,192 Australia 1,043 Japan 681 | 1,150 | 4,436 | South Africa 745 Japan 2,658 Australia 493 |
| Oil exporting | 645 | 6,447 | Saudi Arabia 1,361 Nigeria 1,225 | 1,036 | 3,454 | Saudi Arabia 1,447 Nigeria 356 |
| Developing | 1,571 | 6,571 | India 805 Hong Kong 732 | 1,421 | 5,899 | Hong Kong 872 Brazil 444 |
| Centrally planned | 308 | 973 | USSR 355 Poland 133 | 332 | 1,326 | USSR 645 Poland 151 |
| TOTAL | 9,602 | 55,538 | | 11,072 | 56,940 | |

(Based on information from *Annual Abstract of Statistics* Table 12.5 HMSO)

(a) Identify the key changes in the direction of British exports from 1972 to 1982.

(b) Identify the key changes to the direction of British imports from 1972 to 1982.

(c) With which areas of the world did Britain appear to have a trade surplus in 1982?

(d) From the data provided, which countries did Britain have the biggest trade deficit with in 1982.

(e) Account for the changes identified in (a) and (b) above.

**7 UK balance of payments accounts, 1972 to 1983**                    Figures in £m

| | 1972 | 1973 | 1974 | 1975 | 1976 | 1977 | 1978 | 1979 | 1980 | 1981 | 1982 | 1983 |
|---|---|---|---|---|---|---|---|---|---|---|---|---|
| Visible balance | − 748 | −2586 | −5351 | −3333 | −3929 | −2284 | −1542 | −3449 | +1233 | +3008 | +2119 | − 500 |
| Invisible balance | + 971 | +1607 | +2073 | +1820 | +3093 | +2338 | +2700 | +2796 | +2002 | +3539 | +3309 | +2549 |
| of which | | | | | | | | | | | | |
| Services balance | + 701 | + 786 | +1075 | +1515 | +2503 | +3338 | +3816 | +4071 | +4267 | +4249 | +3844 | n.a. |
| Interest, Dividends and profits | + 538 | +1257 | +1415 | + 773 | +1365 | + 116 | + 661 | + 990 | − 186 | +1257 | +1577 | n.a. |
| Transfers | − 268 | − 436 | − 417 | − 468 | − 775 | −1116 | −1777 | −2265 | −2079 | −1967 | −2112 | n.a. |
| CURRENT BALANCE | + 223 | − 979 | −3278 | −1513 | − 836 | + 54 | +1158 | − 653 | +3235 | +6547 | +5428 | +2049 |
| CAPITAL ACCOUNT | − 673 | + 178 | +1602 | + 154 | −2975 | +4166 | −4263 | +2157 | −1887 | −7594 | −2851 | −2044 |
| Balancing Item | − 815 | + 89 | + 105 | − 106 | + 183 | +3141 | +1979 | + 206 | − 156 | + 202 | −3861 | − 821 |
| BALANCE FOR OFFICIAL FINANCING | −1265 | − 771 | −1646 | −1465 | −3628 | +7361 | −1126 | +1710 | +1192 | − 845 | +1248 | − 816 |
| Allocation of SDRs | + 124 | | | | | | | + 195 | + 180 | + 158 | | |
| Changes in reserves* | + 692 | − 228 | − 105 | + 655 | + 853 | −9588 | +2329 | −1059 | − 291 | +2419 | +1421 | + 603 |
| Other official financing | + 449 | + 999 | +1751 | + 810 | +2775 | +2226 | −1203 | − 846 | − 901 | −1732 | − 137 | + 213 |
| Effective exchange rate | 124 | 111 | 108 | 100 | 86 | 81 | 82 | 87 | 96 | 102 | 90 | 83 |
| $:£ exchange rate | 2.6 | 2.5 | 2.3 | 2.2 | 1.6 | 1.8 | 1.9 | 2.1 | 2.3 | 2.0 | 1.8 | 1.5 |
| Growth | 2.3 | 7.5 | − 1.1 | − 0.5 | 3.7 | 1.3 | 3.2 | 1.5 | − 1.4 | − 0.1 | 1.0 | 2.0 |
| Inflation | 8.6 | 7.5 | 14.9 | 26.7 | 15.2 | 14.1 | 11.4 | 15.1 | 18.7 | •13.0 | 12.0 | 4.6 |

[*(−) = additions to; (+) = drawings on reserves]                (Based on information from *Annual Abstract of Statistics* Table 13.1 (HMSO)

(a) Explain the terms:
   (i) Visible balance
   (ii) Invisible balance
   (iii) Balancing Item
   (iv) SDRs

(b) Describe UK performance on:
   (i) Visible Trade
   (ii) Invisible Trade
   (iii) Current balance.
   Explain the key changes that occur in the period 1972 to 1983.

(c) Is it possible to show any link between the balance of payments on visible account and
   (i) the rate of the inflation,
   (ii) the exchange rate,
   (iii) the rate of growth?
   What would you expect the relationships to be?

(d) Which section on the accounts shows the biggest fluctuations? What factors affect these flows?

**8 Essay**

What is meant by saying that a country has a balance of payments problem? Is such a problem only for the government concerned?

# Review

## Unit 17 will have helped provide answers to the following questions

1 On what, according to the theory of comparative advantage, should patterns of international trade be based?
2 Why do countries not allow their trade patterns to be determined entirely by free market forces?
3 What methods do countries employ to protect their industries?
4 What are the main sections of conventional balance of payments accounts?
5 What policy options are available to governments to improve their balance of payments position?
6 What are the costs to the economy of using these policy options?
7 What have been the main trends in UK trade, by composition of the trade, and direction of the trade?
8 What have been the key developments on the UK balance of payments accounts since 1972? What were the main causes of these changes?

## Unit 17 has introduced the following terminology

Absolute advantage (disadvantage)
Balance for official financing
Balance of trade
Capital account
Comparative advantage (disadvantage)
Current account
Deflation
Devaluation
Discretionary government
    procurement
Dumping
Embargoes
Exchange controls
General Agreement on Tariffs and Trade (GATT)
Hot money
Infant industries
International Monetary Fund (IMF)
Invisible Account
Local Content Laws
Official financing
Orderly marketing agreements
Portfolio capital flows
Quotas
Reflation
Relative efficiency
Revaluation upwards
Tariffs
Terms of trade
Visible account
Voluntary Export Restraints

## Multiple choice questions

1 The table shows the production possible from identical units of resources of two products in two countries.

| Country | Good S | Good T |
|---------|--------|--------|
| X       | 30     | 40     |
| Y       | 40     | 60     |

Which of the following is a true statement?
(a) Country X has an absolute advantage in the production of S.
(b) Country X has an absolute advantage in the production of T.
(c) Country X has a comparative advantage in the production of S.
(d) Country X has a comparative advantage in the production of T.
(e) Country X has a comparative advantage in neither S nor T.

2 Which of the following measures to restrict imports does so by switching the relative prices of imports and domestically produced goods?
(a) Voluntary export restraints (VERs).
(b) Orderly marketing agreements (OMAs).
(c) Health and safety regulations.
(d) Subsidies paid to domestic producers.
(e) Discretionary government procurement.

3 Governments may indulge in protectionism in order to achieve long run economic growth by:
        (i) raising profits in existing industries
       (ii) protecting infant industries
      (iii) protection of jobs in declining industries
(a) (i) only
(b) (ii) and (iii) only
(c) (i), (ii) and (iii)
(d) (ii) only
(e) (iii) only

4 Which of the following would not be recorded on the invisible account?
(a) Tourist expenditure within the UK by people from overseas.
(b) Government expenditure on overseas diplomatic activity.
(c) Government receipts or refunds from the EEC.
(d) Government repayments to the International Monetary Fund.
(e) Inflows of dividends from shares owned by British people in overseas companies.

Questions 5, 6 and 7 refer to the data in the table which are the only items in a country's Balance of Payments accounts for a given year.

| | |
|---|---|
| Visible balance | + 300 |
| Invisible balance | + 100 |
| Capital account | − 250 |
| Balancing Item | − 50 |
| Additions to reserves | + 100 |

5 What is the value of the balance of trade?
(a) + 300 (b) + 400 (c) + 150 (d) + 100
(e) cannot be determined from this data

6 What is the balance for official financing?
   (a) + 300   (b) + 400   (c) + 150   (d) + 100
   (e) cannot be determined from this data

7 What are the terms of trade?
   (a) + 300   (b) + 400   (c) + 150   (d) + 100
   (e) cannot be determined from this data

8 Portfolio investment outflows refer to:
   (a) unrecorded imports
   (b) imports of services
   (c) purchases of shares and securities overseas
   (d) exports of capital to finance the purchase of factories overseas
   (e) changes in the level of reserves held by the Bank of England

9 A devaluation of the exchange rate will improve the balance of trade if:
      (i) the sum of the price elasticities for exports and imports adds up to more than one,
      (ii) there is some spare capacity in the economy,
      (iii) exporters do not take the opportunity to raise their profit margins.
   (a) (i) only
   (b) (ii) only
   (c) (i) and (ii) only
   (d) (iii) only
   (e) (i), (ii) and (iii)

10 If the marginal propensity to import in an economy is 0.2, and the government raises the level of national income by £1000m what will be the effect on the level of imports?
   (a) fall by £200m
   (b) rise by £500m
   (c) rise by £1000m
   (d) rise by £200m
   (e) no change

11 The movement of the UK's current account on the balance of payments into surplus in 1980 was due primarily to:
   (a) imports of oil drilling machinery
   (b) revaluation of the exchange rate
   (c) rise in the exports of manufactured goods
   (d) sales of North Sea oil
   (e) reduction in food imported from the EEC

12 Which of the following is consistent with a favourable movement in the terms of trade?
   (a) Export prices rise by 10%, import prices stay the same.
   (b) Export volume rises by 10%, import volume stays the same.
   (c) Export prices fall by 10%, import prices stay the same.
   (d) Export volume falls by 10%, import volume stays the same.
   (e) Export prices fall by 10%, import prices fall by 10%.

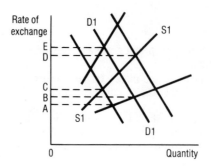

**Figure 17.1**  Influences on the exchange rate

Questions 13 and 14 refer to Figure 17.1
D1 and S1 are the original demand and supply curves for sterling.

13 What will be the new exchange rate of sterling if new voluntary export restraints are observed by exporters to the UK?
   (a) A   (b) B   (c) C   (d) D   (e) E
14 What will be the new exchange rate for sterling if more tourists come to the UK for their holidays?
   (a) A   (b) B   (c) C   (d) D   (e) E
15 Which of the following government measures will tend to increase the exchange rate of sterling in the short run?
      (i) raising the rate of interest
      (ii) subsidising fuel costs for domestic industry
      (iii) re-imposing controls on availability of foreign exchange
      (iv) re-imposition of HP and credit controls in the UK
   (a) (i) and (ii) only
   (b) (iii) and (iv) only
   (c) all four
   (d) (i) and (iv) only
   (e) (ii) and (iii) only

## Answers

### Exercise 1

1 (a) A has an absolute advantage in both goods.
   (b) NZ has an absolute disadvantage in both goods.
   (c) Wool—A is almost twice as good at making wool (10:6) but only just better at making cars (6:5).
2 (a) Both shirts and coffee. Figures here relate to opportunity costs, hence the lower the figure the higher the level of efficiency.
   (b) Shirts—PNG is twice as good at making shirts.

**3**

| (a) | | WM | F |
|-----|-----|-----|-----|
| | WG | 300 | — |
| | Sw | — | 400 |

| (b) | | WM | F |
|-----|-----|-----|-----|
| | WG | 150 | 100 |
| | Sw | 150 | 300 |
| | | (all gain to Sw) | |

| (c) | | WM | F |
|-----|-----|-----|-----|
| | WG | 200 | 200 |
| | Sw | 100 | 200 |
| | | (all gain to WG) | |

| (d) | | WM | F |
|-----|-----|-----|-----|
| | WG | 175 | 125 |
| | Sw | 125 | 175 |
| | | (gains shared) | |

**4** (a) US—chemicals, Can—machines.
 (b) 25 chemicals, 30 machines.

**5** 20 videos. After complete specialisation production is:

| | V | M |
|-----|-----|-----|
| J | — | 60 |
| GB | 80 | — |

but original supply of medicine was only 40, so J can make 40 units of medicine using only 1.33 units of her resources, and make videos with the remaining 0.66 unit of resources, i.e. 40 extra videos, making final position with partial specialisation

| | V | M |
|-----|-----|-----|
| J | 40 | 40 |
| GB | 80 | — |
| TOTAL | 120 | 40 |

**6** (a) Nil—there is no comparative advantage.
 (b) No it does not. There may be economies or diseconomies of scale or other externalities to be considered.

## Exercise 2

**1** See table below

| | Protectionism | Reason | Costs |
|-----|-----|-----|-----|
| (a) EEC agriculture | Import levies<br>Guaranteed prices<br>Support buying<br>Grants (See *Unit 19.4*) | Strategic industry<br>Employment protection<br>Balance of payments<br>considerations | More expensive<br>food<br>Over production<br>Retaliation |
| (b) Jet trainers | Discretionary govern-<br>ment procurement | Strategic reasons<br>Employment protection | Quality of<br>product |
| (c) Micro-<br>electronics | Directed finance<br>through MITI | Infant industry<br>Employment protection | Loss of finance<br>to other industry<br>Retaliation |
| (d) Cars | VER | Balance of payments<br>Employment | Lower quality<br>goods |
| (e) Shipping | Local content laws | Merchant shipping<br>a strategic industry<br>Invisible inflows for<br>Balance of payments | Increased costs |
| (f) Cars | Government funds<br>Nationalisation | Job protection<br>Balance of payments | Opportunity cost<br>of use of funds |
| (g) Insurance | Nationalisation<br>Sole rights to<br>domestic business | Invisible inflows<br>for Balance of<br>payments<br>Prestige | Less efficient<br>service |
| (h) Airlines | Licensing of<br>routes<br>Nationalisation<br>Price cartels | Prestige | Cost of support<br>Over capacity |
| (i) Food | Health and other<br>administrative<br>requirements | Protection against<br>dumping<br>Employment protection<br>Balance of payments<br>considerations<br>Strategic industry | Retaliation<br>High prices |
| (j) Textiles | Quotas | Employment protection<br>Balance of payments<br>considerations | Reduced choice<br>Higher prices |

**2 Suggested essay plan**

Definition of terms:   GATT set up after World War II to restore free trade.
Was to become International Trade Organisation.
Has become a bargaining shop.

Main paragraphs: Main initiatives known as Kennedy Round (1964–7) and Tokyo Round (1973–9) to work on tariff and non-tariff barriers.
Extra pressure to protectionism from recession and balance of payments difficulties following energy price rises. (See *Unit 17.3*)
Types of protectionism (See Unit 17.3)

Conclusion.   Problem areas still, e.g. agriculture, services, multi-national companies.

## Exercise 3

**1**

| | Item | Section of Balance of Payments accounts |
|---|---|---|
| (a) | VW Car | Visible outflow |
| (b) | French holiday | Invisible outflow |
| (c) | Rome embassy | Invisible outflow |
| (d) | IMF loan repayments | Official financing |
| (e) | Hot money | Capital (short term) inflow |
| (f) | Oil exports | Visible inflow |
| (g) | CAP receipts | Invisible inflows |
| (h) | Scottish whisky | None—transaction involves no financial flows beyond Britain |
| (i) | Teesside factory | Capital (fixed) inflow |
| (j) | British Airways | Invisible inflow |
| (k) | Reserves | Official financing |
| (l) | Shares | Capital (portfolio) inflow |
| (m) | Profits for ICI | Invisible inflow (part of dividends, interest and profits) |
| (n) | Unrecorded | Balancing item |

**2**
(a) − $20m. Visible exports—visible imports.
(b) − $10m. Visible balance plus invisible balance.
(c) + $100m. Current balance plus capital flows plus balancing item.
(d) + $75m. Additions to reserves plus repayment to IMF must equal balance for official financing.

## Exercise 4

**1** £5b (£20b × 0.25)
**2** Balance of trade would strengthen, there would be more demand for the country's exports than the country showed for extra imports.
**3** (a) 16,000 DM (4000 × 4)
   (b) £400,000 (4000 × 100)
   (c) Devaluation
   (d) 12,000 DM (4000 × 3)
   (e) 120

(f) £480,000 (change in demand = 20% i.e. up to 120, following 25% price cut and given price elasticity of demand of 0.8).

**4** (a)

| | Change of exports | Level of exports | Change in imports | Level of imports | Balance of trade | Sum of elasticities |
|---|---|---|---|---|---|---|
| Original | — | 500 | — | 1000 | − 500 | — |
| Situation 1 | up 2% | 510 | up 7% | 1070 | − 560 | 0.5 |
| Situation 2 | up 4% | 520 | up 6% | 1060 | − 540 | 0.8 |
| Situation 3 | up 5% | 525 | up 2% | 1020 | − 495 | 1.3 |

(b) Sum has to be greater than one (the Marshall–Lerner condition).
(c) (i) There would be no change in exports, thus balance of trade would not improve as much.
   (ii) Export prices would fall by an equivalent of only 5% (assuming constant profit margins) and imports would be relatively only 5% more expensive.
   (iii) Capital outflows are not on the balance of trade, but the initial worsening of the balance of trade following a devaluation could cause further problems for the balance of payments overall.

**5** (a) (i) Free on board (i.e. excluding transport and associated costs).
   (ii) Carriage, insurance and freight (i.e. including such costs in valuation of goods).
   (iii) Standard Industrial Classification, as amended in 1980 (Series 1 was produced in 1965).
(b) 1972 − £ 748m (on balance of payments basis).
1982 + £2119m (on balance of payments basis).
(c) Exports:  (i) Rise in oil exports (from 2.5% of total to 20%).
      (ii) Fall in manufacturing exports (84% down to 67%).
      (iii) Small increase in food exports (from 3.5% to 4.5%).
   Imports:  (i) Rise of manufacturing imports (54% to 65% of total).
      (ii) Rise of fuel imports (11% to 13%).
      (iii) Drop in importance of raw material imports (11% to 6%).
      (iv) Fall in food imports (19% to 11%).
(d) Countries should specialise according to relative levels of efficiency. Clearly Britain is not specialising, as many goods are imported and exported. European-wide figures might give a clearer picture of overall specialisation. The theory of comparative advantage will only become operative if suitable trading arrangements can be made, and there are no additional reasons for wishing to restrict international trade flows.

(e) No longer true. Britain now imports and exports manufactured goods; imports and exports food and raw materials.

6 (a) Exports: (i) Rise in importance of EEC (30% to 42%).
   (ii) Rise of oil exporting countries (6% to 11.5%).
   (iii) Fall of exports to other developed countries (9.5% to 5.7%).

(b) Imports: (i) Rise of imports from EEC (31% to 44%).
   (ii) Small reduction from developing countries (12.7 to 10%).

(c) North America, oil exporting countries and developing countries.

(d) West Germany and Japan.

(e) Membership of the EEC involved the progressive removal of tariffs with other EEC countries after 1973. Oil exporting countries experienced greatly increased incomes following the oil price rises of 1973 and 1979, and spent some of this on British exports, e.g. of machinery.

7 (a) (i) Visible balance involves inflows and outflows resulting from imports and exports of goods.
   (ii) Invisibles are inflows concerned with services, tourism, government expenditure overseas, interest dividends and profits and transfers.
   (iii) Balancing item (akin to the residual error in the national accounts) accounts for financial flows that cannot be allocated elsewhere in the accounts.
   (iv) Special Drawing Rights are IMF created international assets, used by member countries for the settlement of debts, up to certain limits.

(b) (i) Increasing deficit to 1974, steady improvement to 1978, bad year in 1979, before moving into surplus in 1980.
   (ii) Always in surplus, good years in 1976, 1981 and 1982.
   (iii) Changes reflection of visible account, record surplus of £6.5b in 1981.

(c) (i) Information about rates of inflation in other countries also needed. Relatively high inflation would cause British goods to become price uncompetitive in world markets.
   (ii) Look for exchange rate effects after 1972–77 depreciation and after revaluation after 1979 (see *Unit 18.7 (2)*).
   (iii) Growth leads to balance of payments problems after a time lag, e.g. after the record growth in 1972–3.
   But there are clearly other factors that affect the visible account, e.g. oil prices, and oil exports.

(d) Capital account (e.g. between 1977–8 and in 1981). Affected by interest rate changes, and expected changes in exchange rate levels, on short term flows; direct flows affected by profitable opportunities and exchange controls.

8 Suggested essay plan
Definition of terms: Balance of payments accounts. Constituent parts (Visible, Invisible, Capital). General position normally described either as:
   (i) Basic balance (Visible + Invisible + Long term capital).
   (ii) Balance for official financing (Visible + Invisible + all capital + Balancing item).

Main paragraphs: Objective for balance of payments: not a surplus, reduced standard of living; not a deficit, need to have finance. Ideally a restriction free, balance on balance of payments in the medium term, with the economy operating at full employment. Correcting a deficit involves changes for all citizens, e.g. deflation causes unemployment. Borrowing may involve conditions, e.g. from the IMF, concerning government economic policy.

Conclusion: Accounts only reflect economic activity. Everybody is concerned with trade position as it reflects relative levels of growth and inflation.

## Multiple choice answers

1 (c) X is 3/4 as good at making S, but only 2/3 as good at making T.

2 (d) Subsidies make domestic goods relatively price competitive.

3 (d) Others will hamper long run growth by keeping resources in inefficient areas.

4 (d) It would be part of official financing.

5 (a) Visible balance is the same as the balance of trade.

6 (d) The same value as the level of official financing.

7 (e) Terms of trade refers to relative value of export prices to import prices.

8 (c) By definition.

9 (c) The aim is to sell more exports and cut down imports so spare capacity is needed.

10 (d) £0.2m worth of imports for every extra £ of income (1000m × 0.2).

11 (d) See the statistics in Exercise 4, number 5.

12 (a) Terms of trade are calculated as an index of unit export prices divided by unit import prices.

13 (e) Reduced imports cuts down the supply of sterling, and raises the exchange rate.

14 (b) Extra tourists increases the demand for sterling, and raises the exchange rate.

15 (c) Although (ii) might take slightly longer to have an effect.

# UNIT 18 The finance of international trade

## 18.1 Preview

1  *Unit 17* described how international trade could lead to increased prosperity for the countries taking part.
2  International trade requires a system for the exchange of one country's currency into another's.
3  If the rate at which one currency can be exchanged for another never alters, changes in economic circumstances in the countries concerned cannot be accommodated, but if exchange rates are always changing trade might be disrupted as businessmen withdraw from the risks of trade.
4  Since World War II the International Monetary Fund has attempted to police the exchange rate system and to promote international trade.
5  From 1944 to 1972 international trade took place with relatively fixed exchange rates, but since 1972 rates of exchange have become much more flexible.

## 18.2 The International Monetary Fund (IMF)

1  The IMF was set up in 1944. It now has about 130 members which include all developed countries and most of the developing countries, but not the centrally planned countries.
2  Originally the aims of the IMF were:
(a) *to establish a system of convertible currencies,* i.e. so that one currency could be exchanged for another and used as a settlement of international debts,
(b) *to monitor and control the system of convertible currencies* to develop confidence in international trade,
(c) *to increase international liquidity,* i.e. those assets which were acceptable as means of payment for international trade,
(d) *to promote international co-operation.*
3  With the move to floating exchange rates after 1972, aim (b) above has been adapted to that of general policing of floating exchange rates.
4  The IMF operates in three important areas.
(a) In helping countries to finance and correct balance of payments deficits.
(b) In increasing the level of international liquidity.
(c) In establishing and policing an appropriate system of exchange rates.

## 18.3 The IMF and finance for balance of payments deficits

1  A country with a balance of payments deficit and insufficient reserves of foreign currency needs to borrow foreign currency if it is to be able to continue trading.

2 The IMF provides foreign currency, under certain conditions, by:
   (a) exchanging a member country's quota or subscription (originally paid into the IMF in that country's own currency) into foreign currencies,
   (b) arranging additional lending of foreign currency.

3 **Basic drawing rights** are provided in five separate tranches or slices, each of 25% of the country's quota. The early tranches are provided automatically, but later tranches are provided under increasingly tight conditions, conditions which, for example, prescribe certain domestic economic policies which must be followed by the borrowing country. These conditions are ratified by the debtor country in a 'Letter of Intent'. Thus basic drawing rights are available up to 125% of the country's quota, normally for a period of about two years.

4 **Additional 'borrowing windows'** have been developed, e.g. by the IMF borrowing from Saudi Arabia, to meet needs for foreign currency in special circumstances, i.e.:
   (a) to help countries whose export earnings have been hit by fluctuating world commodity prices (known as the *Compensatory Financing Facility*),
   (b) to help countries hit by the rising price of oil (known as *Supplementary Financing Facility or Witteveen Credits*),
   (c) to help countries to establish buffer stocks of primary products to help them stabilise world price levels (known as the *Buffer Stock Facility*),
   (d) to help countries with longer-term deficits (known as the *Extended Fund Facility*).

   The availability of these additional channels for borrowing foreign currency means that countries can borrow up to about 450% of their quota for three or more years.

5 The conditions attached to loans by the IMF do not always seem suitable for the debtor countries. Standard solutions of money supply control, and the reduction in government borrowing, may be unacceptable to some countries. The developing countries in particular, feel that the IMF's solutions are dominated by the thinking of the Group of Ten, the ten richest and most influential member nations of the IMF.

# 18.4 The IMF and the level of international liquidity

1 International liquidity, assets which are acceptable as payment for the settlement of international debts, comprise:
   (a) *gold,*
   (b) *reserve currencies*, i.e. currencies acceptable to third parties as settlement of a debt, e.g. a French company accepting US dollars as payment from a Japanese company,
   (c) *IMF drawing rights*, i.e. access to foreign currency through the IMF's normal and additional channels,
   (d) *Special Drawing Rights (SDRs)*—an artificial currency created by the IMF in 1969.

2 The amount of international liquidity is considered to be a problem.

(a) Its supply is unpredictable, e.g. holders of foreign currency in their reserves could lose confidence in the value of that currency in certain economic circumstances.

(b) Its supply is not growing in proportion to the growth of world trade, i.e. it is becoming relatively scarce.

(c) Its supply is not linked to the size of countries balance of payments deficits, and hence not linked to the demand for it.

3 SDRs were created as a response to the agreed widespread reserve shortage in the 1960s. They were a way of increasing international liquidity without some countries having to run balance of payments surpluses (so that their currencies would become strong and would be acceptable), which in turn would cause other countries to run deficits (and therefore to demand additional international liquidity). Initial SDR allocations to member countries ran at 3b SDR (about $3b) between 1970 and 1972 each year. No more were allocated until 1979, when 4b SDRs were issued each year up to 1981.

4 Further supplies of international liquidity are made available by individual countries agreeing to lend currency to those in need, e.g. through the General Arrangement to Borrow (GAB), or stand-by credits.

## Exercise 1

1 (a) From where does the IMF get the foreign currency which it lends to countries needing to finance balance of payments deficits?

(b) If a member country has a quota of SDR 400,000 how much foreign currency would they be able to borrow under the normal drawing rights arrangements?

(c) What additional sources of foreign currency borrowing would be available through the IMF to a developing country that was experiencing a balance of payments deficit because:

(i) there had been a sharp rise in the price of energy imports,

(ii) the value of the exports had fallen through lower world commodity prices during a recession.

2 **A new allocation of SDRs**

The IMF has the power to increase the level of international reserves by issuing Special Drawing Rights (SDRs). It has not exercised that power since 1981. Since then the world has experienced the deepest recession since the 1930s, a major decline in the rate of inflation, and a severe debt crisis.

These developments call for a reconsideration of the decision taken in 1981 to suspend the issue of SDRs.

The SDR was invented by the imaginative financial statesmen of the 1960s in order to allow reserve supply to be expanded in response to widespread reserve shortage, without any need for payments surpluses by some countries (and corresponding deficits in other countries).

This they believed would enable the world to sidestep the deflationary threat that could materialise if countries embarked on competitive policies (whether of protection, fiscal contraction, interest rate escalation, or devaluation) aimed at trying to secure more reserves than actually existed. In such a situation the IMF would allocate SDRs to all its participating members in proportion to their quotas. Since each participant has an obligation to accept SDRs from other countries when 'designated' to do so by the IMF (to a total of twice its cumulative allocation) these SDRs are liquid assets that can replace the need to earn reserves from other sources.

The world was right to be cautious in exploiting the SDR mechanism in the inflationary 1970s. But it would be wrong to fail to recognise that circumstances have changed. Inflation has fallen dramatically. A large part of the world economy, namely the capital-importing developing countries is desperately short of reserves.

(Based on information from *Guardian Economics Agenda*: 4.4.84)

(a) What are Special Drawing Rights? When have they been issued by the IMF?

(b) Excluding SDRs what are the other major sources of international liquidity? Why does the expansion of these sources depend on some countries running balance of payments surpluses?

(c) Explain the link between 'the deflationary threat' to the world economy and the competitive policies listed, i.e. protectionist measures, fiscal contraction, interest rate rises, and devaluations.

(d) Do countries have to accept payment of international debts with SDRs?

(e) Why was 'the world right to be cautious of the SDR mechanism' when inflation was high during the 1970s?

(f) What is the importance of an adequate supply of international liquidity for developed and less developed economies?

# 18.5 Exchange rate systems

1  From 1944 to 1972 the IMF operated a system of exchange rates which had several features.

(a) Countries pegged their exchange rates to the US dollar, which in turn was pegged to the official price of gold.

(b) Rates were allowed to fluctuate within a narrow band of $+/-1\%$ of their value (widened to $+/-2.25\%$ after 1971).

(c) Rates could be adjusted if countries were experiencing a 'fundamental disequilibrium' in their balance of payments.

(d) Finance was to be provided by the IMF for countries so that they had time to correct their balance of payments positions through appropriate domestic policy measures, e.g. through deflation, or controlling their domestic inflation levels.

2  This system, known as the Bretton Woods adjustable-peg system, continued to operate successfully until the late 1960s. Countries began to break away from the Bretton Woods system in the early 1970s for reasons outlined in *Unit 18.6*. Currency values were determined by the interaction of supply and demand on the

international currency markets. Not all currencies 'float'. Some are linked to other currencies, some to a 'basket' of other currencies. Some are stabilised through currency block agreements such as the European Monetary System (EMS) (see *Unit 19.5*). About 80% of world trade is conducted through floating exchange rates.

## 18.6 Reasons for the breakdown of the Bretton Woods system

1 Countries abandoned the adjustable-peg system in 1972 and 1973. The system had been under strain for a number of years. Attempts to perpetuate the system at the Smithsonian Agreement (December 1971), which involved the introduction of new alignments of exchange rates and wider bands, delayed the breakdown for only a few months. There were good reasons for the breakdown.

(a) *The lack of confidence in the US dollar.* The US dollar was at the heart of the Bretton Woods system as all currencies were linked in value to the US$ and the dollar was an important reserve currency. The world's confidence in the US economy and hence the value of the dollar was affected by:

(i) the so-called 'dollar overhang'—the increasing value of US$ held in Europe without adequate backing of foreign currencies in the United States,

(ii) the large US balance of payments deficits—caused by the high value of the US$ which the United States government felt could not be adjusted,

(iii) the poor performance of the United States economy, e.g. its high rate of inflation caused by government expenditure on financing the Vietnam War.

(b) *The shortage of international liquidity.* Reserve currencies formed the major part of international liquidity and the key currencies were becoming less acceptable to countries, e.g. the US$ and the £UK. If means of financing deficits was limited countries had to look for ways of adjusting or correcting the balance of payments imbalances, i.e. in this case by greater flexibility of exchange rates.

(c) *The reluctance to adjust.* Even though balance of payments imbalances arose, e.g. through high and divergent rates of inflation, countries seemed reluctant to adjust both:

(i) the level of domestic economic activity, largely because of the threat to growth and employment,

(ii) their external exchange rates, as this was seen as a form of economic failure.

The tendency of countries to delay re-adjustment until it was forced on them led to further balance of payment problems, notably:

(i) to leads and lags—exporters were paid as late as possible while imports were paid for as quickly as possible to avoid possible currency losses,

(ii) to destabilising short term capital flows—again to avoid currency losses should an exchange rate change take place.

(d) *The basic asymmetry of the system*
   (i) Deficit countries were forced to act to correct their balance of payments imbalances, because they had a shortage of reserves, but surplus countries did not have to react. Surpluses in some countries inevitably means deficits in others.
   (ii) However, surplus countries tended to experience large inflows of short term capital which forced growth in their domestic money supply which in term threatened inflation.

## 18.7 Floating exchange rates in action

1 Economics textbooks written before 1973 could only speculate as to the effect of the breakdown of the adjustable-peg exchange rate system and a movement towards more freely floating exchange rates. The experience since 1973 has shown that some of the advantages expected of floating rates have not been forthcoming, but neither have some of the disadvantages.

2 Balance of payments adjustment under floating rates has not been at all automatic. There have been five main reasons for the perpetuation of balance of payments imbalances despite floating exchange rates.
   (a) Some countries, e.g. UK and Italy, have suffered from *significant non-price uncompetitiveness*, hence changes in prices of imports and exports following exchange rate adjustment have a relatively inelastic effect on the quantities of imports and exports demanded. The Marshall-Lerner condition may not be met (see *Unit 17.7[6]*).
   (b) The response of demand to price changes following a currency revaluation will, at best, be sluggish, e.g. as firms take time to adjust to new channels of distribution. In the short run, therefore, the Marshall-Lerner condition will not be met, and a devaluation will actually make the balance of trade situation worse. Later, as demand responds to the new price opportunities, the Marshall-Lerner condition will be met, and the balance of trade will start to improve. *This is known as the J-curve effect.*

*Observations from Figure 18.1*
□ Devaluation occurs at time X.
□ Import prices rise and export prices to foreigners fall, but initially demand is price inelastic, so the balance of trade falls further into deficit.
□ As time progresses so demand becomes more elastic and the Marshall-Lerner condition is met by time Y.
   (c) The initial deterioration in the balance of trade following devaluation may *induce speculative activity* against the currency, and an outflow of short term capital. The economy may never reach the tail of the J-curve.
   (d) A depreciation of the exchange rate is likely to cause *cost-push inflation* through higher import prices. This inflationary pressure might spark off further inflationary movements, e.g. higher wage demands, which will erode the price advantages given by the currency depreciation.

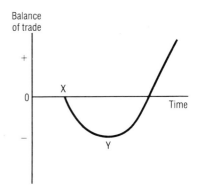

**Figure 18.1** The J-curve

**Vicious Circle**

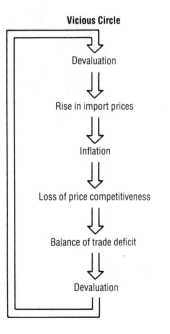

Devaluation

⇓

Rise in import prices

⇓

Inflation

⇓

Loss of price competitiveness

⇓

Balance of trade deficit

⇓

Devaluation

**Virtuous Circle**

Revaluation upwards

⇓

Fall in import prices

⇓

Low inflation

⇓

Gain in price competitiveness

⇓

Balance of trade surplus

⇓

Revaluation upwards

(e) This may become reflected in *vicious or virtuous circles* (see left).

**3 Freedom for domestic economic policy making**

Economics textbooks used to suggest that countries would:

(a) be free to pursue whatever internal economic policies they chose without the need to worry about the external balance of payments constraint,

(b) therefore, not co-operate closely in economic activity.

However, experience has shown that:

(a) countries still have to operate certain domestic policies to defend their balance of payments position, e.g. the need to fix their rate of interest at a level that will attract short term capital,

(b) countries will still co-operate in economic matters, e.g. countries co-operated to manage their exchange rates after the OPEC oil price rises in 1973.

**4 Inflation**

Economics textbooks used to state that fixed exchange rates imposed a discipline on governments requiring them to control their rates of inflation. Undoubtedly inflation was high in the period from 1973 to 1980 but the inflation was not directly attributable to the new freedom to float exchange rates.

There is evidence that some countries, e.g. West Germany and Switzerland, benefited from virtuous circles after 1973 (see above).

**5 Destabilisation**

Economics textbooks used to state that floating rates would:

(a) disrupt international capital flows,

(b) restrict international trade.

There have, indeed, been big exchange rate swings since 1973, but overall world trade has continued to grow faster than world GNP, and capital flows still occur. Destabilising capital flows were endemic in the operation of the Bretton Woods system as well.

## Exercise 2

1  (a) In what ways did the US dollar lie at the heart of the Bretton Woods exchange rate system?

   (b) If countries felt that they could not improve their balance of trade position by changing their exchange rate what other options were open to them?

   (c) If the effect of the Bretton Woods system was basically asymmetrical, was the main effect experienced by deficit or surplus countries?

   (d) What is the chief source of international liquidity? Why did the supply of this source become relatively scarce in the 1960s?

2  In a system of freely floating exchange rates what would you expect to happen to the value of a country's rate of exchange in the following circumstances? Explain your answer by drawing a series of diagrams showing the changes in supply and demand for the currency in each situation.

   (a) An outflow of short term capital following a cut in interest rates.

   (b) A rise in export earnings following increased productivity.
   (c) An increase in the level of interest, dividends and profits earned overseas by British investment projects.
   (d) An increase in the level of British tourist expenditure overseas.
   (e) A fall in imports due to lower inflation in Britain relative to rates in other developed countries.

3  A country devalues its exchange rate by 10% in time period 1. In period 1 price elasticity of demand for imports is zero, and so is the price elasticity of demand for exports. The import elasticity rises by 0.3 each period to a maximum of 2.1, and the export elasticity rises by 0.2 each period to a maximum of 1.4.
   (a) In period 2 will the balance of trade position be better or worse? Explain your answer.
   (b) In what period will the balance of trade stop deteriorating?
   (c) When will the balance of trade be stronger than its original position?
   (d) What is the name of the condition which states that the sum of the price elasticities for imports and exports has to add up to more than one for a devaluation to improve the balance of trade position?
   (e) What curve describes the behaviour of the balance of trade following a devaluation if elasticities behave as indicated above?

# 18.8 The IMF and the world banking crisis

1  Many less developed countries have experienced significant balance of payments difficulties since the oil price rise of 1973.
2  There were three main reasons for this.
   (a) Developing countries relied on imports of oil from the Middle East.
   (b) The general world recession caused a fall in demand for raw materials and commodities, lowering their price, and hence the export revenue of many developing countries who exported these very goods.
   (c) World recession and unemployment in developed countries led to protectionist moves amongst the developed world, reducing further their demand for developing countries exports.
3  In the mid-1970s the IMF was unable and unwilling to lend foreign currency to these countries on a significant scale. The developing countries turned to private banks for their finance which led to the following problems.
   (a) Rates of interest were high.
   (b) Little thought was given to the schedule for repayments of the principal.
   (c) There were no conditions attached to the loans regarding the nature of economic policies to be followed by the borrowers.
   (d) The country's balance of payments position was often insufficient to generate sufficient foreign currency to repay even the interest payments required.

(e) There was no security for the loans apart from the loans of the
   private banking system.

4   Several countries, e.g. Peru, Jamaica, Nicaragua, Zaire and
    Turkey, are in danger of defaulting on their loans and interest rate
    commitments, or are seeking a rescheduling of their repayments.

5   The effect of a collapse of these international debt arrangements
    would be far-reaching. For example:
    (a) further loans to the developing countries would dry up,
        leading to a curtailment of growth and a drop in living
        standards in countries where standards are already low,
    (b) demand for the exports of the developed countries would fall,
    (c) a loss in confidence in the lending banks from the developed
        countries would lead to higher interest rates and slower
        growth in the western world.

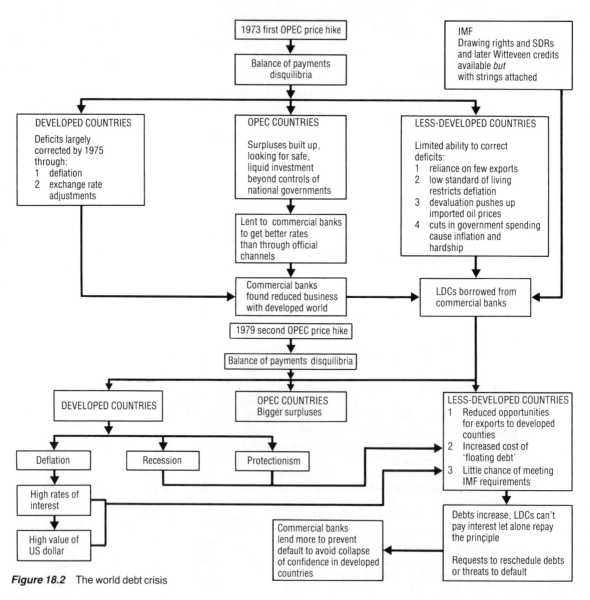

***Figure 18.2***   The world debt crisis

# Exercise 3

## 1 Diary of a debtor country

| | |
|---|---|
| Nov. 1982 | Brazil runs out of foreign currency.<br>Negotiates bridging loans from commercial bank ($2.3b), Bank for International Settlements (BIS) ($0.5b) and US treasury ($0.8b).<br>IMF asked for $4.9b, and commercial banks for a long term loan for $4.4b. |
| Jan. 1983 | Brazil signs 'Letter of Intent' with IMF.<br>BIS provides a further $0.9b bridging finance. |
| Feb. 1983 | US treasury provides a further $0.4b.<br>Commercial banks supply the required $4.4b.<br>IMF approves loans subject to promises by Brazil to reach prescribed economic targets and introduce required policies, e.g. reduction in wage indexation. |
| May 1983 | Brazil fails to meet IMF targets.<br>IMF freezes its loans. Commercial banks follow. |
| July 1983 | Brazil passes decree that wage increase will be limited to 80% of the inflation rate. |
| Aug. 1983 | Brazil's debt arrears (repayments of previous loans and interest) stands at $2.5b. |
| Sept. 1983 | A new $11b loan package announced–$6.5b coming from commercial banks. |
| Oct. 1983 | Decree law on wage indexation modified by Brazilian congress. |
| Nov. 1983 | IMF approves new economic programme.<br>IMF releases $1.17b of loans which had been held back since May. All of this goes straight to the BIS in repayments. |
| Dec. 1983 | Commercial banks release $1.8b of their Feb. 1983 loans. All goes straight back to the commercial banks in repayments for past loans.<br>New long term loans agreed for Brazil by commercial banks and the IMF. |

By the end of 1984 Brazil had foreign currency debts of over $100b. Interest and repayments required during the year were $18.7b. This money was found from:

(a) achieving a balance of payments surplus of $9b compared to 1983's level of only about $6.5b.
(b) renegotiating rates of interest charged on their loans,
(c) rescheduling some of their debts,
(d) raising new loans for about $5b.

Brazil cannot tolerate much more recession. Although the goals agreed with the IMF are being met it is politically impossible for Brazil to keep on course much longer.

Inflation shows no sign of falling from the 10% per month, 200 plus a year level. Massive street demonstrations of the past few weeks reflect the growing discontent with the economic situation. Average per capita income has shrunk by 12.6% in the past four years and by as much as 5.7% last year alone.

The very measures which have brought about the record trade surplus now boost inflation, and have united with the previous culprit, high government spending, in keeping the spiral going.

Brazil's export earnings are up 8.2% on 1982 and imports are being held down to last year's very low levels which cannot be managed much longer.

This is being achieved by the government devaluing the cruzeiro by at least the rate of inflation so that Brazil's exports have become more competitive abroad. But this policy means that imports cost more every time there is a devaluation, now almost weekly. Oil derivatives have to go up 25% every ten weeks or so. This increase is immediately fed through to affect all other prices, particularly food, public transport and building materials.

Utility prices have also to be raised to keep pace, as the public sector has been Brazil's great foreign borrower and the state prices have to be raised constantly to pay off debt instalments. The removal of food subsidies means that food prices are rising faster than most.

All this might be an acceptable price to pay if it could be demonstrated that inroads were being made into the $100b debt, but even if all goes to plan, and the hoped for $9b trade surplus is achieved, Brazil will need to borrow more this year to meet commitments.

And there are many signs that the foreign trade success may be short lived. Extra exports are nearly all to one market, the United States. Exports to Latin America have slumped, markets in Africa have disappeared, EEC exports remain static under threats of new taxes on soya as expensively produced home crops become available. In the United States there are calls to prevent Brazil 'dumping' her goods there.

(Based on information from *Times* 10.5.84)

(a) Explain the following:
   (i) rescheduling debts
  (ii) bridging loans
 (iii) Letter of Intent
 (iv) wage indexation
  (v) Bank of International Settlements
 (vi) devaluation

(b) Why were commercial banks prepared to lend currency to Brazil? Why was Brazil prepared to borrow from the commercial banks?

(c) Why do you think that wage indexation was such a crucial issue for the IMF? Have the measures insisted on by the IMF brought about a reduction in the rate of inflation in Brazil?

(d) Why was it important for Brazil to achieve a Balance of Payments surplus? What problems did Brazil experience in trying to achieve this surplus by:

(i) deflation
(ii) devaluation
(iii) expanding exports
(e) Even with all the measures Brazil's debts were still increasing during 1984? What could be done to ease her debt problems?

# Review

## Unit 18 will have helped provide answers to the following questions

1 What is the role of the International Monetary Fund?
2 How does the IMF provide help for a country with a balance of payments problem?
3 How has the IMF sought to increase the level of international liquidity?
4 What are floating exchange rates?
5 To what extent has the experience of floating exchange rates confirmed economic textbook expectations?
6 Why did the Bretton Woods adjustable-peg exchange rate system break down?
7 What is the origin and what are the possible consequences of the so-called world banking crisis?

## Unit 18 has introduced the following terminology

Adjustable-peg (exchange rate system)
Borrowing windows
Bretton Woods system
Buffer stock facility
Compensatory (and supplementary) financing facility
Credit tranche
Destabilisation
Dollar overhang
Extended fund facility
Floating exchange rates
General arrangement to borrow
Group of Ten
International liquidity
International Monetary Fund
J-curve
Leads and lags
Marshall-Lerner condition
Rescheduled debts
Reserve currencies
Special Drawing Rights
Stand-by credits
Vicious and virtuous circles
Witteveen Credits

## Essays

1 How has the role of the International Monetary Fund adapted to the introduction of floating exchange rates? How successful has it been in dealing with international economic problems?

2 Why have floating exchange rates not eliminated balance of payments imbalances?

## Multiple choice questions

1 Which of the following could not perform a reserve currency role for France?
(a) United States dollar
(b) Japanese yen
(c) British pound
(d) West German deutschmark
(e) French franc

2 Which of the following was not an original objective of the International Monetary Fund?
(a) To establish a system of convertible currencies.
(b) To promote a system of stable exchange rates.
(c) To increase the level of international liquidity.
(d) To lend finance to developing countries for development projects.
(e) To promote international trade.

3 J-curves occur because:
(a) there is no spare capacity in the country whose exchange rate changes.
(b) the sum of the price elasticities of demand for imports and exports always adds up to less than 1,
(c) initially the sum of the price elasticities of demand for imports and exports is less than 1, but after a certain time period they add up to more than 1,
(d) exporters and importers react quickly to changes in prices,
(e) exporters may react to the exchange rate change by increasing their profit margins.

4 A currency that is freely convertible is one:
(a) whose value is determined by free market supply and demand for the currency,
(b) which can be exchanged into another currency without any quota restriction,
(c) which can be exchanged for gold at the central bank,
(d) that countries are willing to hold as a reserve currency,
(e) which is perfectly divisible.

5 Which of the following policy options is not available to a country with a balance of payments imbalance, that is obliged by international treaty to maintain a fixed exchange rate, and which wishes to correct the payments imbalance?

(a) deflation
(b) direct controls, e.g. quotas
(c) exchange controls
(d) revaluation
(e) improvement of the efficiency of domestic industry

**6** The IMF imposes restrictions on countries which borrow foreign currency:
    (i) so that corrective payments policies are introduced by the debtor country,
    (ii) so that the IMF has reason to expect the loan to be repaid after a reasonable period of time,
    (iii) so that private commercial bank loans are more likely to be forthcoming.
    (a) (i) only
    (b) (ii) only
    (c) (i) and (iii) only
    (d) (i), (ii) and (iii)
    (e) (i) and (ii) only

**7** Developing countries find IMF loans unacceptable at times because:
(a) conditions of the loan which require deflation are inappropriate in countries where the standard of living is very low,
(b) the length of the standard loan was too short for countries with severe payments problems to correct their deficits,
(c) decisions regarding the size and terms of the loans are made by a group of ten relatively rich developed countries who have a lack of sympathy for the situation,
(d) a revaluation of the exchange rate of developing countries increases the price of essential imports and thereby reduces the standard of living in those countries,
(e) all of the above.

**8** SDRs increased international liquidity without countries having to run balance of payments surpluses because:
    (i) SDRs were created by the the IMF and were allocated to all member countries,
    (ii) the value of SDRs does not depend on the value of one particular reserve currency,
    (iii) IMF members are obliged to accept SDRs as settlement of international debts up to a prescribed limit.
    (a) (i) only
    (b) (i) and (ii) only
    (c) (i) and (iii) only
    (d) (iii) only
    (e) (i), (ii) and (iii)

**9** Under the Bretton Woods adjustable-peg exchange rate system countries could adjust their exchange rates:
(a) whenever they liked as long as their balance of payments accounts showed a deficit,

(b) in circumstances of fundamental disequilibrium of the balance of payments after consultation with the IMF,
(c) with agreement with the IMF as long as certain economic policies were followed,
(d) if the balance of payments was in disequilibrium for at least two years in succession,
(e) in no circumstances at all.

**10** Which of the following is not an explanation for the collapse of the Bretton Woods exchange rate system?
(a) A growing lack of confidence in the United States dollar.
(b) A growing surplus of international liquidity.
(c) The reluctance of countries to adjust their exchange rates.
(d) Pressure to adjust was felt initially by countries with balance of payments deficits who were short of reserves.
(e) Surplus countries experienced large inflows of short term capital.

## Answers

### Exercise 1

**1** (a) Subscriptions (or quotas) of member countries, and from additional borrowing, e.g. from OPEC countries.
    (b) 500,000 SDR, i.e. 5/4 of its subscription level.
    (c) (i) Supplementary Financing Facility (Witteveen Credits)
        (ii) Compensatory Financing Facility

**2** (a) SDRs are IMF created assets which form part of international liquidity as they are accepted as payments for international debts, up to prescribed limits.
    (b) Reserve assets, i.e. currencies of countries which are acceptable to third parties: gold, IMF Drawing Rights.
    (c) The competitive policies would lead, in their various ways, to a fall in overall aggregate monetary demand, which is deflationary and would cause a fall in living standards and a rise in unemployment.
    (d) Member countries are obliged to accept SDRs up to a level of twice their cumulative allocation of SDRs by the IMF.
    (e) SDRs were a straightforward rise in the world money supply, and hence could have caused inflation, or allowed countries to operate domestic policies that were inflationary.
    (f) Without assets to settle international debts trade has to be restricted. The well being of developed and less developed countries depends on international trade flows.

## Exercise 2

**1** (a) (i) The rates of exchange of all countries were pegged to the US dollar, which in turn was pegged to gold.
  (ii) US dollars were an important part of international liquidity.
 (b) (i) Deflation
  (ii) Direct controls
  (iii) Improvement of competitiveness of their industry
 (c) Both. Deficit countries had to deal with deficits before they ran out of appropriate sources of finance, surplus countries suffered from large inflows of short term capital which inflated their money supplies.
 (d) Reserve currencies because the chief reserve currencies were themselves under pressure, i.e. the US dollar and the £ sterling.

**2** (a) Fall—shift of supply curve to the right.
 (b) Rise—shift of demand curve to the right.
 (c) Rise—shift of demand curve to the right.
 (d) Fall—shift of supply curve to the right.
 (e) Rise—shift of demand curve to the left.

**3** (a) Worse—import bills would rise by 7%, but export revenue will rise by only 2%.
 (b) Time period 3.
 (c) Time period 4, the 5% improvement in this time period compensates for the 5% loss in time period 2.
 (d) Marshall-Lerner condition.
 (e) J-curve.

## Exercise 3

**1** (a) (i) Arranging a new time schedule for the repayment of debts.
  (ii) A short term loan to cover the gap between the end of one loan and the arrangement of a new permanent loan.
  (iii) A statement by a country of agreement to the terms of an IMF loan.
  (iv) Linking wage rises to the level of inflation.
  (v) BIS has the role of providing a forum for discussion amongst central banks. It has helped arrange currency swaps, and undertakes general surveillance of international banking.
  (vi) Reducing the value of your currency against other currencies, e.g. one unit of your currency can be exchanged for fewer units of other currencies.
 (b) High rates of interest for the banks. Static demand for loans in the developed world. Countries got loans without the IMF-type string attached.
 (c) Breaking into the inflationary spiral. Devaluation and government spending cuts fuelled more inflation (e.g. increasing prices of imports, cutting food subsidies).
 (d) Need to raise foreign currency to pay the

interest on loans. Problems included:
  (i) deflation causes lower living standards and political unrest
  (ii) devaluation causes inflation
  (iii) the rest of the world is unable or unwilling to take extra goods from Brazil as they have their own economic problems.
 (e) Lower interest rates. Transfer loans out of US$. Increase international liquidity of LDCs, e.g. through more SDRs. At the extreme Brazil might simply refuse to pay.

## Suggested essay plans

**Essay 1**
Role of the IMF: pre-Bretton Woods break-up, post-Bretton Woods break-up (see *Unit 18.2*)
Main paragraphs: Liquidity issues. Orderly exchange rate operations. Promotion of international trade. Balance of payments adjustment; but, debts of less developed countries. Destabilising swings of floating exchange rates. Operations dictated by the leading 10 IMF nations.
Conclusion.

**Essay 2**
Definition of terms: Floating exchange rates. Balance of payments imbalances.
Main paragraphs: Why might floating exchanges be expected to eliminate imbalances? Qualification that rates are not freely floating.
Problems of adjustment, e.g. Marshall-Lerner condition not satisfied, J-curve effects, outflows of short term capital after devaluation, inflationary pressures caused by devaluation, profit taking by exporters, virtuous and vicious circles.
Conclusion: At best floating exchanges operate with a time-lag, many other factors affect the balance of payments position at any particular time.

## Multiple choice answers

**1** (e) A reserve currency refers to a currency that is acceptable to third parties.
**2** (d) This was the role assumed by the World Bank.
**3** (c) Elasticities increase with time.
**4** (b) By definition.
**5** (d) Fixed exchange rates and revaluation is a contradiction in terms.
**6** (e) Commercial banks may be more prepared to lend in such circumstances but the restrictions by the IMF are not designed specifically to encourage such activity.
**7** (e) These are four commonly presented criticisms of the way the IMF operates.
**8** (e) All the statements are accurate, surpluses increased the supply of some reserve currencies, but meant other countries had to carry deficits.
**9** (b) 'Fundamental disequilibrium' was an IMF term but never formally defined.
**10** (b) International liquidity was in short supply.

# UNIT 19 The European Economic Community

## 19.1 Preview

1 The European Economic Community (EEC) was established in 1957, and the rules for its operation were outlined in the Treaty of Rome.
2 The UK joined the community at the start of 1973.
3 In 1984 EEC members were France, West Germany, Italy, Belgium, the Netherlands, Luxembourg, Denmark, Ireland, Greece and the UK. Spain and Portugal became members in 1986.
4 Political and social considerations of EEC operations tended to be relegated in importance to economic issues. The economic issues included:
(a) concern about the level of expenditure on agricultural support,
(b) concern about the control and uneven incidence of the EEC's budget,
(c) the existence in the EEC of a stable exchange rate system,
(d) the EEC's relationship with the rest of the world.

## 19.2 The aims of the EEC

1 The EEC has sought to:
(a) *Establish a customs union or common market,* i.e. to remove trade barriers between member nations and to impose common barriers to non-member countries.
(b) *Protect the 'four freedoms' within the community,* i.e. the freedom of movement for people, goods, services and capital.
(c) *Develop common policies,* e.g. for tax, fisheries, energy, agriculture and currency.
(d) *Promote fair competition* between producers within the community.
(e) *Prepare a common association with the rest of the world,* e.g. by allowing preferential trade arrangements with developing countries (the Lomé Convention).

## 19.3 The EEC budget

1 The EEC receives revenue from four sources.
(a) *VAT receipts* of member governments (up to 1.4% of these after the Fountainebleau Agreement of June 1984).
(b) *Customs duties* levied on goods imported by members from outside the EEC.
(c) *Agricultural levies* on food imported by members from non-EEC members.
(d) A *sugar levy* on countries where sugar is produced within the EEC.

2  EEC expenditure involves the following areas.
   (a) *Agricultural support* through the Common Agricultural Policy (CAP) (see *Unit 19.4*).
   (b) *Regional policy grants*—e.g. grants for the establishment of industry or the development of infrastructure in areas designated by national governments.
   (c) *Social policy grants*—e.g. to support national programmes for retraining, housing schemes, youth opportunity schemes (YTS) and education initiatives.
   (d) *Research, energy, industry and transport* programmes, e.g. funding of the European Torus research into nuclear fusion.
   (e) *Development aid*—e.g. to the sixty-three African, Caribbean and Pacific countries which have signed the Lomé Convention which allows preferential trading arrangements for these countries with the EEC.

3  Budgetary difficulties came to a head in 1984. The main issues involved were:
   (a) the sources of EEC revenue were proving inflexible, e.g.
      (i) duties and levies depended on the volume and direction of international trade,
      (ii) VAT revenue could not be increased because Britain would not agree to increasing revenue until expenditure reforms had been agreed for agricultural support programmes.
   (b) national contributions to the budget were uneven, and were, apparently, unrelated to a country's ability to pay, e.g. West Germany and Britain were the only net contributors to the budget while the other eight members were net recipients (see Exercise 1, question 2).
   (c) Expenditure was dominated by operations of the Common Agricultural Policy.

4  Britain's contribution was relatively high because:
   (a) Britain has a relatively small farm sector, so that CAP receipts were relatively small,
   (b) Britain pays a relatively high sum into the EEC budget as a fixed percentage of its VAT receipts,
   (c) Britain imports a relatively large amount of food from outside the EEC, e.g. from New Zealand, and thus has to pass on the agricultural levies to the EEC,
   (d) as a sugar producer, Britain has to contribute the sugar levy.

5  A solution to these budgetary difficulties was reached in the Fountainebleau Agreement of June 1984. The main elements of the agreement were:
   (a) The UK received an *ad hoc* refund of £590m for 1984, to be paid in 1985.
   (b) With effect from 1986 the UK will get a refund each year of 66% of the difference between its VAT contribution and money received from EEC expenditure.
   (c) The Community's VAT revenues were increased from 1% to 1.4%, with a further increase to 1.6% planned to meet the extra costs of Spain and Portugal's membership.
   (d) Measures to guarantee 'effective budgetary discipline' were to be introduced.

# Exercise 1

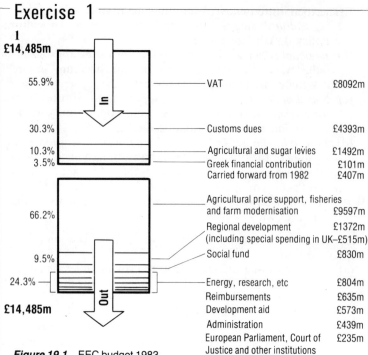

**1**
£14,485m

55.9% In ——————— VAT £8092m

30.3% ——————— Customs dues £4393m

10.3% ——————— Agricultural and sugar levies £1492m
3.5% Greek financial contribution £101m
Carried forward from 1982 £407m

66.2% Agricultural price support, fisheries
and farm modernisation £9597m

Regional development £1372m
(including special spending in UK–£515m)

9.5% Social fund £830m

24.3% Out Energy, research, etc £804m
Reimbursements £635m
£14,485m Development aid £573m
Administration £439m
European Parliament, Court of £235m
Justice and other institutions

**Figure 19.1** EEC budget 1983

(Source: *Economist*)

(a) Explain how the EEC receives money from:
(i) VAT,
(ii) Customs duties,
(iii) Agricultural and sugar levies.
(b) Why are the sources of EEC revenue inflexible?
(c) What proportion of EEC expenditure was on agricultural support programmes in 1983? How might you assess the opportunity cost of so high a degree of expenditure on agricultural support?
(d) What kind of programmes are supported with expenditure from the Social Fund?
(e) In 1982, what was the surplus on the EEC's budget? Could the EEC run a budget deficit like national governments?

**2** The profit and loss account of EEC members is shown in the table. (Figures are in £s sterling and relate to 1982.)

| | Net repayments or receipts | Per head of population | GDP as percentage of EEC average |
|---|---|---|---|
| Belgium | 152m | 16 | 107 |
| Denmark | 177m | 35 | 126 |
| W.Germany | − 1200m | − 20 | 123 |
| Greece | 411m | 42 | 44 |
| France | − 11m | na | 114 |
| Ireland | 439m | 125 | 58 |
| Italy | 970m | 17 | 71 |
| Luxembourg | 153m | 421 | 108 |
| Netherlands | 182m | 13 | 111 |
| UK | −1200m | − 22 | 98 |

The total net payment Britain has made since joining the EEC is approaching £5b. Since 1980 Britain has been granted special refunds on a year by year basis, which have totalled, by 1983, £2617m, so without these refunds the net contribution would have been half as much again.

(Based on information from EEC Commission)

(a) Is the UK the only country to either pay in or take out an unfair share from the EEC budget?

(b) Why is Britain's net contribution so large?

(c) What could the EEC budget contribution be linked to, to make it fair for all member governments?

# 19.4 The Common Agricultural Policy

1 All countries support their agricultural industry. For the economic theory behind the support given to agriculture refer back to *Unit 6, Exercise 4*.

2 **The original aims of the CAP were to:**
(a) increase agricultural productivity
(b) guarantee a fair standard of living for farmers
(c) ensure secure supply of food
(d) stabilise food markets
(e) maintain reasonable consumer prices

3 **The CAP incorporates the following features:**
(a) guaranteeing prices to producers,
(b) support (or intervention) buying,
(c) special 'green' or farming exchange rates,
(d) Monetary Compensation Amounts (MCAs) which act to dampen out the effect of green currency exchange rate levels on the value of CAP support policies,
(e) variable import levies, to protect EEC farmers from the import of cheaper food from outside the EEC,
(f) export subsidies to encourage farmers to export some of their surplus production,
(g) structural aid, e.g. for land clearance or for drainage programmes.

4 **The CAP has achieved some degree of success** in meeting its original objectives. For example:
(a) production per acre has increased on average by 2% a year over the last ten years,
(b) it has helped sustain farmers' incomes although not for all types of farmers and not during the recession,
(c) the community is self-sufficient in practically all farm goods that can be grown within the EEC,
(d) the large swings in world food prices have been avoided within the EEC.

The cost of all this is higher prices than need be to the consumer, e.g. butter is 50% higher within the EEC than on world markets and wheat prices are 33% higher.

5 **Criticisms of the way the CAP operates**
(a) The high cost of agricultural support—each year, up to 1984, agricultural support prices were increased which had the

effect of increasing the overall support bill by an even larger amount because:
(i) the increased guaranteed prices stimulated increased output,
(ii) the surplus food was stored in intervention stores which cost money to operate.
So, for example, the 8% average food price rises in 1983 led to a 28% increase in CAP spending on agricultural support.
(b) The production of the food surpluses ('mountains', 'rivers' and 'lakes') which:
(i) have to be stored
(ii) destroyed, e.g. wine turned into industrial alcohol
(iii) or sold outside the EEC at reduced, subsidised prices, e.g. to the USSR or to central and southern Africa.
(c) The support given to national specialities, e.g. to Britain's 'milk factories' (highly mechanised dairy units where the cows are fed imported feedstuffs).
(d) The high guaranteed prices which are paid to all farmers within the EEC, so efficient farmers are handicapped by having to sell their output at high prices but helped by the receipt of CAP subsidies.
(e) The dominance of agricultural support of the total EEC budget (see *Unit 19.3*).

6 The first steps to reform the CAP and to restrict the growth of spending came in 1984. Reforms included:
(a) the introduction of production quotas for milk production. (1983 production levels of 103m tonnes to be progressively reduced to 98.4m tonnes by 1985, and then pegged at this level.),
(b) the extension of production quotas for sugar beet, cereals, some oil seeds and for processed tomatoes,
(c) the reduction of imports of agricultural products, e.g. of foodstuffs from the United States and of butter from New Zealand,
(d) the reduction of the level of guaranteed prices by an average 0.5% (as compared to an average increase of 8% in 1983),
(e) the phasing out of the system of MCAs.

7 These reforms only begin to tackle the problem, and for the forseeable future agricultural expenditure will continue to dominate the EEC's budget.

8 For the UK, membership of the EEC and the impact of the CAP has meant:
(a) the protection of jobs in agriculture (298,000 in 1972, 294,000 in 1982),
(b) growth in agricultural incomes and of the share of agriculture on gross national product,
(c) structural change in farming, e.g. less horticulture and new crops introduced like oilseed rape,
(d) high food prices to the consumer, through the British government's attitude to fixing its green currency rate and the level of MCAs,
(e) the encouragement of technological advances and expansion of output, e.g. of cereal production in East Anglia.

# Exercise 2

**CAP payments by crop: 1983**

Total: ECUs ‡ 15.5b *

Milk products 30.3
Cereals 15.9
Sugar 9.2
Fruit and vegetables 7.0
Wine 4.1
Beef and veal 9.5
Other 24.0

*Excluding MCA payments

**Self-sufficiency index** 1978–81 averages

100 = self-sufficiency†

130 — Sugar
120 — Wheat / Butter
110 — Skimmed milk powder
100 — Beef and veal / Pork
90
80 — Rice
70 — Maize
60

†EEC production over consumption

**CAP payments by country: 1982**

Total: ECUs ‡ 12.4b

France 23.0
Belgium/Lux 4.3
Denmark 4.5
W.Germany 15.6
Ireland 4.0
Netherlands 11.4
UK 10.4
Italy 21.2
Greece 5.6

‡ECU = European Currency Unit

**Figure 19.2** Carving the CAP

**1** (a) Why are agricultural prices unstable?
   (b) Why would farm incomes tend to fall over time without government support programmes?
   (c) What are the social arguments for agricultural support?
**2** (a) On which three agricultural products does the CAP spend most money?
   (b) In which three products does the EEC have the largest excess production over consumption within the EEC?
   (c) Which three countries benefit most from CAP aid? Why is this so?
   (d) Why cannot all surplus food (e.g the butter mountain) be sold at reduced prices to consumers within the EEC?
   (e) Why have the food surpluses developed?
   (f) What reforms to the CAP would eliminate the food surpluses?

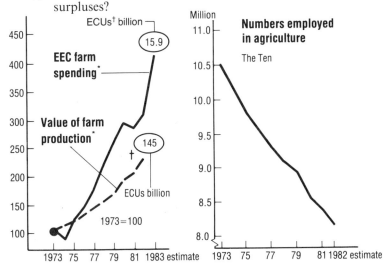

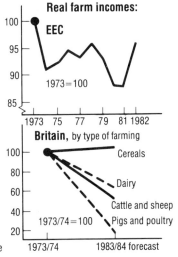

*Excludes Greece before 1980 †1982
†ECU=European Currency Unit

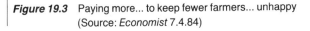

**Figure 19.3** Paying more... to keep fewer farmers... unhappy
(Source: *Economist* 7.4.84)

3 (a) Describe the trends in the value of farm production and of farm spending in the EEC. Why has expenditure followed this trend?

   (b) To what extent has the CAP been successful in maintaining real farm incomes?

   (c) Which group of farmers in Britain have benefited most from the CAP?

   (d) What has happened to the level of employment in agriculture within the EEC since 1973? Was it an objective of the CAP to protect farm jobs?

   (e) In general has the CAP achieved its original objectives?

# 19.5 European Monetary Union

1 A basic aim of the EEC was to bring about increased trade between member nations.

2 The movement towards floating exchange rates threatened the growth of trade, and the disintegration of the economic policies of the EEC member countries.

3 Fixed exchange rates would encourage trade between members, and would force closer co-operation between member countries. Taken to an extreme, if rates were to be permanently fixed, the national currencies could be replaced by a single European currency. Such developments were outlined in the Werner plan, which commited the EEC to seek monetary union by 1980.

4 The present European Monetary System (EMS) is only a small distance along any route to monetary union. The EMS has developed from the 'snake in the tunnel' arrangements of 1972 and has the following features.

   (a) *Membership of the EMS is voluntary* and not all EEC members belong to the EMS arrangements.

   (b) *Exchange rates are pegged through a double network:*
   (i) bilaterally, e.g. the French franc to the Duch guilder
   (ii) with the ECU.

   (c) *The ECU (European Currency Unit) is the unit of account* within the EEC, and derives its value from a trade-weighted basket of European currencies.

   (d) *The ECU was created by Fecom* which is developing a role as the European Monetary Fund (along the lines of the IMF). Countries have swapped 20% of their gold and foreign currency reserves for ECUs.

   (e) Within the double network of pegged rates currencies are allowed *narrow bands for fluctuation* of $+/- 2.25\%$ as in the last months of the Bretton Woods system. (Italy is allowed to float the lira by $+/- 6\%$).

   (f) *Divergence indicators* signal to governments that currencies are moving towards the limits of the flexible band and that some form of corrective policy is necessary.

   (g) *Periodic realignments* of exchange rate pegs occur with the agreement of the member countries.

5 The EMS has operated since 1979, superseding the more informal arrangements of the snake and the Benelux 'worm'. The more fixed exchange rates have not brought about a convergence of inflation rates in Europe or eliminated balance of payments

problems, but there has been an element of short term currency stability and trade amongst members has continued to grow.

6 Britain did not join the exchange rate arrangements of the EMS, but did contribute gold and currency reserves to Fecom. The reasons for non-participation by Britain include:

(a) *The Atlantic connection*—Britain's trade and the value of currency was thought to be dominated by the United States and not by Europe.

(b) *Petrocurrency status*—sterling's value is influenced by movements in international oil markets whereas the other EMS currencies are largely unaffected.

(c) *Destabilising speculation*—speculators would return to the one-way option of the Bretton Woods system, i.e. because currency changes are delayed they would know which way a currency was going to change, if at all.

(d) *Deutschmark domination*—the EMS has worked, it is argued, because the rates in Europe are dominated by the German Mark. The introduction of a second 'heavyweight' currency into the parity grid might destroy the relative stability achieved.

(e) *Domestic monetary management*—the British government is reluctant to reduce the country's capacity to control the growth of the domestic money supply, and inevitable result of being forced to maintain a specific rate of exchange for sterling.

However British membership of the EMS would:

(a) show a political commitment to Europe in general,

(b) put the reserves of Fecom at the disposal of the British government to counteract speculation against the pound.

(c) promote trade within Europe.

Key factors in any decision to join the EMS would be the initial rate for sterling in the parity grid, and the size of the bands within which sterling would be allowed to float against the other EMS currencies.

# 19.6 The impact of EEC membership on the British economy

1 There is always a problem in economics in assessing the impact on the economy of something like EEC membership because there is no way of knowing what the present economic situation would have been if the UK had not become a member.

2 Certainly the main problems facing the British economy since 1973, e.g. deindustrialisation, world recession, difficulties with a high exchange rate and the impact of high oil prices, were not of European origin or directly to do with EEC membership.

3 It is equally clear that the optimism which heralded British EEC membership was misplaced.

4 Some of the impact of EEC membership can be examined with reference to the standard macroeconomic objectives.

(a) *Growth*

(i) UK has increasingly attracted direct overseas investors from non-member countries, keen to establish a production plant within the EEC tariff barrier. For example in

1984 it was estimated that 70,000 jobs in Scotland, and over 25% of the jobs in Northern Ireland were with United States-owned concerns.

    (ii) The lowering of trade barriers within the EEC has led to a growth in trade, which has, in turn, increased living standards.

    (iii) The UK agricultural sector has benefited specifically from the CAP.

(b) *Employment*

    (i) Growth of economic activity, as described above generates employment.

    (ii) Structural changes have been caused by changing trade flows, e.g. jobs in the food and drink industries have expanded but those in textiles have contracted with EEC membership.

    (iii) In 1984 an estimated 2.5m jobs in Britain were directly concerned with exporting goods and services to the EEC.

(c) *Inflation*

    (i) CAP has raised the price of food above levels that would have existed if Britain had been free to buy all her food on world food markets, and by causing a switch in support methods from deficiency payments to support buying. However, much of the increased food prices has been a deliberate choice of the government (through its fixing of the green exchange rate and the level of MCAs) in order to boost farm incomes.

    (ii) Tariff reductions on goods and services imported from the EEC have probably offset any inflationary effect of increased food prices.

(d) *Balance of payments*

    (i) There has been a change in direction of British trade in favour of the EEC. Nearly 50% of British trade is now with EEC countries.

    (ii) The balance of trade in 1973 was in deficit by £1.3b with EEC countries, and by 1982 the deficit had increased to £2.1b.

    (iii) The balance of payments has benefited from the inflow of direct capital mentioned above.

    (iv) The net contribution to the EEC budget is recorded in the accounts as an invisible outflow.

# Review

**Unit 19 will have helped provide the answers to the following questions**

1 What were the original objectives of the European Economic Community?

2 What are the main sources of revenue, and forms of expenditure for the EEC?

3 Why is the EEC budget a problem area?

4 Why does the EEC devote so much attention to agricultural support policies?

5 What are the main methods of agricultural support used in the EEC?

6 What reforms to the CAP are advocated?

7 Why was European Monetary Union considered an important objective?

8 What are the features of the European Monetary System?

9 What has been the effect of EEC membership on the British economy?

**Unit 19 has introduced the following terminology**

Common Agricultural Policy (CAP)

Customs union

European Currency Unit (ECU)
European Monetary Fund (EMF)
European Monetary System (EMS)
European Monetary Union (EMU)
Green exchange rates
Lomé Convention
Monetary Compensation Amounts (MCAs)
Snake
Support buying (or intervention buying)
Variable import levies

## Essays

1 Europe's budget difficulties inevitably involve reform of the Common Agricultural Policy. Discuss.
2 What are the economic effects of Britain's membership of the European Economic Community?

## Multiple choice questions

1 Food mountains have developed in the EEC because:
   (a) the CAP guaranteed a minimum price to farmers for all their food
   (b) food is stored in intervention stores
   (c) free market prices for food have consistently been below the CAP guaranteed prices
   (d) deficiency payments are made to increase farm incomes
   (e) green currencies are used to fix agricultural prices

2 Food prices would tend to be unstable without intervention because:
   (i) supply is unpredictable due to factors beyond the farmer's control, e.g. climate and disease,
   (ii) in the short run supply tends to be price inelastic,
   (iii) the demand for food tends to be price inelastic.
   (a) (i) only
   (b) (ii) only
   (c) (i) and (iii) only
   (d) (i) and (ii) only
   (e) all three

3 If the green pound is valued below the actual pound then it follows that:
   (a) food imported from within the EEC is cheaper than would otherwise be the case, and British farmers' incomes will be lower,
   (b) food imported from within the EEC will be cheaper, and British farmers' incomes will be higher,
   (c) food imported from within the EEC will be more expensive and British farmers' incomes will be higher,

   (d) food imported from within the EEC will be more expensive and British farmers' incomes will be lower,
   (e) green currencies have no effect on food prices or on farmers' incomes.

4 Britain has become a major contributor to the EEC budget because the country:
   (a) has an inefficient farm industry
   (b) imports sugar from non-member countries
   (c) has to send a bigger proportion of VAT receipts to the EEC than other members
   (d) imports relatively large quantities of food from outside the EEC
   (e) does not get a fair share of regional and social fund expenditure

5 A group of countries (like the EEC) which allows free trade amongst its members and imposes a common external tariff against non-members is called:
   (a) a free trade area
   (b) a customs union
   (c) a trading zone
   (d) a currency bloc
   (e) a multinational zone

6 By 1984 the EEC had developed common policies for:
   (a) fishing
   (b) indirect taxation
   (c) competition in industry
   (d) agriculture
   (e) all of the above

7 Which of the following is not a feature of the European Monetary System?
   (a) A double network of exchange rate pegs.
   (b) Compulsory membership for all EEC members.
   (c) Use of divergence indicators to signal the introduction of corrective economic policies.
   (d) Periodic realignments of the exchange rate pegs.
   (e) Use of the ECU as the unit of account.

8 EEC membership has contributed to an improved standard of living in Britain through:
   (i) the attraction of direct capital from outside the EEC
   (ii) the protection of agricultural incomes
   (iii) trade creation within the EEC free trade area
   (a) (i) and (ii) only
   (b) (ii) and (iii) only
   (c) (i) only
   (d) (iii) only
   (e) (i), (ii) and (iii)

9 The variable import levy:
   (a) keeps out all food imports from non-member countries,
   (b) keeps out food imports until the EEC price has risen to a set level,

(c) raises the price of imported food so that EEC produced food stays competitive,

(d) keeps the price of domestic food low,

(e) lowers the export price of surplus food.

10 Which of the following is not a true statement?

(a) Britain joined the EEC in 1973.

(b) Britain did not join the EMS when it was set up in 1979.

(c) Britain was a large net contributor to the EEC budget between 1973 and 1983.

(d) British farmers have not benefited from the CAP because they are more efficient than their European counterparts.

(e) Britain has experienced an increase in its growth rate due to EEC membership.

# Answers

## Exercise 1

1 (a) (i) Member countries all impose VAT and up to 1.4% of revenue collected goes to the EEC.

(ii) Member countries collect duties on goods imported from outside the EEC, and the revenue is passed to Brussels.

(iii) Member countries collect the variable import levies imposed on food imported from outside the EEC, and pass this through to the central budget.

(b) The sources of revenue depend on factors beyond the EEC's direct control, e.g. the level of world food prices, the value of goods imported from outside the EEC, the level of economic activity and expenditure within the EEC.

(c) 66%. The jobs or economic growth that could have been created in other areas of the economy if this money had been spent elsewhere.

(d) National government's retraining programmes, housing schemes, day-care centres for the disabled and mentally ill.

(e) £407m was carried forward from the previous year. If people are prepared to lend there is no reason why not, indeed in mid-1984 the EEC was trying to borrow £1.4b to make ends meet.

2 (a) Fairness is a subjective concept. It was all fair in the sense that it was legal and what member countries agreed to when they joined the EEC. However, the level of contributions do not correlate with the other figures shown for all countries.

(b) Britain pays in a relatively large sum because we import food from outside the EEC (e.g. from Australia and New Zealand) and we import a bigger proportion of goods from outside the EEC. We get out a relatively small amount because we have a small agricultural sector and the EEC expenditure is dominated by agriculture.

(c) GNP/head? GDP levels compared to EEC average levels? Or leave it as it is, and reform the CAP?

## Exercise 2

1 (a) Unpredictable supply (e.g. loss of orange crop in America in the hard winter of 1984) coupled with price inelasticity of demand. Plus cobwebs, and a relatively low quantity traded internationally.

(b) Increased technology and knowledge increases supply, but food demand increases only slowly due to its relative income inelasticity.

(c) Farmers are immobile, without jobs in agriculture they would become structurally unemployed.

2 (a) Milk, cereals, beef and veal, or sugar if the veal is excluded.

(b) Sugar, wheat and milk products (butter and skimmed milk powder) very similar to the list in (a) above.

(c) France, Italy and West Germany. They have the highest numbers of people in farming.

(d) The guaranteed prices are achieved by support buying which requires that the excess food be kept off the EEC food markets.

(e) The guaranteed prices are constantly set above the market price, so that supply is generated without reference to the level of demand at these prices.

(f) Switch to deficiency payments. Introduction of quotas on the production of food. A reduction in the level of guaranteed prices relative to the free market (or world) level of prices.

3 (a) Food production values have risen constantly, but the cost of providing the food has risen by even more.

(b) The CAP has in general maintained real farm incomes, but not completely during the recession, and not for all farmers.

(c) Cereal farmers.

(d) Numbers have fallen from 10.5m to 8m. Increasing food production and increasing efficiency in farming have helped protect employment opportunities in agriculture but clearly overall numbers have fallen.

(e) Yes—the main qualification would be the cost of food to the consumer. Is it reasonable to ask consumers to pay 50% more for their butter and 33% more for wheat than in the rest of the world?

## Suggested Essay plans

### Essay 1

Definition of terms: EEC, EEC budget, CAP

Main paragraphs: Budget problems: Inflexible sources of revenue. Rising expenditure, shortage of money. Uneven national contributions.

Agriculture: Importance of agriculture in EEC spending. Balance of contributions/receipts linked to size of agricultural sector in countries, efficiency of their agriculture, special arrangements for specific crops/products, amount of food imported from outside EEC.

Reforms: Reduced guaranteed prices. Quotas. Control of the surpluses.

Conclusion: Agriculture takes 66% of total EEC spending so bound to be the chief target for reform, unless the budget itself can be transformed.

### Essay 2

Definition of terms: EEC membership from January 1973, but transition arrangements in operation until 1977. Economic effects analysed with reference to basic macroeconomic objectives.

Main paragraphs: See *Unit 19.6*.

Conclusion.

## Multiple choice answers

1 (c) It is relationship between the guaranteed price and free market prices which determines whether surplus has to be bought up by the intervention authorities.

2 (e) All three operate to make free market food prices unstable.

3 (c) Lower exchange rate increases the price of imported goods, pushing up prices obtainable by British farmers in the UK.

4 (d) Import levies collected by Britain (e.g. on food imported from New Zealand) are transferred to the CAP.

5 (b) By definition. A free trade area does not provide for common external tariffs.

6 (e) Although member nations were able to adapt the general policies.

7 (b) Membership of the EMS is voluntary. Britain contributes to the European Fund but is not a full participating member of the EMS.

8 (e) All three stimulate economic activity.

9 (c) Food from non-EEC countries is subject to a variable import levy to raise its price to the CAP prices.

10 (d) British farmers have benefited considerably from the CAP because they receive high guaranteed prices for the food they grow, plus assorted improvement grants.

# UNIT 20    Economic growth

## 20.1 Preview

1 Economic growth refers to an increase in the level of economic activity within a country.
2 Growth is thought to be desirable for most economies so that there can be a rise in the standard of living of the citizens of that country.
3 For less developed countries, with increasing populations, growth may be necessary to maintain living standards.
4 In developed countries growth will be important to allow the industries of the countries to remain competitive.
5 The discovery of North Sea oil, was expected to give Britain's growth rate a major boost, but the effect of the oil revenues is not all beneficial to the economy.

## 20.2 Economic growth

1 Economic growth can be considered in two ways.
  (a) In the short run simply as an increase in the level of economic activity, with the economy making fuller use of existing resources.
  (b) In the long run as an increase in the production capacity of the economy, through the expansion of resources or the more efficient use of existing resources.
  *Observations from Figure 20.1*
  ☐ AA is the economy's production possibility curve for the production of goods and services.
  ☐ At point 's' some resources are unemployed.
  ☐ A movement from 's' to 't' represents an increase in the levels of economic activity, but growth cannot continue in the long run without an increase in the capacity (or production potential) of the economy.
  ☐ Curve BB represents an increase in productive capacity. Further economic growth can take place, represented by a movement of the economy from point 't' to point 'u'.

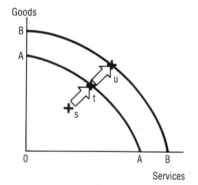

**Figure 20.1**  Economic growth

## 20.3 Growth as a macroeconomic objective

1 Economic growth is normally thought desirable for several reasons.
  (a) Greater output means that more of people's wants can be satisfied.
  (b) This leads to an increased standard of living within the country.
  (c) If other economies are growing, a country will have to achieve economic growth to maintain the competitiveness of its output. Slower growth than competing countries leads to a fall in the rate of increase in the standard of living.

(d) Growth rates are considered to be a measure of success in economic performance, so growth has a prestige value.

(e) Growth creates wealth which can be distributed to less prosperous areas of the economy.

2 Some people, however, question the desirability of striving for economic growth because:

(a) extra production damages the environment and creates pollution,

(b) extra material output (and the consumption of this output) does not necessarily lead to an increase in welfare for people in a country (see *Unit 10*),

(c) growth involves a change in the structure of the economy which will leave immobile resources structurally unemployed,

(d) growth may require investment expenditure which can only be undertaken if present rates of consumption are reduced.

## 20.4 Sources of economic growth

1 Economic growth may occur as a result of *additional resources* becoming available for economic use, e.g. through the discovery of new natural resources like oil in the North Sea, through immigration, or through investment expenditure on the creation of more capital goods.

2 Economic growth may also occur through the *more efficient use of existing resources*, e.g. through technological advances, through better education and training of the workforce and through the abolition of restrictive work practices.

3 Often the two sources of economic growth come hand in hand, e.g. investment expenditure creates increased capital goods which may involve the embodiment of technological advances.

4 Growth will not occur unless there is sufficient demand in the economy to absorb the increase in production. Growth involves a cumulative process in the economy as illustrated on the left.

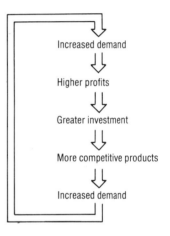

Increased demand

Higher profits

Greater investment

More competitive products

Increased demand

## ┌ Exercise 1

1 For each of the following situations state what the likely effect would be on a country's rate of economic growth. Explain each answer.

(a) A shift or resources from manufacturing to the service sector of the economy.

(b) A shortage of long term risk capital for industry.

(c) An increase in government expenditure on non-marketed output, e.g. on health and education.

(d) An increase in private sector investment expenditure in technically advanced fixed capital.

(e) An increase in the level of population.

(f) A removal of controls of the international movement of foreign exchange, allowing more investment finance to flow overseas.

(g) A fall in the number of hours worked each week (assuming the level of employment remains unaltered).

(h) A situation where any increase in the level of economic activity leads to balance of trade difficulties for the country.

Gross domestic product 1960–1980.
Index 1970 = 100.

|  | 1960 | 1970 | 1980 |
|---|---|---|---|
| UK | 76 | 100 | 120 |
| US | 68 | 100 | 132 |
| W. Germany | 63 | 100 | 132 |
| France | 58 | 100 | 144 |
| Italy | 58 | 100 | 148 |
| Japan | 35 | 100 | 168 |

(*Whatever Happened to Britain?*
1982, Eatwell J., BBC/
Duckworth, p13.)

(i) A government economic policy which aims to lower inflation by controlling the growth of the money supply.
(j) An increase in the world price of a raw material as yet unexploited within the economy.

**2** See table on left.
(a) How does British economic growth compare to the other countries shown in the table?
(b) What factors might explain the different rates of economic growth?

## 20.5 Why is the level of economic growth uneven?

**1** Fluctuations in the level of economic activity have been an observed feature of economies for centuries. The cyclical changes have been called trade or business cycles.

**2** **A possible growth path** for an economy can be seen in Figure 20.2.

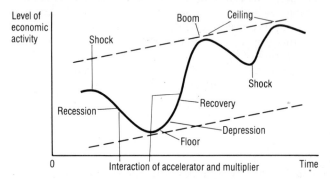

**Figure 20.2** Growth path for an economy

*Observations from Figure 20.2*
☐ Phases of the cycle can be labelled as boom, recession, depression and recovery.
☐ Once the level of economic activity changes a cumulative process may become established involving a combination of the multiplier and acceleration effects (see below).
☐ There exist in the economy forces which provide a floor and a ceiling to these cumulative movements in economic activity.
☐ The whole process is subject to periodic shocks, i.e. a major event that influences economic activity.

**3** **Periodic shocks** in the post-1970 period would include:
(a) the × 15 rise in the price of OPEC oil from 1973–80.
(b) the 41% increase in the value of sterling from 1979–81.
(c) the discovery and move to self-sufficiency in oil in Britain by 1980,
(d) the implementation of deflationary 'monetary' policies by Margaret Thatcher's and President Reagan's governments.
(e) industrial disputes, e.g. miner's strikes in 1973–4 and 1984–5.
Shocks possibly to come include:
(a) the end of supplies of oil in the seas around Britain,
(b) the defaulting of major debtors, e.g. Argentina or Poland, and a collapse of the world banking system,

(c) a move towards protectionism by developed countries faced with continuing high levels of unemployment,

(d) a break-down of the exchange rate system, causing a down turn in international trade flows.

4   **Cumulative processes** at work in the economy involve the interaction of the accelerator and multiplier effects.

(a) *The multiplier* links the final change in national income to the expenditure change bringing it about.

i.e. dNY = M × dEx

where dNY = the change in national income
M = the value of the multiplier
dEx = the change in the level of autonomous expenditure

(b) *The accelerator* links changes in the level of investment expenditure with the rate of change of national income.

i.e. I = a(dNY)

where I = the value of investment expenditure
a = the value of the accelerator
dNY = the change in national income

(c) So when combined together:

dI → dNY → dI → dNY etc.

5   The cumulative process is arrested by the existence of *ceilings* and *floors* within the economy.

Ceilings will include:

(a) shortages of skilled labour,

(b) bottlenecks in the capital goods industries,

(c) a shortage of finance leading to a rise in the rate of interest,

(d) automatic stabilisation effects of fiscal policy, i.e. the higher the level of economic activity the higher the tax take and the less the need for some forms of government expenditure,

(e) constraints from the balance of payments if imports rise faster than exports as a result of the economic expansion.

Floors will include:

(a) the need for some firms to undertake replacement investment expenditure,

(b) falls in the level of withdrawals from the circular flow in the form of less tax payments and reduced savings,

(c) the increase in government expenditure on transfer pay-ments, e.g. on unemployment benefits,

(d) technological advances that generate new investment opportunities.

## 20.6  The effects of North Sea oil on UK growth

### 1   The discovery of new natural resources

*Observations from Figure 20.3.*

☐ AA shows the production possibility curve before the discovery of the oil reserves in the North Sea.

☐ AB shows the new production possibility curve, indicating a possible rise in the production of oil and oil-related goods.

☐ The new resources increase Britain's production potential. There has to be sufficient demand in the economy for this potential to be realised.

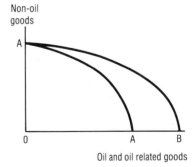

**Figure 20.3**  Production possibility curve for North Sea oil

In 1984 the value added by oil production from the North Sea contributed about 5% of GDP.

2  **Tax revenue**

The exploitation of the oil reserves has generated tax revenue for the government from the following sources:

(a) royalties (12.5% of the value of oil produced),

(b) Petroleum Revenue Tax (PRT) (70% of profits after various allowances),

(c) Supplementary Petroleum Duty (SPD) between 1981–3 (a further 20% of profits),

(d) corporation tax (levied at usual rates on any profit remaining).

This new source of revenue for the government could have been used in the three main ways.

(a) *Option 1—cut borrowing* which might be expected to:
  (i) lead to lower rates of interest
  (ii) more investment expenditure in 'wealth creating' private sector industry
  (iii) allow better control of inflation which in turn would reduce savings and stimulate export earnings.

(b) *Option 2—cut taxation on other areas* (or, as it turned out, avoid the need to increase taxation on other areas) which might be expected to:
  (i) increase disposable incomes and stimulate demand in the economy
  (ii) lower inflation through reduced wage demands which would lead to more competitive goods and more export earnings.

(c) *Option 3—raise government expenditure* on, for example:
  (i) investment expenditure in manufacturing 'sun-rise' industries (through the creation of a National Investment Bank or an expanded role for the British Technology Group),
  (ii) on improvements in the state of British social services such as health and education provision,
  (iii) on public works programmes such as further electrification of the railways, building new roads, more houses, or new sewers.

These measures might lead to:
  (i) increased employment
  (ii) increased economic activity through the multiplier effect
  (iii) increased welfare from the expenditure undertaken.

3  **Removal of the balance of payments constrain on growth**

By 1980 when the balance of payments on visible account moved into surplus, oil exports formed 10% of Britain's total exports. In 1981 oil exports raised about £10b, the current account was in surplus by £6b, so other trade flows were in deficit. Attempts to stimulate growth in the 1960s and early 1970s through government reflationary programmes had invariably been cut short by balance of payments problems.

4  **Inflow of capital and expertise**

Over 75% of the capital employed in the North Sea is foreign owned, representing a genuine addition to investment expenditure.

**5 Petrocurrency status and the Dutch disease**
Exports of oil, and the inflows of capital associated with it, have pushed the value of sterling to levels above those which allow other manufacturing industries to stay competitive in world markets. The inability of Britain to export sufficient goods to pay for the level of imports that would be demanded at levels of full employment is a key feature of the process of deindustrialisation in Britain.

**6 Deficits elsewhere in the world**
If Britain is operating a balance of payments surplus elsewhere in the world there must be a corresponding deficit. These deficit countries will be forced to deflate their economies and reduce the demand for British exports.

**7 Outflows of capital**
Oil flows have allowed outflows of other capital from Britain without generating balance of payments problems. These flows would have generated economic activity in Britain if they had not gone overseas.

**8 Currency instability**
As a major exporter of oil, the value of the pound is susceptible to changes in the world price of oil. Currency instability is likely to reduce exporters' confidence.

# Exercise 2

1  See table on left. North Sea revenues (£m)

| | 1982–3 | (estimated) 1983–4 |
|---|---|---|
| Royalties | 1630 | 1600 |
| SPD | 2600 | — |
| PRT | 3280 | 5250 |
| Corporation tax | 500 | 1000 |
| TOTAL | 7810 | 7850 |

(Based on information from *Expenditure White Paper*.)

   (a)  What is the difference between royalties and Petroleum Revenue Tax?
   (b)  In 1983 income tax raised about £35,000m for the government when the basic rate of income tax was 30%. If the oil revenue was not available what do you estimate would have to be the basic rate of income tax to raise the necessary revenue?
   (c)  In extreme circumstances it was possible for the marginal rate of tax on oil companies operating in the North Sea to be greater than 90%. What would be the result of the government setting tax rates so high that they eat into the companies transfer earnings rather than scooping off their economic rent? Explain your answer.
   (d)  What would happen to the government's revenue from North Sea oil if there was a fall in the world price of oil?

2  **Essay**
   Why did the exploitation of North Sea oil not stimulate significantly faster economic growth in Britain?

## 20.7 Growth in less developed countries

1  There is a large gap between living standards in developed countries and those in less developed countries, the so-called North/South divide.

**2** In 1976 it was estimated that there were twenty-two countries in which GNP/head was less than US$175 but eighteen countries where GNP/head was greater than US$5600.

**3** Some of the problems experienced by less developed countries in increasing their level of economic growth include:
  (a) *Rate of population growth.* Poorer countries experience high rates of population growth which literally swallow up any increase in production.
  (b) *Population structure.* Almost 50% of the population in poor countries comprises children, dependent on the production of the rest.
  (c) *Lack of investment funds.* At low levels of income there is no opportunity to save, so financial capital does not accumulate.
  (d) *Misplaced investment projects.* High technology schemes are inappropriate in countries with abundant supplies of labour. Intermediate technology schemes can harness the plentiful labour source more efficiently.
  (e) *Narrow base of exports.* Foreign currency earnings may be based on only a few exports, which are subject to price fluctuations and changes in the level of demand of developed countries.
  (f) *Trading difficulties.* The developed world has increasingly developed trading blocs which isolate the less developed non-member countries.
  (g) *Lack of infrastructure*, e.g. banking systems, transport, networks.
  (h) *Lack of education, skill and training.*
  (i) *Low productivity.* Production is often hampered by entrenched social attitudes and structures.

**4** Policy options available to help produce a more equal distribution of wealth and income in the world include:
  (a) *Development aid*—e.g. financial aid from governments or commercial banks to finance investment projects.
  (b) *Trade arrangements*—e.g. allowing less developed countries preferential access to the markets of the trading zones, e.g. the Lomé Convention and the EEC.
  (c) *Commodity stabilisation schemes*—e.g. the establishment of buffer stock facilities or trading cartels.
  (d) *Finance for countries in balance of payments difficulties*—e.g. the provision of foreign currency to allow countries to run deficits without the need to deflate their economies.

**5** **The World Bank** (the International Bank for Reconstruction and Development) intends to encourage growth by the promotion of investment projects aimed at reconstruction or development of the infrastructure.
The World Bank obtains its money from:
  (a) members' subscriptions
  (b) selling bonds on world markets
  (c) chanelling private funds
Other agencies, e.g. International Development Association, European Investment Bank, national governments and commercial banks provide funds for similar projects in less developed countries.

# Review

## Unit 20 will have helped provide answers to the following question

1 What is economic growth?
2 Why is economic growth desirable?
3 Is economic growth always desirable in all circumstances?
4 What are the sources of economic growth?
5 What is the cause of cyclical economic activity?
6 What has been the effect on British growth rates of the discovery of North Sea oil?
7 What are the problems experienced by developing countries in achieving economic growth?
8 What can be done by developed countries to help promote economic growth in less developed countries?

## Unit 20 has introduced the following terminology

Boom
Business cycle
Depression
Petrocurrency status
Petroleum Revenue Tax
Recession
Recovery
Royalties
Trade cycles
World Bank

## Multiple choice questions

1

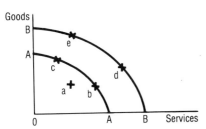

**Figure 20.4**  A shift in the production possibility curve

In Figure 20.4, AA is the original production possibility curve for a country. BB shows the production possibility curve five years later. Which of the movements of the economy would normally be considered to be an example of long term economic growth?
(a) a to b  (b) c to a  (c) b to c  (d) b to d
(e) d to e

2 Which of the following are costs associated with economic growth?
   (i) Extra production causes damage to the environment.
   (ii) Growth involves change and the generation of structural unemployment.
   (iii) Investment expenditure to generate growth will involve a reduction in consumption levels in the short run.
(a) (i) and (ii) only
(b) (iii) only
(c) (i) only
(d) (ii) and (iii) only

(e) (i), (ii) and (iii)

3 Which of the following would not tend to limit economic expansion?
(a) a shortage of skilled labour
(b) the multiplier effect
(c) bottlenecks in the supply of machinery
(d) a high marginal propensity to import
(e) automatic fiscal stabilisation

4 Cumulative changes in the level of economic activity are produced by:
(a) the interaction of the accelerator and the multiplier effects,
(b) the accelerator effect alone,
(c) the interaction of the multiplier and changes in the rate of interest,
(d) the interaction of the accelerator and the rate of interest,
(e) the multiplier effect alone.

5 Which of the following has not been a source of tax revenue for the government from North Sea oil operations?
(a) Petroleum Revenue Tax
(b) Royalties
(c) Corporation tax paid by the oil companies
(d) Supplementary Petroleum Duty
(e) Petroleum excise duty

6 The Dutch disease refers to a situation where:
(a) the exchange rate rises due to the output of one highly competitive industry,
(b) a fall in the exchange rate due to poor performance in manufacturing trade,
(c) a loss of manufacturing exports due to membership of the Common Market,
(d) restrictive trade practices by workers in exporting industries,
(e) the exchange rate falls due to outflows of short term capital.

7 Which of the following are reasons why less developed countries find it difficult to raise living standards?
   (i) high rates of population growth
   (ii) plentiful savings but limited financial infrastructure
   (iii) shortage of labour resources
(a) (i) and (ii) only
(b) (ii) only
(c) (i) and (iii) only
(d) (i), (ii) and (iii)
(e) (i) only

8 The international institution established after World War II to fund long term investment projects in less developed countries is:
(a) the EEC
(b) the Bank of International Settlements
(c) the International Monetary Fund
(d) the International Bank of Reconstruction and Development

(e) the General Agreement of Tariffs and Trade

**9** Which of the following is not a source of economic growth in Britain associated with the exploitation of North Sea oil?
(a) increased inflows of direct capital
(b) the removal of the balance of payments constraint on growth
(c) increased availability of natural resources
(d) increased tax revenue for the government which has allowed other tax rates to be held down
(e) increased rate of exchange for sterling

**10** North Sea oil production has affected the British balance of payments in all but one of the following ways:
(a) by attracting inflows of direct capital
(b) by increased inflows of short term capital
(c) through exports of oil
(d) through the reduction of imports of oil
(e) through increased exports of manufactured goods to other countries who have to import expensive oil

## Answers

### Exercise 1

**1** (a) Manufacturing industry is considered by some to be 'the engine of growth' because:
  (i) there is a high income elasticity of demand for manufactured goods
  (ii) there are opportunities for economies of scale in manufacturing processes
  (iii) there is scope for technological innovation which stimulates further investment expenditure.
Service industries tend to be less efficient. There are clearly exceptions to the above.
(b) Growth would be held back. This reason is sometimes put forward as an explanation for slow British growth rates, but committees of enquiry (e.g. the Wilson Commission) found no such shortage of risk capital existed.
(c) The basis of the Becon and Eltis resource crowding-out theory, which seems to be refuted by evidence and common sense, e.g. spending in these areas creates demand for output from the private sector, and in what sense can education be anything else but wealth creative?
(d) Good for growth. It will only happen if there is sufficient demand for the goods produced.
(e) Extra population increases labour resources (if by natural means after a time-lag) and generates extra demand for produce. GNP/head may not rise though.
(f) Exchange controls were removed in 1979 allowing investment capital to flow overseas more easily. Overseas investment generates interest, dividends and profits but investment here would stimulate domestic economic activity

through the multiplier effect. If profits at home were insufficient to attract investment funds the expenditure might not take place at all if controls existed.
(g) Less growth, unless productivity rises, e.g. as in the 3-day week of 1974.
(h) Slow growth. The constraint of the balance of payments led to British stop-go economic management in the 1960s and early 1970s.
(i) The initial impact of the deflation or restricted money supply may be to slow growth, but reduced inflation increases price competitiveness and attracts export orders which in the longer turn stimulates growth.
(j) Faster growth. The increase in world price means that the resource becomes worth exploiting, increasing natural resources, and attracting capital inflows.

**2** (a) Poor comparison.
(b) Different resources, different levels of productivity, different shifts of resources within each economy, different levels of investment expenditure, different government economic policies.

### Exercise 2

**1** (a) Royalties are levied on production values. PRT is levied on profits.
(b) To make up the lost £8b income tax would have to be raised to about 38%.
(c) Too high tax rates would put off new oil exploration, but once it is in operation the companies would be bound to carry on getting out the oil unless tax rates were leaving them with less than their variable costs.
(d) Fall—royalties would fall, as would the level of profits for the oil companies and hence their PRT and corporation tax payments.

**2** Suggested essay plan
Definition of terms: North Sea oil—from 1975, self-sufficient since 1980. Growth.
Main paragraphs: North Sea oil's beneficial effects: (i) inflows of capital, (ii) new natural resource, (iii) tax revenue generated for government, (iv) removal of balance of payments constraint
Damaging effects: (i) effect on the exchange rate, (ii) our surpluses caused deficits in other countries, (iii) allowed outflows of capital without balance of payments difficulties
Other problems for growth: (i) World recession, (ii) Effect of the MTFS, (iii) Government decisions as to how to spend the oil revenue.
Conclusion.

### Multiple choice answers
**1** (d) An outward movement of the production possibility curve allows LT growth.
**2** (e) All three are problems associated with economic growth.

**3** (b) This helps create the cumulative effect, with the accelerator effect.

**4** (a) See *Unit 20.5(4)*.

**5** (e) Excise duty is levied on sales of all petrol.

**6** (a) As with gas in the Netherlands, and oil in Britain.

**7** (e) There is plentiful labour, and limited savings.

**8** (d) More commonly known as the World Bank.

**9** (e) A higher rate of exchange has inhibited exports of other industries.

**10** (e) As above.

# INDEX